INFINITE AUTONOMY

INFINITE AUTONOMY

The Divided Individual in the Political Thought of G. W. F. Hegel and Friedrich Nietzsche

Jeffrey Church

THE PENNSYLVANIA STATE UNIVERSITY PRESS
UNIVERSITY PARK, PENNSYLVANIA

Publication of this book has been supported by the
Jack Miller Center for Teaching America's Founding
Principles and History.

Library of Congress Cataloging-in-Publication Data

Church, Jeffrey, 1978– .
   Infinite autonomy : the divided individual in the
   political thought of G.W.F. Hegel and Friedrich
   Nietzsche / Jeffrey Church.
      p.   cm.
   Includes bibliographical references and index.
   Summary: "Argues that G.W.F. Hegel and Friedrich
Nietzsche share a concept of individuality that combines
autonomy and community, but that they develop this
concept in opposite directions, leaving an irreconcilable
tension between political means of individual
fulfillment"—Provided by publisher.
   ISBN 978-0-271-05075-1 (cloth : alk. paper)
   1. Hegel, Georg Wilhelm Friedrich, 1770–1831—Political
and social views.
   2. Nietzsche, Friedrich Wilhelm, 1844–1900—Political and
social views.
   3. Individuality.
   4. Autonomy.
   I. Title.

JC233.H46C57   2012
320.01—dc23
                     2011023349

The Pennsylvania State University Press is a member of the
Association of American University Presses.

It is the policy of The Pennsylvania State University Press
to use acid-free paper. Publications on uncoated stock satisfy
the minimum requirements of American National Standard
for Information Sciences—Permanence of Paper for
Printed Library Material, ANSI Z39.48–1992

This book is printed on Natures Natural, which contains
50% post-consumer waste.

To EMILY

CONTENTS

Preface		ix
List of Abbreviations		xiii
Introduction		1
1	Three Concepts of Individuality	8
	1.1 The Natural Individual	10
	1.2 The Formal Individual	17
	1.3 Rousseau and the Historical Individual	22
2	Hegel's Defense of Individuality	25
	2.1 The Distinctively Human Subject and the Good Life	28
	2.2 The Autonomy of the Laboring Subject	32
	2.3 The "Infinite Worth" of Individual Character	44
3	Hegel on the Ethical Individual	56
	3.1 The Origin of Community	57
	3.2 The Nature of Community	63
	3.3 Politics as the Highest Ethical Community	78
4	Hegel on the Modern Political Individual	84
	4.1 The Ancient Versus the Modern State	85
	4.2 Expansion of Desire in Modern Commercial Society	87
	4.3 Estates and Corporations as Ethical-Political Communities	96
5	Nietzsche's Defense of Individuality	111
	5.1 The Problem of Individuation in Nietzsche	113
	5.2 The Will to Power and the Development of the Distinctively Human	117
	5.3 Individuality as a Narrative Unity	129

6 Nietzsche on the Redemptive Individual   140
   6.1 The Tension in the Bow and Human Community   141
   6.2 Silenus' Truth   146
   6.3 The Aesthetic Justification of Existence   149
   6.4 The Individual's Redemption   154
   6.5 *Eros* and *Eris* of Community   162

7 Nietzsche on the Antipolitical Individual   170
   7.1 Historical Development of State and Culture in Modernity 171
   7.2 On the Nature and Function of the Modern State   179
   7.3 The Possibilities of Modern Culture   190

Conclusion   199

Notes   211
References   249
Index   259

PREFACE

I began thinking about a project on the modern individual several years ago as a way to get to the bottom of the disputes between liberalism and its many critics. I found that the claims and counterclaims—about individual rights, the liberal community devoted to defending these rights, and the ethos of self-reliant "individualism"—were based on different conceptions of what an individual is and ought to be, and were not fully intelligible apart from them. A Christian view of an ensouled human being, for instance, results in a very different political self-understanding than a Hobbesian view of individuals as bundles of passions. This project was motivated, then, by the age-old desire for self-knowledge, to understand who or what the modern individual is, and, more deeply, whether the modern individual fulfills what it means to be a human being or whether it corrupts or dehumanizes us.

Yet I found that the most powerful challenges to liberal individuality from the nineteenth century to the present held that individuality is not real but an illusion. How can one understand the individual if it vanishes under the force of these criticisms? These criticisms of liberalism in late modernity are familiar: advanced commercial societies dissolve individual freedom by submitting human thought and action to commodity fetishism, ever more specialized and benumbing forms of labor, and manipulative and reifying forms of technology. Mass democracies undermine individual freedom with a tyranny of social custom and the disciplinary apparatus of the modern state. Structural patterns of inequality strip individuals of effective agency while ever reproducing and deepening these same patterns. At a deeper philosophical level, universal "determinism"—the view that all events, including individual actions, are determined by previous natural or cultural causes—threatens individual agency as the "uncaused cause" with "ultimate causal responsibility" for its actions and with the capacity "to do otherwise" for any particular choice.

Though powerful, these criticisms nonetheless seemed to me to be flawed in not revealing a way out, a way to foster individual agency and defend the institutions of modern public life through a decisive response to these malaises of modern liberalism. What I was looking for, then, was a theory of the individual that could weather these storms. Happily, I came then to deepen my knowledge of the classical German philosophers Kant, Fichte, Hegel, Marx, and Nietzsche, who examined the nature and basis of individual freedom in a much deeper and more satisfying way than I've encountered in other theorists past or present. These philosophers deployed a deep, modern skepticism about fanciful models of the human self, while nonetheless defending the irreducible agency of subjectivity and the boundlessness of human reflection. They themselves leveled many of the same cultural and philosophical criticisms of individual agency and modern community, but yet designed creative ways to avoid the usual problems and dichotomies.

Hegel and Nietzsche came to be the central figures of this project because they defended a notion of modern individuality—what I call the "historical individual"—that could resolve these modern problems. Hegel and Nietzsche's key contribution was to historicize human subjectivity while nonetheless retaining a normative standard of "perfection" internal to its nature. I call Hegel and Nietzsche's notion of individuality the "historical individual" because the individual is not pregiven by nature nor is it any kind of "substance" or "thing," but rather an achievement of accumulated individual and communal historical meaning. Their shared view of individuality as a historical creation helps us understand the late modern challenges to the individual—if history shapes the individual, then oppressive and alienating communal practices will construct distorted human personalities. Yet this view also points toward a solution, in that we can design communal practices that can help construct complete human lives according to the standard internal to human subjectivity. Instead, then, of opposing individual and community as theorists from Socrates to Mill have done, Hegel and Nietzsche argue that they can be mutually reinforcing. At the same time, neither Hegel nor Nietzsche thinks that cultivating genuine individuals is an easy task. On the contrary, they both argue that individuality is difficult to achieve. To be more precise, for these philosophers, individuality is not an all-or-nothing affair, but rather achievable according to degrees of success.

I was motivated, then, in this project by a philosophical aim, namely, to argue that Hegel and Nietzsche can help us see how a robust theory of individuality is both possible and desirable in late modernity. But like many scholars working in the history of political philosophy, I also wanted to contribute to our historical understanding of these authors' texts and aims. The scholarship on both thinkers is vast and flourishing. Hegel continues to gain ever more widespread acceptance among contemporary political and philosophical writers, while Nietzsche never ceases to accumulate a diverse scholarly following of approaches and interpretations. In writing this book, I did not want to offer another commentary on any one of the authors' texts, but rather to reconstruct the arguments of these philosophers on this theme of individuality. In so doing, I sought to challenge the current scholarship by arguing that Hegel and Nietzsche should be regarded more as philosophical allies than enemies (or rather "evil twins," as I suggest in the introduction). Moreover, I wanted to make the case that Hegel and Nietzsche are both concerned with harmonizing individual and community, not, as is sometimes thought, choosing one over the other. Finally, I set out to complicate the tendency in the scholarship toward political camps of "Left" and "Right" Hegelians and Nietzscheans by arguing that both philosophers were profoundly ambivalent about the modern age and hence recognized the perils of both progressive and conservative approaches to politics and society.

Many thanks to the smart and caring people who helped me conceive and execute this project, though I feel I would do an injustice to their influence by limiting my gratitude to their help on this project alone. I would not have been motivated to embark on a career studying political philosophy if it were not for my mentors at Ursinus College, Paul Stern, Stewart Goetz, and Roger Florka, who revealed to me the great depth of philosophical texts and the wonder of the big questions. In addition, this book has benefitted from Stern's continued guidance and inimitable Socratic midwifery.

At the University of Notre Dame, through many seminars and reading groups, Michael and Catherine Zuckert demonstrated charismatic teaching, rigorous textual analysis, and a humble appreciation for the wisdom of philosophy's history. This book and all my work owe them an immeasurable debt. They have generously read, reread, and even re-reread many portions of this manuscript in its several stages of development. Dana Villa read and offered penetrating comments on the work and helped show me how all the pieces of my own thinking went together. He is a model of a scholar with a charming, ready wit. Ruth Abbey provided many insightful remarks on the whole manuscript and pushed me to clarify my view of Nietzsche's politics while revealing to me the problems with the "Left" Nietzsche interpretation. Karl Ameriks taught me a great deal about Kant and the classical German literary and philosophical tradition, and he helped me articulate the philosophical problems at the heart of the book. I also learned to appreciate the Continental philosophical challenges to individual subjectivity under Fred Dallmayr, who commented on an early version of this work.

My colleagues in political theory here at the University of Houston— Sue Collins, Jeremy Bailey, Greg Weiher, and Don Lutz—have graciously supported this work in its final stages and have coached me through the publishing process. The University of Houston New Faculty Grant was invaluable in giving me the time to make the final revisions to the work. Robert Ross and Bruce Hunt assisted me in the nitty-gritty details of preparing the manuscript for publication.

Several other friends and colleagues have read and provided thoughtful comments on the work: Laurence Cooper, Peter Euben, Richard Velkley, Alex Downes, Joel Schlosser, Catherine Borck, Alex Duff, Matt Holbreich, and Kevin Cherry. Many thanks to the two anonymous reviewers for Penn State Press, whose comments helped me improve the work considerably.

The *AJPS* has given permission to reprint a portion of chapter 4, which is a revision of "The Freedom of Desire: Hegel's Response to Rousseau on the Problem of Civil Society," vol. 54, no. 1 (January 2010): 125–39. Thanks also to the Jack Miller Center for a generous subvention grant to help fund the book's production.

Finally, I could not have completed this project without my devoted family. My mother and father taught me to commit myself to what I love and to love the truth. And my wife, Emily, to whom this book is dedicated, has inspired more of these thoughts and ideas than I can count and has tested these arguments in innumerable discussions. She has healed my mangled prose. She has a soulful care for the big questions and for my grief in failing to live up to them. If my muse could also be my coauthor, it is she.

ABBREVIATIONS

In quoting from the major texts, I have employed the standard English translations, but have altered the translation when necessary. All translations from the German texts are my own.

Hegel

Aesthetics
Vorlesungen über die Ästhetik, vols. 13–15 of G. W. F. Hegel, *Werke in 20 Bänden,* ed. Eva Moldenhauer and Karl Markus Michel (Frankfurt am Main: Suhrkamp, 1970).

Aesthetics: Lectures on Fine Art, trans. T. M. Knox (Oxford: Clarendon Press, 1975). Cited by page number of English translation.

EL
Enzyklopädie der philosophischen Wissenschaften I, vol. 8 of *Werke.*

The Encylopedia Logic: Part I of the Encyclopedia of Philosophical Sciences with the Zusätze, trans. T. F. Geraets, W. A. Suchting, H. S. Harris (Indianapolis: Hackett, 1991). Cited by paragraph number.

EN
Enzyklopädie der philosophischen Wissenschaften II, vol. 9 of *Werke.*

Hegel's Philosophy of Nature: Being Part Two of the Encyclopedia of the Philosophical Sciences, trans. A. V. Miller (Oxford: Oxford University Press, 2004). Cited by paragraph number.

ES   *Enzyklopädie der philosophischen Wissenschaften III*, vol. 10
       of *Werke*.

       *Hegel's Philosophy of Mind: Being Part Three of the Encyclo-
       pedia of the Philosophical Sciences*, trans. William Wallace
       and A. V. Miller (Oxford: Oxford University Press, 1971).
       Cited by paragraph number.

ETW   *Early Theological Writings*, trans. T. M. Knox (Philadel-
       phia: University of Pennsylvania Press, 1971). Cited by
       page number.

HP   *Vorlesungen über die Geschichte der Philosophie*, vols. 18–20
       of *Werke*.

       Lectures on the History of Philosophy, 3 vols., trans.
       E. S. Haldane (Lincoln: University of Nebraska Press,
       1995). Cited by volume number, page number of
       English translation.

PH   *Vorlesungen über die Philosophie der Geschichte*, vol. 12 of
       Werke.

       The Philosophy of History, trans. J. Sibree (New York:
       Dover, 1956). Cited by page number of English
       translation.

PhG   *Phänomenologie des Geistes*, vol. 3 of *Werke*.

       Phenomenology of Spirit, trans. A. V. Miller (Oxford:
       Oxford University Press), 1977. Cited by paragraph
       number.

PHI   *Die Vernunft in der Geschichte*, ed. Johannes Hoffmeister
       (Hamburg: F. Meiner, 1955).

       Lectures on the Philosophy of World History: Introduction,
       trans. H. B. Nisbet (Cambridge: Cambridge University
       Press), 1975. Cited by page number of English
       translation.

PR   *Grundlinien die Philosophie des Rechts*, vol. 7 of *Werke*.

            Elements of the Philosophy of Right, trans. H. B. Nisbet
            (Cambridge: Cambridge University Press, 1991). Cited
            by paragraph number.

PS   *Lectures on the Philosophy of Spirit 1827–1828*, trans.
            Robert Williams (Oxford: Oxford University Press,
            2007). Cited by page number.

PW   *Political Writings*, trans. H. B. Nisbet (Cambridge:
            Cambridge University Press, 1999). Cited by page
            number of English translation.

SEL   *System of Ethical Life*, in *System of Ethical life (1802/3) and
            First Philosophy of Spirit (Part III of the System of Specula-
            tive Philosophy 1803/4)*, trans. H. S. Harris (Albany: State
            University of New York Press, 1979). Cited by page
            number of English translation.

SL   *Wissenschaft der Logik*, vols. 5–6 of *Werke*.

            Hegel's Science of Logic, trans. A. V. Miller (Amherst:
            Humanity Books), 1969. Cited by page number of
            English translation.

VPR   *Vorlesugen über Rechtsphilosophie, 1818–1831*, 4 vols, ed.
            Karl-Heinz Ilting (Stuttgart: Frommann-Holzboog,
            1973). Cited by volume number, page number.

VPR17   *Die Philosophie des Rechts: Die Mitschriften Wannenmann
            (Heidelberg 1817–1818)*, ed. Karl-Heinz Ilting (Stuttgart:
            Klett-Cotta Verlag, 1983).

            *Lectures on Natural Right and Political Science: The
            First Philosophy of Right*, trans. J. Michael Stewart and
            Peter C. Hodgson (Berkeley: University of California
            Press, 1995). Cited by paragraph number.

VPR18   *Die Philosophie des Rechts: Die Mitschriften Homeyer (Berlin
            1818–1819)*, ed. Karl-Heinz Ilting (Stuttgart: Klett-Cotta
            Verlag, 1983). Cited by page number.

VPR21   *Die Philosophie des Rechts: Vorlesung von 1821–1822*, ed.
             Hansgeorg Hoppe (Frankfurt: Suhrkamp Verlag, 2005).
             Cited by paragraph number.

Kant

Ap   *Anthropology from a Pragmatic Point of View*, trans. Victor
             Lyle Dowdell (Carbondale: Southern Illinois University
             Press, 1978). Cited by page number.

CJ   *Kritik der Urteilskraft*, in vol. 5 of *Kants gesammelte
             Schriften: Akademie Ausgabe* (Berlin: Walter de Gruyter,
             1902–).

             Critique of the Power of Judgment, trans. Paul Guyer and
             Eric Matthews (Cambridge: Cambridge University Press,
             2000). Cited by page number of English translation.

CPR   *Kritik der Reinen Vernunft*, in vols. 3–4 of *Kants gesammelte
             Schriften*.

             Critique of Pure Reason, trans. Paul Guyer and Allen
             Wood (Cambridge: Cambridge University Press, 1998).
             Cited by *Kants gesammelte Schriften* page number.

CPrR   *Kritik der Praktischen Vernunft*, in vol. 5 of *Kants gesammelte
             Schriften*.

             Critique of Practical Reason, trans. T. K. Abbott
             (Amherst, N.Y.: Prometheus Books, 1996). Cited by
             page number of English translation.

GMM   *Grundlegung der Metaphysik der Sitten*, in vol. 4 of *Kants
             gesammelte Schriften*.

             Groundwork for the Metaphysics of Morals, trans.
             James W. Ellington (Indianapolis: Hackett, 1981).
             Cited by *Kants gesammelte Schriften* page number.

KPW   *Political Writings*, ed. Hans Reiss, trans. H. B. Nisbet
             (Cambridge: Cambridge University Press, 1991). Cited
             by page number.

MM   *Metaphysik der Sitten*, ed. Hans Ebeling (Stuttgart: Reclam, 1990).

            Metaphysics of Morals, trans. Mary Gregor (Cambridge: Cambridge University Press, 1996). Cited by page number of English translation.

Nietzsche

A   *Der Antichrist*, in vol. 6 of *Kritische Studienausgabe*, ed. Giorgio Colli and Mazzino Montinari (Berlin: Walter de Gruyter, 1980).

            The Anti-Christ, in *The Anti-Christ, Ecce Homo, Twilight of the Idols*, trans. Judith Norman (Cambridge: Cambridge University Press, 2005). Cited by section number.

AOM   *Vermischte Meinungen und Sprüche*, in vol. 2 of *Kritische Studienausgabe*.

            Assorted Opinions and Maxims, in *Human, All Too Human*, trans. R. J. Hollingdale (Cambridge: Cambridge University Press, 1986). Cited by aphorism number.

BGE   *Jenseits von Gut und Böse*, in vol. 5 of *Kritische Studienausgabe*.

            Beyond Good and Evil, trans. Judith Norman (Cambridge: Cambridge University Press, 2002). Cited by aphorism number.

BT   *Die Geburt der Trägodie*, in vol. 1 of *Kritische Studienausgabe*.

            The Birth of Tragedy, trans. Ronald Speirs (Cambridge: Cambridge University Press, 1999). Cited by section number.

D   *Morgenröte*, in vol. 3 of *Kritische Studienausgabe*.

            Daybreak: Thoughts on the Prejudices of Morality, trans. R. J. Hollingdale (Cambridge: Cambridge University Press, 1997). Cited by aphorism number.

EH   *Ecce Homo*, in vol. 6 of *Kritische Studienausgabe*.

Ecce Homo, in *The Anti-Christ, Ecce Homo, Twilight of the Idols*. Cited by section name, number.

FEI   *Über die Zukunft unserer Bildungsanstalten*, in vol. 1 of *Kritische Studienausgabe*.

On the Future of Our Educational Institutions, trans. Michael W. Grenke (South Bend, Ind.: St. Augustine's Press, 2004). Cited by page number of English translation.

GM   *Zur Genealogie der Moral*, in vol. 5 of *Kritische Studienausgabe*.

On the Genealogy of Morality, trans. Caroline Diethe (Cambridge: Cambridge University Press, 1994). Cited by essay, section number.

GrS   "Der griechische Staat," in vol. 1 of *Kritische Studienausgabe*.

"The Greek State," in *On the Genealogy of Morality*. Cited by page number of English translation.

GS   *Die Fröhliche Wissenschaft*, in vol. 3 of *Kritische Studienausgabe*.

The Gay Science, trans. Josefine Nauckhoff (Cambridge: Cambridge University Press, 2001). Cited by aphorism number.

HC   "Homer's Wettkampf," in vol. 1 of *Kritische Studienausgabe*.

"Homer's Contest," in *On the Genealogy of Morality*. Cited by page number of English translation.

HH   *Menschliches, Allzumenschliches*, in vol. 2 of *Kritische Studienausgabe*.

Human, All Too Human, trans. R. J. Hollingdale (Cambridge: Cambridge University Press, 1986). Cited by aphorism number.

KSA   *Kritische Studienausgabe*, ed. Giorgio Colli and Mazzino Montinari (Berlin: Walter de Gruyter, 1980). Cited by volume, notebook number, entry number.

L   *Selected Letters of Friedrich Nietzsche*, trans. Christopher Middleton (Indianapolis: Hackett, 1996). Cited by page number.

PTA   *Die Philosophie im tragischen Zeitalter der Griechen*, in vol. 1 of *Kritische Studienausgabe*.

   Philosophy in the Tragic Age of the Greeks, trans. Marianne Cowan (Washington, D.C.: Regnery, 1962). Cited by page number of English translation.

TI   *Götzen-Dämmerung*, in vol. 6 of *Kritische Studienausgabe*.

   Twilight of the Idols, in *The Anti-Christ, Ecce Homo, Twilight of the Idols*. Cited by section number, aphorism number.

UM   *Unzeitgemässe Betrachtungen*, in vol. 1 of *Kritische Studienausgabe*.

   Untimely Meditations, trans. R. J. Hollingdale (Cambridge: Cambridge University Press), 1997. Cited by meditation number, section number.

UUM   *Unpublished Writings from the Period of Unfashionable Observations*, trans. Richard T. Gray (Stanford: Stanford University Press, 1995). Cited by notebook number, entry number.

WP   *The Will to Power*, trans. Walter Kaufmann and R. J. Hollingdale (New York: Vintage Books, 1967). Cited by entry number.

WS   *Der Wanderer und sein Schatten*, in vol. 2 of *Kritische Studienausgabe*.

   The Wanderer and His Shadow, in *Human, All Too Human*. Cited by aphorism number.

Z   *Also Sprach Zarathustra*, vol. 4 of *Kritische Studien-ausgabe*.

                     Thus Spoke Zarathustra, trans. Walter Kaufmann (New York: Penguin Books, 1966). Cited by part number, title of speech.

Rousseau

E   *Emile*, trans. Allan Bloom (New York: Basic Books, 1979). Cited by page number.

SC   *On the Social Contract*, in *The Basic Political Writings*, trans. Donald A. Cress (Indianapolis: Hackett, 1987). Cited by page number.

SD   *Discourse on the Origin of Inequality*, in *The Basic Political Writings*. Cited by page number.

INTRODUCTION

Within each modern liberal regime, there are considerable disagreements about every manner of policy issue, every step in foreign affairs, every vision of the nation's future. Yet one feature of modern life is shared by even the bitterest political rivals—a moral and political commitment to the value of the individual. This commitment is quite striking and relatively new. No longer does political order have the aim of glorifying or appeasing the gods, nor of expanding the authority and might of the empire, nor of reinforcing and transmitting ancestral traditions and practices. Rather, liberal states have as their ultimate end the protection and promotion of individuality, individual identity, dignity, and rights. For instance, the German *Grundgesetz* asserts that "inviolable and inalienable human rights" are the "basis of every community" and that to "respect and protect" human dignity "shall be the duty of all state authority." The French Constitution upholds the "attachment to the Rights of Man," while the American Declaration of Independence declares "that all men are created equal, that they are endowed by their Creator with certain unalienable rights." All these foundational political documents enshrine in law liberalism's commitment to individual equality and liberty, our desire to lead our own lives, to pursue happiness in our own way, to associate and exchange with whomever we want, to assert our own voice in public and think for ourselves—rather than finding ourselves subject to the will of another, our life planned by another and our identity scripted by some authority, our voice stifled and our own thoughts suppressed.

At the same time, just as our foundational documents profess support for individualism, the very notion of liberal individuality—along with what kind of social and political order is entailed by such a notion—has become a matter of great dispute in the contemporary world. The standard liberal understanding of the individual as a self-sovereign, rights-bearing person has been challenged from many theoretical and political perspectives. The communitarian movement has criticized the liberal "unencumbered self" as too abstract and "atomistic," as encouraging an individualistic self-image divorced from those communities in which our personalities are shaped and achieve fulfillment.[1] Conservatives argue that the ideal of the "autonomous" individual gradually erodes those traditional sources of morality that transcend and bring harmony to individual wills.[2] On the left, progressives hold that classical liberal individualism obscures the social and economic conditions required to enjoy individual rights, thereby perpetuating the structural inequalities of class, race, and gender.[3] Multiculturalists worry that the individualist ethos of liberalism undermines attachment to traditional cultures and engenders the anomie of a deracinated self.[4] For postmodernists, the self-sovereign individual is an illusory goal, as identity is always already constituted through differentiating oneself from another, and these identities are constantly being renegotiated through engagement with many different others. Hence the attempt to endow individuals with self-sovereign control is undesirable as it involves a domination of this endless process of identity negotiation.[5] Finally, outside of the academy, perhaps the most pervasive criticism is the religious or traditionalist critique of the very notion of Western individuality. According to such a criticism, the dedication to individualism is decadent, corrupt, or immoral in that it dissolves traditional customs and encourages the flouting of divinely ordained commands.

In reaction to both non-Western and Western critics of individuality, this book offers a defense of the individual.[6] My strategy will not, however, be to respond directly to these critics, since many critics rely on quite different conceptions of the "individual." In order to get at the heart of the matter, I return to the basic question, what is individuality? Indeed, as Lukes (1973) has detailed, this vague term has at least seven different meanings, from political to economic to methodological individualism, all of which are lumped together in one ambiguous term within both critiques and defenses of individuality, leading to a great deal of confusion and talking past one another. However, this book does not aim to cover the same ground that Lukes does. Rather than offering an analytic survey of the different meanings of individualism, in this book I adopt a historical approach to this notion. I trace the philosophical development of this concept in its three different stages in the modern age. Since the meanings of "the individual" we contemporaries employ derive ultimately from historical philosophical disagreements, such a historical perspective can provide us with the needed philosophical context for assessing contemporary critiques. At the same time, I do not aim just to articulate the historical development of individuality in the modern age, but also to defend individuality of a certain sort, which I call "the historical individual."

In chapter 1, then, I sketch the historical development of this concept in what I argue are its three modern incarnations—the "natural," "formal," and "historical" individual. All three of these models of individuality have the same goal—the liberation of the individual—and each corrects the mistakes or one-sidedness of its predecessors. The "natural" individual, found in the empiricism and classical liberal thought of Locke, Hume, and other early moderns, supplanted the authority and aims of traditional or premodern, Christian society. However, in rooting individual freedom in naturally given desires, the defenders of this model fail to liberate the individual from nature. The "formal" individual of the rationalists Kant and Fichte frees itself from this natural desire by transforming its will in accordance with a universal moral law discerned by reason. However, the abstractness and generality of the moral law saps individuals of their concrete distinctness from one another and hence enchains them to a rigid and austere general will.

I introduce the "historical" individual, developed by G. W. F. Hegel and Friedrich Nietzsche, briefly in chapter 1, but the remainder of the book is devoted to explicating and defending it. The "historical" individual begins with the argument that individuality is not something given to all human beings, a set of natural capacities or a self that lingers like a phantom behind appearances. Rather, individuality only comes to be through certain historical practices that cultivate capacities and traits for individual independence and respect for individual uniqueness. Individuality is then not just a legal unit, but also a goal to be achieved by both community and individuals. This goal always involves different degrees of realization, depending on the structure and character of the community. In other words, the "historical individual" doctrine is first and foremost an ethical view, a view about what makes for the good life of human beings, and that is to foster a certain kind of individual character and actions suitable to the dignity of human beings. In particular, as we will see, this individual character must combine independence, autonomy, and personal uniqueness with a dedication to historically established public or common purposes. In developing personal traits of independence and autonomy, the individual liberates himself from nature, whereas by actively participating in a (certain kind of) historical community, the individual frees himself from a slavish attachment to society. The promise of the historical individual, then, is that since individuals are thoroughly formed by the historical communities in which they live, individual and community need not be opposed ideals as they have been in the history of political philosophy. On the contrary, so long as we structure community in the right way, individuality and community can be mutually reinforcing. With this understanding of individual and community, Hegel's and Nietzsche's aim is to retrieve the ancient dedication to communal excellence and human perfection on modern individualist grounds.

In eliciting this shared notion of individuality, this book contributes also to the historical scholarship on Hegel and Nietzsche. Indeed, many have considered these two thinkers to represent the opposing poles of nineteenth-century philosophy.[7] According to the traditional story, in the early part of the nineteenth century, the arch-rationalist Hegel conceived of his titanic philosophical system, which holds that a cosmic "spirit" closely resembling the Christian god achieves fulfillment and satisfies human striving in the modern state. In the later part of the century, Nietzsche waged war against Hegel and the Hegelians on nearly every count—he declared most of German philosophy to be the excrescence of an oppressive Christian morality, upheld an intractably antisystematic philosophy and writing style, and argued that those putative victories of reason actually indicate a wholesale decline in the quality of human life into a regularized, homogenized herd-like thinking. At the turn of the twentieth century in Europe, practical men found themselves with two options, either the rational collectivism of the Hegelian strand or the irrational individualism of the Nietzschean strand.

Yet my argument in this book is that Hegel and Nietzsche share the important foundational notion and aim of defending "historical individuality." I develop their similarities in a way unexplored in the literature by showing how this basic premise is developed in broadly similar ways by both thinkers.[8] My aim is to challenge the traditional account portraying a radical opposition between these two thinkers, and indeed convince the reader that their agreements are a good deal more prevalent and interesting than their disagreements. Accordingly, I have structured my discussion of the two German thinkers in order to bring out as clearly as possible the considerable degree of convergence in their thought.

Chapters 2 and 5 concern Hegel's and Nietzsche's defenses of the historical individual. For both, I argue, individuality is good because it is the good life for human beings. They arrive at this notion of the human good by eliciting the fundamental structure of what is distinctively human, our free subjectivity, by tracing the emergence of the human out of nature. They then make the case that this subjectivity has a necessary, immanent aim. This aim is that human subjects should realize themselves in the world. To do so, human subjects must autonomously craft a unified, independent individual character not compelled by the outbursts of natural passions or the dominance of tradition or custom. Individuality, in other words, is not something given to human beings, but a goal implicit in the very notion of the distinctively human subject, a goal to be achieved in order to lead a full human life, yet an aim that one is always on the way to achieving, a task achievable by degrees.

In chapters 3 and 6, I make the case that for Hegel and Nietzsche, subjects cannot become individuals through selfish or solitary activity, nor through independent, countercultural activity as in J. S. Mill's "experiments in living." Rather, individuality only comes to be through ethical participation in communal purposes. The reason is this: human beings are the products of our biological and social history. There is no kernel or substratum of my "real self," but rather my self comes to be only in my interactions with others. In order to free ourselves from nature and society, to carve out a space for our own uniqueness and freedom, we must make those interactions constitutive of our identity "our own." To do so, we must participate in the constitution of communal meaning, thereby investing what is common with my own subjectivity. We then submit ourselves to the pursuit of common purposes, and in so doing we follow our own will as the general will. For Hegel, the community in question is the (properly structured) modern state, whereas for Nietzsche, this community is culture.

Finally, chapters 4 and 7 take up Hegel's and Nietzsche's views of modern politics, since the modern state plays an important role in grounding the harmony between individuality and community and hence fostering the good life for human beings—that is, at least, for Hegel. Hegel's view is that we lead a good life by participating in modern politics since the modern state protects individual diversity while also rooting these differences in a common identity. The modern state's "mediating institutions" are the main mechanism for ensuring this harmony. By contrast, for Nietzsche, the modern state homogenizes individual distinctiveness. Only through individual participation in a culture that exists far from political influence can the individual lead an independent life. Private, classical education that resists the abstract rationalization of the modern state can provide, for Nietzsche, the mechanism to bring individuality and cultural community into harmony.

As we can see, although Hegel and Nietzsche share a kinship on this basic premise, they are something like evil twins, developing this premise in opposing directions. Their familial difficulties originate in

Rousseau, who articulated the idea of the historical individual in an inchoate form—Rousseau argued that it was not nature, but human history and society that are responsible for the successes and failures, virtues and vices, booms and busts of human civilization. Yet we also find in Rousseau the origin of the disagreement between Hegel and Nietzsche. For Rousseau, there were only two models for the good life of an individual in human society: the opposed ideals of citizen and the solitary dreamer. Hegel and Nietzsche adopted Rousseau's basic premise and thereby saw the difficulties involved in the notion of the historical individual. Yet in trying to remedy these difficulties, each grasped one of these imperfectly reconcilable strands of Rousseau's thought. For Hegel, who developed the "citizen" model of individuality, the historical individual can only achieve liberation and the good life through participating in the modern state. For Nietzsche, transforming the "solitary dreamer" model, the historical individual is enslaved by the modern state and can only find freedom and the good life outside of its boundaries in culture.

This divergence, as we will see, came from competing assessments of the rationality of the historical human subject. For Hegel, human subjectivity can come to create a rational human world through history, while for Nietzsche, history and human institutions will always be imperfectly rational, always suffused with incompletely rational irruptions of individual creativity and psychological malaise. These contradictory assessments shape and are shaped by differing views of the nature and character of politics. Hegel is optimistic about the capacity of the political state to be at once an ethical community, while Nietzsche sees the political state to be the sphere of selfish, material desire masquerading as spiritual fulfillment.

Neither of these possibilities is thoroughly satisfactory, I argue ultimately. Hegel uncovers our fundamental desire to lead ethical lives in communities with other human beings, our drive to find meaning and fulfillment in such communities. Yet Hegel fails to grasp that these communities can suppress the cultivation of difference and individual uniqueness. Hegel underestimates the individual desire for separation from and transformation of community, that individuals desire solitude or the transcendence of parochial states. Nietzsche develops this strand of individual longing, the desire to lead a unique, self-determined life, one wholly different from that of friends and compatriots and from the parochial "common good" that often forces each of us to give up something essential about ourselves. Yet Nietzsche fails to understand that modern human beings desire a rational, ethical community to afford them a sense of belonging and solidarity and a place for sharing a notion of the good life. My argument, then, is that the concept of individuality as represented in exemplary form by Hegel and Nietzsche is not without serious problems. Their inability to ground this concept indicates that the notion suffers from a deep internal wound that is, I argue, irreconcilable in theory. In sum, even if the historical individual improves upon its predecessors in redeeming and liberating individuality, we still must be aware of its internal tensions and limitations.

Finally, the reader will notice that I employ the third-person masculine pronouns to describe the individual. In doing so, I am making no political or philosophical statement. Rather, Hegel and Nietzsche argued that individuality was the privilege of men, not women. Accordingly, as I was writing, it seemed rather strange to describe Nietzsche's "sovereign individual," for instance, as a "she." This issue is a complicated one, beyond the scope of this book, yet one I think Hegel and Nietzsche are wrong about—I think we have seen that in the contemporary world men as well as women are able to achieve individuality equally. Yet regardless of whether they were right or wrong on this matter, I defer to their views and pronouns in interpreting them.

1

Three Concepts of Individuality

Individuality is in many ways the foundational modern concept. Consider by way of illustration the derivative character of individuality in "premodern" societies, which are founded and sustained based on appeals to supraindividual entities or ideals, such as tradition, nature, or God.[1] In premodern societies, individuals' social function and duties, their political rights and responsibilities, their honors and their shame, their personal identities and sense of place in the universe, are all established by their role or station within tradition or nature or the "Great Chain of Being." For the premoderns, "community" precedes "individuality" in at least three senses. First, premodern community provides individuals with an identity or self-understanding such that individuals think of themselves first and foremost as members of a community—as Spartans or Athenians, for instance. Second, the community is the source of legitimate binding authority on individuals. The church, or the elders, or nature itself declares that I have certain duties to perform, certain rules to abide by, and hence I must follow this authority whether or not I happen to disagree or even have a say in the matter. Finally, the community sets the ends for individual action, the function for its members' lives. Traditional communities contain certain roles that individuals occupy and strive to live up to with excellence or virtue, such that the failure to perform one's role is regarded as a failure to lead a good life. These ends are ultimately rooted in something like an Aristotelian natural science or a Great Chain of Being, a metaphysical edifice in which human beings are situated and which grounds our specific role or meaning, the standard for living a complete human life.

By contrast, modern individuality challenges premodern community on all three fronts, seeking thereby to liberate the individual from these premodern constraints. First, moderns argue that individuals should be free to choose their own associations, craft their own identities, and hence be recognized in virtue of their own self-developed identity rather than one developed for them. Individuals should have this freedom because, second, individuals are the only legitimate authorities over themselves. I am thereby obliged to obey a social or political norm only insofar as I acknowledge this norm as binding upon me. Finally, individuals do not (or rather, should not) derive the meaning of their lives from some external metaphysical or political structure, but rather craft for themselves an understanding of the good life. These basic normative ideals are the basis for a liberal institutional design—for instance, a civil society of estates and associations open to the free choice of all, the administration of justice blind to class or gender differences among individuals, regular elections and the rotation of offices.

As we will see, though the philosophers of the modern age agree about these basic features of the individual, they nonetheless disagree vehemently about how this ideal can be realized in the political world. The notion of individuality, I argue, undergoes a development in the history of modern philosophy, and this development occurs in three stages, each stage dialectically building on the previous one. In this chapter, I briefly articulate the first two conceptions of individuality in the modern age, what I call the "natural" and "formal" individuals. Each of these views is seeking to solve a problem posed by the previous understanding, and so part of the task of this chapter will be to clarify the main objections to these first two models of individuality in an attempt to set the stage for a defense of the "historical" individual in the remainder of the book.

My account of this development follows Hegel's own views. For Hegel, there are "always only two possible viewpoints" to develop a theory of the individual and community. First, one can "proceed atomistically and move upward from the basis of individuality [*Einzelheit*]" to community. Or one can "start from substantiality" (PR 156Z) or from community and work down toward individuality. The second is Hegel's own position, whereas Hegel attributes the first to his modern predecessors such as Hobbes, Locke, Rousseau, and Kant. These "atomists" come in two varieties, what I will refer to as the "natural" and "formal" individuals, following Hegel's own presentation in his early essay "On the Scientific Ways of Treating Natural Law." The main problem with naturalist and formalist "atomism" is, as we will see, that this "viewpoint excludes spirit, because it leads only to an aggregation, whereas spirit is not something individual [*nichts Einzelnes*] but the unity of the individual [*Einzelnen*] and the universal" (PR 156Z). In other words, the atomistic approach to individuality cannot make intelligible the ethical commitments that make up what Hegel calls "Spirit," and hence fail ultimately to ground individual freedom.

1.1   The Natural Individual

The early modern thinkers, from Machiavelli through Hobbes, Locke, and Hume, articulated an understanding of individuality in reaction to the problems of the premodern view of individuality. For these philosophers, as Hegel put it, the premodern community regarded "individuality as such [as] nothing, and simply one with absolute ethical majesty."[2] The objections to the premodern view are many and well known, so I will briefly enumerate two. First, premodern community stifled the development of human knowledge that can master nature, better society, and relieve human suffering. Instead of relying on inherited custom to understand the world outside of the individual, the early moderns argued, the individual should grasp the world based on his own senses and reason. The empiricism of Hobbes, Locke, and Hume rooted human knowledge not in tradition or revelation, but in the direct encounter between individual mind and the world. A consequence of this shift was that the new modern science led ultimately to a modern view of nature and the cosmos not as sustaining any objective moral order "out there" but rather as consisting in nonmoral mechanistic interactions of cause and effect. A core feature, then, of the premodern justification of community over individuality was stripped away, and individuals were cast back upon themselves without any "metaphysical" connection to a higher power or transcendent purpose.

The second objection to the premodern demotion of individuality is that it is not conducive to stable political order. As Machiavelli famously argued in chapter 15 of *The Prince*, the "gap between how people actually behave and how they ought to behave is so great that anyone who ignores everyday reality in order to live up to an ideal will soon discover he has been taught how to destroy himself, not how to preserve himself" (Machiavelli 1995). Premodern societies aim too high and seek to fulfill cosmic ends and noble purposes. If we lower the sights of political order and seek, not to reform the souls of individuals, but merely what individuals already want, that is, preservation of life and protection of property, we can be much more successful and happy.

Based on these criticisms, these thinkers developed a new notion of individuality that precedes tradition, custom, indeed all social and political order, in the hypothetical "state of nature." The early modern empiricists stripped the individual human being down to his universal basic nature—essentially consistent with all other animals in nature, the human individual is constituted and guided by a set of passions, the most powerful of which is the fear of death. Moved by these passions alone, human beings have been engaged in one melancholy conflict after another for most of human history. Fortunately, individuals also possess a reflective, instrumental rationality which helps us overcome the chaos of the state of nature. Accordingly, as Hegel puts it, philosophers like Hobbes "sought to derive the bond which holds the state together . . . from principles which lie within us, which we recognize as our own" (HP 3, 316).[3] Our natural passions, especially those of fear, honor, and the desire for happiness—those that are so elemental that we must think of them as "our own"—become the basis for norms of political order.

Social and political order, then, are understood not as serving the ethical or metaphysical aims of some supraindividual entity. On the contrary, the early moderns regard political order as a contract among individuals preceding that order. The social contract is an ingenious theoretical model, ensuring individual freedom and communal order. Each individual can freely give his consent to a group of equals in a social contract, which establishes the authority of a general government in order to avoid the "inconveniences" of the state of nature, such as the lack of an indifferent judge.[4] Thus, this contract preserves the freedom and self-ownership of each individual by tracing the legitimacy of governmental coercion back to individual freedom itself, rather than back to a claim of nature, God, or tradition—"obedience to the laws of the state, as the rational basis of volition and action, was now made into a principle. In this obedience, human beings are free, for the particular [now] obeys the general" (PW 204). At the same time, since individuals in a truly "rational" state will come to pursue their own "natural" desire for a "commodious living"—rather than the traditional, premodern goals of nobility and excellence foisted upon them by their societies—individuals can engage in a commercial society that supplies a wealth of material goods and reduces the likelihood of physical conflict.

Philosophers from Rousseau through Hegel and Marx criticized this model of the "natural individual" for two reasons, the first having to do with the authority and the second with the aim of the individual.[5] First, the natural individual cedes its authority over moral norms to nature. The defenders of this view of individuality crafted their empiricist science of natural law in accordance with the growing modern scientific understanding of nature as nonteleological, as mere matter-in-motion governed by necessary laws. The empiricists thus cast the individual into the deterministic matrix of natural causes and effects. The inevitable question for these philosophers became how to reconcile our free, purposive moral and political lives with the mechanistic scientific worldview. If nature is simply a deterministic matrix of efficient causes, and nature is all there is, there seems to be no place for what Aristotle called "final causes" at all. Nature just is—there is no normative purpose that natural things strive toward and by which we can assess them. But then how do we square a purposeless world with purposive human lives and with the moral and ethical claims we make on one another?

The philosophical empiricists, much like contemporary naturalists, strive to explain our normative lives within a purposeless universe. For the most part, they claim, explanations of human behavior based on nature are easy. Human beings get angry, sad, boastful; we feel and respond to pleasure and pain; we seek food and shelter and seek to preserve ourselves. We share all of these qualities with animals, and we can locate the sources of these passions in psychological traits or determinate features of our bodies, and, more recently, in precise locations within our brains. Thus, empiricists conclude that these qualities are "natural," built in to the biological constitution of animals. In particular, early modern philosophers explained human behavior as more or less complex responses to pleasure and pain, to our desire for happiness and our fear of death. Accordingly, a human outburst of anger can be explained through efficient causation, just like the wrath of a lion. Natural desires such as self-preservation cause human beings or lions to lash out in certain cases—when they are threatened, for instance.

When we come upon more complex forms of human interaction, naturalistic reduction gets trickier. The stumbling block for empiricists is reason. Human beings do not always or even primarily act like animals, thoughtlessly pursuing our own natural pleasures. Rather, we exchange reasons with one another, deliberating about what would be "good" for us to do, whether we "ought" to act on our pressing animalistic desire or not. This introduction of reason is challenging to the empiricist because it appears to interrupt the deterministic matrix of efficient causation. Nature apparently does not cause human beings to act in the way it causes animals and plants and rocks to move. Human beings still feel the pull of natural desire, but we are not determined to act on this desire. We can decide whether or not we ought to act on the desire.

Empiricists "instrumentalize" reason, just as they do to social and political institutions. The individual stands externally to reason just as he stands externally to his political and social institutions, ready to put it to good use in the satisfaction of his naturally given desires. Reason is a later addition to human development, a biological advantage we have evolved that can help us better satisfy our desires. It serves as the "scout and spy" of the natural passions, or the "slave to the passions," in finding more prudent, efficient, and elaborate ways to satisfy our desires.[6] Reason and language bring human beings together and show us that we would be better off restraining the immediate satisfaction of our natural needs. If we would all agree to regulate our natural desires according to certain artificial rules—what we come to call the just and the unjust— then we would all benefit more than how we would otherwise fare in the state of nature.

In other words, the empiricists locate the phenomenon of human reason in the picture of a deterministic matrix of efficient causation by making reason the tool of this efficient causation. Nature, the empiricists argue, is imperfect. As Hegel glosses Hobbes, the "natural condition is not what it should be, and must hence be cast off" (HP 3, 318). Nature supplies human beings with desires that, when pursued, leads to wholesale misery. The system of efficient causation must thereby be transformed by human reason such that the aggregate result of the system is the greater overall satisfaction of naturally given desires. Two hallmarks of modern science—the modern conquest of nature and modern social science—are expressions of instrumental reason's attempt to transform the given matrix of causation into a "better" one. In the first case, modern natural science as Bacon described it was founded on the project of improving the system of efficient causation such that it becomes more amenable to naturally given human desires.[7] Improvements in medicine and technology with the aim of the prolongation of human life and the increased comfort of human beings are examples of such transformations. In the second case, modern political science is the attempt to find increasingly better artificial or institutional matrices of efficient causation. Taking human beings as we are, not as we ought to be, is a recurring refrain in modern political science.[8] Institutions are designed so as to direct pregiven natural desire in the right sort of ways, that is, in ways in which we refrain from harming one another and gain the most satisfaction possible.

So, in short, empiricists reduce what appear to be final causes, the claims of the right and the good, to efficient causes. Human beings give and exchange reasons because we ultimately want to satisfy our given natural desires, and we find that holding ourselves to conventions will more effectively satisfy natural desires. The index of good and bad regimes, then, boils down to how well these regimes fulfill naturally given desires. The question of the just or the unjust in itself or apart from human convention makes no sense, then.[9] It would be like asking whether or not it was just for the lion to devour its prey. Final causes are thus epiphenomena of human conventions. In all cases of the norms within conventions, we can tell a developmental story in which human beings imposed these norms upon ourselves in order to better satisfy some pregiven needs. The only standard of assessment we have ultimately, then, is the standard of those given natural desires.

However, Hegel asks, how can human nature or natural desires serve as a normative standard if these desires are by definition the efficient causes of nature on us?[10] What makes our desires any more worthy of satisfaction than the lion's, or the cow's, or the goldfish's? The natural individual has no more bedrock standard by which to evaluate his basic natural passions, cannot question whether they are good or bad passions to have at all, cannot ask whether nature as such is a good authority to follow. Instead, the empiricists attempt to pass off their contingent natural desires as "necessary" and "universal" standards of human conduct. Their argument defending their normative claims is a characteristically empiricist inductive one—empiricists infer from the given data of human activity the general moral norms that should structure their society. Yet as the empiricist Hume had argued, nothing "necessary" or "universal" can arise from induction.[11] The demands of nature can at best tell us what we want to do, not what we ought to do.

Yet the natural individual cannot transcend nature in order to bring his own standards of assessment to bear on the content given to him by nature. There is always a limit of the reflective determination of the individual will, as when Hume encounters his "philosophical melancholy" in reflecting too much.[12] This limit is supposed to indicate that nature is the final sovereign arbiter of the determination of the individual will. The individual does not act in accordance with his own self-determined choices, but rather with the impulses nature supplies to him. The whole edifice of human society that we are responsible for is an elaborate causal result of the human pursuit of naturally given desires. When a natural individual acts on what he deems to be "just" or "unjust," he is acting based on principles that are instrumental to the satisfaction of pregiven desires.[13] The individual becomes sovereign in name only. Yet it is precisely this kind of illusion and unfreedom that modernity aimed to overcome.

The second problem of the natural individual concerns his aim, or, we might say, the kind of individual and communal character likely to be produced by this view. Hegel argues that the conception of the individual as preceding and hence willfully choosing his social and political associations shapes a character who thinks he is "external" to these conventions.[14] The natural individual thereby comes to think of his social and political institutions as a craftsman stands to his produced instrument. This relationship of *techne* involves a producer who builds an instrument to satisfy the pregiven needs he possesses. Without this instrument he would not be able to satisfy his needs. For instance, a craftsman needs to drive in a nail, and has been advised not to do so with his fist. He thus produces a hammer in order to drive in the nail. Similarly, the naturalist individual builds social and political institutions so as to satisfy his basic needs and allow him a free space to pursue life, liberty, and happiness. Without these institutions, the individual becomes lost in a chaotic state of nature.

The naturalist individual thus understands his institutions as the craftsman understands his hammer. The relationship of individual to community is an "inorganic" or technological one. The naturalist individual "uses" his mechanistic institutions by consenting with others to erect and obey the laws. The institutions of government are thus a "formless external harmony" that "remains something formal, which merely hovers above the multiplicity without penetrating it" (PW 113). Individuals obey the laws because they suit their pregiven needs, and become annoyed when laws ask them to do something onerous or counter to their needs. According to Hegel, communal order and stability are thereby threatened when the individual understands his basic relationship with others as accidental or contingent, because the tenuous communal bond may at any time break down and leave the individual stranded once again in the state of nature. According to Hegel, the social contract method of knitting individuals together based on pregiven interests should be only a temporary and insufficient solution. Unfortunately, this conception of the individual is the "reflective standpoint of our time, this atomistic spirit, the spirit that consists in taking pride in one's individual interests and not in what is communal." The deleterious result of this self-understanding is that countries "distintegrate into atoms" and "empires [go] into decline" (VPR17 121A).

Hegel saw the toxic effect of this philosophy at work in his contemporary Germany. At the end of the eighteenth century, Germany was not a unified state, but a loose confederation of principalities with feudal pedigrees. The "modern" view of "constitutional law" gave up looking for a rational principle to ground national unity and settled for a "description of what is present empirically" (PW 6). The whole of constitutional law, then, became a description of "rights against the state" (PW 15). For Hegel, this political atomism led to a dissolution of the unified political sovereignty of the state and hence a weakening of each individual principality itself, as there is every reason to think that such atomistic fragmentation would continue at the principality level. Though the problem of the "German Constitution" was not initiated by modern thought, it was exacerbated by empiricist atomism. The "atomistic spirit" of empiricism allowed each principality to "behave as an absolutely free and self-sufficient power" (VPR17 121).[15] However, this self-understanding is a complete illusion and hence a failure of self-knowledge. Each principality is "unaware of the fact that all of them are instruments in the hands of higher powers—primordial fate and all-conquering time—which laugh at their supposed freedom and self-sufficiency" (PW 51). Throughout his corpus, from his *Logic* to the practical philosophy, Hegel elicits the self-contradiction involved in the hubristic claim to atomistic self-sufficiency—agents think of themselves as self-sufficient, yet their very self-understanding presupposes a larger communal practice in which such a self-relation is possible.

Hegel elaborates on this self-contradiction in his section on "Abstract Right" in the PR. For Hegel, the abstract atomistic individual of Hobbes and Locke—described as the "person" in "Abstract Right"—cedes sovereign authority over contract exchange to a will shared in common with another.[16] However, each individual agrees to the terms of the contract in word or deed only. Accordingly, "it is purely contingent whether [the individuals'] *particular* wills are in conformity with" the norms of the contract (PR 81). The individual's will remains "external" to the general will created to regulate the stipulations of the political contract. The individual does not *internalize* the norms of the contract. In cases of conflict between the general duty to adhere to the contract and the individual's natural desires, the individual may come to see the contract as a mere obstacle to circumvent for the satisfaction of these desires. For Hegel, this understanding of individuality leads inevitably to "crime" and hence the negation of "right" itself.[17] Unless the individual can internalize the common will and hence transform his given, natural desires into moral desires, right itself will have no foundation, and all individuals will return to a basic state of nature. The same worry persists in Hegel's mind in a more concrete setting in the "inward rebellion" of the "rabble," those impoverished individuals who blame the government for their woe, and hence see the state as external and oppressive (PR 244Z). For Hegel, as soon as individuals view the state as external to their basic identities, the maintenance of the contract simply rests on the fragile bond of economic incentive, the tenuous harmony of institutional norms and natural desires, a bond easily broken through the vicissitudes of the market or the cunning of the knave. For Hegel, the problem originates in the early moderns' emphasizing the critical project of liberating the human mind from prejudice, and hence focusing on a notion of liberty for the individual as freedom from social authority. They thus set aside an older conception of liberty that prized our freedom from natural desires, the individual's capacity for self-mastery and self-determination. In short, then, the defenders of natural individuality succeed in one way, but fail ultimately to meet the ideal of modern individuality, that of the liberation of the individual.

1.2   The Formal Individual

According to the natural individual model, human beings are naturally full of bad passions. We are selfish, power-hungry, and vain. The defenders of natural individuality argue that the best, most prudent response to this is that we should not seek to better our moral character, but rather to arrange society and politics to satisfy natural needs as well as we can. However, Rousseau, Kant, and Fichte break from this understanding of the natural individual. For Kant, the aim of the natural individual—the satisfaction of material desires—does not differentiate human individuals from sheep. The natural individual does not, Kant says in speaking about Herder, "give a satisfactory answer to the question . . . of whether it would not have been just as good if this island had been occupied by happy sheep and cattle as by happy human beings" (KPW 220). But human beings are greater than and distinct from natural individuals. As Rousseau puts it, "freedom" represents what is distinctively human, our capacity to act in opposition to natural stimulus—nature "commands every animal, and beasts obey," while the human being "feels the same impetus, but he knows he is free to go along or to resist" (SD 45). We can resist natural urges, call these desires into question, even try to cultivate for ourselves different sorts of desires. For instance, human beings have the capacity to turn against absolutely everything in nature. Kant gives the example of a man who can stake his very life for a rational ideal (CPrR 45), and Hegel suggests that the human being is the only animal that can take its own life (PR 5Z).

In other words, the early modern thinkers highlight the continuity of the human being with nature's aims (the passions) and authority (the satisfaction of natural desires). By contrast, Kant seeks to restore the dignity of humanity as having a greater authority and higher aims than nature. Kant does not ground this dignity in a premodern understanding of the "function" of humanity in an ordered cosmos. Rather, Kant seeks to deepen the modern project to liberate the individual. For Kant, the source of normative authority does not come from "out there" in the world, but rather comes from us, from the commands we as rational beings give to ourselves. Reason has this authority because it is the only possible basis for a nonquestion begging normative authority. All other claims to normative authority—tradition, nature, and God—at bottom rely on some claim about the goodness of tradition, the goodness of nature, or the goodness of God's commands. Yet all these authorities can be called into question, dragged before the court of reason as the final "unconditioned" arbiter. It is "unconditioned" because any attempt to call reason into question from some more basic perspective would necessarily involve dragging reason in front of the court of reason. The Kantian "Copernican Revolution" in philosophy eliminates standards of judgment deriving from the structure of the universe or from human nature as possible sources of normativity (CPR Bxvi). Instead, Kant argued, reason is self-grounding or self-legislating. It is legislator, judge, and jury all in one, the ultimate and authoritative source of moral norms.

For Kant, then, being a free individual means being rational. Yet "rationality" here is not the "instrumental" rationality of the early moderns, but rather a reason that can autonomously generate rules for human action. Reason can liberate individuals both from natural impulse and social conformity by providing them with rational aims. These rational aims can be derived by investigating the necessary "formal" conditions for acting rationally at all. As Kant puts it, "since I have deprived the will of every impulse that might arise for it from obeying any particular law, there is nothing left to serve the will as principle except the universal conformity of its actions to law as such" (GMM 402). For an action to be rational, in other words, it must be lawlike—it cannot be based on whim or impulse, which, as in the animals, have their basis in natural desires. Human actions are performed for reasons—they are structured according to lawlike principles or "maxims" that can be applied generally. For instance, the firefighter who puts himself in harm's way to save a child performs this action for a reason that can be articulated in terms applicable to and assessable for all firefighters (e.g., "just doing my job" or "because each child is an end in herself" could be candidates for a reason for such an action).

For Kant, the "test" for whether my reason for acting is a good one or not—and hence whether I am acting rationally—is whether my "maxim" can be universalized without contradiction (GMM 402). Kant uses the example of a person who willfully breaks a promise to illustrate this famous "categorical imperative" of reason. The intentional promise breaker follows a law that is self-contradictory. In order to break a promise, the person does two things—first, he abides by and hence binds himself to the laws constitutive of the practice of promising, which includes the law that one must follow through on one's own side of the promise. Second, at the same time, he exempts himself from these same laws. He both submits himself to the law and claims that he is above the law (GMM 403). As Kant puts it, his maxim "destroys itself" in the process of universalization (CPrR 5:28), which means that his subjective intention or "maxim" cannot be made into a coherent law of action, but remains hopelessly self-contradictory. The person who acts in a self-contradictory way fails to be rational, and hence, since reason is the judge of how we ought to act, he fails to be moral.

For Kant, then, every individual is a being capable of freeing itself from natural impulse and social tradition. Accordingly, a "rational being" is that being "who obeys no law except what he at the same time enacts himself" (GMM 434). An individual can only act rationally by acting based on his own reason. In acting based on the moral law, such an individual makes our distinctive humanity visible to all others. By contrast, an individual guided or coerced by an authority is little different from an animal caught in the natural nexus of cause and effect. The only way to demonstrate my autonomy, moreover, is to be given an unfettered space in which to exercise it (KPW 73–74). Therefore, the individual duty to be rationally autonomous grounds a "right" on the part of individuals in politics to act without coercion from fellow citizens. Furthermore, in the moral realm, Kant argues that the humanity within each individual implies that we must treat all other rational agents as "ends in themselves" rather than means to our own ends (GMM 433). This is because in order to promote their own humanity, rational individuals must recognize that humanity resides in all individuals, as there is no rational reason to privilege their own humanity over that of others. For Kant, history is intelligible as a progression of the human species toward this "kingdom of ends," in which our empirical, passionate natures described by the early modern defenders of the natural individual are gradually transformed by pure practical reason such that the moral law becomes "second nature" for us (KPW 51).[18]

For Hegel, the formal individual marks a distinct advance on the model of natural individuality, but is nonetheless subject to problems of both authority and aim. First, the authority of reason is an overly abstract and empty authority. The formal individual is just an empty I spinning about in his empty world in a "serene unity with itself, without any substantive principles to act upon" (ES 413Z; cf. PhG 167). Kant's view of practical reason as conforming to a formal, universal law amounts, according to Hegel, to a principle of noncontradiction in moral action (PR 135A), that is, that I should not contradict myself in my own principle of action. Yet for Hegel, this formal procedure of assessing the moral worth of actions is insufficient to offer guidance for the substance of one's actions (PW 123–24). What maxim should I choose in the first place, before I submit it to a universalization test? Reason is empty of such guidance, and hence, Hegel argues, the practical principle of noncontradiction is consistent with behavior devoid of ethical conduct (PW 125–26). That is, there is no contradiction in being a completely consistent egoist, the person who declares, I do not treat others as means to my own ends; I just don't care about them.[19]

Indeed, for Hegel, the authority of abstract reason encourages the development of such an unethical, internalized character who shuns the external world, called the "beautiful soul" (PhG 632ff.; cf. PR 140A).[20] Hegel argues that the "infinite" will of the formal individual abstracts from all concrete, determinate content, since "any content presupposes a heteronomy of the arbitrary will" (PW 124). The formal individual comes to regard the finite world as fallen, corrupt, unworthy of his will. The individual thereby eschews public, ethical action, not wanting to tarnish his infinite will containing infinite possibilities by choosing some finite content which will never measure up to his infinitude. Instead, the beautiful soul basks "in the glory of [its] self-knowledge and self-expression" (PR 140A). Yet the problem with this "beautiful soul" is a version of the same problem of abstractness—since the beautiful soul never engages in determinate activity, he can never be sure what his beauty consists in. His beautiful nature is empty. Indeed, he can never know whether the beauty that he perceives by introspection is in fact beauty at all, or whether it is a carbon copy of some effete aesthete in some other Parisian salon.[21] In "this transparent purity of its moments, an unhappy, so-called 'beautiful soul,' its light dies away within it, and it vanishes like a shapeless vapor that dissolves into thin air" (PhG 658).

The abstract authority of reason further encourages an unethical character because it is unstable. Hegel argues that the formalist individual comes to stand toward his content with arbitrariness, that he could easily have chosen otherwise than he did (PR 15). As a result, the formalist individual dangerously slides into a position of "irony" toward his own autonomously given laws (PR 140A). The individual as lawgiver gives himself a law, but he could have easily given himself another law. No content completely satisfies the individual because the individual's formal, choosing will always has many possible choices in front of him. Since the content that the individual actually does choose is made on a whim (on what other basis can the rational will choose the substance of its behavior?), then he *qua* infinite will has not bound himself to this content, but always already stands at a reflective remove from it. He sees arbitrariness or randomness in his content, not his own autonomous will. Therefore, the infinite autonomy of the individual never fully commits itself to any finite law or content. The individual "has a relation to this objectivity [of finite law], [but] it at the same time distances itself from it and knows itself as that which wills and resolves in a particular way but may equally well will and resolve otherwise" (PR 140A). Consequently, Hegel worries, the individual will never fully commit to the principles constitutive of social and political life. He may follow the laws of the land, or he may not—what he does is a matter of arbitrariness. He "merely plays with them as with my own caprice." This individual is "empty of all ethical content" (PR 140A).

Finally, Hegel argues that the authority of abstract reason deteriorates into a kind of Romantic subjectivism. The return to one's immediate sentiment is itself a project of realizing self-sufficiency—only by being with oneself in one's "heart" can one truly rely on oneself alone. Yet Hegel argues that this immediate sentiment destroys the autonomy of individuality in appealing to sentiment and not to lawlike reason. The man who appeals to the "oracle within his breast" remains enchained to the "merely animal" nature (PhG 69). His natural feelings do not provide concrete principles of conduct nor applications of this conduct in the manifold situations of modern life, but rather supplies the individual with the "mush of 'heart, friendship, and enthusiasm'" (PR Preface, 16). The individual relies not on himself, but on the claims of nature, which land him squarely back in the camp of the empiricist individual. He stands possibly in a worse situation, however, because at least the empiricist individual was willing to listen to instrumental reason to tell him that the rule of law was a good mechanism to satisfy pregiven desire. The appeal to immediate sentiment does not allow for such instrumental calculation, but in fact turns strongly against it, enjoining the individual to a hatred of law as a *"dead, cold letter* and a *shackle*," which is the precise antithesis of his "warm," lively, particularistic "heart" (PR Preface, 17).

The second problem with the formalist individual concerns the aims of abstract reason. For Hegel, abstract reason leads to abstract aims that are destructive of all existing institutions and practices. For Hegel, the truly terrorizing consequences of a *Willkür*-like general will emerged in the application of this formal general will in the aftermath of the French Revolution (and, in forms Hegel did not witness, as in the internment and death camps, the gulags, and so forth). The abstract moral judgments of reason condemn all finite content for failing to meet the demands of the moral law. As Hegel argues, all existing political arrangements will contain inequalities antithetical to abstract reason, since social and political inequalities are shaped by the necessary natural inequalities among human beings (PR 49A). All concrete everyday content contains difference, rank, nuance, whereas the general will contains only sameness, equality, simplicity from its most abstract principles.[22] Since no attempt to "correct" these inequalities will ever completely succeed, the general will assumes a project of total destruction of everything concrete and particular (PR 5A). Hegel understands the "'Terror" following the French Revolution to be the necessary working out of the logic of abstract reason's aims in the French Revolution itself.

According to Hegel, these problems stem ultimately from the "atomism" of the formalist individual, the problematic ontology of the individual which the formal individual shares with the naturalist individual. In attempting to liberate the individual from society and nature, both views quite sensibly conceive the individual as independent of nature and separable from the society and politics he may elect to join. The formalist individual demonstrates the problem, however, with this "atomistic" ontology, in that the formalist individual dialectically undermines the very purpose this "atomism" sought to serve. Whereas "atomistic" individualism sought to free individuals, the problems with the formalist individual reveal that "atomism" results in an abstract, empty moral law that is both unstable and destructive, an atomism that abstracts human beings from the concrete political world and fails to return them to it.

1.3   Rousseau and the Historical Individual

Hegel and Nietzsche, I argue in the rest of this book, articulate and defend a third development in the concept of individuality, the "historical individual." In defending this concept, these philosophers seek to deepen the modern project and thereby truly liberate the individual while not turning back the clock to a premodern moral order. Accordingly, Hegel and Nietzsche incorporate the insights of their predecessors by situating the other aims of individuality within a historical community animated to produce complete human individuals. As Hegel argues, individual authority and aims are not the result of some predetermined private choice, but are always already negotiated through individual participation in an ethical community. Paradoxically, then, it is only through ethically participating in a community that individuals can become complete individuals. To be a complete individual involves harmonizing the three elements of a complete human being—in Hegel's language, the "particular" material desires, which derive from nature and constitute the kind of freedom characteristic of the natural individual; the "universal" moral will, which derives from human reason and which makes up the freedom of the formal individual; finally, the "individual" narrative, which weaves universal norms and particular desires together into determinate ethical actions and practices.

This will undoubtedly sound rather vague before I flesh out the notion more fully in the rest of the book, but perhaps it will be helpful if I provide two points of context. First, the historical individual represents Hegel's and Nietzsche's attempts to restore an ancient ethos of nobility or excellence to the modern age without giving up on its commitment to individualism. From their point of view, neither the natural nor the formal individual succeeded on its own terms, nor do they provide an adequate response to the premodern form of ethical community. Both previous models of individuality failed to take on the ancient view on its own grounds, that is, that the goodness of community does not reside in how well it preserves individual bodies or spaces for freedom of movement, but rather in how well it fosters a full or complete human life.[23] In this regard, the bodily desires of the natural individual fail to do justice to the dignity of distinctively human longings. The abstract rationality of the formalist individual discourages the development of the totality or completeness of the human being as a composite of both reason and passion.[24] Leading a complete life involves—for Hegel and Nietzsche, transforming the ancient position—sharing sovereign normative authority and aims in a properly structured ethical practice. Such a practice will nonetheless be built on modern foundations—on what Hegel calls the "infinite" value of individuality—precisely in order to incorporate the advances of modern individualism in a project of cultivating complete individuals. Modern life can "aim higher" than its humble origins in Machiavelli's fifteenth chapter of *The Prince* suggest. In fact, modernity can accommodate premodern aims on its own individualistic grounds.

The second point of context is related to the first. The historical individual did not emerge fully formed out of the minds of Hegel and Nietzsche, but arose in an inchoate form in Jean-Jacques Rousseau. In Rousseau we can see rather clearly the above dedication to redeeming the modern age. The ancient world, especially Sparta, successfully "denatured" human beings, allowing them to lead ethical lives as "part of the unity" of community (E 40). Yet the fact that individuals served as merely an appendage of a social whole injured the inherent dignity of individuality. However, the modern world, built on the foundations of liberating individuality, actually deepens the enslavement of individuals, Rousseau reasons, this time to an excessive, slavish dependence on public opinion stemming from our *amour-propre*, our desire for social approval. Rousseau's task is to design modern institutions (especially a state based on the modern "social contract") that will reshape the character of this *amour-propre* such that individuals come to seek public approval in civic-minded activities.[25]

Rousseau offered his *Social Contract* and his Romantic *Solitary Walker* as two different models of modern redemption. However, Rousseau's *Social Contract* and his Romantic sentimental *Walker* are still nonetheless rooted in a formal understanding of individuality, with its attendant problems. Nonetheless, Rousseau introduces for Hegel and Nietzsche both the problem the historical individual is meant to respond to—the redemption of an unethical modern age—and the adumbration of two solutions to this problem. These two solutions involve the realization of what Rousseau calls "civil liberty" and "natural liberty" (SC 151).[26] The "civil liberty" path of the participant in the *Social Contract*'s general will was taken up by Hegel. Along this path, the historical individual can only lead a full individual life through participation in the state.[27] By contrast, the "natural liberty" path of the *Solitary Walker* was taken up by Nietzsche. Here, individuals are enslaved by the public norms of society and politics, and can only find completion in the context of culture.[28] Rousseau, then, indicates already in the eighteenth century that this inchoate concept has two very divergent strands at bottom. It was the task, then, of Hegel and Nietzsche to pursue these different paths to their contradictory end points.

2

Hegel's Defense of Individuality

Hegel may seem to be a strange choice as a champion of individuality. He does, after all, liken the state to a "substance" and individuals to its "accidents" (PR 145Z). Leading a proper ethical life, Hegel argues, "consists in fulfilling the duties imposed upon [an individual] by his social station," and the "worth of individuals is measured by the extent to which they reflect and represent the national spirit" (PHI 80). Further, only a professional elite civil service is competent to oversee the universal concerns of the state and thereby maintain the existing rational social structure.[1] The task of political philosophy is to reconcile individuals to the modern state by "comprehending and portraying the state as an inherently rational entity" (PR Preface, 21). Though scholars of Hegel have long since dispensed with the view that Hegel holds a protofascist view of the state, nonetheless Hegel's modern rational state, in which nonexpert "citizens have only a limited share in the universal business of the state" (PR 255Z), and in which the democratic elements of public opinion and universal suffrage are denigrated, seems to leave a severely circumscribed role for individuality (PR 317–18).

However, my aim in what follows is to challenge this interpretation of the passive Hegelian individual kowtowing to the rationality of the state. Indeed, I claim in what follows the very opposite, that is, that Hegel envisioned individuals as key participants in the political process. Individuals must serve such a role, for Hegel, because the good life for human beings can occur only through political participation. Only by cultivating this good life for individuality, I argue, can the modern social and political order be justified.[2] Accordingly, as I stressed in the previous chapter, Hegel owes a great deal to Rousseau's model of the active citizen leading a good life in politics. As we will see later, however, the political activity is institutionally dispersed and structured for Hegel, which distinguishes his model of individuality from Rousseau and indeed from the ancients.

This interpretation that Hegel defends an active citizenry contrasts with a good deal of literature that reads Hegel as closer to the liberal tradition.[3] Yet this interpretation contrasts at a deeper level with recent scholarship on Hegel. For in order to make good on this interpretation, I argue that "active citizenship" is justified based on Hegel's philosophical view of the good life for human beings, and hence that modern politics is justified as providing the best institutional system for the good life. For a long while in Anglo-American Hegel scholarship, the general assumption was that Hegel's political reflections could be useful independently of Hegel's logic and hence his basic justification for modern individuality and community. In recent years, however, this debate has lapsed, and Hegel's logic has returned to the study of his political thought.[4] The main disagreement in the literature now concerns how to understand Hegel's project of justification, whether as a metaphysical or nonmetaphysical project.

On the one hand, the metaphysical interpreters of Hegel, such as Peperzak (2001) and Beiser (2005), argue that the systematic development of the categories of human thought outlined in Hegel's *Logic* can only be justified for Hegel if this structure of thought is not just the structure of how we view the world, but how the world in itself is.[5] On the other hand, the nonmetaphysical "Left Hegelians" like Pippin (1989), Pinkard (1996), and Brandom (2002) argue that Hegel was a "post-Kantian philosopher," by which they mean that Hegel found traditionally metaphysics, understood as the search for or discovery of a substantive structure of the world as it really is in itself, to be impossible after Kant's first *Critique*. Rather, for this "new Left," Hegel's notion of "Spirit" is a historically developing "space of reasons" sustained and transformed by structures of mutual recognition among individuals. Spirit, in other words, consists of a system of rules and norms according to which individuals understand themselves and their highest aspirations and within which individuals seek these aims and perform intelligible actions according to shared reasons.

I do not seek to adjudicate this controversy, which will take us too far afield, though my sympathies lie with the nonmetaphysicians.[6] However, the metaphysicians are right to push the nonmetaphysicians on the question of justification, the point where the latter are weakest. The nonmetaphysical Hegelians are at the end of the day unable to justify the modern social and political order "in itself," since all justifications involve inferences from other reasons, and so there can be no absolutely foundational norm immune from contestation. Yet Hegel himself was keenly and explicitly interested not just in justifying modernity "in itself." For Hegel, the historicists like von Savigny who argue that right is "entirely grounded in and consistent with the prevailing circumstances and existing legal institutions" do not go far enough, since the normative system as a whole might be "contrary to right" (PR 3A). In this way, readers like Rockmore (1986) get Hegel wrong when they argue that Hegel defends a "coherentist" conception of truth. As McDowell (1994, 11) argues, the purely coherentist understanding of truth leaves us in a sorry state of "frictionless spinning in the void." There must be something in the world, Hegel argues, that our truth-claims get wrong or right.[7]

My strategy is to split the difference between the metaphysicians and nonmetaphysicians. I agree with the metaphysicians that Hegel saw that justification "in itself" was necessary, but I disagree with them and agree with the nonmetaphysicians that "spirit" is a human, historical structure. My argument is that Hegel's defense of historical individuality is the cornerstone of his defense of the modern social and political order. The individual serves as the objective standard for Hegel's justification of modernity "in itself." What many readers of Hegel miss is that he engaged in an old-fashioned form of justification, one that hearkens back to Plato and Aristotle and was given new life by Schiller.[8] That is, Hegel justifies modern life by arguing that it fulfills what it means to be a complete human being. For Hegel, the "fundamental characteristic of human nature is that man can think of himself as an ego" (PHI 50), and the satisfaction or completeness of human subjective agency is precisely what modern individuality and community provide. Setting Hegel's concerns about the ambiguity of "nature" aside for the moment (VPR17 2A), my claim here is that Hegel defended a modern form of "natural law," that there is something in the nature of things—I argue, the structure and aim of human subjectivity—that can render communal practices better and worse objectively.[9]

We can understand Hegel's defense of the goodness of an individual life led in political activity and the goodness of the modern state in which this life can be led most fully in three stages. First, Hegel defends the idea that subjectivity contains a natural standard for leading a good life. This is a rather formal standard at first, that subjective agency demands that it realizes and finds itself in the world, specifically in an individual life (this chapter). Second, Hegel argues that an individual life must consist in an ethical life, which itself consists in participation in a good community, specifically a political community (chapter 3). Finally, Hegel claims that that the individual good life is only possible in the modern state redeemed by a restored harmony between individual and ethical community (chapter 4).

2.1   The Distinctively Human Subject and the Good Life

Like his predecessors, Hegel supports the modern aspiration to liberate the individual, and follows them in denying that nature in itself has a metaphysical or teleological structure in which human beings understand their moral function. Much of Hegel's and his successors' work consists in showing how these metaphysical understandings were themselves the expressions of the needs and aspirations of particular historical communities. Sitting squarely in the modern camp, however, Hegel must face his predecessors' problem—how to grasp individual authority and aims in a purposeless Newtonian universe. He rejects, as we have seen, both options available to him. He agrees with the formal individualists in thinking that the natural individual fails to do justice to human freedom, reducing us to clever animals directed by our natural passions. Yet he disagrees with them because for him they dodge the central problem of the modern age by positing a spooky transcendental ego persisting behind appearances.[10] Instead, adopting Rousseau's strategy, Hegel returned to the origin of the human being out of nature in order both to maintain the continuity between the natural and the human being, and to discern what is distinct about human beings.[11] The distinctively human subjectivity provides, I argue for Hegel, an immanent standard for what makes for a full human life.

Natural beings and human beings are both subjects. Hegel defines "subject" as a "being which is capable of containing and enduring its own contradiction" (EN 359A). A subject, then, is a being that orders and commands its various components into an interdependent harmony and that acts for ends set by the subject itself.[12] The subject achieves such wholeness by subjecting the various, often "contradictory" material around it into parts under one commanding authority. This squirrel or dog or elephant, for instance, has subjected or ordered all the multifarious bodily processes that constitute it into a kind of hierarchical totality. Its subjectivity thus appears as the "shape" of what Hegel calls its "substance," or the contentful determinations and desires that constitute an organic body, the "richness of all content" (EL 151; cf. PhG 18).

Like Kant of the third *Critique* and his Romantic successors, Hegel sought to replace the Newtonian understanding of nature with one that includes complex, natural organic systems or functional wholes that resist reduction to atomistic or mechanistic cause and effect (EN 245Z).[13]

For Hegel, an organic "subject" is not some pregiven self that subsists behind appearances, but it is rather an achievement of organic activity. This dog Fido, who wags his tail when he is happy, is the result not of a "pattern" of self or personality derived from heaven or hidden within him, but of a "process" of growth and response to stimuli over the course of its lifetime (EN 356). The "identity" of Fido as a subject is the net result of these many bodily processes and experiences cohering into one unified organic creature. In other words, the material parts of Fido are all that "really"—in the sense of tangible bodily material—exist. Nonetheless, Fido's actions are unintelligible apart from the subjective whole that is the structuring principle guiding the material interdependence. In this way, we can say that Fido's subjectivity is what truly exists, the "idea" in Hegel's language that makes sense of the "real."

Subjectivity is an achieved agency, a victory over the forces of entropy and undifferentiated chaos. The wholeness of the organic being is constantly threatened from all sides with "contradiction," with the rejection of its ordered harmony. In Hegel's terms, the "subjectivity of the animal contains a contradiction" or lack of wholeness and hence feels an "urge to preserve itself by resolving this contradiction" (ES 381Z). From within, it experiences pangs of hunger, a distinct "lack" or incompleteness that it seeks to restore to wholeness (EN 359); from without, it fears predators and hence is "dependent" on the exterior world to supply food and shelter (EN 359Z). Finally, some "contradictions" cannot be overcome—disease "contradicts" the order of an organic subject to the point at which the latter cannot "maintain and endure" the contradiction any longer. Death is the dissolution of subjectivity.

Thus, subjectivity is inescapably an agent, never a passive spectator on the world. Subjectivity is an achievement, but it is constantly in need of further achievement. For Hegel, then, the nature of all subjectivity is to fight against internal contradiction and to realize its subjectivity in the world. This aim is the immanent aim of all subjects, the aim, in other words, that all subjects have simply in virtue of being subjects (not, that is, an "external" function assigned to it by tradition, nature, or God). This aim encompasses and explains all particular aims that an organic being has. Hunger, one of Hegel's favorite examples, is for him the feeling of incompleteness, which is overcome by extending my subjectivity into the world and—literally—incorporating another being. This object ceases to be an alien object in the world and becomes a part of my own biological system: "The negation of myself which I suffer within me in hunger, is at the same time present as an other than myself, as something to be consumed; my act is to annul this contradiction by making this other identical with myself, or by restoring my self-unity through sacrificing the thing" (EN 245Z).

Thus, Hegel redescribes the central organic desire not as self-preservation, but as the extension of subjectivity, which incorporates more and more of the world. Indeed, for Hegel, the more extensive the subjectivity, the higher the being, because it is highly difficult to reconcile the many contradictions present in a complex creature. Some creatures, like insects and amoebae, are simple organisms with little agency, that is, with not much scope or ability to extend their individual selves into the world. The "higher" animals can persist with a longer lifespan, engage in a wider variety of activities, even form certain basic communicative patterns and social groups amongst others of the same species. It is a "privilege" to exist as a "contradiction," Hegel argues (EN 359Z), because contradiction "is the root of all movement and vitality; it is only in so far as something has a contradiction within it that it moves, has an urge and activity" (SL 439). Thus, the greater the contradiction, the more complicated and vivacious the forms of activity that result and the greater effort needed to unify one's subjectivity.

Yet at the same time, the "higher the nature, the more unhappiness it feels" (EN 359Z). The more "endlessly and tremendously [the subject] is divided against itself, and the more lacerating are the contradictions in which it still has to remain firm in itself," the more "the intensity and depth of subjectivity come all the more to light" (Aesthetics 178). Nature is an "unresolved contradiction," a vale of tears, because the higher animals, those in whom "subjectivity come all the more to light," are the ones that suffer the most, and this suffering has no apparent purpose or meaning (EN 248A). For Hegel, the redemption of this suffering, the "solution to the problem of evil," comes in the highest and hence unhappiest of beings, human beings (EN 359Z). The reason why human beings can justify this suffering is because we can construct for ourselves a human world in which this suffering becomes meaningful.

For Hegel, then, nature gives rise to creatures that rebelled against it, creatures who form our own independent agency against the push and pull of nature's instinct, and who eventually narrated the development of nature itself as a story that led up to our own self-understanding.[14] Just as for Kant in "Speculative History," so too for Hegel, the "Christian fall from grace" should be understood as a "fortunate fall," one from the immersion in natural instinct into the reflective ability to create and reform our own natures based on our commonly shared reason. As Hegel puts it, "man must have eaten of the tree of knowledge of good and evil . . . in order to become what he is, having overcome this separation between himself and nature" (EN 246Z). Far from being absolutely distinct from nature, then, for Hegel, human beings are the culmination of nature's development—mindless nature gives to itself a mind in human beings, such that nature's longing for the realization of subjectivity is finally realized in nature's fundamental transformation of itself in the human world.[15] Human beings hence are consistent with nature in that we are embodied beings subject to hunger, disease, and death. Yet at the same time, human beings possess a distinctive kind of subjectivity, a "spiritual" as opposed to bodily subjectivity (PR 190). "Spirit," for Hegel, is not some ghostly substance that suddenly descended upon nature at some point in history. Rather, spirit is a complex self-formation of nature itself, the point at which agents can begin to rebel against the impulses of nature by giving themselves general norms of conduct.[16] Nature is spirit's "beginning point," but spirit is the "true being" of nature, and spirit exists by "making itself"; it "is itself only through its own work [*Werk*]" (VPR 1, 231).

Though the human subject is distinct from nature, it nonetheless retains the same formal, immanent aim as natural subjectivity, that of realizing its subjective agency in the world. Yet human beings are able to be successful at realizing this aim in a way that animals are not. The human subject is a "thinking" subject, rather than an instinctual subject (EL 2). The first distinctively human or spiritual characteristic, then, is freedom (cf. Rousseau, SD 44). We are able to call natural desires into question and assess how we should act based on reasons. The human subject "places the ideal, the realm of thought, between the demands of the impulse and their satisfaction." Hence, "man acts in accordance with ends and determines himself in light of a general principle" (PHI 49). Second, the human substance is "perfectible" (SD 45, PHI 125, 149). For Hegel, human nature is malleable, able to be transformed by our first characteristic, freedom. This trait is in contrast to natural substances, for whom there is "nothing new under the sun"— they exist in a perpetual cycle of generation and decay (PHI 124). Human beings can achieve the aim of our subjectivity by transforming our natures such that they bear the image of our subjectivity—subjective thought embeds itself in natural desire and thereby transforms it. Such a transformation is self-conscious in the sense that our subjectivity recognizes and approves of its own subjectivity in the substantial identity we have created in the world. Ultimately, for Hegel, the subject has "made itself what it is by means of its own activity" (PHI 50). As we will see, this formal criterion requires that subjects achieve individual lives in order to lead a fully human life. Just as organic beings needed to produce and maintain an interdependent harmony among their biological parts to realize their subjectivity in the world, so too must human beings generate the same interdependent harmony. Yet the crucial difference is that the "parts" of the human subject's substance are features of a human identity expressible in a narrative form, an independent, persisting form in which the subject can self-consciously recognize itself as the author.

2.2   The Autonomy of the Laboring Subject

Absolute Negativity

Let us examine more closely, then, these features of subjectivity in order to see why, for Hegel, an individual life is the immanent or "natural" aim of human subjectivity. "The *essence* [Wesen] of spirit . . . is freedom" (ES 382), Hegel claims. What is distinctively human—our spiritual nature—is that we are free subjective agents, in other words, that normative authority as to how we should act resides in us, not in nature or society.[17] Freedom means for Hegel that human subjects have "absolute" or "infinite negativity." We can call into question the impulses nature presses upon us and the pressures society imposes on us, such that "what confronts the subject . . . is nothing alien and it is not a limitation or a barrier; on the contrary, the subject finds himself in it" (Aesthetics 97). We have the capacity to free ourselves from the demands of our bodies and the claims of our time-bound societies, even if, as a matter of fact, such questioning is extremely difficult to accomplish for most people concerned much more with practical affairs. But Hegel's point is that for any passion that we might experience (e.g., the desire for another slice of cake) or any conventional norm expected of us (e.g., proper table manners), we can always ask the question, "why should I?" A reason is warranted in response (e.g., eat the cake because it tastes good; have good table manners because it is base not to), but I may return with a similar question, "Why?" The questions of "why" may keep coming again and again, until no further reasons can be given.[18] From a sufficiently skeptical distance, all natural passions and social norms may appear as expressions of oppressive authority, seeking to bend the will of a free subject with pure force.[19] As Hegel points out, the fact that human beings can commit suicide—that, unlike nature-bound animals, the "human being alone can abandon all things, even his own life: he can commit suicide" (PR 5Z)—attests to our freedom to jettison all things, even our natural bodies.[20] For Hegel, the subject's freedom soars far above any natural or social claim upon us, whether any particular human being realizes it or not. This "infinite" negative freedom is implicit in the very nature of human subjectivity.

Thus, for Hegel, the human subject possesses a certain nature, that is, there is no set or determinate limit to its questioning. There is no final limit in principle as to what and who the subject can interrogate. There are, of course, many practical reasons for us to stop questioning—we are, after all, embodied beings in society with needs and reputations, and maintaining these things means that we need to stop asking questions and just act upon the information we have. Yet the practical, everyday activity of human beings does not eliminate the fact that each one of us is a subject which has the capacity to question everything, a subject that is often revealed to us when our usual way of comporting ourselves is radically cast out of joint. In such cases—when we lose a job, lose a relative, fear for our very lives—the "infinite" nature of subjectivity reveals itself to us, that we are so much more than any particular event, material good, or personal relationship we experience. For Hegel, the experience of death most profoundly establishes the infinitude of subjectivity, in which we come face to face with our own nothingness, that everything about our natures and societies can melt away in an instant: "It [the slave] felt anxiety [*Angst*] about its whole being, for it has experienced the fear of death, the absolute Lord. In that experience it inwardly dissolved [*aufgelöst*], had trembled in every fiber of its being, and everything fixed has been shaken to its foundations. But this pure universal movement, the absolute melting-away of everything stable, is the simple, essential essence [*Wesen*] of self-consciousness, absolute negativity, *pure being-for-self*, which consequently is implicit in this consciousness" (PhG 194). Subjectivity reveals itself to us in these moments with its profound question mark, its "absolute negativity" of all things existing.

Socrates was, according to Hegel, the first person to harangue his fellows with the ruthless negativity of the I (PR Preface, 20). Socrates was, after all, famous for inquiring into the ground of all opinions great and small. Meanwhile, the Athenian elites wanted Athenian tradition to be accepted unquestioningly by the youth, as unconditionally normatively binding. Of course, Socrates revealed Athenian tradition to be what all traditions are, finite assertions or claims of particular peoples that aim, as Nietzsche says, to preserve the community (D 9). When the Athenian elites found themselves unable to provide a rational justification for their claims, they got upset. Yet in getting upset at Socrates, they implicitly recognized the legitimacy of Socrates' questioning, the normative "ground" of the I, and the groundless or finite claims of their tradition.[21] That is, they recognized that their own subjectivities longed for the same kind of negativity, the same kind of answers, that Socrates called for, yet they were unable to satisfy this repressed longing of their subjectivities. No wonder they were so outraged at this gadfly of Athens.

In Hegel's language, pure human subjectivity is "*pure indeterminacy or . . . the 'I''s pure reflection into itself, in which every limitation, every content, whether present immediately through nature, through needs, desires, and drives, or given and determined in some other way, is dissolved [aufgelöst]; this is the limitless infinity of absolute abstraction or universality*, the pure *thinking* of oneself" (PR 5). In negating all particular or finite things, the I assumes a "pure *thinking* of oneself." The I thus stands in simple, abstract identity or unity with itself, what Hegel calls, following Fichte, the "I = I" (PhG 167, ES 424Z). At this idealized standpoint, the I has attained for itself pure form, without content.[22] In other words, the I recognizes that it is completely "other" than its content (ES 413), a clear reference to the formalist model of individuality we examined in the previous chapter. Its distinctive "activity consists in transcending and negating its immediate existence so as to turn in again upon itself" (PHI 50). The I finds itself thus poised at a reflective level of remove from its content, utterly indifferent to it. It sees that it is absolutely unique in being a wellspring of negativity in contrast to the "positive" claims of content.

This formal, indeterminate subjectivity is an important initial stage in thinking through the longing of the distinctively human. In particular, it points to the fact that individuals themselves have the right to make up their own minds about how to live and not have their decisions made for them. The authority of individuality remains paramount. However, we must not identify this formal authority with the full realization of subjectivity as such, or with the achievement of a full individual human life. We misunderstand what is human if we think that our true selves are endlessly distorted by social interactions or by natural desires, that "who we are truly" exists somehow independent of our upbringing, historical circumstances, political backgrounds, held deeply within me in some spooky "true self." For Hegel, we misunderstand what the nature of the "infinite" in subjectivity is if we take the subject to these formal extremes. Such is the failure, as we have seen, of the "formal individual." For Hegel, the human being is finite, because our bodies, like the societies in which we live, come to be and pass away. By contrast, our self-consciousness, what is distinctively human, can become infinite. Because of his endless questioning of tradition, for instance, Socrates became the first "infinite personality" (PR Preface, 20). Yet as Hegel points out, the meaning of the "infinite" is ambiguous. According to Hegel, there are two forms of "the infinite": a "bad" and a "good" infinite. The bad infinite is "nothing but the negation of the finite" (EL 94), that ruthless questioning and abstractive longing we have been discussing thus far.

The pursuer of the bad infinite experiences dissatisfaction because he undermines the very task he assigns for himself. Absolute negativity may become after a while, Hegel admits, a pointless naysaying. The Sisyphean nature of absolute negativity gets us to the heart of why the bad infinite is bad after all. It is bad because the act of constant negation is a "progress ad infinitum" that "does not go beyond the expression of the contradiction." Hence the negated finite determination "arises again in the same way" to be negated once again, only to arise again and again (EL 94). The absolutely negative I can no more achieve its infinite negation than one can count to infinity. One will always remain confronted with an endless series of finite numbers or determinations. One is always on the way to infinity, but never quite makes it. Stuck in the bad infinite, the I remains mired in what is finite, forever incomplete. For Hegel, then, this bad infinite is a "spurious infinite" since it remains within the "sphere of the finite" after all (EL 94Z).

The Laboring Subject

For Hegel, then, the human subject is not a passive spectator indifferently evaluating the world as this infinite negativity suggests, as such "freedom" is in fact self-defeating. Rather, the human subject, like the animal subject, is at bottom a practical agent that must realize its subjectivity in the world. Indeed, such subjectivity does not precede action as some kind of substratum or thinking thing behind appearances. Just as in the case of Fido, above, subjectivity appears only through action as an achievement of an organic interdependence of parts. For Hegel, then, the human "true self," that which brings subjectivity into the world, is not hidden deep within me, but exists in public, emerging out of the series of actions that I perform among others in particular historical contexts. As Hegel puts it, "what the subject is, is the series of its actions" (PR 124).

To defend this notion of subjectivity, Hegel appropriates Kant's account of the unity of apperception, which Hegel takes to be "one of the profoundest and truest insights to be found in the *Critique*" (SL 584). Kant's unity of apperception—"the original synthetic unity of apperception, as unity of the I think, or of self-consciousness" (SL 584)—helps explains this basic nature of this synthetic agent. Kant argues that we cannot help but think of the human subject as the original, unified, spontaneous synthesizer of parts and wholes that constitute intelligible experience (CPR B133–34). We can have no direct empirical apprehension of this transcendental synthesizing agent (who can see the I?), but in order for coherent experiences or actions to occur, we must posit a unity that effects such coherence. Within every experience or action, a judgment is made, namely, that this bundle of sensations is an object, or that this series of bodily movements I am to perform adds up to a coherent action.[23] In order to be able to see a tree as an instantiation of a general concept tree, for instance, a subject must bring a general concept whole to bear in making coherent the various sensible parts—the bark, the leaves, the branches—that the subject sees. In order to sign over the deed to my house, I must synthesize a set of general rules that structure the practice of buying and selling a house to the particular array of bodily motions and speech patterns that will properly execute this action. The "subject," then, is not some thinking thing behind appearances, but is the formal posited unity accompanying coherent experience or action that makes the idea that something can be "my" experience or action possible (CPR B139–40, 158).[24]

I do not want to rehearse the details of Kant's arguments, but rather to describe the main way in which Hegel transforms this feature of the synthetic subject. He transforms the subject by making it more practical than Kant had envisioned.[25] In particular, Hegel transformed the synthetic subject who combines premade parts and wholes into a laboring subject who produces new parts and wholes that bear his identity.[26] I use "labor" here in a broad sense, referring to the human capacity to transform what is "other"—such as untilled nature—into something intelligible to the human mind and useful to human need. Hegel describes this laboring subjectivity in a different metaphor in his Berlin *Phenomenology*: "Ego, as this absolute negativity, is in itself identity in otherness: the ego is itself that other and stretches [*greift*] over the object (as if that object were in itself *aufgehobenes*)—it is *one* side of the relationship and the *whole* relationship—*the light*, which manifests itself and the other too" (ES 413). In other words, for Hegel, the human I does not apply concepts to pregiven material, but rather transforms the world in accordance with the subject's own purposes. Human beings give the "light" of meaning to the world by incorporating the world itself into the subject's plan. In its primordial state, nature is "darkness," without meaning, without significance.[27] Or, in our "laboring" metaphor, the world "out there" is malleable, open to radical transformation by human labor. The strong division between subject and object erected by early modern philosophy is broken down in Hegel's mind as the subject inscribes its own subjectivity in the object of labor.

The most primordial form of the human subject's "labor" is that of bodily consumption. In the Jena *Phenomenology*, Hegel speaks of the primal human self-conscious relation to the natural objects he consumes, characteristic of human "desire" (*Begierde*) (PhG 167). The act of consumption is an act of negation because it negates the independence of those finite things of nature, replacing their own given structure with the structure of my own subjectivity (PhG 174). The subject (literally) incorporates the object into himself, such that the object "is no longer something independent, no longer a being over and against me" (PS 184). In externalizing itself in this way, the I "gives itself content [which] coincides with itself, gives itself objectivity and makes itself actual. Self-consciousness proves its freedom in relation to its consciousness, and this is at the same time realization, since it gives itself an objectivity that is identical with subjectivity" (PS 184). That is, the subject must extend itself out into the world in order to overcome the "contradiction" of its felt "desire." In transforming an object of the world into its own structure of subjectivity (by eating it), the subject can see its own subjectivity realized in the external world. Both human subject and natural object, then, are essentially constituted such that the subject transforms and the object is able-to-be-transformed to bear the image of subjectivity. The object is not something given, inaccessible, or unchangeable. Hegel's gibe against Kant's thing-in-itself is instructive here. He says that "even the animal has gone beyond this realist philosophy, for it consumes things and thereby proves that they are not absolutely self-sufficient." As Hegel puts it, "I give the living creature . . . a soul other than that which it previously had. I give it my soul" (PR 44Z).

For Hegel, a higher form of the laboring subject's activity is labor in the narrower sense of the term. The problem with consumption is that ingesting one's object fails to leave a lasting testament to one's subjectivity in the world, and indeed one's hunger—that contradiction to subjectivity—will return again and again. Labor is a human means of sustaining one's subjectivity in a more lasting way in the world. As Hegel puts it, in labor, we take up a "negative relation to the object," relieving it of its independence and transforming it in accordance with a subjective purpose. This "negative relation to the object becomes . . . something permanent, because it is precisely for the worker that the object has independence" (PhG 195). Instead of ingesting the object the subject transforms, in other words, the subject labors on the object but in so doing gives it independence, a permanence that will sustain subjectivity in the world, thereby realizing in a practical way the Kantian unity of apperception, in which the "I think expresses the act of determining my existence" (CPR B157n). "Through work," Hegel argues, one can "become conscious of what he truly is" (PhG 195). Indeed, when I construct my own home, for instance, I come to see my own subjectivity in it as the creator of this object. In seeing my subjectivity, I possess a strongly felt attachment to this object, since it is part of me, part of my identity.

In language, we represent this laboring nature of subjectivity. We describe my personal identity, who I am—that set of beliefs, desires, relationships, duties—as "me" (Aesthetics 123). My identity is an object out there in the world for others to understand and interact with, but there is no gap between this object and the subject. My personal identity—my "me"—is constituted insofar as the subject posits this belief or this desire as its own, as parts of a coherent character. In language, we represent this intimate connection by making this object a first-person pronoun. Furthermore, the objects I produce with my own hands or that I purchase with my labor are "mine."[28] That is, the object's identity is so thoroughly pervaded by my own subjectivity that we refer to it in the first-person possessive. This house is not simply a collection of bricks and mortar, but this material is intelligible only as parts of the whole brought into being by the laboring subject. For Hegel, the right to private property rests at bottom on this connection to personal identity construction. The human subject seeks to externalize itself in the world, and its identity englobes objects in the world as it labors on them. Taking these objects without the subject's permission amounts to a denial of the "mine," the subject's transformation of this object, and hence a denial that the subject is a human subject at all.

In laboring, one transforms the world, posits one's subjectivity in it, yet this very laboring transforms personal identity. The construction of one's personal identity does not follow a "blueprint" as building a house might. Rather, labor transforms one's identity in unexpected ways. First, labor "educates" the human self in that through activity, we acquire capabilities we didn't have before we started. Hegel does not mean simply that we learn how a plumbing system works, but rather, more deeply, work requires that "desire [be] held in check," that we work in collaboration with others, that we produce an object with a tool, both of which in principle can be used to satisfy another's desires, not just our own (PhG 195, 190; SEL 113). All of these requirements of labor transform us from natural, selfish creatures to independent ethical beings sharing a community with others. Furthermore, labor, like artwork, is creative, in that production sometimes can yield a surprising result, something that I had not intended when I set about on this project, but yet something that satisfies my purposes better than what I had in mind in the first place. This new unexpected "mine," however, stands in tension with my identity, with my "me." It challenges to some degree what I believed and thought before. The laboring subject is dissatisfied by such a "contradiction" in its own identity and hence desires to engage in a kind of second-order laboring on its own identity. That is, it desires to harmonize those different parts of its identity into a coherent individual personality, a whole in which the subject can appear.

We have been discussing two forms of the laboring subject's activity—consumption and labor—in order to grasp its structure and immanent aim. The most important form of the laboring subject's activity, however—and a form of activity that is in fact always already embedded in human consumption and laboring—is "normative labor," acting upon, exchanging, and assessing reasons. It may seem odd to think of reasoning as a kind of labor. Hegel's predecessors envisioned the reasoning subject as a detached and passive observer of the world "out there." Yet Hegel argues that reasoning is an eminently practical activity having the same form as consumption and labor. Hegel argues that even the *"comprehension* of an object consists in nothing else than that the ego makes it its *own* [eigen], pervades it and brings it into *its own form* [seine eigene Form]" (SL 585).

To see why this is, we must return again to Kant's transcendental unity of apperception to grasp Hegel's view of the basic nature of a normative subject. For Kant, representational experience—the experience of objects—is made up of two components, contentful intuition and formal concepts. Intuition supplies us immediately with a multitude of individual sensations arrayed in space and time. Yet these sensations do not yet form themselves into objects with particular normative meaning; that is, we cannot yet judge this tree as subsumable under a concept "tree." For us to make sense of objects, we must deploy concepts, abstract or general norms that help us identify this aggregate of sensations as an instantiation of a general norm. Concepts, then, are formal wholes that render sensations intelligible by gathering them together within their general categories. For Kant, experience must consist of both, because "thoughts without content are empty, intuitions without concepts are blind" (CPR B75/A51). Furthermore, for this experience to be mine—and not partially mine and partially someone else's—the "I must be able to accompany all my representations" (CPR B131). We must posit a unified subject who synthesizes parts and whole, intuition and concept, to make a coherent experience.

There are two problems with Kant's view, according to Hegel. First, it is not clear what the basis of these categories that subjects spontaneously deploy to make intuition intelligible are. Why this set of categories and not others? Why this table of judgments and not some other one? Second, the notion that intuition is somehow distinguishable from the categories we apply to them is incoherent. What is intuition separable from a concept? Any imaginable intuition always already comes loaded with normative intelligibility. Even if we try to imagine a raw plenum of natural determinations, a buzzing chaos of sensation, we still nonetheless have deployed various concepts ("raw," "plenum," etc.). Stripping away all these concepts leaves us with silence, emptiness. By contrast, Hegel historicizes both concept and intuition. On the one hand, he argues that subjects deploy concepts that are not universal or ahistorical, but are the categories structuring the particular historical practices in which one makes objects intelligible. Historical practices have certain practical goals that structure the categories we deploy to make sense of the world and ourselves.[29] On the other hand, Hegel argues that intuition is not separable from the subject, but the subject's "property," the result of the subject's "labor." The objects that seem to be simply given from the world are actually pervaded by the subject's purposive will. For instance, the object we call a "bank" is not something given by nature—it is not that material array of bricks and mortar—but rather it is intelligible as an object for a subject's purposes, such as cashing checks, saving money, getting a loan, and so forth. When we "intuit" the objects of the world, we are grasping objects that are always already loaded with normative meaning.

As we will see in the next chapter, the condition for the possibility of an individual I is that a universal I or a "we" must ground the rules for any practice in which individuals can perform meaningful actions. Indeed, Hegel points out that my use of the personal pronoun "I" is only possible insofar as I can make myself intelligible to others, which means obeying linguistic rules that transcend my individual will.[30] "I," then, both refers to me, this particular author, and is a universal linguistic unit, capable of being deployed properly (in referring to other human individuals) or improperly (referring to plants or rocks). What is most personal, the I, is at the same time "universal in and for itself," shared among all other human beings (EL 20A).[31] Hegel argues that these rules that make intelligible utterances and action possible are not ahistorical, but actually situated within particular historical practices that make up what he calls "Spirit."[32] These historical practices—such as churches, professional organizations, states—are systems of intelligibility in which any particular action performed within it is intelligible according to the rules or aims immanent to the practice.[33] The bank teller's cashing a check, for instance, is intelligible not as the mere material motion of a hand dispersing slips of paper, but rather as a normatively loaded action explicable and assessable according to the practice's rules. Accordingly, we posit a universal subject—a "collective subject"—that unifies the various material actions occurring within this bank as parts of a whole system, just as we posit a particular I, this individual subject, who unifies the various components of my identity to produce a coherent personality, just as we posit the animal subject who fights off disease and hunger to sustain its subjectivity. These practices in which we make sense of the world have certain practical aims—just as animal and human subjects do—that shape the system of intelligibility for those within it.

The human capacity for reasoning, or what Hegel calls "thinking," consists in grasping, assessing, and applying the rules of a practice. For Hegel, "thinking" is what distinguishes the human being from the animal because the human subject may transcend natural desire in a human action in which he temporarily occupies the standpoint of a universal subject (EL 2A). "Only man can [say 'I'], because he is thinking itself," Hegel argues, whereas "animals cannot say 'I'" and think because their actions are initiated by nature and natural laws (EL 24Z1). Only human beings act based on "thinking," or what we call reasons, on a conception of what is right, not expedient, in which "what is right" is established and maintained within a historical practice.

Much of the normative activity of an individual, laboring subject is rather humdrum. One's "duties . . . can be recognized without difficulty" (PHI 80)—if presented with a check from a valid customer, the bank teller should cash the check. However, that the bank teller can fail to disburse the customer's funds tells us something important about the individual I acting within the universal I. That is, the individual human subject who acts according to his duties is an achievement. For instance, it is possible that the recently hired bank teller is really a crook and hence follows his natural, selfish, greedy desire to embezzle the money of his customers. In such a case, the individual subject has not internalized the norms of the practice to which he belongs such that his identity would be shaped by these norms—the individual I fails to act as an individual subject here, but rather falls to the level of natural animality. Alternatively, we could imagine a bank teller whose good performance goes unrewarded, whose benefits and pay are shabby, who is treated almost as a slave by management. In this case, it is not the individual I who fails, but the universal I, whose structure systematically undermines the capacity of the individual I to find itself within the practice. The final, successful case is of the happy employee who rises above natural instinct and spontaneously does his duty and in doing so is recognized, respected, and rewarded. In such a case, the human subject is satisfied, since the subject finds itself in the action it performs and the practice in which this action is received. The subject's identity has been shaped and "educated" in and through successful activity within this practice, such that it comes to identify itself with the practice itself and see things from the perspective of the universal I.[34] Accordingly, it sees itself in its actions because the human subject—*qua* universal I—gives itself a set of norms that it—*qua* individual I—follows. Hegel compares this identification of the private with the general will to artistic "ecstasy" (*Begeisterung*), the elevation of the subject to what is universal or general (VPR21 2). We can call this the "top-down" model of autonomy.

Yet such a top-down model of autonomy is not sufficient for satisfying the human subject. The top-down model suffers the same problem plaguing the formalist individual, that the universal normative authority ignores the distinctness of the individuals carrying out its aims. The performer of the categorical imperative is completely fungible, as is the completely obedient bank teller. The individual subject hence becomes swallowed up in the universal I, such that the individual subject can no longer differentiate himself from his fellows. In other words, the top-down model is necessary for a free individual action, but it is insufficient—it must be supplemented by a "bottom-up" model in which the individual I is encouraged to make creative (yet intelligible) moves within the practice. For Hegel, the subject possesses the right to autonomy, to "know only his own law," to "recognize only what is his own [*das Seine*]" (VPR 3, 110). If the subject obeys a law that is not his, but rather nobody's in particular, this will begins to seem alien and abstract. The subject ceases then to recognize itself in its own law and hence is dissatisfied. Yet Hegel argues that the "universal" or "general" (*Allgemeinen*) rules of a practice can rarely be simply read off in any one "particular" (*Besonderen*) situation. "Individuality" (*Einzelheit*) must often engage in a kind of interpretive process to discern what would be the spirit of the right action here, as the letter of the law gives no guidance, may be inappropriate, or may simply be out of date (EL 163; Aesthetics 109).[35] In being the "ground" of its determinations, as we will see, the individual comes to be the "identity of the ground with itself in the grounded" (SL 461). That is, its subjectivity comes to extend itself into its determinations such that it sees itself in those objects of its labor and its property.

Robert Brandom's (2002, 13–14) helpful example on this score is common law judgment, in which there is no written law to bind one's actions, but rather individuals must creatively interpret the norm that is applicable in this situation. Such an interpretive process is not arbitrary or random, but neither is it a command-authority, deductive process of reasoning. Instead, it involves individual, bottom-up interpretation, which itself involves understanding the nature and aims of the historical practice before acting. Accordingly, for Hegel, even such normative activity is laboring in the sense that it is the practical, creative transformation of the world and oneself as a result.

I will have much more to say about all of this in the next chapter, but the central point is the following. Human subjects are "thinking" subjects with "absolute negativity," which means that human subjectivity is dissatisfied when any norm does not meet its rational approval. Good reasons for action do not come from an abstract pure practical reason, but from the embedded rationality of the universal I that structures human practices. When a subject comes both to identify with this universal subjectivity and to differentiate itself from it by tweaking its norms from within, it acts based on reasons that it has (in effect) given itself. It therefore satisfies its own demand for a legitimate authority (which can, for modern individuality, only be itself) and for its own immanent end. It recognizes its own subjectivity in its actions and in the rules and performance of the practice with which it identifies itself.

Furthermore, individuals in the modern age engage and identify themselves with many practices, which means that the subject's personal identity is fragmented among a number of different normative systems—I may be, for instance, a churchgoer, a neighborhood association treasurer, a friend, a senator, an American, a firefighter, each of which has a set of rules for proper behavior and comportment. The subject must seek to harmonize these various components of its identity in order to make a whole personality that bears the trace of its subjectivity. This is no easy task because the many different practices shape the character of their participants in very different, often contradictory ways. For Hegel, the "boundless extravagance" of modern civil society, in which the "particularity" of different opinions, desires, and norms can "develop and express itself in all directions," makes such a unification difficult (PR 185Z, 184). In engaging in this richly diverse modern world, the subject may find himself lost in this multitude—as the "system of ethical life" is "lost in its extremes" (PR 184)—not aware of what makes "me" "me." "Who I am" in my occupation might be quite different from "who I am" at home and even further from the "me" at city hall. In Hegel's mind, however, the multiplicity of different practices the individual belongs to in the modern age—family, civil society, religion, and the state—make possible the kind of creative individual we have been describing independent yet engaged in these many practices.[36] I will elaborate on the latter claim further in chapter 4.

2.3   The "Infinite Worth" of Individual Character

Thus far in this chapter, we have been discussing the subject in the abstract, both the basis of its authority in absolute negativity and its immanent aim to realize itself in the world. Yet at the same time, we have seen that for Hegel the subject arises only in and through action. The subject is not something we can "see" empirically with our eyes. Nor is the inference that the I is an internal homunculus residing in the brain somewhere a legitimate inference, a claim that Hegel develops from Kant's "Paralogisms" (EL 47). The human subject, then, cannot see itself in its solitude; there is no kernel of the true self that stands behind my public actions. The I is "activity *überhaupt*," as Hegel puts it (VPR 3, 118).[37] Otherwise put, "action is the clearest revelation of the individual, of his temperament as well as his aims; what a man is at bottom and in his inmost being comes into actuality only by his action" (Aesthetics 219). Subjectivity is the unified posited agent to which we apply the harmony among these parts. But the subject is not "real," standing behind appearances, any more than Fido or the United States is (which both count as subjects, for Hegel).

However, it is difficult to see how we can make sense of this subject's labor or autonomous agency if it does not precede but only arises only through action. Isn't all this talk of individual freedom, then, an illusion, such that individuals are at bottom determined by natural causes or by social forces? In order to make sense of Hegel's self-bootstrapping subjectivity, we have to turn in this part to his view of the human substance, which is distinguished from animal substance in its perfectibility. Substance, you may recall, is the complement to subjectivity. It is the set of determinations—bodily features, capabilities, desires, beliefs, character, and so on—that constitute the content of this subject's identity. The substantive determinations of a subject are either "particular" or "universal" in character. For instance, in an animal's substance, the animal possesses a wide array of particular desires for food, drink, shelter, and bodily traits and capacities to run, fly, swim, and so forth. At the same time, its general or "universal" characteristics concern its belonging to a certain species of animal. The "individual" subject is then responsible for bringing together these particular needs and universal traits in preserving and reproducing itself. The animal substance never changes, according to Hegel, because it never raises itself above nature to act within historical practices that change over time.

For Hegel, the human substance is perfectible. Our perfectibility is our nearly infinite capacity to labor on and transform our own identities and natures.[38] Not only do the "universal" or general norms change over time depending on the historical practice a subject lives in, but the "particular" desires and capacities one has changes as well. By way of contrast, consider Kant's view of the human "substance." For Kant, human beings indeed are distinct from animals in legislating for ourselves the "universal" rational norm we follow (rather than pursuing the end of the species instinctively), but our "particular" natural desires are not qualitatively different from an animal's. Self-love is the basic natural drive, and it appears in many forms—pride, self-preservation, greed, and so forth (Ap 155ff.). As a result, reason and inclination are sharply opposed, as inclination has no moral value—if we perform a good deed because it benefits us financially, for instance, Kant argues that this deed is not really moral after all. However, for Hegel, this sharp distinction between the two guarantees that the human subject can never achieve wholeness, perpetually divided between reason and inclination (PhG 623). Worse, for Hegel, Kant leaves us without any explanation of how reason could possibly defeat inclination in its struggle over our souls—if acting out of duty is supposed to be devoid of inclination, what actually motivates us to act morally?[39]

Hegel's view of the perfectibility of substance overcomes these Kantian problems. Human beings initially begin both in history and as children as immersed in "particular" natural desire, in our "first nature." However, he argues that this desire can be restrained, reformed, or "educated" to become a civilized "second nature." According to Hegel, "education is the art of making human beings ethical: it considers them as natural beings and shows them the way to be reborn, and to transform their original nature into a second, spiritual nature" (PR 151Z; cf. PHI 50, 57). Indeed, the subject longs to effect such an education of its character, to restrain and harness its desires, since its immanent aim is to be a unified, whole being whose many parts harmonize to produce this whole. Natural desires are indeed, as Kant worried, wayward, tempting the human being away from the discipline required to fulfill his duties, advance in his career, create a satisfying and ethical, rather than merely pleasurable, life. Hunger and sexual desire, for instance, tempt us to escape those various forms of rational order we impose upon them, such as dieting and monogamous relationships. Yet Hegel does not suggest that desires are to be extirpated through the process of education—Hegel associates such an ascetic ideal with Kant. On the contrary, education harnesses the "energy" of these "particular" inclinations and puts them in service of one's "general" normative duties. The example of the happy bank teller from above illustrates this point—the bank teller has shaped his character such that he does not see his duties as in conflict with his natural desires to sleep in, indulge his appetite, and so forth, but rather he acts out of his duty with pleasure, since the fulfillment of duty and inclination are one and the same.

In this way, Hegel's model of the changeable character of human beings avoids Kant's problem of the division between the "universal" and "particular." Hegel's view is Aristotelian, in that moral theory is not concerned with judging isolated actions, but rather with habituating human character such that it acts spontaneously for the good. In adopting this approach of addressing human character or substance and not just action, Hegel finds a way to avoid the subject's "self-bootstrapping" problem. The subject is not some external entity who can mysteriously perform an uncaused moral action. Rather, the human subject is inseparably connected to its substance—it is the "form" to the "content" of character. It shapes and is shaped by its character. On the one hand, it shapes its character by "laboring" upon it, that is, by transforming the natural bits of one's character into something human, into a "part" that harmonizes with all the other parts of one's personality. This labor, then, has the very same structure as the kinds of labor we saw above, that of the subject incorporating something "other" and thereby producing a coherent identity that realizes the human subject in the world. On the other hand, a subject's character or substance shapes the subject by supplying it with the principles and desires that animate and guide the actions that it performs. Some human characters possess such an internal harmony that there is an effortless harmony of duty and inclination and a unified subject is expressed in every action. Yet other characters are torn between particular desires and duties, and such a character resembles more a hodgepodge of different drives and adumbrations of other people's personalities. The subject of such a character is dissatisfied, as it fails to appear in the world as a coherent personality.

For Hegel, as for Aristotle, such formation of character occurs through habituation. By repeated performance of these norms, we "habituate" ourselves to this way of acting—we even begin to desire and enjoy this way of acting (PR 151).[40] We come to inhabit and love this law and act upon it without reflecting. We do not have to go through the exhausting trouble of thinking about how to act before every action, because the principle of the good has been trained into us, a "consciousness" that has become embedded in, "quivering in every muscle," as Nietzsche puts it (GM.2.2). The training and disciplining of one's body to produce a rational, moral character is, for Hegel, the main way in which we can become rational human creatures. Constantly thinking and reflecting about our every move is too arduous, and, indeed, conscious reflection or rational injunction is often too impotent to change our existing passions anyway. Instead, our "rational" part should not fight against our "passionate" part (a battle it can hardly win), but rather it should structure our passionate nature as an architectural form comes to structure a block of marble, so that the rational "ethical" law "is the actual lifeblood [*wirkliche Lebendigkeit*] of self-consciousness" (PR 147A). In Hegel's terms, the "universal" norm comes to occupy and structure the "particular" desire, such that we witness the "elevation of the particular to universal truth" (PHI 81).[41] Desire or inclination becomes "ennormed," such that in following a properly shaped desire, I actually am following a law that I have given to (embedded in) myself.[42] As we will see in the next two chapters, such "particular" desire that is shaped by "universal" concerns is ethical desire.[43]

The end point of such education is that particular desire is transformed in accordance with general norms. Yet, as above in the case of the individual's authority, so too here in the individual's character, this self-formation follows the top-down model of autonomy.[44] For Hegel, when such habituation to general rules works too well, the vitality of the subjective longing begins to disappear: "human beings even die as a result of habit—that is, if they have become totally habituated to life and mentally and physically blunted . . . for they are active only in so far as they have not yet attained something and wish to assert themselves and show what they can do in pursuit of it. Once this is accomplished, their activity and vitality disappear, and the loss of interest which ensues is mental or physical death" (PR 151Z). The individual subject desires not only that it see the universal will shaping its particular desires, but also that its own individuality impress itself on its particular desires. As I put it above, the individual subject must supplement the top-down autonomy with a bottom-up autonomy of character formation.

In order to understand the individual subject's contribution to its character formation, we must investigate a little more closely Hegel's peculiar cyclical understanding of the relationship among the universal, particular, and individual, the three formal elements that characterize the furniture of the human world. For Hegel, each element is unintelligible apart from its relationship to the others. Universal norms must be embodied in particular practices and within certain human desires in order for them to escape the formalist problem of emptiness. The norm of "honor thy father and mother," for instance, makes sense or is compelling in human life because I have a natural affective attachment to my parents that renders this norm important to me.[45] Yet such particular desires are never simply natural instinctual passions, but always already shaped by some historical practice according to certain rules, such as, in this case, the institution of the bourgeois family in the modern, post-Christian world. The "universal" norms are "interpenetrated" (*durchdringt*) by "particular" desires, and vice versa (VPR 4.121). For Hegel, the logical moment of "individuality" is absolutely central and necessary to bind together what would otherwise be a stale and lifeless opposition between universal norms and particular desires. The moment of individuality belongs to my subjectivity and is the moment of judgment (EL 165). "Individuality" is the "self-determination of the I," the moment in which "particularity" is "reflected into itself and thereby restored to universality," all the while maintaining a smooth self-unification (PR 7). In short, individuality mediates general norms and particular desires by applying norms appropriately in particular circumstances. How do I know, for instance, how to apply the general norm of "honor thy father and mother" in particular circumstances? The general norm does not apply itself for me. Rather, I must take the initiative and discern how to employ this ideal appropriately. I may, for instance, send flowers on Mother's Day, or visit my family more often, or write my mother a nice thank you note.

One might think that judging the right thing to do involves a kind of Aristotelian prudence, an on-the-ground knowledge of how to apply this or that norm in the right time and place. Yet applying a general norm is not simply a matter of finding out what the situation demands (we'll adopt such a "practice-centric" approach in the next chapter). This is because the "situation" is not separable from who I am as the potential actor performing this deed. My long-lost sister, for instance, sending flowers on Mother's Day has quite a different meaning than my dutiful brother doing the same. Thus, the proper judgment that brings together universal and particular in this situation will be based in "who I am," and my identity is the series of intelligible actions I have performed in the past combined by me into a coherent whole. The subject desires to perform actions on the basis of its identity, as it affords the subject the opportunity to further realize itself in the world and maintain its coherence as a whole over time. The subject becomes dissatisfied when it is encouraged or coerced to act in a way indifferent or contrary to its identity.

I take this to be a rough and ready way of understanding Hegel's cyclical logic of the "concept."[46] For Hegel, the concept is not something abstract and distant from the concrete world—it is "what is altogether concrete," containing a general conceptual whole structuring material parts, rendering this action or experience intelligible to us. For instance, the concept of a "rose" already contains a number of particular qualities of color and smell, the material parts, associated with a universal form or structural whole that weaves these qualities together. Yet for the human being, each individual person is not simply deduced from the concept of man. Rather, after Christianity, we have come to treat other human beings as we deserve, in our "infinity and universality" (EL 163Z1). "This individuality," Hegel argues, "is in fact none other than the concept itself" (PR 7A). Each of us hence consists of a character structured as a concept—with "general" moral beliefs that have been embedded in "particular" desires. Yet what brings universal and particular together is not some kind of natural species determination, but my unique, individual history and the I as the author of it.

Admittedly, Hegel uses the term "concept" to refer to a much vaster agent than individual human beings. The concept is for Hegel the most general system of normative intelligibility, that is, system of norms that is the condition for the possibility of all sense-making (EL 160; SL 590ff.). Thus, he sees the concept as a high-altitude notion. Hegel refers to only one concept because for him all normative claims are themselves only intelligible within certain historical practices, but the norms structuring this practice are only intelligible in contrast to other practices in terms of a higher practice, and so forth, until we reach the most universal norm of intelligibility that makes sense of and is the standard for the evaluation of the historical practices, the universal human I. Despite this high-altitude use of the concept, however, Hegel indeed applies the structure of "concept" to the rational "will" of particular states in the PR (PR 1A). That is, even if political states are not the ultimate system for the validation of inferences, they as general I's nonetheless have a similar structure to that most general, human I, and hence must be understood accordingly.

It stands to reason, then, that individual wills possess this same conceptual structure. Indeed, this is what I take to be the meaning for Hegel of the Christian development that each individual contains "infinity and universality" (EL 163Z1).[47] For Hegel, the "good" infinite refers to a subject's or concept's actualizing itself in the world and hence obeying its own laws or "remaining at home with itself in its other" (EL 94Z). The infinite subject becomes normatively independent in the sense that it negates any and all norms "external" to its authority and follows only those norms that it itself has authorized. The individual subject's construction of a personality reproduces this very same structure. The individual subject becomes normatively independent when its actions are best intelligible and assessable according to canons internal to the subject's character history. In his discussion of "character" in the *Aesthetics*, Hegel defends the claim that individual subjects have the structure and moral salience of concepts. For Hegel, an individual self "appears as the form immanent in the reality and corresponding with the nature of that reality, the form giving itself an outward shape," when the subject weaves together the different parts of his life into a unified personality (Aesthetics 115). For Hegel, this individual character "can be known only from the whole series of his actions and sufferings," so long as this series is intelligibly narrated, given a coherent meaning, by a subject (Aesthetics 147).[48]

The "concept" structure of individual subjectivity hence points toward the kind of life best for human individuals and thereby provides a justification for individuality. So for Hegel, the "infinite worth" of each individual—that bedrock principle of the modern age—is rooted in the individual subject's immanent longing for such a complete, self-guided life. The denial of the subject to lead its own life would amount to a denial of the humanity of the agent, as the very nature of a human subject is to pursue a life of just this sort. Accordingly, this "infinite worth" of the individual grounds, according to Hegel, the infinite right of subjective freedom (PR 185A). According to this freedom, the individual subject "determines himself in the light of a general principle," and it is "up to him to decide what end to follow" (PHI 49).[49] In acting thus autonomously, the individual is "determined by whatever conceptions he has formed of his own nature and volitions" (PHI 49–50). In its most developed form, this freedom consists in the ability of human beings to negate all "external" forms of authority—even "its own externality, its very existence"—and to respond only to norms that "internally" I give myself (ES 382). The conscience is the modern fruit of this autonomy, and Hegel's argument is that this conscience deserves to be protected as it is a necessary feature of leading a full human life. As Hegel puts it, "Conscience expresses the absolute entitlement of subjective self-consciousness to know *in itself* and *from itself* what right and duty are, and to recognize [*anerkennen*] nothing but what it thus knows as the good" (PR 137A).

What does it mean to act based on the Hegelian conscience? How can we distinguish it from, on the one hand, a kind of willful arbitrariness that Hegel associates with Schlegel and, on the other hand, an internalized "superego" of the community's general will? Hegel argues that individual, subjective autonomy requires interpretation of my life as a narrative whole.[50] It requires interpreting how I—as this individual being with a unique history—should apply these general rules in this particular situation. My personal history has morally salient guidance on our judgment—we should not attempt to judge from pure practical reason, which gives us no determinate direction for action, but nor should we think for this reason that our judgment would be "up for grabs" or willfully arbitrary. Rather, I should act so as to complete the next stage in my life's narrative, to act from the perspective of this "encumbered me," and thereby to continue to render consistent this sequence of actions as parts of a whole personality.[51] Like an "artist," the individual "must act creatively and . . . give form and shape throughout and from a single casting to the meaning which animates him" (Aesthetics 174).[52]

I can indeed fail to live up to the subjective demand for narrative coherence—I may obey a norm inconsistent with my personality (a thoughtful father whose rare gambling stint with friends forces him to forget to pick up his children from the airport), or I may misinterpret the kind of action that would be consistent with my character.[53] Alternatively, I may surrender entirely the process of acting based on my own life history. I may act by imitation, by slavishly conforming to what everyone else is doing in this circumstance, and thereby fail to constitute myself as an individual subject. Indeed, such failures occur all the time, and it is difficult to live up to such a lofty demand for narrative coherence. However, Hegel's response to this problem of all-too-high standards would likely be the one he gives to the utopian critics of modern institutions. It is easy to criticize the lack of coherence and rationality a nation possesses, he argues, and hard to recognize the deep structure that exists (PR 268Z, Preface, 11). For Hegel, all individuals possess a certain core, determinate personality that testifies to their subjectivity alone, but every individual character can always be brought into greater coherence.

This is not to say that the self-narrating individual is like an author who knows in advance what his book means and what the various parts of the book should be to make this meaning shine forth. Indeed, we may perform actions that we think are consistent with our character, but that result in effects that strain the limits of our narrative, forcing us to transform it in sometimes very fundamental ways. Alternatively, an individual may perform an action that he considers to be exciting, pushing the boundaries of his own narrative, but that turns out to be quite ordinary after all. The individual never has a complete picture of the whole or parts of his life, but only inklings as he writes the account of his "true self." As Velleman (2005) has put a similar point, the individual self-narrating agent is analogous to an actor improvising the story of a life. In making real our "true self," we may find ourselves staking a position within our story that we find unexpected but illuminating of our own views, just as when we, in discussion with our fellows about politics or philosophy, come to find ourselves expressing a position that we had never thought of, but one that better expresses our "true" feelings than any we had thought of before. Whenever the individual "externalizes" himself in the form of action, he may discover something surprising about himself, just as the author may find himself writing an unexpected turn in his novel.[54] Much of this opaqueness of the self to itself stems from the individual's belonging to structures of meaning that are not subject entirely to his will, a topic we'll take up in the next chapter.

For Hegel, the subject's life as a whole—not just each individual action—also should conform to a narrative structure. When an author sits down to write a book, she has only a hazy sense of its whole and parts. As she goes about writing the book, this whole and these parts take on determinate meaning and flesh. Thus, the author finds that in the later moments in the story, when characters have run their course and themes have been developed, there is much less range for radical change or re-development. Yet this moment is at once the moment of self-knowledge, when the author finally realizes (in the sense of both "creating" and "discovering") what the book has been about all along. Similarly, in his youth, the individual has a tremendous range of possibilities of the person whom he can become, the principles that he will hold most dear. Thus, he only has the vaguest of ideas of what the central narrative line of his life will be. As he runs the course of his life, as he develops those principles and desires and hopes that mean so much to him, he closes off many possibilities he once had. Later in life, as the whole and parts of his self harden into solid shape, the individual self comes to fruition at last as a determinate being, and the individual can gain knowledge of what his whole life had been about—as the owl of Minerva flies at dusk.[55] That is, we come to see that the individual self comes to be through the very process of his activity, just as "spirit" "makes itself" in "its own deed or creation," and hence "becomes its own object, and has its own existence before it" (PHI 58). The individual creates himself throughout the course of his life by struggling to harmonize the whole and parts of his identity, and hence he makes a self for himself.

Two important paragraphs in Hegel's *Phenomenology* bring out the nature of Hegel's hermeneutic approach to individual self-creation. In PhG 401, Hegel discusses the nature of individual action. The ego is pure negativity or "nothing," and hence is not a substantive substratum of content. Thus, the "individual cannot know *what he is* until he has made himself an actuality [*Wirklichkeit*] through the deed [*Tun*]." The individual is caught, then, in a kind of "circle" in which "each moment already presupposes the other, and thus he seems unable to find a beginning, because he only gets to know his original essence, which must be his purpose, from the deed [*Tun*], while, in order to act, he must have that purpose beforehand." In other words, individuals cannot reach deep down into some hidden nature or identity of themselves—rather, their identity, their "me," is constantly being negotiated among their various internal components and by the different members of a public. The individual may have an inchoate sense of what he wants to do in performing this action, but the full ramifications of his actions do not come to light until the action has already been performed. For Hegel, normative meaning itself is created, maintained, and constantly revised by a public consciousness, and so individuals can never be wholly sure how their actions will be understood by their fellows. As Hegel puts it in the context of "spirit," "the business of spirit is to produce itself," yet it "produces and realizes itself in the light of its knowledge of itself"—the tentative knowledge it has now—and "it acts in such a way that all its knowledge of itself is realized" only after the action. Spirit is never a "completed entity. On the contrary, it is by nature active, and activity is its own end; it is its own product, and is therefore its own beginning and its own end" (PHI 48). Individuals, too, as *geistig* beings, are never fully "complete" selves, but always shape their identity in the very activity of coming to find their place in the world.

Similarly, in PhG 665, Hegel describes the "actuality of the individual," which arises out of the negotiation between the individual's own testimony of his intentions and the judgment of the meaning of his actions by others. For Hegel, the individual can never be sure before acting that his actions are going to express his freedom and unique individuality. It may turn out that his action is tinged with a strong element of "fame," and so the "outer aspect" of the action redounds to the individual's self, constituting him as one who has a "desire for fame." The "doer," then, "attains an intuition of *himself* in objectivity, or to a feeling of self in his existence [*Selbstgefühl in seinem Dasein*]." He has no way of knowing, in other words, what "real self" is going to emerge as a result of his actions.

The "arch-rationalist" Hegel may seem at first to be in tension with this "hermeneutic" understanding of individual self-realization. However, as Redding (1996) and Speight (2001) have argued, Hegel's phenomenology and logic are peculiar in precisely the ways I have been examining, that since spirit is never a "completed entity," there can be no complete rational account of human thought.[56] Furthermore, for Hegel, individual human beings are an unusual mixture of body and mind—we have finite bodies that grow, change, and dissolve, yet we also have infinite minds that can participate in the "infinite objects" of "freedom, spirit, and God" (EL 8). Thus, our embodied finite natures can never be made wholly rational. The human "individual" exists within an ever-shifting system of particular desires and universal norms that it must struggle to piece together within a consistent narrative. The human being is still a "living organism," which, as Hegel puts it, "has itself as the product of its activity." But unlike natural organisms, the authority and aim of its actions lie in its history, with its own character as a product of that history. How I am to act here is justified in light of my immanent subjective aim to realize myself in the world. My action is guided by my past history and projects a coherent identity into the future. Individuals must author their own stories for themselves—they are not appendages or epiphenomena of society or nature, but rather infinite subjects who must demonstrate and achieve this infinitude to themselves in creating a self, an "activity [that] constitutes the individuality of self-consciousness, which posits itself as negativity and is the free ego, infinite relation to itself" (VPR17 123A).

However, the literary analogy incompletely expresses the life of the historical individual. One of Hegel's great worries about the modern individual is that abyss of the ego will tempt the individual to Promethean world creation or willful irrationality, a dark vision Hegel attributes to his Romantic contemporaries like Fichte, Schlegel, and Fries.[57] Hegel worries that if nature, tradition, and God do not legitimately direct the individual, if the individual himself is the only legitimate source of authority, what prevents him from sliding into such Dostoevskian excesses? If the only binding requirement on individual action is consistency, harmony, diversity, then a very creative thief or murderer could fulfill these requirements, and do so with élan. Yet for Hegel, this creative individuality is necessary but not sufficient for the individual subject to lead a full life. Rather, the individual subject leads a full human life as this creative individual participating in common, rational forms of ethical life. Hegel envisions the individual simultaneously as a whole unto himself and also as a part of a general societal whole. Defending this claim will be the topic of chapter 3, while defending Hegel's claim that the modern age provides a mutual harmony between creative individual and common life will be the subject of chapter 4. For if the demands of individual coherence and the normative demands of our historical practices do not harmonize, one must give way—and the human subject would in such a case not find satisfaction but rather would lead an incomplete, distorted human life.

3

Hegel on the Ethical Individual

In the last chapter, we saw that, in contrast to the traditional under-standing of Hegel, our Hegel is a defender of a robust form of individu-alism, both in terms of an individual's right to follow only those laws he has given himself (his autonomous authority) and in terms of our respect for each individual's uniqueness of character (the unity of his character as aim). Individuality is good and ought to be defended, Hegel argues, because it is the necessary, immanent aim of the distinctively human subjectivity. It is, for Hegel, the "good life" of a human being. Success-fully leading an individual life entails that one has created a human subject in the world. Failure to lead an individual life means failing to live a fully human life. At the same time, not recognizing this human being as a human subject amounts to treating him as other than what he is. There are several degrees of achievement of this norm, as "individu-ality" is not given to human beings, but is rather the accumulated achievement of human effort, the creation of a more or less coherent character bearing the trace of a single subject.

However, we get the wrong impression if we think of Hegel as some kind of Romantic individualist like John Stuart Mill encouraging "ex-periments in living." Indeed, Hegel was a sharp critic of this brand of Romanticism of his day, as he makes clear in the prefaces to PR and PhG. Rather, subjects can only be individuals by leading an ethical life through participation in community. "Ethical life" is not merely the precondition for freedom and self-realization, as some scholars argue, but rather the individual's aim.[1] That is, Hegel does not just argue that community precedes individual in a temporal sense, but also in an eth-ical sense. Ethical activity is virtuous activity in the Greek sense of *arête* or excellence—ethical action is part and parcel of what it means to be an individual. The standard for excellence and hence the aim of the individual's ethical action is the common good jointly established and maintained within community.[2] It is only by acting ethically in this way—and, specifically, politically—that individuals lead complete human lives.[3] This is what I take Hegel to mean when he says that it is the "destiny of individuals . . . to lead a universal life" and that "it is only through being a member of the state that the individual himself has objectivity, truth, and ethical life" (PR 258A).[4] This chapter is dedicated to articulating Hegel's defense of his claim that the destiny of individuals is to lead an ethical life.

3.1   The Origin of Community

The claim of this chapter is that ethical action is necessary in fulfilling individual subjectivity and hence leading a good life. At the outset, I should adumbrate the meaning of the "ethical" for Hegel, because I think it remains still rather obscure in the scholarship. This is partially due to the fact that many readers highlight the term *Sitte* related to Hegel's *Sittlichkeit*, thereby emphasizing the concrete customs or mores that make up *Sittlichkeit*. By emphasizing that institutions and *Sitte* are preconditions for individual freedom, scholars argue that Hegel's view is more concrete, less atomistic and deracinated than the overly abstract, rational rules of Kant's political philosophy.[5] This claim is true so far as it goes, but the problem is that it leaves underdetermined what happens to the individual after such preconditioning.

My view is that the *Sitte* is not as important as the *sittlich* element in *Sittlichkeit*. That is, Hegel is alerting us, in using the term *Sittlichkeit*, that this is a community of individuals who act *sittlich* or ethically. Ethical action is distinguished in Hegel's mind from, on the one hand, self-interested or "selfish" action of natural desire (ES 433) and, on the other hand, the coerced heteronomous action under a political tyrant or social conformism (PHI 204).[6] Rather, ethical action involves freeing ourselves both from nature's impulses and from social pressures to act for what Hegel calls the rational "living good" or common good constitutive of *Sittlichkeit* (PR 142). An ethical individual is one who sees his community not as a means to his selfish, private ends, but as an end in itself. Under the proper conditions, ethical action is regarded by the individual's fellows as virtuous activity, activity not performed for the instrumental goal of satisfying individual "utility," but rather in bringing into appearance a form of human life in a display of public excellence. Hegel sees "ethical life," then, as a bond not according to a self-interested contract nor force, but rather one of love, friendship, and honor (ES 436Z).

Just as in the previous chapter, so too here we must examine the origins of human subjectivity in order to see why the human subject can only become truly fulfilled through such ethical activity.[7] For Hegel, the primitive human being exists submerged in his natural "desire" (*Begierde*), wholly part of nature or "life" (PhG 167).[8] In this primordial condition at the dawn of humanity, the naked drives of his bodily passions guide his actions, while human interactions do not exist for him. As we saw in the previous chapter, this natural desire involves a "lack" (*Mangel*) and hence a felt need for completeness (EN 359). The natural desire hence has the aim of appropriating or "negating" other objects of nature to fulfill one's natural incompleteness. One gains completeness by extending one's subjectivity out into nature, replacing the alien objects of the world with one's own subjectivity (PhG 174). In fulfilling our desires, we employ a primitive form of instrumental rationality that allows us to act in the world by mastering it, rather than by following natural instinct within it. We use our cunning and manipulate nature to use it against nature's hardships: we make tools out of nature to hunt the things of nature and to protect us from natural evils, for instance. Nature seems, then, to belong to man. The human is independent, while nature is dependent on him. Every object bends to the human will. As Sophocles puts it, the human "has a way against everything, and he faces nothing that is to come without contrivance" (*Antigone*, ll. 358–60; cf. Hegel's citation at EN 245Z).

Rousseau, who influenced Hegel considerably on the speculative origins of human history, argued that the natural human being achieves wholeness as the "numerical unity, the absolute whole which is relative only to itself or its kind" (E 39). However, Hegel argues, this natural wholeness is only apparent. In truth, the primitive human comes to find himself imprisoned by the cycles of natural desire. Even if he considers himself sovereign over the wild berries and beasts of the wilderness, he remains utterly dependent on nature for the character and objects of his desire, while the wilderness does not depend on him at all for its persistence. That is, no matter how much the natural human being fulfills his incompleteness, his natural desires, those same natural desires invariably return. The human being finds himself enslaved to the pangs of his hunger. Human beings are thus maintained in a state of pure "desire" (*Begierde*) in which their "satisfaction is always destructive [in form], and in its content selfish." As Hegel points out, selfish desire is never truly satisfied, because "the desire is again generated in the very act of satisfaction" (ES 428). That is, as soon as I sate my hunger, my body starts to process the food I have eaten, and my hunger begins to return again, as my body needs a constant intake of fuel. The cycle of desire and consumption never provides stable satisfaction for an infinite consciousness—for the human being who seeks freedom—but instead lands the natural human being in the same kind of "bad infinite" we found in the last chapter, that of constant negation, constant destruction, without any positive claim in which his infinite consciousness can find a stable object that will reflect his infinitude back to him. For Hegel, this critique of bodily pleasure holds true also against hedonistic human beings in modern society, that this notion of the good as "pleasure" is ultimately dissatisfying to human beings.[9] As we will see in the next chapter, however, the modern age tends to cultivate a love for the "particular" natural desires in civil society, a development that requires correction, in Hegel's view.

This cycle of desire and consumption is dissatisfying even for the most primitive human beings, who possess a faint awareness of the categorical difference between human freedom and natural need, the "tremendous difference on the one side of the 'I,' this wholly simply existence, and on the other side, of the infinite variety of the world" (ES 425Z). This awareness gives rise to the "*impulse* [Trieb] to realize what it is in itself, by giving its abstract self-awareness content and objectivity, and in the other direction to free itself from its sensuousness, to sublate [*aufheben*] the given objectivity and identify it with itself" (ES 425).[10] Natural objects of consumption fail to provide the human with this self-awareness, the "truth" or objective testimony of my agency to match the "certainty" of our difference from nature (ES 416Z), so human beings long to find something else that will "realize [the] implicit nature" of our freedom. Subjects, in short, cannot yet realize ourselves in the world.

It is in encountering another human being that we discover the possibility of overcoming nature and asserting our freedom.[11] We discern this possibility when we see that the other human being is not a natural object like any other, mutable according to my whims, without an essence or will of its own. As an infinite center of natural desire, a willful being, the other human being responds unpredictably to my approaches and encounters.[12] The encounter with the other human being is both exhilarating and terrifying in that it contains the "highest contradiction" in life (PS 187). On the one hand, I am drawn to the other because I discern that he has an ego as I do. He masters nature by extending his infinitely negating ego over all the objects of nature. In this way, his infinite ego resembles my own so that "in that other as ego I behold myself" (ES 430). I finally have confirmation of the certainty of my own freedom—I see my own subjective superiority or sovereignty over nature reflected back at me, and hence I feel a measure of satisfaction.

On the other hand, however, I am also attracted with a terrible anxiety to him as well, since he shows "infinite resistance" to my desires (PS 187). This other ego is "absolutely independent of me and opposed to me" (ES 430) since I see that I cannot fold him under my own activity of desirous negation. The other ego is not pliable and dependent on my will as the objects in nature are. I know this because even if I treat the other's body as I would the bodies populating the rest of nature, the other is infinitely more than his body. I am sure of his own transcendence over his body because I am "certain" of my own infinite transcendence of my body, and this other is just like me.

Furthermore, what is truly terrifying in the primordial relationship of human to human is that both egos make identical claims to the totality of nature. That is, each human being extends his subjectivity indefinitely over nature. Each, in turn, sees the other as always already engaged in a project of the subjective, laboring transforming nature into "his" world amenable to "his desires." The relationship is a "contradiction" because each makes an infinite claim on the very same objects in nature—and since the human being is a composite of body and consciousness, each human being makes a claim on the body of the other as well. As a result, each primitive human being's world is threatened in every way—down to every wild berry and every beast, to my own body—of being swallowed up by the world of another, of belonging to the will of another, of becoming an object of nature rather than a sovereign over it. The natural being's project of transforming nature is therefore not challenged from within nature—as in, for instance, the appearance of a bear or a tiger surprising one in one's usual hunting ground. Rather, the very *possibility* of my transforming nature is challenged. The very possibility of my desire as such is negated and called into question, when I see myself as an object in the eyes of the other.[13] This meta-challenge of another human being compels me to defend my desire, for I can never escape the infinite reach of another's absolute negativity. When the other sees my infinite subjectivity as an object, I have the "impulse to show [myself] as a free self, and to exist as such for the other" (ES 430). I must affirm my own desirous self by negating his self, or rather by getting the other to recognize the validity of my own desires. I seek, in other words, his recognition.

In this standoff, all I know is my own material desire, so I cannot sit down and talk peaceably with my competitor. Rather, I must fight against him.[14] So what might amount to a proof of my rightful claim in a fight? We might say that strength would win out, yet for Hegel, "might makes right" is actually no reason at all—it simply confuses natural or material power with spiritual norms. Rather, for Hegel, the competitors seek to prove their freedom from nature—from being a mere thing in nature like any other—and hence their rightful sovereignty over it by staking their natural life in a fight to the death (ES 431Z). Courage, then, is the first distinctively human virtue, the first component of leading a good human life. In staking his natural life, each combatant seeks to show that he has mastered the most powerful pull that nature has over him—the fear of a violent death and the desire for self-preservation. That is, if he is successful, the combatant shows that his subjectivity infinitely transcends the most powerful impulse of nature, and hence this subject is not a thing like any other, but rather is due recognition of it being a free no-thing. However, the fight to the death is ill-conceived because one combatant is left standing, while the other is killed. The fallen one achieves no satisfaction at all for his freedom, since he is dead. Yet the victor also is left as dissatisfied as before—his agency does not find a permanent place in the world but rather encounters another natural object, the corpse of his enemy, dissolving back into the rest of a defiant nature (PhG 188).

In other words, all the primitive human being knows is the model of his appetitive desire, which only destroys or negates natural bodies (including offering up his own for possible negation). The combatant who eventually becomes a slave ironically makes a revolutionary leap in the development of ethical life. In anticipating his loss of the combat and hence his own death, the slave chooses his natural life over his freedom and hence renounces his claim to recognition as a free being. In so doing, he recognizes the master as a free being. The slave thereby offers a public or objective testament to the master's freedom by carrying out the master's will. Such recognition is initially very satisfying to the master—much more satisfying than nature—since the slave offers a permanent home for the master's self-consciousness. The master sees again and again his own free subjectivity reflected back at him when the slave does his bidding, thereby realizing his own will in the world. The slave's recognition of the master's law consists of the slave's "negation of itself in itself" (PhG 175). That is, in contrast to the things of nature, which are negated by the master, the slave negates his own natural body in recognizing the master. Such recognition as self-negation consists in negating one's own natural desires, transforming them in accordance with a general norm of conduct set by the master. Recognition, as we can see, is the activity of making one's own self-consciousness a home for another will, so that the other will can inhabit it. It means setting aside one's natural selfishness, one's all-destroying instinct, one's sub-sumption of the world under one's ego, and submitting oneself to a higher law. It comes eventually to involve sentiments of what we call trust, care, solicitude, and respect in supporting and fostering the oth-er's leading a good life in more reciprocal forms of human community. As Hegel puts it, this "subjugation of the slave's selfishness forms the *beginning* of true human freedom" (ES 435Z). Such recognition, then—the sharing of a self-consciousness with another—is an essential social condition in developing our autonomy, the capacity to order and master one's natural being according to a self-given law.

In this way, the master and slave exemplify two features of free sub-jectivity. The master creates and gives a moral law—a law not dictated by nature—that adjudicates the conflict between them. The slave ne-gates his natural self and follows this human law.[15] Yet the problem with this primitive community—the master lawgiver and the slave law fol-lower—is that these two elements of human subjectivity do not coexist in one self. For Hegel, the form of recognition that exists here, a "one-sided and unequal recognition" (PhG 191), from the slave to the entity that is "higher" than the slave, the master, does not satisfy the subjec-tivity of the master. The master succeeds in legislating a law, and hence acting out of his subjective freedom, but he does not give the law to himself. This is because the master has willfully created this law—he does not achieve a sufficient distance from his own law such that the law would appear as binding upon him, authoritative over his will rather than revocable at his whim. Instead, the master finds himself slavishly dependent on his natural desires in the same way he had been in the state of nature.[16] He is slavishly dependent on his natural desires be-cause his "formal recognition" from the slave—that is, recognition that he is a free subject, that he can stake his life when he needs to—does not shape his character such that he can be a truly self-determined ethical being. This is because he does not receive "substantive recogni-tion" from the slave—that is, recognition through a common substan-tive principle of the good life which binds and shapes both participants' wills (PS 192). In other words, the master can do whatever he wants with his slave, and this kind of unbounded arbitrariness does not ultimately satisfy the master's subjectivity, which itself longs to master and order his natural desires. "Mind" is separated from "body"—it does not per-meate or transform the latter, and hence fails to find a genuine home in nature (PS 192). The slave does not judge the master's freedom from a normative perspective—rather, the slave gives him recognition out of nature, a natural fear of death. It is only by encountering legitimate resistance from the other that I can come to be satisfied, since here I can discern the limits of my subjectivity—otherwise, if the slave recognizes any and all of my actions, regardless of what I do, I have no positive guidance for my will's actions, no sense of the boundary between the good life and a selfish or base life.

On the other hand, the slave successfully overcomes his natural self in the face of death, which reveals to him the utter contingency of his natural life to his free subjectivity (PhG 194), as well as in light of his labor upon nature, in which he comes to see himself in the permanence of his institutional creations (PhG 195). The slave can create himself in nature because he labors on it. His labor differs from the labor of the natural human being because he works for his master, or for a rainy day, not for his immediate consumption. In other words, he disciplines nature (including his own natural desires) to a human law, to an idea of the good (the pleasure of the master). At the same time, however, the slave's subjectivity is fundamentally incomplete because this law that he follows is not his own. He is internally divided—on the one hand, he sees himself through the master's eyes as a mere natural tool to be disposed of as the master sees fit. On the other hand, he is "certain" that he is a free subjectivity far transcending nature. The law of the master, then, appears to him as an oppressive, alien force that attempts to erase his subjectivity and replace it with a natural tool. Thus, the subjectivity of each is fundamentally thwarted because each falls into the enslavement of one of the two pitfalls perennially threatening human individuality— nature or society. Nature reveals itself like Teflon to the master, incapable of having his agency stick there; "society" (in the form of the master) shows itself to be a force entirely external to the slave's will, and hence the slave sees nothing of himself in this law. For Hegel, to make a complete subject, the subject must be simultaneously master and slave, not one or the other.

3.2   The Nature of Community

How is it possible to overcome this problem? Each person requires the recognition of the other for his freedom. Though we are each of us "certain" of our own freedom, since our subjectivity only appears through action, we cannot be assured of the truth of our subjective freedom without getting validation from the other. Therefore, the best way to ensure free subjectivity on both sides is for each party to recognize the other as a free subjectivity. That way, each should receive back the opinion of himself that corresponds with his "certain" inkling each has about his own subjectivity. This mutual recognition does not consist in a contingent "intersubjective" agreement of empirical subjectivities. Mutual recognition is not like a cease-fire between two warring nations, especially in the cases in which we expect the nations to return to battle after a short respite. Such an agreement—such as, for instance, "My territory is over those hills and yours is to the edge of this forest"— leaves the combatants fundamentally unchanged and hence still enslaved to their particular natural desires, still threatened by the other, now within a particular territory. The empirical agreement appeals simply to their instrumental reason, rather than to the substance of their selves. For Hegel, the ethical conception that the other holds about me fundamentally shapes who I am and hence can reveal my own free subjectivity for me, and so I am interested in belonging to this other, in the sense that I belong to a shared ethical community.

Rather, to avoid both the problem of the master and that of the slave, we must submit ourselves to a will whose authority transcends both of us yet nonetheless a will that we both share in common, a will through which we can recognize one another as free beings. In other words, mutual recognition involves the mutual subsumption under a *"universal self-consciousness,"* which is, as Hegel puts it, the "affirmative awareness [*Wissen*] of self in an other self" (ES 436). Mutual recognition brings about that famous Hegelian notion of "spirit, this absolute substance which is the unity of the different independent self-consciousnesses which, in their opposition, enjoy perfect freedom and independence: *I* that is *we* and *we* that is *I*" (PhG 177). For Hegel, the only way to be free from both nature and from power-hungry masters is for everyone to submit themselves to a norm of the good life that is binding equally on all members and sustained in the laws and ways of a community or practice, that is, to the "form of consciousness which is the *substance* of all true spiritual life—in family, fatherland, state" (ES 436). In doing so, each follows his own law (and hence avoids enslavement to society), and each follows a way of life that itself transcends the way of natural desire (and hence avoids enslavement to nature). Mutual recognition, then, only takes place as mediated through this "spirit" or communal will. As members or parts of this community, we each of us have a principle of the good upon which to recognize the other as equal and free.[17] ("Spirit," then, for Hegel, is not some quasi-mystical substance, but the system of norms and dispositions that make up an ethical community.)

In other words, mutual recognition involves three steps, and the human subject only finds completion upon taking all three. First, each of us must negate his own natural selfish desire, just as he negates the things of nature to display his freedom. We negate our own consciousness, opening and disciplining it to the ethical, universal self-consciousness we share in common. This universal self-consciousness we share cannot be my or our personal property, subject entirely to my or our will, but it rather transcends it. Otherwise, there can be no objective, neutral testament to my and our freedom, and my will will remain immersed in nature. In negating my own natural will, I surrender both my aims as a selfish natural being and the "authority" of nature—the natural "laws" governing my biological needs are trumped by the communal laws of ethical behavior. Ethical behavior is higher than natural behavior because it involves the "self-consciousness" of subjectivity—the universal subject "finds itself" in the human world of institutions and customs that it constructs for itself.

Second, each must embody the universal subject in his own identity. The universal subject creates a human world animated by the pursuit of a particular form of the good life which becomes the standard for free human action. The public recognition of this good life thus allows participants in the community to witness the truth of their own freedom in the approving reception of their ethical actions by the other participants. In Rome, for instance, two Romans mutually recognized one another when they saw one another as fellow courageous men willing to put their lives on the line for the Republic. Each Roman, then, saw his own free subjectivity in the other and was satisfied thereby. We need not resort to fighting one another to prove our freedom from nature—we can simply act based on a human principle of the good to attest to our freedom.

Finally, each of us must be equal partners in this activity of mutual recognition. If there is serious inequality of recognition, in which the standards for leading a good life are unequally applied, then we encounter the same problems of asymmetrical recognition discussed above. However, when each person recognizes the other equally, there obtains the condition Aristotle describes as "ruling and being ruled in turn." Each person gains back from this surrender to the other an independence as equally part of a communal whole that is self-legislated. For this reason, Honneth (2008) describes this condition of mutual recognition as mutual "respect," in which each subject comes to publicly grasp the other as an infinite self-consciousness, and thus both subjects come to assume the freedom of this infinite subjectivity (88). As Hegel puts it, in "relating myself to the *other* I am immediately *self*-related" (ES 436Z).[18]

The key point is this—subjectivity only comes to be through its actions. The human subject cannot be free within himself. Only by transforming one's "particular" desires in accordance with a "universal" notion of the good life can the subject pursue aims that transcend nature. Such "ethical" actions—those which follow the communal notion of the good life and hence aim at the common good—allow subjectivity to appear in the recognitive gaze of the other.

Universal Identity

Human beings hence have a longing to act ethically, so that our subjectivity can be recognized by the other. Yet such ethical action is impossible if there is no standard of ethical action and a set of institutions and customs with an independent history that can make such a standard intelligible and realizable. In order to understand the character and aim of individual ethical action, we must investigate the nature of the universal subject that gives shape to the ethical will. As I have argued already, the universal subject is not the product of agreement by preexisting human wills (the natural individualists were wrong on this count), but nor is it an ahistorical, noumenal "faculty" given to all human beings (the formalists were wrong here). Rather, Hegel argues, the genesis and development of this self-consciousness always occur "behind the back" of individual subjects in history. This is not to say that the universal I is some spooky substratum, but that this universal I does have an aim and authority that is not identical with any one individual I. Yet this universal I is remarkably similar in structure to the individual I we discussed in the previous chapter—Hegel thinks of nations, for instance, as individuals with a certain identity, history, set of preferences, and vision of the good (PHI 56–60). Only by understanding the relationship between the universal and individual I's can we understand how the individuality we discussed in the previous chapter can be completed in this ethical participation.

A universal or "general" (*Allgemeinen*) subject is a collective agent structuring what we referred to in the previous chapter as a historical practice. The universal subject and the substantive practice it produces are the source of normative intelligibility for the participants within that practice. Yet these norms are not given from on high, but rather are generated by the universal subject in service of producing the good that it seeks. We can see here, then, how the universal subject reproduces the same structure of subjectivity as the animal and the human being. The universal subject is first and foremost a practical agent—it is not a passive onlooker or a mere set of rules, but an active seeker after a certain good, a set of rules established in order to create some good. That good is formally describable as maintaining and enduring inner contradictions, extending itself outward and incorporating parts of the world such that it can come to see itself as realized in it. Now, unlike animals and like human beings, the universal subject can free itself from natural inclinations and obey this set of norms that it gives to itself. In other words, the "parts" that make up a whole universal subject are not biological elements but rather determinations of normative thought, such as laws, institutions, and customs.

However, normally we do not attribute agency to a collective will in this way. Indeed, speaking of a collective agent as seeking to realize itself in the world and legislating for itself certain norms borders on the mysterious, if not mystical. However, I want to insist that this collective subject is not spooky, existing antecedently of the group, the family, the nation, but rather it arises only through human actors who represent—or embody—the collective subject. Thus, Hegel is not speaking metaphorically when he says that there are collective agents, but he does want to offer an unusual notion of subjective agency that arises only through the actions of interdependent parts. Just as the "subject" Fido or my personal whole identity is not a substratum persisting indifferently beneath appearances, so too here the collective subject appears in its actions. For instance, we may speak of collective agents such as the United States (going to war in Afghanistan, bailing out the banks, having this and such aim or identity, etc.), corporations (getting bailed out by the government, compensating its employees with taxpayer money), sports teams (winning and losing certain games, playing well), without reducing these collective agents to one or any number of individual wills, and without assuming that there is a ghostly substance "the United States" persisting behind appearances.

However, it is true that collective agents require human beings for their embodiment. The collective subject "the USSR" has ceased to be because there are no more human beings acting as agents of this collective subject within institutions that it has created. Human subjects are the most important "parts" of this collective whole because our subjectivity is naturally moved by ethical concern, and maintains and advances the common good as a result. The most fundamental way in which collective subjects embody themselves in human agents is through the profession of identity, that I as an agent belong to, or am a member of, this group. Such an identity claim is of fundamental importance because subjects naturally seek to create a coherent identity among their parts. Individual agents can express their own belonging to this group—and hence embody the group's practical agency—in any number of ways, from holding a certain legal status all the way down to waving a flag. But the central form of identification in Hegel's mind is acting based on the notion of the good life shared by this community, the good life that expresses the aims of the collective subject. It is only on the basis of a common identity of acting for an ethical good that we can recognize the other's (and my own) actions as free from nature and as distinctively human (SL 412). The clearest examples of such ethical identity are the premodern regimes, in which Rome or Athens had distinct notions of what it means to be a citizen; members of these groups were expected to live up to this notion of the good, and in doing so they made this collective subject a reality. But for Hegel, these are not the best or highest instances of such identity—that distinction belongs to the modern regime, as we will see.

The relationship between universal subject and individual subject initially, then, takes the "top-down" form we spoke of in the last chapter. The individual subject has a basic ethical longing, a desire to be free from nature. This ethical longing is shaped within historical practices, such that the longing takes on a particular content, that of the good of this community. Participants desire to seek the common good because they have internalized the universal subjectivity of their community. They feel they must act ethically because they will then be judged by the public, who themselves have also internalized this universal subjectivity. In short, the individual subject pursues this notion of the good because he will be recognized as a free being by others, in whom he can therefore see the reflection of his own free subjectivity. Yet in so doing, the individual subject himself realizes the aims of the universal subject in which the universal subject—in the form of the onlooking community—can take satisfaction. For instance, heroic figures such as Achilles become expressions of communal virtue that other Greeks—*qua* universal subject—can see themselves.

In this moment of ethical "identity," the ethical actor and the audience identify themselves with the universal purposes of the collective subject, and hence they have an "intuition of their *determinate identity with each other*" (ES 436Z). Indeed, for Hegel, the feelings of solidarity, care, honor, and love are prototypical ethical feelings in that they stem from our elevating our own "particular" affective natures into harmony with the "universal" purposes. The "trust" and "national pride" that "I am a Prussian, an Englishman," for instance, mean that I have been raised to the universal I, "that I am that which the state is, [and] the state is my being [*mein Sein*]" (VPR 4.641). These bonds form the "substance of ethical life," that which is the object of subjective satisfaction (ES 436Z).[19] In other words, for Hegel, acting for the common good is not a matter of ascetic self-denial, of "selflessness" or "altruism." Rather, ethical action consists in the pursuit of a spiritual good for another, such as honor or friendship, which makes ever more real in the world a common subject that I share with another. Similarly, when we witness this higher subject in motion—whenever, for instance, a member of the whole acts as a mouthpiece of the community with a particular kind of virtue, setting aside his natural desires and "risking one's life in a universal cause"—each member thus feels "honor" in the community, or what Hegel calls in a more specific context "honor of estate" [*Standesehre*] (PR 253; cf. ES 436Z).[20] In short, just as the individual subject identifies itself with the collective subject, so too is the individual character shaped by the collective notion of the good life. Insofar as this honor and love of the good exist objectively in the "dispositions" of individuals, Hegel argues, the good of the community and of individuals has already been partially achieved (PR 267–68). Solidarity, honor, and friendship are not just promptings for actions, then, but rather forms of individual subjective satisfaction, in which the subject finds its own good existing all around it in the virtuous character of its fellows.[21]

Hegel's notion of recognition of "identity" is exemplified in the phenomenon of "team spirit" in sporting events. On a winning high school soccer team, for instance, each teammate implicitly recognizes all the others as "free beings," as beings responsible for making this team a success thus far. Each teammate recognizes the others as parts of the whole because each is importantly "identical" to one another in contributing to the whole greater than all the members. The mutual recognition structuring this community takes the affective form of mutual support, encouragement, high-fiving, trust, and so forth. This particular winning soccer team, like all others, has a particular "personality," a "we," that transcends the personality of any one of its member (designated in its colorful name, its jersey, its vocal pregame cheers, its unique game play), which in turn comes to shape and mold the personality of the individuals within the group. There is a certain standing "good," a certain "common self" characterized by its history of experiences, wins and losses, and so forth that is possessed by the group and that binds the group together in solidarity. But also, this standing good at once arouses the players to "virtuous" activity when the time comes. During the game, each strives to gain recognition from the others for embodying the "personality" of the team, for ever more realizing and completing the good that they share as a whole—that is, scoring a goal, playing excellent defense, achieving victory. When our teammates perform some excellence on the playing field, they bring to appearance and complete what had been persisting in an inchoate form all along, that is, the good of the collective subject itself. In other words, we honor our teammate by honoring his virtuous embodiment of the collective subject "team" that appears through his action and thereby comes subsequently to suffuse our relationship with our teammates.

For Hegel, subjects find satisfaction in such ethical behavior, as in contributing to the "common good" of the team. Consider what happens, for instance, when subjects do not pursue ethical ends. Some teams consist of players who do not play for the team, but rather play for themselves. These "ball hogs" think of the team as a loose aggregate of self-sufficient wholes, rather than, as in the case of the spirited team, parts of an overarching whole. In a team full of ball hogs, no player recognizes any other, and hence no player succeeds in accruing recognition from the other when he succeeds on the field, in, for instance, scoring a goal. When I play only for myself, my actions do not take on significance since they are not part of some system of ethical relationships that could confer significance on them. I am dissatisfied by my own conferral of significance on my actions, similar to the way that the master is dissatisfied—there is no objective or set standard for the excellence of my behavior. If I set my own standard, then no action will fail to meet that test. But if no action can fail, then no action can truly succeed, either. My teammates, whom I use as instruments to my own ends rather than as ends in themselves, do not offer objective criteria of success or failure, since I subsume them under my own will. Instead, the ball hog becomes ever more dissatisfied and incomplete in longing to be recognized as free, but failing to submit himself to a general will shared with others that is the necessary condition for such recognition. The ball hog falls back on the natural pleasures, developing a corrupt, hedonistic, and selfish character on the field and off. Or consider the player consistently recognized as unequal by his fellow players for reasons irrelevant to his game play (for instance, because of the color of his skin). This player acts like all the others, wears the same jersey, performs just as well as the others, but is systematically excluded from the adulation, the high-fives, the pats on the back. He takes himself to be part of the whole, but the whole itself rejects him. He sees a diminished form of himself in the eyes of the others, and hence his attachment to others and to the team as a whole frays. Accordingly, he loses respect and honor in himself, and his deeds appear to take on no meaning.

For Hegel, individual human beings have the natural desire to be a "somebody," to be a member of a particular communal whole in which we exist within a good life and pursue a common good jointly with others who recognize and admire our efforts. We desire, in other words, to be recognized as embodying and as desiring to live up to a common will that we share with others. In concrete terms, we desire to be "similar" to or "equal with others" according to the criteria of living a good life within one's community (VPR17 95A). If I, by contrast, cease to be part of a community that recognizes me and admires my efforts, then I no longer find my own agency recognized by concrete fellows, and hence my actions begin to lose significance or meaning. I come to think of myself not with honor and self-respect accorded to me by the recognitive gaze of others, but as a "nobody," whose actions mean little and who has little motivation to act either for others or to craft my own self.

Individual Difference

However, this initial understanding of the relationship between universal I and individual I—that of "identity"—must be deepened, because its top-down approach to the satisfaction of subjectivity would fail to satisfy the subject as an individual. That is, individual subjects cannot be satisfied ultimately through mere identification with others, since they would then be unable to see their own distinctive subjectivity in the world. For Hegel, the individual subject seeks identification with the common good, but the subject also wants to identify with the collective subject in its own way, thereby making its own distinctive mark on the collective will. Each of us seeks "to assert [himself] through some distinctive quality" (PR 193), since we long to see our own particular subjectivity reflected back at us in the whole.

For Hegel, there is a deeply dialectical relationship between identity and difference. He argues that "reason is nothing more than a loom on which it externally combines and interweaves the warp of say, identity, and then the woof of difference" (SL 412). The different way of each is not, then, a matter of independent, arbitrary choice on the part of each member or the dictates of powerful elites. Rather, the common good of the community comes to be divided in its history into a functionally rational system of divided labor.[22] Even the most primitive communities tacitly understand that the most sensible way to achieve the common good is to assign individuals to particular stations or tasks. Accordingly, the form of the "good life" will differ depending on, say, whether one is a farmer, a craftsman, or a bureaucrat (PR 201). Indeed, for Hegel, ironically, it is essential for the wholeness of the community for each of us to recognize the distinct and different forms of the good life achieved by different members of the whole.[23] In this way, Hegel pairs the recognition of "identity" against this recognition of individual "difference."

Indeed, since subjectivity organizes its substance organically—its parts possessing an interdependent harmony—difference is necessary to perform the various functions that make up the whole. In the human body, for instance, the heart plays a very different function than the brain, and hence they are quite different in character. Subjectivity hence seeks such internal differentiation, because the more inner complexity it displays, the more apparent (and hence nobler) the subjectivity for being able to unify these otherwise contradictory parts. The subject must employ, then, a functional rationality to bring its parts into harmony. Such a functional rationality works by dividing the task of pursuing the good into smaller functions each of which is necessary to the fulfillment of this good. Hence, in order to be rational and whole, the subject seeks to assign its parts—for instance, brain, heart, lungs, hands—different functions that are indispensable not only in producing the good as a whole, but in maintaining the functioning of the other parts. The death of the heart or the brain does not lead just to the loss of that specific contribution to the common good of the organism, but to the death of the organism as a whole and all its parts. It is for this reason that Aristotle argued that a severed hand is not really a hand, because a hand is defined as performing a specific function within a total system—its nature is indivisible from this totality.[24] As Hegel puts the point, each member of the organic whole is explicable only in terms of its relationship to the whole and hence to all the other members within it.[25] Hence, for Hegel, each member "exhibits the totality" of the whole in a properly constituted organism (EN 354Z).

Universal subjects work the same way, except that, as we have seen, their whole and parts are not biological, but ethical.[26] The community possesses a common good, and in order to realize it, the community assigns its different human agents to different vocations or tasks, such as farmers, merchants, sailors, statesmen (PR 201). Each task is indispensable to producing the common good, and each task is indispensable to the continuation of the others—for instance, if we get rid of all the statesmen, we will no longer have a state and hence farmers and merchants will no longer be able to trade. Accordingly, each individual's vocation is intelligible only according to its connection to the common good and hence to every part within the whole.[27]

In describing this moment of "difference" and the functional rationality of the collective subject, we are again not imputing a personal agent behind the scenes lining up its pawns as a chess champion does. Rather, the collective subject comes to be through the action of its members. How does such membership become coherent, then? There are two ways in which functional rationality is produced and maintained, and in both cases, as we will see, the individual subject comes to find itself in the social world. The first is through the maintenance and transformation of institutions, while the second resides in the ethical disposition and action of individual subjects. First, for Hegel, human beings do not spontaneously do their duties. On the contrary, since we are a composite of bodily and spiritual beings, our natural, selfish desires often lead us away from our duties to our community. Accordingly, the vocations we perform as parts of the common good transcend our own individual wills. My vocation, say, as a statesman—a president, congressperson, city council member—is independent of my will. It is occupied and occupiable by many more wills than my own because it contains normative rules that bind any will. These rules are designed through history and human design to shape the will of the participant into a proper part of the whole, or in other words, to make my will ethical. On this point, the quotations we began our discussion of Hegel's defense of individuality with are relevant—the "worth of individuals is measured by the extent to which they reflect and represent the national spirit, and have adopted a particular station within the affairs of the state as a whole" (PHI 80). Each citizen's "morality" consists "in fulfilling the duties imposed upon him by his social station" (PHI 80). Institutions and mores provide the content of ethical behavior in which subjects can be free.

Some of these rules remain at the level of mores and are regulated by the stigma of public opinion, whereas some are codified and enforced by public coercion. In either form, they take on the normative binding force of moral laws. The "moral law" amounts to doing my duty, which is distinguished from the "ethical good," which involves cultivating a good life (though the first is an integral part in the second). Hegel here appropriates Kant's moral theory by bringing it down to earth and embedding its logic in historical practices. For Kant, as for Hegel, moral norms are only legitimately binding if they are self-legislated by the individual.[28] Accordingly, for Hegel, individuals must be able to be free in their selection of their vocation (PR 206). In freely choosing their occupation, individuals effectively legislate for themselves the system of rules, duties, and rights that structure the practice of their occupation. For instance, in becoming a lawyer, I bind my own will to the norms of the bar association, such that it does not make any sense for me to declare that its rules are an unjust imposition on my sovereign will. Such a statement would amount to both willing the norms of the practice and exempting myself from them at the same time. However, not all rules within historical practices are rational. In order to be rational and hence arouse the spiritual interest of a human subject, such rules need to meet the test of functional rationality. That is, they must not serve "particular" interests, but must—in a suitably efficient fashion—be justified as serving the "universal" or common good.

Just as these institutions should shape my will to make it ethical, so too should the individual will be able to shape the institutions it belongs to. In other words, the top-down model of institutional autonomy must be supplemented by a "bottom-up" form of individual autonomy in order for me to be able to identify my own will in the activity of the practice as a whole. That is, for Hegel, individuals must be able to revise the rules of the institutions they belong to when these rules become inefficient, outmoded, or otherwise inappropriate. In revising these rules in accordance with the individual's own notion of the relationship between the whole and its parts, the individual comes to "labor" on this institutional whole and hence transform it to bear the trace of my individual subjectivity. Even the slightest change in rules can have deep ramifications in these organically structured institutions, which makes such individual revisions meaningful for the individual subject.

Yet for the same reason, Hegel counsels great restraint in such revisions. For him, institutions should shape characters to be primarily reverent for their community and for their institutions, identifying with it, and only secondarily be mistrustful of its rules (VPR17 136A). Hegel argues that precisely because communities and institutions have a complex, organic structure whose parts cannot easily be replaced or changed without a comprehensive knowledge of the total system, individual revisions should be made only after considerable deliberation, and even then with prudence and restraint.[29] Hegel's worry on this point is similar to Burke's—the modern individual who considers himself an ahistorical, rational self-maker comes to find the deep historical meaning and rules embedded in institutions to be irrational, not in conformity with an abstract notion of "equality" or "freedom" the individual has. Accordingly, such an individual seeks to dissolve these organic structures, replacing them with an understanding of society as a mechanism whose parts can be replaced without consequences.[30] Yet for Hegel, the individual fails to grasp the larger ethical system in which he is shaped and whose deep historical meaning is the very fabric his own subjectivity weaves to produce a good life. Without this historical meaning and institutional norms, the individual is, as we will see in the next chapter, cast back upon himself and his natural, selfish desires.

The second way to produce and maintain functional rationality is through the ethical "disposition" of members (PR 267). Once the different vocations are established within a community, each vocation takes on an ethical meaning in virtue of its connection to the common good. Virtuous behavior, then, is also connected to our different occupations, since these occupations are themselves connected to the identity we all share. Thus, just as individual subjects long to express their identity with their fellows, so too do they desire to express their distinctness. This latter desire hence emerges by belonging to these different occupations, and is fulfilled through ethical action, living up to the good assigned to this particular vocation—at "his standpoint [he] must do only what the standpoint requires" (VPR17 70A). In taking up this vocation, the individual seeks to be "recognized [*anerkannt*] that he belongs to a whole which is itself a member of society in general, and that he has an interest in, and endeavors to promote, the less selfish end of this whole" (PR 253).[31]

Such ethical action is sustained and promoted by a similar kind of ethical feeling we saw above—individuals of similar stations or vocations feel solidarity, "love, self-forgetfulness" with one another, as they belong to a common part in distinction from the other parts within the community (VPR17 70A). However, such ethical feeling may undermine the functional rationality of the system if individuals come to identify with their parts in opposition to or at the expense of the whole. Yet for Hegel, such a development would in turn undermine the ethical action of these seceding individuals, since a part of the whole—even vocations or classes—requires the whole for its ethical action, just as a hand requires the functioning of the other parts in the whole body. By contrast, by performing his distinct task within a properly organized totality, the individual subject comes to see his own subjectivity expressed in the common good of the community. The individual's virtuous action for his vocation is at the same time a virtuous action for the community as a whole, given that the community is structured as an organic totality.[32] Thus, the individual subject is at once identical with the universal subject but also distinct from it as well. There is a perfect harmony or reflection between individual and community, such that the "objective and the subjective will are then reconciled, forming a single, undivided whole" (PHI 97). Each individual is, in Hegel's image of the Greek polis, a mirror of the whole in its own activity, as each part embodies the activity of the whole as differentiated within his own station.[33]

Now that we have investigated the nature of the universal subject and its relationship to the individual subject, let us take a moment to apply these abstract concepts to an example. Communities can range from very private relationships, the bonds of love, to the social and public relationships of friends and co-workers, to the political relationships among citizens (ES 436). The "community" of lovers is an example of Hegel's argument that the good is something possessed, but always to be achieved. Each lover recognizes the other as part of the whole love that they have constituted together. The relationship they have formed and sustained transcends each as separate embodied beings—it is what Hegel calls the "immediate ethical relationship" (PR 161).[34] Yet the "whole" of the relationship is not some ghostly metaphysical substance, even if it stands all around them, in their shared history and memories together, experienced again and again in videos and reminiscences and enjoyed in those long gazes into one another's eyes. The common relationship is constituted by their mutual recognition of its significance, but this common relationship in turn constitutes their very identities as lovers. The relationship is the living good that makes each one whole, that "constitutes" them as "a single person" (PR 162). The relationship is like another self, a common self, that has a history, a personality, longings all on its own. The lovers' selves largely share in this common self, even if each is not perfectly immersed in the whole (one lover may continually harbor doubts about their collective desire to own a dog, for instance). Each lover understands himself in light of how the other understands him; and each gains his ethical satisfaction by crafting his self as the common self in the eyes of the other. As Hegel puts it, "within a love relationship, the individual is conscious of himself through the consciousness of another; he renounces his own self, and in this mutual renunciation, each gains not only the other self but also his own self in return, for the latter is united with that of the other" (PHI 100).

The good is all around them in the relationship that is their common self, but at the same time, the good is something always on the way to being achieved—what "ought to be is, and at the same time is not," as Hegel puts it (SL 132). Lovers continually bring flowers and chocolates to one another, they whisper sweet nothings into their ears, they travel to exotic places and discuss artwork and politics with one another. The lover's goal is to act for the good; and in this context, acting for the good means ever more realizing that common self, the relationship, that the lovers share, that constitutes both their personalities. Acting well means acting in accordance with the desires and longings of the collective subject of the relationship, as well as rendering consistent one's own actions with the actions of the collective subject in the past. Each lover has his or her particular role to play within the relationship as it is established in the history of that relationship, and the relationship itself has a particular narrative identity that always serves as the basis for the lover's actions. The identity of the common self and their distinct roles within this self are open to deliberation based on this commonly shared narrative history. Yet acting based on this collective self means acting freely or autonomously, since this collective self bears the trace of my own self. Acting for the good of the relationship, however, means each action of one of the lovers changes ever so slightly the nature of that relationship. Momentous actions that are accomplished as part of the relationship—such as getting married or having a child—change the identity of the collective subject considerably. In turn, then, the lover's action that changes the collective subject changes his own identity, insofar as he himself is shaped by the collective subject. Finally, this whole "collective subject" of the relationship is itself conditioned by historical, shared self-understandings, customs, and institutions larger than itself that provide ethical guidance for living in a successful relationship.

Teleological Rationality and the Unity of Community and Individual

We have investigated the nature of the universal subject, which differentiates its substance into a whole identity and functional parts. The individual subject gains satisfaction and comes to lead a complete human life only by striving to make this universal subjectivity real in its whole and parts. However, this account of the individual subject's satisfaction seems to be a complete reversal of the conclusions of the last chapter, in which the individual's unique personality was the basis for his actions and the aim of his life. Can universal subjectivity satisfy what we described as the "absolute negativity" of the subject? That is, how can these conventional rules and goods sustain the gaze of the completely skeptical subject? Isn't Hegel's ethical view of individual satisfaction a return to premodern forms of community? Furthermore, is the universal subject able to satisfy the infinite value of individual subjectivity, especially if the universal subject shapes the individual will to be ethical on its terms, to be identified with its view of the good life and differentiated into stations of its design?

For Hegel, a universal subject can meet this standard of the absolute negativity and infinite value of the individual subject only if it is rational in an additional sense than the "functional rationality" we have been describing. The universal subject must display also what we may call a "teleological rationality," that is, that the good towards which these parts tend must be the right or rational one.[35] Many different universal subjects have very different aims—some associations, like the family, seek to foster the love among family members as the good, or the association of Rome sought to achieve a glory of the empire, and so forth. These goods always have an ethical component to them, which means that they are shaped by human norms or "thinking." Yet at the same time, many goods are still partially mired in nature—for example, the courage involved in the glory of Rome still has an element of the natural about it, in that it involves the forceful application of one's freedom against enemies, the coercive application of norms to subjects, both hallmarks of the master-slave relationship, which forms the exemplary "partially natural, partially ethical" relationship.[36]

Instead, a communal good is rational in this "teleological" sense if it has human thinking itself as its goal elevated wholly out of nature. That is, its good must be shaped entirely by human thought, such that pure thought itself becomes the aim. This good, for Hegel, must be none other than the promotion of individual subjective freedom itself. As Hegel puts it, the end of "spirit" is "the freedom of the subject to follow its own conscience and morality, and to pursue and implement its own universal ends; it also implies that the subject has infinite value and that it must become conscious of its supremacy. The end of the world spirit is realized in substance through the freedom of each individual" (PHI 55). That is, Hegel argues that the true end of universal subjectivity can be none other than the true end of human subjectivity itself. The true end of human subjectivity is to find itself reflected back at itself in the world. Thus, the universal subject must cultivate independent individuals, those individuals who extend their unique personalities out into the world through their ethical participation with other individuals engaged in the same activity. As we will see in the next section, such activity is only possible in modern politics.

3.3   Politics as the Highest Ethical Community

For Hegel, individual subjects lead full lives only by participating in community, that is, by acting ethically. Yet not all communities provide the right conditions for ethical action, as we have seen—they must meet certain standards of rationality for the individual subject to gain satisfaction within them. Indeed, for Hegel, true communities, like true individuals, are achievements of human effort and hence actualizable according to degrees of success. Some communities fail to be fully communities by not being functionally rational, and hence these communities are likely to fall apart internally. Other communities fail to be fully teleologically rational. That is, they fail to respect and cultivate—or may indeed be hostile to—independent, autonomous individuals.

Hegel argues that political communities are the highest form of ethical community, that which best actualizes human rationality and the good life for individuals. As Hegel puts it, "it is also the purpose of all individuals that this essence [of the universal spirit or state] . . . should be, that it should be continually brought forth" (VPR17 129A). In concluding this chapter, we must investigate Hegel's argument for this surprising claim, since it is one that Hegel commentators often overlook and since it seems an outlandish claim.[37] Our liberal intuitions balk at this claim for at least two reasons—first, we tend to think that individuals should be free to decide what ethical associations will fulfill them the most. Family life, friendship, the accumulation of capital all are more popular forms of association than the political community in the modern world. Second, we tend not to think of the state as an ethical association, but rather as a legal association, an artificial authority established to maintain justice among individuals. Hegel's "atomistic" predecessors, from Locke through Fichte, all thought of political "right" in opposition to "morality," in which the former concerns our "external" duties to one another, whereas the latter deals with our "inner" pursuit of moral perfection.

By contrast, Hegel argues that the political community is the highest form of human ethical association, and that this political community is the structuring whole in which all other associations participate and hence gain their ethical value. Thus, the subject leads a full life through participation in politics, and indeed indirectly acts for the political common good through its participation in subpolitical associations. These are seemingly radical antiliberal claims that redound to ancient understandings of community in which the political community was the foundation of its members' identities and the ultimate aim of all its pursuits. Hegel seeks, I argue, to recover this ancient understanding of political community and its elevated sense of the good life to rejuvenate a modern community that has "aimed low" (at satisfying the mere bodily desires or at best tweaking the individual consciences of its members). Yet

Hegel seeks to elevate the modern state on distinctly modern grounds, that is, on the liberal grounds of individuality.

How does Hegel defend these radical claims? The first question we must investigate is what the "state" means for Hegel, since he means a lot more by it than the institutions of government. The latter make up only the springs and cogs of the state, its material "reality" (PHI 116). Following Montesquieu and Herder, Hegel includes within the notion of the state a way of life, a *Volksgeist,* a set of customs, institutions, characters, forms of the good life that coalesce into a particular "identity" of a nation. This collective identity, enshrined in our mutual recognition through memories, symbols of victory and defeat, inequalities, public documents, is formed through, as Hegel puts it, "the position of the country, its history, national character, religion, trade, climate" (VPR 4, 84–85). It is the "sacred bond which links men and spirits together" (PHI 97), the "determinate content" of the nation's shared identity that we also call "the nation's culture" (PHI 97). Only in the context of this identity does the legal apparatus of government arise, such that laws and customs are not interchangeable among nations, but rather part of the organic totality of the state. In other words, Hegel argues that in every group of people there is a universal subject that legislates a principle of the good life that comes to constitute the identity of the people—both the good life they have achieved and the good that is still to be achieved. In almost all times and places, this universal subject is embodied in the institutions and offices of the state. It is for this reason, then, that Hegel conceives of the political community as an ethical community, a community in which individual subjects act virtuously and hence lead full human lives.

However, one may object that this understanding of the state's ethical role is a nationalist part of the past that we have overcome—why ought we retain it? Hegel's answer would be that the state—particularly the modern state—expresses what is highest in us, our rationality or "thinking." Hegel, like Aristotle, argues that politics is the highest form of human association, since its aim involves realizing the answer to the question posed by the distinctively human subject, that is, how ought I to live my life?[38]

What is distinctive about the modern state in particular is that the "spirit does not assume the form of love and emotion, but of consciousness, volition, and knowledge" (PHI 100). That is, the universal subject of the modern state gives to itself a principle of the good that stems from free human thinking, not natural desires. This good is, as we have seen, the good life of human subjectivity itself, the distillation of human freedom as opposed to nature. The good is based, then, on nothing but pure human subjectivity. As Hegel puts the point, the universal subject of the state—and hence the universal subject we come to embody in our character—"obeys itself and is self-sufficient and therefore free" (PHI 97). It possesses, then, the highest form of autonomy or freedom, the ability to give itself, unfettered by nature, its own notion of the good and then go about realizing its notion of the good life in the world, the kind of autonomy requisite for an individual subject to lead a full life. When the state develops institutions and customs devoted to the good of individual subjectivity, it becomes that "substantial unity" which is the "absolute and unmoved end in itself" (PR 258).

This good is realized in the universal subject in the ways we saw above. A group of individuals in a modern state identify with one another based on their common belonging to an aspiration for individual freedom and an experience of the good life of individual freedom around them. Not only subjective dispositions but also objective institutions testify to the existence and aspiration for this good of individual subjectivity. The rule of law disregards the accidental and the arbitrary and treats individuals equally according to the "formal rationality" of the will (PR 100A). The institutions of the modern state educate new individuals to respect individual conscience and rights. The modern state educates human beings to relate to one another and to the state through this community of rational laws. We relate to laws, in contrast to how we relate to men, rationally. We reflectively assess these laws, render judgments on how they can be improved for the total good of the nation. Accordingly, the nation of laws affords individuals with a "position of independence within the state; for they are knowing subjects, in that they can distinguish between their own ego and the universal" (PHI 101)—we are not beholden to others because of any tradition or custom or unreflected-upon norm. The laws are present for all to see and critically assess and call into question. The state asks us not to take anything on faith, but to realize to its fullness the nature of our absolute negativity, the radical questioning of all general norms from the perspective of my ego. Once I come to see that the state's view of the good and its internal differentiation is rational, I can endorse this institutional system. In endorsing the system, I "obey the laws," and in doing so I obey myself, since the "unity" between individual and state is "consciously willed" (PHI 101).[39] Only in the state, Hegel argues, "are the powers of internal reflection developed" (PHI 101). Hegel's Rousseau-inspired claim, then, is that only if we surrender ourselves to the ethical will of the modern state can we then be shaped as independent rational beings who can participate, bring the universal subject of the state continually into being, and hence find ourselves in its institutions.

In light of the modern state's claim to be the highest form of ethical association, we can then see why it is that other forms of associations gain their ethical meaning as derivative from it. That is to say, the individual subject leads a full life in the modern state because only in it can he realize himself fully in the world. Other associations may allow for degrees of the good life, or partial realizations of it, but only the state provides for a full human life. It is the "ethical whole" (PR 258Z), the "focal point of all the other concrete aspects of the spirit"—all other forms of community—"such as justice, art, ethics and the amenities of existence" (PHI 93). For instance, our private relationships of marriage and friendship satisfy certain elements of our total personalities, such as our desire for love and companionship. Our associations of civil society, such as those in our voluntary associations or our workplaces, satisfy other parts of ourselves, such as our desire to be recognized for quality labor and our desire to feed our families. Our religious or artistic associations fulfill still other parts of ourselves, such as our wonder about the nature of the universe or about human beings. None of these on their own fulfill the totality of the human life. The political association, however, in containing all these associations, ensures that we have a rational ethical connection to all other individuals within our state, while also allowing each to pursue his distinctness within this rational community.

Accordingly, then, these derivative associations are justified or not based on their place within the organic ethical-political system. The state is the authoritative "form to which everything in it is assimilated" (PHI 96–97). Some associations may find their way into modern politics that thoroughly denigrate the autonomy and infinite value of individual subjectivity, and hence have no place within the modern state. More likely, however, associations fulfill one element or another of individual subjectivity, and their ethical goodness stems from their contribution to the common good. These associations are the interdependent organic parts of the whole, and yet sometimes these associations break off from their ethical dependence on the state and attempt to assert self-sufficiency. Hegel's main example of such a development is that of the fragmented German states and the remaining estates of the feudal order (PW 66; VPR17 121A). For Hegel, however, the ethical activity of these associations is intelligible only as a part of the state whole. The good of the farming estate, for instance, is only intelligible as a contribution to the common good, the "resources," of the whole nation (PR 199). Hence such a claim to self-sufficiency fails, and these associations begin to become corrupt, as their good ceases to be the animating principle, re-placed rather with natural, selfish needs. As we will see in the next chapter, the task of the state in this case is to reconcile these parts back to itself by elevating their "particularity" back up to "universality."

To sum up the kind of view Hegel has in mind, let us look for a moment at Hegel's view of the Greeks, since they offer a clear exemplification of what Hegel wants to recover in the modern world. In Athens, each individual gave his all to the community, and the community itself reserved a place for individual voice and debate. Pericles' Funeral Oration is an example of this ethical activity, a speech Hegel describes as a "profound description of Athenian life. . . . [Pericles] paint[s] the character of Athens, and what he says is most profoundly thoughtful, as well as most just and true" (PH 261). For Pericles, the Greek good does not involve achieving security or peace or welfare, but rather it is about the promotion of the Athenian way of life. It is about sending individuals into war in which they must test their mettle as human beings. But not just any human beings: Pericles says that Athenians are naturally courageous. They fight for their city out of a spontaneous love for it. They balance often competing human impulses and bring wholeness to human existence.[40] Thus, when Athenians die in service to the city, they beautify it by bringing to appearance the Athenian way of life as a life free from the natural desire for self-preservation and dedicated to ethical freedom. In this way, others can "look instead at the power our city shows in action every day, and so become lovers of Athens."[41]

My aim in this chapter has been to defend Hegel's claim that the individual subject we discussed in the last chapter can only be realized through ethical-political action. For Hegel, the only individuality worth having is the individuality we share in ethical institutions of public life. In interpreting Hegel in this way, I challenge those readers of Hegel like Pippin, who argues that there is "very little for the state actually to do, and so very little it actually asks of citizens" (2008a, 262). In the next chapter, I will suggest that there is indeed a great deal that the state must do, and hence a great deal that citizens themselves must do as well in order to shape the universal will of the state and hence achieve the modern autonomy constitutive of the good life.

4

Hegel on the Modern Political Individual

Hegel offers a refreshingly unusual defense of individuality on the basis of what fulfills human subjectivity, or rather, what perfects the distinctively human. Neither the whimsical particularisms of an individual nor the ascetic rationalism of the moralist fulfills human subjectivity, but rather only the individual life, which is shaped by and shapes a modern ethical-political community, can be the best life for human beings. Hegel's two-part argument, then, is that the individual subjective conscience is the only rational end of communities, and that individuals can only achieve a good life through ethical participation. Yet such a harmony between individuality and community is difficult to achieve in practice. For most political theorists, the relationship between individuality and community is deeply problematic or even antagonistic—Socrates, Locke, and Mill comes to mind initially. For Hegel, the solution to this tension is not "more individuality" or "more community," but more of both. According to Hegel, the modern state is the best regime because it provides the maximum possible of both, balanced and unified within individual subjectivity: "The principle of modern states has enormous strength and depth because it allows the principle of subjectivity to attain fulfillment in the *self-sufficient extreme* of personal particularity, while at the same time *leading it back to substantial unity* and so preserving this unity in the principle of subjectivity itself" (PR 260). But how is this ambitious union of individuality and community possible? Is it even likely? Isn't this ultimately a utopian theory?

Not so. Hegel is keenly aware of the great difficulty of combining these features of the good human life. In fact, he agrees with Rousseau's criticisms of modern life: that modern commercial society leads to individual selfishness, corruption, and dehumanization. Hegel seeks to elevate the modern state to higher purposes and thereby satisfy the immanent longing of individual subjectivity. It is only by bringing the ethical back into political life that the modern state can cultivate whole human individuals—those who can combine "universal" norms with their "particular" desires, not fragmented and dehumanized ones.

However, unlike Rousseau, Hegel does not return to the ancient valorization of community over individuality.[1] How, then, does Hegel envision communities overcoming the dehumanizing problems of commercial society while still securing individual rights? One popular interpretation since Marx is that for Hegel a rational system of governing laws and institutions staffed by rational experts will secure individual, subjective freedoms, and hence individuals will come to be reconciled to the rationality of this state. Though Hegel does advocate for such a "top-down" institutional solution, my argument is that Hegel's "bottom-up" democratic solution is the better response to Rousseau's problem, a better way for Hegel's political community to satisfy the needs of individual subjectivity, and truer to Hegel's own views—indeed, Hegel argued that "universal patriotism . . . must come about through *Standesehre*," our honor and participation in our mediating estates (VPR17 132A). The "mediating institutions" of modern civil society, I argue, provide the mechanism for the mutual interdependence we have been looking for—that is, among the "particular" interest of commercial society, the infinitude of "individual" subjective self-creation, and the "universal" freedom of the state (EL 198A).[2]

4.1   The Ancient Versus the Modern State

This harmony of individuality and community is exceedingly rare in human history before the modern age, according to Hegel. The great exemplar of such harmony was the Greek polis. Within the Greek polis idealized by Hegel and his contemporaries, there was a perfect harmony among parts and whole. Individual members performed virtuous deeds by participating in the common good, and were recognized as equals in the joint activity of political self-determination (thereby freeing themselves from the enslavement to society). At the same time, they acted upon an ethical principle of the good life—the rigorous life of, say, a "Spartan"—rather than a material natural aim (thereby freeing themselves from nature). The Greek city glorified the community's origin, identity, and aims and cultivated ethical individuals reverent of the common good. In Hegel's mind, Plato's *Republic* is the philosophical attempt to capture the Greek ethical life (PR Preface, 20).[3] In the *Republic*, for instance, Socrates argues that the happiness and beauty of the whole, rather than the parts, are what is important to promote (420b–c).

At the same time, Socrates revealed the essential and "greatest of contradictions" at the heart of the harmonious Greek community—the Greek city freed individuals to live an ethical life within their parochial community, but it did not satisfy their rational natures as thinking beings, as beings who can radically call into question any and all claims of community (PHI 203). Greek individuals indeed were free, but their freedom was "substantial," by which Hegel means that individuals existed in "unreflecting habit and custom in relation to the basic unity" of their community (PHI 197). They were immersed in the "substance" of the universal subject, and hence each individual subject remained at bottom dissatisfied. The Greek world was a "most serene yet inherently unstable structure," an "ephemeral and quickly passing flower" (PHI 202), yet we should not, Hegel argues in contrast to his Romantic contemporaries, attempt to return to such a premodern harmony. Such a return would give up on the gains of the modern age in making real what Socrates, that "infinite personality" (PR Preface, 20), anticipated—namely, "subjective freedom," in which "individuals are reflecting personalities and subjects who exist for themselves" (PHI 197).[4] However, the achievement of the Greek world is not to be overlooked, in that it so profoundly balanced individual and community and hence provides a historical model for the modern state to live up to on its own subjective ground.

However, according to Hegel, the modern state may fail in a different way than the ancient polis in reconciling individual and community. The root of the ancient failure was that the ancients did not recognize and accommodate "subjective particularity," that is, the particular desires of individuals (PR 185A). This omission left the individual subject without a full range of "universal" norms and "particular" desires through which his "individuality" can be deepened through the activity of marrying these divergent elements of the concept. The "principle of the self-sufficient and inherently infinite personality of the individual, the principle of subjective freedom" is thereby "denied its right" in the ancient world (PR 185A). By contrast, the moderns unleash the particular desires in civil society, a free space upholding private property, voluntary associations, and commerce. Indeed, the liberal "atomists" we spoke of in the first chapter restrict individual freedom to these particular desires, identifying individuality with this distinctively modern celebration of particularity. However, as we will see below in Hegel and Rousseau's critique of modern civil society, particular desires on their own fail to satisfy human sub-jectivity, which requires ethical action based on "universal" norms. For Hegel, a modern institutional design of ethical mediating institutions remedies this problem while also allowing the modern state to cultivate both "universal" ethical commitments and "particular" desires that the individual can weave together to make a unique personality.[5]

4.2   Expansion of Desire in Modern Commercial Society

While studying at the Tübingen Seminary, G. W. F. Hegel found his intellectual hero in Rousseau, whose *"Emile, Social Contract*, and *Confes-sions* he read constantly."[6] Hegel displayed an avid interest in Rousseau throughout his intellectual career, and scholars have recently detailed how the Genevan political philosopher decisively shaped Hegel's thought.[7] What is overlooked in the literature, however, is a decisive strand of Hegel's response to Rousseau that bears directly on our con-cerns here. Namely, Hegel was sympathetic to Rousseau's critique of modern commercial society and sought to find a way out of this critique by redeeming modern institutions, designing them so that they could cultivate full, not incomplete human lives.[8]

I explicate Hegel's critique of commercial society next to Rousseau's for a few reasons. First, in examining this critique, we can come to un-derstand the nature of the ethical flaws and dissatisfaction with modern society, and hence grasp the root of the reactive impulse to it that per-sists to this day. Indeed, for Hegel, Rousseau's worries are the perennial pathological tendencies of modern life. As Hegel puts it, Rousseau made us aware of the sources of the "corruption of states—when . . . the citizen no longer lives in the universal, but rather only seeks his own [*das Ihrige*] at the expense of the universal, so selfishness, arbitrariness have their ground" (VPR 1, 308; cf. VPR18 90Z).[9] Second, in his engage-ment with Rousseau, Hegel shows that a defense of commercial society attentive to its deep flaws is possible.[10] This defense is only possible, I will argue, on the basis of making an "ethical" turn in liberalism, that is, by infusing modern institutions and individual subjectivity with ethical goals that thereby "aim higher" than modern concerns with self-preser-vation by retrieving the ancient spirit of community on modern grounds.

There are two main strands of Rousseau's criticism that Hegel adopts. First, commercial society has the tendency to expand individual, selfish "particular" desire to the point at which this desire becomes insatiable, in which we have become "infinitely aroused" (*unendlich erregt*). The more these desires are satisfied, the harder it becomes to feel ultimately complete, and the more emphatically one must think of oneself over the welfare of others in order to seek this elusive fulfillment.[11] Second, this increasing selfishness undermines individual civic attachment to the common good. Individuals become too embroiled in considering what is expedient for them and lose the inclination and even capacity to deliberate about what is good for the political community as a whole. Individuals thus cannot satisfy themselves, and at the same time they lose the capacity to support and participate ethically in the community in which they live—both "particular" and "universal" longings of individuality are thwarted. Civil society becomes a "spectacle . . . of excess, misery, and physical, ethical, and communal decay" (VPR 4.477).

The Nature of Desire

Both Rousseau and Hegel begin their critique of modern commercial society with desire. They argue that the foundation of the modern age lies in desire, our selfish desire that is aroused when we leave the immediate unity of familial love and pursue wealth and esteem in an institutional arena of free exchange (PR 181). However, this desire comes in two types: animal or natural desires and human or spiritual desire. Animal desires are those basic desires we have for survival, reproduction, and increasing pleasure and minimizing pain (PR 190), summed up in Rousseau's mind by the phenomenon of *amour de soi*. Human desire, by contrast, is the desire for another's desire, the desire to be recognized by another. Rousseau describes this desire as *amour-propre*, the "relative" love of ourselves as mediated through the gaze of another (SD 106). As we saw in the previous chapter, for Hegel, this human desire is the desire to be recognized as a free being by another. Even though there are these two different types of desire, there are three parts to desire and its satisfaction as such: first, the initial feeling of incompleteness that fuels subjective action (impulse), second, a sense of what kind of object would satisfy this feeling (the means), and third, the acquisition of this object and hence the feeling of wholeness (the end). In the case of natural desire, nature supplies the feeling of incompleteness (e.g., hunger), the sense of what would sate this desire (e.g., wild berries), and then the ability to completely satisfy this feeling (e.g., the bodily strength and capacity to gather food and eat it). In the case of animals or natural humans with circumscribed needs, they can achieve satisfaction of their desires without remainder (E 39).

By contrast, the "spiritual" or "imagined" needs of human life are quite different from animal desires (VPR17 98). They arise in part from the division of labor, which, as we saw in the last chapter, differentiates the common good into many smaller tasks. Our increased ability to perform our own vocation results in increased dependence on others for the satisfaction of our natural needs. But the division of labor has the effect of abstracting from our natural needs—as we saw before, the slave holds his natural desires in abeyance and pursues a more abstract need, that of satisfying the master.[12] Similarly, to be recognized as a free being, a worker must perform his task well, which requires many conditions that are social in nature—that we be on time to meetings, wear the appropriate fashion, "produce means whereby others can be satisfied" (PR 192). Accordingly, natural desires come to be replaced by these spiritual or "imagined" social desires surrounding the ethical commitment to perform my duty well.[13] In other words, "particular" natural desire comes to be transformed by and loaded with "universal" or general norms and aims.

These desires are distinctive, then, in that their origin, object, and end are not as clearly delineated as in natural desire. We each of us desire recognition from one another because our subjectivity longs to extend its free agency into the world—this is the "origin" of the desire and the "impulse" for subjectivity's self-realization. By acting in accordance with the good life of my community and with the particular norms of my station, I gain the recognition from others that I so desire (i.e., the means). That is, what would sate this desire is becoming a certain ethical character or performing set of ethical actions, rather than consuming any particular object. Finally, my desire for recognition can be satisfied when I judge the recognition I receive to be sufficient. For instance, if I engage in (what I take to be) the right kind of activity and receive an indifferent shrug from my fellows, or, worse, contempt from them, I am not able to judge my agency a success. Instead, it appears as if I have failed in some way, even though I may be "certain" of my own success. I must be able to judge the recognition of my actions as significant and commensurate with my intuitive sense of them—I must attain the "truth" of my actions, not just the feeling of "certainty" (i.e., the end).

The source of desire, then, is the only element of "spiritual desire" that resides wholly in the individual subject, as the subject's own longing for freedom. By contrast, the means and end of spiritual desire arise out of the interactions between individual and community. The individual's desire for subjective satisfaction is in society a longing to be recognized as a "somebody" (PR 144)—that is, the individual desires to perform meaningful ethical actions, seek the common good, and identify with the good life around him. To do this, he must meet standards of ethical excellence that are embedded in the norms, customs, and institutions—the "substance"—of the community (PR 144). Furthermore, the judge of whether the individual fulfilled these standards is the public itself, the embodiment of the universal subject. Accordingly, an individual's ethical desires and his own understanding of his success are thus fundamentally formed and satisfied in his ethical relationships in public. Hegel claims that "what I am, I am not for myself but have my reality through another," and hence "if the individual attains his end in civil society, it belongs to this end that he be recognized [*Anerkanntsein*]" (quoted in Williams 1997, 231). For example, a university professor is recognized as a member of the higher education establishment in virtue of gaining a Ph.D. and procuring a job at a university. Yet at the same time, this professor desires still further recognition, to be recognized as an expert in his or her field. This desire is formed, regulated, and satisfied by the norms of the university system and recognitive judgments of its members. The professor can succeed with his research and successfully be recognized by others and hence gain satisfaction. Alternatively, the professor can either fail with his research or fail to garner recognition with his research (because it is unintelligible to his colleagues, because his colleagues dislike or are prejudiced against him, etc.), in which case he will not be satisfied in his spiritual desire.

The Expansion of Desire

For Rousseau and Hegel, the problem in the modern age is that these spiritual desires expand far beyond our capacity to fulfill them. The "particularity" of human desire, in Hegel's phrase, "indulg[es] itself in all directions" and expands without limit (PR 185). For Rousseau and Hegel, there are two main ways in which human desires in general can expand (PR 190). First is the relatively innocuous "refinement" of human desire—human beings can concentrate and analyze the different parts of a whole pleasurable experience. We can then desire to increase the quality of these different parts so that the whole experience adds up to something greater (PR 191). The refinement of one's taste in wine is an example of the expansion of desires—one desires the right type of grape, the proper level of tannins, an excellent "nose"—such that if any one of these components is missing, one's desire for wine is thwarted. Alternatively, we can "refine" not just our subjective taste, but the array of particular different comforts we enjoy. Natural needs like shelter and clothing can be satisfied with the austerity of Hercules, merely with a "lion skin." But we can also refine this natural desire by rationally breaking down the human body into its different parts—"head, neck, feet—[which are] given particular clothing, and so one concrete need is divided into many needs and these in turn into many others" (VPR17 93).

But there is a second, more important way in which human desires can expand (PR 192). Desires "multiply themselves" (*vervielfältigen sich*) when individuals attempt to gain recognition for being equal to all others within their community, and for being different from them at the same time (VPR 4, 488).[14] As we saw in the previous chapter, in order to be recognized, individuals must be "similar" or "equal with others" in the sense that they follow the same principle of the good as all other individuals (VPR17 95A). Yet recognition also requires that we distinguish one individual from another, which requires that we recognize differences among them (VPR17 96). To return to the clothing example, not only do we divide needs for the purpose of comfort, but also—and more importantly, given the fashion world's propensity to put many in discomfort—to express our similarity and difference from others. We wear similar clothes to others in order to be recognized as a "somebody," but we also appropriate these clothes and wear them in our own unique way so as to be recognized as this unique "somebody."

To explain further: in order to be recognized as equal, individuals desire to follow all the customary norms by affecting the popular traits of others, such as wearing the fashionable clothes of the time and eating at all the right restaurants. Individuals attempt to display all the symbols of commonality, but also of success and prosperity in a community. Thus, all "particular" aspects of human life—even down to the mundane—take "on a social [*Gesellschaftliches*] character" (PR 192Z). An individual's success at following these general norms ensures recognition of his equality, recognition that, yes, he is one of us, he is a "somebody." The desire for equality creates a multitude of desires for similar dress, habit, comportment, and so forth, so that one can fit in among all others. For Hegel, our desire to "imitate" others—rooted in our desire to be "recognized" (*Anerkanntwerden*) as a "somebody" (*etwas*)—"becomes the further source for the multiplication of desires [*Bedürfnissen*] and their expansion" (VPR 1, 312; cf. VPR18 95).[15] Rousseau bemoans this development, arguing that human beings tend to become alienated from themselves through the incessant need to be recognized based on shared norms of behavior. Furthermore, if individuals cannot live up to the norms hovering over them (or, rather, more precisely, within them), they long to "affect them," which introduces cunning, vice, and deception into human affairs (SD 67).

This socializing of desires would not expand desires very far, how-ever, were it not for the fact that it exists in a dialectical relationship with the need for individuals to assert their difference from all others.[16] Individuals are not content with mere similarity or equality to all others, since their subjectivity longs to be recognized as this individual subject. Particular human beings are distinct from one another in many ways, and so an individual seeks "to assert [himself] through some distinctive quality" (PR 193).[17] "Particularity," according to Hegel, lies at the root of "vanity" (*Eitle*) (VPR 1, 313). Yet this assertion of particularity intro-duces an element of competition into society, another point inherited from Rousseau. For individuals to "stand out" or to be unique among others, they must outdo others in certain generally recognized pursuits. Rousseau portrays this development in terms of the "one who sang or danced the best, the handsomest, the strongest, the most adroit or the most eloquent became the most highly regarded" (SD 64). The desire for particularity multiplies desire because we each must continuously desire to do more and to garner more recognition than others. If I seek to be a unique and talented musician, for instance, my desire for more and more training increases as I see that my competitors are training more vigorously than I do.

For Hegel, the expansion of desire is salutary to a point, since the in-creasing number of desires drives the creation of jobs to satisfy all these new desires, which in turn produces prosperity, luxury, and leisure, which in turn creates more desires, and so forth. In recognizing the dia-lectical relationship between the expansion of desire and the creation of a human world through labor in which these desires can be satisfied, Hegel incorporates the modern political economy of Mandeville, Smith, Stuart, and Ferguson into his broadly Rousseauan developmental ac-count.[18] According to this British political economy, the unleashing of selfish particular desire in society actually produces wealth for all through a certain "wonder of inner necessity" (VPR 3, 614). Indeed, as Bernard Mandeville argued in his *Fable of the Bees*, the more expansive and selfish our desires become, the more the public benefits through the creation of ever new markets and products. Hegel glosses this Mandevillian posi-tion when he argues that "subjective selfishness turns into a contribution towards the satisfaction of the needs of everyone else," that private vices become public benefits (PR 199).

However, for both Rousseau and Hegel, modern commercial society threatens to expand our desires far beyond our capacity to fulfill them and leads ultimately to "physical and ethical corruption" (PR 185).[19] This is because the standard for what satisfies our spiritual desires is comparative in nature. Natural desires, by contrast, have a kind of absolute form of satisfaction—our body tells us when we are full. Spiritual desires require us to live up to a standard established in public by a community. Yet this standard is established in virtue of a certain comparison—we know what makes for the proper performance of this deed because we can distinguish it from a whole host of worse performances. Yet for Rousseau and Hegel, when individuals perform their actions and receive recognition, they can nonetheless still compare this action and this recognition from some imagined better possible outcome. The aspiring musician can always imagine a competitor who can play just slightly better than every effort he puts forward. The human imagination can always come up with better and more expensive handbags, watches, TVs, or cars to set myself apart from those ever persistent Joneses.[20] We keenly feel the limitation of what we have, since we always imagine what is not there, that is, the additional thing we could possess or action we could have performed which would set us apart from others, and "so it goes on endlessly [*Unendliche*]" (VPR 4.491). Human desires are inflamed by this relational norm and hence are infinitely expansive because this relational norm is embedded in the formation and satisfaction of the desire itself. Individuals thus find themselves consistently incapable of finding satisfaction for their desires.

This obsessive incompleteness is fueled by the declining structures of ethical-political community in modern commercial society. For Hegel, in the modern age, the "picture of the state as a product of [the individual's] own energies disappeared from the citizen's soul . . . activity was no longer for the sake of a whole or an ideal. Either everyone worked for himself or else he was compelled to work for some other individual. Freedom to obey self-given laws . . . all this vanished" (ETW 156–57). Modern commercial society destroys community, particularly through the emergence and proliferation of private property and money. Money is an abstract means of making commensurable the contribution of every occupation to the general good. It strips away the concreteness of the occupation and hence its ethical goals through its abstractness. For instance, commercial society's monetary economy encourages bakers no longer to derive their identities or their honor from baking good bread, but rather seek to honor in the accumulation of wealth. Accumulating wealth in a competitive market involves baking bread in the most efficient way possible, which often means a marked decline in quality to increase efficiency. Hence, the baker no longer desires to make the most delicious, crusty baguette as part of some baker's estate which upholds a standard of excellence. Rather, he desires to accumulate a great deal of money in order to prove himself better than all others, including the moneylender and merchant and lawyer.[21] Good-quality bread is no longer an end in itself, but rather becomes instrumental to the pursuit of an abstract good, one that is quantitative (and hence without limit) in nature, rather than qualitative. In short, this abstract or quantitative good atomizes individuals by tearing them away from their identification with their particular occupation and its internal competition. The introduction of money thus increases the expansion of desires exponentially by making all occupations commensurable. This in turn dissolves further the concrete ties of community, ever entrenching the abstract relationships among individuals. With the introduction of money in a commercial society, the worker comes to be increasingly alienated from his occupation and from all ethical ties. As Hegel puts the point: "If individuals are reduced to living as particulars, they must necessarily strive to become recognized in their special activity by others. First they decline into pleasure seeking, and then they must put on an external show. This leads to luxury and excess in the trade which is a necessary consequence of the fact that they lack an ethical engagement with something universal" (quoted in Williams 1997, 257).

Thus, not only does the atomization of individuals produced by the introduction of money forestall the satisfaction of "particular" desire, and it undermines individuals' ethical desires by thrusting them always back into selfishness. This state of selfishness is what Hegel calls the moment of "particularity" divorced from concrete community or general forms of "ethical life." The severing of "particularity" from the other "moments" of the modern age, the "universal" demands of morality and the claims of "individual" self-determination will, lead to enslavement within a "false infinite" (VPR 4.476), what he describes in the social context as the "infinite [*unendliche*] multiplication of need" (VPR 1, 313). The false infinite in this circumstance means that individuals seek satisfaction for their particular desires in a condition not only where they cannot achieve it, but also where it arouses ever more needs and more dissatisfaction, that is, on their own, in isolation from a mutual ethical commitment with others. The "false infinite" appears here as an infinite series of desires without an internal mechanism for satisfaction. Individuals find themselves competing with a faceless crowd of selfish individuals who will never offer recognition but will only defeat every effort of the individual to find completeness.[22]

Single-mindedly pursuing one's own selfish desires in a competitive economy also often undermines our commitment to the common good, as we all witnessed in the recent world economic crisis. Indeed, Hegel even worries that this atomism will give rise to a certain juvenile "notion" according to which individuals recognize the commitment to institutions larger than themselves "as a limitation . . . and as a purely *external* necessity" (PR 207A). Hegel argues that this view is a "consequence of abstract thinking," which itself is a consequence of the gradual atomization and alienation of individuals from a shared life and of the attachment to the abstract ideal of money (PR 207A).

Finally, this abstract thinking gives rise to the liberal "atomistic" view of individuality, which in turn maintains and deepens this loss of ethical life. According to the atomistic conception, freedom simply consists in the subjective right to particularity, and subjects are free to choose (or not) to commit themselves to ethical communities and common goods. Communities that enshrine ethical meaning, such as the state, are regarded as external impositions on individual freedom, not as the necessary constituents for leading a full and satisfying life. This atomistic individuality, then, hampers the development of "particular" desires into ethical ones and hence undermines our means of creating a lasting and ethical society by failing to produce individual ethical characters concerned about the common good. As Hegel puts it, "in contemporary times, we have considered the state [simply] to determine how it should be organized and governed. We have, that is, proceeded to build the upper floors, we have organized from above, but we have in part neglected and in part demolished the foundation of marriage and the corporation. But an organization cannot hang in the air" (VPR 4.628). Rather than hanging in the air, this ethical-political community comes crashing down, leaving individuals without the communal recognition to lead complete human lives.

By contrast, Hegel argues that the transformation of unruly or unfettered desire is the "*liberation*" (Befreiung) of desire, the freedom from my own enslavement to an abstract public standard.[23] He argues that instead of being enslaved to "external necessity, to inner contingency, and to *arbitrariness* [Willkür]," we should submit ourselves to our "*own opinion* [Meinung], which is universal, and to a necessity imposed by [ourselves] alone" (PR 194). Our own opinion—to be our own—can only be formed in the context of ethical norms of judgment and recognition. In other words, only in the common participation in ethical institutions of shared communal life can desires be free, satisfied by the mutual recognition of common goals and goods.[24] Only within a community can I subject myself to my own autonomous judgment, since only within this community can I glean general but concrete, qualitative norms of proper judgment for the satisfaction of spiritual desire.

Only within such a community can the "false infinite" become a "true infinite," in which the series of my desires becomes intelligible as a whole based on the universal or common good that issues from it (EL 95). In short, an individual should not seek "recognition . . . through the appearance of wealth," but rather through ethical action and membership (VPR 4.623). In order for Rousseau's critique to be addressed, Hegel argues, liberalism needs to incorporate ethical considerations, considerations about how institutions can be designed to allow us to lead whole human lives.

4.3   Estates and Corporations as Ethical-Political Communities

My central claim in this section is that Hegel's "mediating institutions" (*vermittelndes Organ* or *Mittelglied*) of civil society—especially the estates and corporations—are the central features of his solution to Rousseau's critique of modern commercial society. These institutions curb the excesses of modern "particularity" by educating desire to its connection with "universal" ethical ends and by encouraging "individual" associations to maintain their own distinct boundaries from the encroachments of the state (VPR 3, 799–800; VPR 4, 618–23). These institutions aim to render our economic exchanges ethical. As Hegel puts it, "in the corporation the corruption of wealth is set aside . . . here [the individual] becomes something through the way he applies his wealth for the sake of his cooperative association . . . in the corporation the individual has his true consciousness" (quoted in Williams 1997, 257). These institutions are not quite a panacea for Hegel. Other rational modern institutions, such as a flourishing bourgeois family life, a robust system of unbiased courts and judges, and a constitutional government of divided powers staffed by civil service experts, are also necessary contributors to realizing human freedom. Yet the mediating institutions are so important because they stand in Hegel's mind at the pivotal point between the unfettered capitalist "egoism" and fervent "patriotism." As Hegel describes these institutions as the "pillars on which public freedom rests" (PR 265), in them "the universal and particular will are united" (VPR17 132A).[25] They are such strong pillars because they allow "particular" desire—that distinctive bedrock of the modern age— free rein within these institutions (PR 260).[26] At the same time, these institutions aim for the high ethical purposes reminiscent of the ancients yet based on lowly but solid modern foundations.[27]

To see how these mediating institutions can help subjects lead a full individual life, let us examine the origin, nature, and function of these institutions.[28] For Hegel, truly effective modern mediating institutions must have their origin in our economic lives, in the pursuit of satisfying our "particular" desires. The most important institutions of modern life for individuals will inevitably be associations and businesses, which form the infrastructure of the modern market economy. These are the associations in which individuals spend most of their waking lives, and they shape and satisfy the "particular" desires of individuals. Our vocation, in other words, puts food on our table and involves long-term, close interactions with co-workers. For Hegel, the associations and practices which house these vocations generate extremely strong attachments through such collaborative laboring. Therefore, Hegel argues, they ought to serve as the central institutions to mediate or rather transform individual desire from sole interest in self-concern to the public good. By attracting and channeling an ever-full and powerful supply of particular passions, these institutions can serve as the backbone for attachment to public institutions.[29] Hegel's thesis stands in contrast, then, to contemporary views that tend to bracket the "market" as a separate sphere entirely and focus on civic associations like community groups and bowling leagues for "social capital."[30] Yet, Hegel would claim, unless we invoke economic associations in support of our community, individual attachment to this community will be rather "free-floating" or detached from their more basic material or "particular" interest (VPR 4.628). As Hegel says, "people take no share in the universal unless it is in their own self-interest" (VPR17 132), and modern people's self-interest is most fundamentally economic in nature. According to Hegel, the contemporary attempt to base "social capital" on voluntary associations will not work in the long run, since individuals will choose their "particular" interest over this "free-floating" communal interest every time, which would gradually lead to an erosion of this communal interest.[31]

The nature of Hegel's mediating institutions is best characterized, I think, as a guild crossed with a labor union. Like guilds, Hegel's institutions provide for members' recognition and education, and, like labor unions, these institutions look out for the members' economic interest. Hegel argued that these associations would emerge naturally, as modern civil society would divide labor into three "estates" corresponding to the three different tasks required of modern human community. First, human beings must work with "given" raw materials of the earth. This sort of task and its attendant occupations of farming, mining, and the like serve as the basis for an "agrarian" estate (PR 203). Second, human beings must form or shape these raw materials and then exchange them, a

wide group of tasks that cohere into institutional form in the manufac-
turing and commercial estate. This estate is the problematic "reflective"
estate, in that it is distinctly susceptible to the problems Rousseau outlined above (VPR17 104). A "member of the business class experiences a
'drowning in possessions and particularity,' a 'serfdom' to money."[32] As
the bourgeois estate that stands at a "reflective" distance from the material it works with and the community of which it is a part, this community must be further subdivided into an internal system of "corporations,"
each responsible for one occupation, in order to foster and shore up a
communal spirit within this estate.[33] Finally, there must be a "universal"
estate that oversees the agrarian processing and bourgeois exchange and
hence looks out for the public interest as a whole (PR 205).[34] For Hegel,
individual workers come to identify themselves with other workers with
the greatest kinship to them in their tasks, forming bonds of ethical solidarity rooted in mutual recognition. These associations, moreover,
should be given an official and institutional status in the modern state
(PR 206–7, 253A). They "represent the communities and various profes-
sions and estates" and are responsible for looking out for the "private
property and interests of these particular spheres" (PR 288). Hence,
their existence must be recognized and preserved by the modern state
against the dissolving tendencies of modern commercial society.

However, the modern state must be vigilant in preventing these institutions, which grew out of the feudal estates and guilds, from declaring themselves self-sufficient and independent of the state. Indeed, in
Hegel's own Germany, the feudal versions of these institutions caused
serious problems for the cohesion of the modern German state. They
resisted unification under a higher state authority. For Hegel, a "miser-
able" guild system threatened to develop, in which associations understood themselves to be self-sufficient and separate from the higher
authority of the state (PR 255Z; VPR 4.628). Under such a condition, the
guilds would understand the state and other guilds around them as instruments for the satisfaction of their interests, in the same vein as the
"natural" individual's view of social and political association.[35] In sepa-
rating itself from the ethical good of the state, the association upholds
its material "interest" as highest. Yet in not upholding an ethical principle regulating this interest, the leaders of industry would become unethical to their own members, understanding their own task within the
whole solely in terms of lining their own coffers.

As we will see further below, Hegel argues that these institutions
must therefore remain ethical to others to be true communities within

themselves. For this reason, the associations of public life must take themselves to be parts of the larger ethical whole of the state, rather than thinking of themselves as atomistic, self-sufficient interest-seekers. For Hegel, such a temptation to defect from the common good is indeed an endemic problem of the modern age, as "subjective particularity becomes the sole animating principle of civil society and of the development of intellectual activity, merit, and honor" (PR 206A). Consequently, the state is constantly in danger of appearing to be an "external necessity," a "coercive power" that burdens the particular activities of civil society. For this reason, the state must not stand to civil society in such an economic, self-interested fashion, as one economic association among others, but rather it "must constantly draw [civil society] back within its substance" (VPR17 128). An important development to promote this ethical relationship, for instance, was to break the feudal guilds' control over individual membership and to liberate individuals to choose which occupation they would pursue.

The function of these mediating institutions is the most important feature for understanding how these associations reconcile individual and community. The function of these institutions is threefold:

1. To sate the particular desires of individuals. That is, the institutions must arrest the ever-expanding desires plaguing the modern age and hence satisfy infinite "particularity."

2. To elevate these particular desires to a "universal" concern. In participating within my particular estate, I at once participate in the universal activity of self-governance and hence in the embodiment of the rational freedom of the state.

3. To promote the "individuality" of the associations and hence of their members.

For Hegel, the plurality of estates and corporations restrains the modern rational community from dissolving all differences into a unified "universal" moral order on the one hand and from fragmenting individuals into a decentered and chaotic "particular" selfishness on the other. Estates and corporations are jealous of their spheres and seek to protect them. In this way, individuals within these estates and corporations are given a model of how they themselves can sustain their own uniqueness in light of how the estates and corporations promote their own.[36]

Function 1: Satisfying Particular Desires

The estates and corporations' first function solves the first problem endemic to modern civil society, that of the perpetual incompleteness of "particular" desire. These institutions supply their members with norms of proper behavior and hence with the capacity to recognize a worker as a "somebody" with a "title" that is an "external sign for all" to recognize him (VPR21 253). In so doing, these institutions make desire satiable by providing the individual with an identity and a circumscribed arena in which his desires are limited and transformed. These desires thereby become satiable because the individual "gains recognition [*Anerkennung*] in his own eyes and in the eyes of others" in these institutions according to a settled standard (PR 207). The burdens of one's labor are given meaning because there are others around me who respect my work, recognize me, and hence reveal to me how my labor contributes to the common good.

These institutions provide such recognition in two main ways, corresponding to the two forms of recognition I introduced in the previous chapter, identity and difference recognition. Since each institution is a community unto itself, it contains both a good already accomplished and always to be accomplished and a set of moral rules structuring the different stations within the community. Each institution is responsible for designating who's in and who's out, that is, by officially declaring conditions of membership based on legal norms which are rooted in the moral rules and ethical good animating the community as a whole. In turn, the institution provides education for the worker "so as to make [him] eligible for membership" (PR 252). Each institution educates its potential members and forms their substantive second natures in accordance with its moral norms, its good, and, in general, the technique by which one carries out the norms of one's station. The community essentially becomes, in Hegel's mind, a "second family" (PR 252) for its members, not just because it supplies the needed welfare protection from the vicissitudes of the market, but, most fundamentally, because it supplies a common self, a good life, of which all members feel themselves a part, which all members gain fulfillment in embodying and striving to live up to. A baker's assistant learns from a baker how to be a great baker, for instance, by embodying certain moral norms (including not cheating customers) and ethical goals (that of producing high-quality bread, not just cheap bread to make a quick buck). Such a community is held together by a qualitative ethical principle of the good—in the case of baking, high-quality bread (rather than high-efficiency production for greatest profit, cutting corners on quality).

As a part of the common self, they respect and applaud and recognize their fellow "parts" within the total endeavor, as team members do in a condition of team spirit. Subjects receive back to them their own subjectivity in performing a successful deed—that is, they gain the "truth" of their own freedom in acting for an ethical principle, rather than out of material desire. This condition of unity, according to Hegel, must be protected from the pathologies of the modern age, in which these ethical communities are dissolved, replaced by the expansive and endless pursuit of the qualitative, nonethical "good" of moneymaking. Hegel worries that the "dissolution of corporations has the . . . consequence that the individual is reduced to his private ends [*Privatzweck*]" (VPR 3, 709). In the latter condition, there is no "common self" to which individuals contribute, and hence they gain no ethical satisfaction for their deeds, but only engage in an endless cycle of natural consumption and despair.

At the same time, the baker's assistant does not just long for recognition of "identity" or "similarity" with other bakers—that of producing high-quality bread and hence as appearing as a somebody—but also longs for recognition of "difference," of what makes him distinctive as a baker (his "secret ingredient," as it were). The dialectic between identity and difference is played out here once again, but this time in a virtuous, rather than vicious, circle. Individuals still seek to assert their "difference" from the others within a regime, and hence they still must strive to produce the highest-quality goods (which happens to be the most desirable in an ethical regime). Accordingly, this institutional design does not mean that the capitalist engine would sputter to a halt. Just as the Rousseauan concern has been answered, the Mandevilles or Adam Smiths of the world should not take offense. Individual desires will expand through the dialectic of identity and difference—admittedly, not as much as in the pathologically feverish capitalist state—though enough to continue the expansion of the nation's economy. Capitalist innovation will continue as well, as each attempts to discern a new way to actualize the ethical good of one's occupation.

Function 2: Elevating Desires to the Universal Good

The second function of the estates and corporations is to transform "particular" desire according to a "universal" concern for the public good. The main mechanism in Hegel's eyes for this transformation is the "disposition" of "honor" (PR 207). As we saw in the previous chapter, honor organically develops out of the condition of mutual recognition in these estate communities. A condition of mutual recognition maintains a "universal self-consciousness," a communal self, that all strive to embody in their actions. When they succeed, they ever more fully realize the good around them, exert their autonomy, and thereby see themselves in the eyes of others (PR 207). These others are also striving equally to embody this whole in their actions. We all see one another, in other words, as part of a common self, and hence this ethical feeling of "honor" is the bond holding together fellow members of a common whole. We all see that each of us harbors "still higher aims" for the common good that trump our particular, selfish concerns (VPR17 107A).

In other words, these institutions should be structured so that our "particular" desires contain within them a desire to realize the common good. Out of our "particular" activity motivated by honor, we achieve not just the satisfaction of our "particular needs," but the "universal" good. Not only do our particular desires have the "accidental" effect of contributing to the common good—as a result of the "invisible hand" of the modern market—but my own conscious ethical perspective is transformed when I come to see my belonging to this whole. When the community, our association, prevails, then we are uplifted by its success. We glory in the glory of our association, to paraphrase Tocqueville (2000, 90). We are uplifted because we see our rational nature realized in an objective form in the world. This institution bears the trace of my subjectivity, my own individual laboring effort. I can "view" this institution "as [my] own" (VPR17 132A). Freedom of "self-determination" fills the individual with honor because he recognizes himself in the fruits of his activity, that he has accomplished this important aim (PR 207). We become autonomous—"we ourselves are our own end"—as we "entangl[e]" ourselves "with the end pursued by all others," the universal or common good (VPR17 107A).[37]

However, since my association's distinctive good only makes sense as part of a more comprehensive political community, the "honor" that I feel extends to the larger community as well. Hegel's defense of this claim is the following: I feel honor in my estate in virtue of its standing out among the other "parts" of the community. Thus, Hegel claims, an individual has "honor in his estate" only when "it is recognized that he belongs to a whole which is itself a member of society in general, and that he has an interest in, and endeavors to promote, the less selfish end of this whole" (PR 253). That is, honor is only possible when there are multiple mediating institutions vying to embody the universal self-consciousness of the state. Only then can I see my own estate or corporation as distinctly worthy of honor, because this association itself gains recognition from the others in realizing the common good all associa-tion share. That is, Hegel imagines a second tier of the struggle for recognition, here among estates that constitute the parts of the organic state whole. This struggle for recognition among members of the estate or corporation resembles the desires for recognition among individuals, such that these associations embody the good only insofar as they live up to their "station" within the whole, insofar as they act for the ethical good of the entire community. As we have seen, these mediating insti-tutions only make ethical sense as differentiated parts from a common good—the production of each institution has "meaning" or "goodness" in light of its contribution to the whole, just as each laborer's work has "meaning" to himself and others due to the same (VPR17 132–33).

This, then, is how each member of the modern state achieves freedom through participation in the state. He does not do so by participating di-rectly in political affairs, since in a complex modern state, "citizens have only a limited share in the universal business of the state" (PR 255Z). After all, individual subjects can only experience their own autonomous self-determination in a human world not "remote from individuals" (VPR17 136), but rather one that is always "proximate" to their interest (VPR17 141). Accordingly, the individual participation in the estates or corporations is supposed to resemble the political self-determination of Greek individuals within their closely knit communities of city states. I lead a full life as an individual only by engaging in honorable ethical be-havior in these associations. Yet this feeling of honor is expanded beyond my own particular surroundings in a properly constructed state. If I see this association as my association, and my association integrally creates and sustains the common good of the state as a whole, then the common good of the state becomes mine as well.[38] In this case, I see the state as the rational foundation of the ethical aims of my community (PR 263). The "laboring" nature of subjectivity is transitive from one community to the larger community in which it is nested and which it helps support. For Hegel, then, my ethical "disposition" and actions will thereby always al-ready include implicitly and explicitly the good for the state as a whole (PR 264). As a result, the ethical disposition of "patriotism" is the founda-tional disposition in my character, one that is mediated through the ethi-cal disposition of the *Standesehre* (PR 268; VPR17 132A).[39]

Function 3: Sustaining Individual Pluralism

For this harmony of particular and universal to obtain, however, the "in-dividual" moment must be developed and deepened. The individual subject creates and maintains itself in action, and, as we have seen, such self-determination occurs through these several ethical institutions that make up the state. In fulfilling their ethical vocations within these associations, individuals craft their own identities. For instance, bakers do not just seek to bake high-quality bread, but rather seek to create high-quality bread that bears the trace of their identity, with their secret ingredient or magic touch. In other words, it is this foundational need for difference that suffuses the whole and maintains the distinctness between universal and particular while still holding them together. The individual, after all, is the moment of judgment, the moment of weaving universal and particular together into a coherent story. In the modern state, universal and particular are both embedded within multiple different mediating institutions, and so within these institutions the individual deepens his own identity in being forced to weave these moments together. Thus, Hegel argues, the moment of individuality restrains the twin temptations of the modern age—the general will cannot appear as the whole into which all the parts dissolve (as in Rousseau's *Social Contract*), but neither can the general will be another instrument for the satisfaction of particular desires. Neither the universalism of modern rationalism nor the particularism of the modern bourgeois market can be allowed to overwhelm the other.

It is then the third function of the associations to foster individuality. This task centrally involves encouraging the kinds of virtues of individuality we discussed in chapter 2. First among those virtues was a kind of rational autonomy, of the individual subject consciously crafting an individual character for himself. Such a virtue requires that the honor and patriotism felt by the individual not be unreflective and knee-jerk. Only when we scrutinize the rationality implicit in the relationship between wholes and parts in my community and participate in making the community more rational can we come to make it our own. Simply "seeing" the rationality of the community is not sufficient to establish our autonomy, though a rational civil service that governs many of the activities of the state is still necessary.[40] This top-down form of autonomy must be supplemented by a bottom-up form, such that I come through my own activity to bring about such rationality in the world. Associations then should invest individuals with a sense of responsibility for the fate of the whole through offering them the opportunity to take up shared ownership over and self-governance of the community.[41] Such cultivation of individual autonomy can easily fail in modern institutions, as the case of the "rabble" (*Pöbel*) makes clear. The poor are not recognized to have any stake in the community, have no education and no opportunity for ethical significance, and hence "feel as if [they] were related to an arbitrary will," to an alien, external will that oppresses them (quoted in Williams 1997, 247).

These associations foster independent individual characters fundamentally through their political activity, through what Hegel calls the state's "democratic moment," in which the different estates and corporations wield power at local and national levels. That this freedom of self-determination is political should not surprise us, because, as we have seen, the sphere of politics is the sphere in which the question of the good—the central question of human subjectivity—comes to the fore. Hegel argues that the mediating associations have two political powers to achieve this self-determination, a negative and a positive power. On the negative side, these associations have a constitutional check on the encroachments of government. In tandem with the monarch, the associations jealously guard their particular purview of power. As we have seen, Hegel argues that the associations of civil society should have power over legislating and executing their internal policies at the local level. As Hegel puts it, "particular concerns as such are in the first place the particular property, aims, and interests of the individual local communities, guilds, estates, and corporations, and are administered by these bodies themselves as a matter of right" (VPR17 141).

This is not to say that the associations should have total control over their members (see VPR17 141A on the "second moment"). Rather, Hegel broadly follows a principle of subsidiarity in the assignment of the proper functions for different levels of administrative authority.[42] In following this principle, Hegel argues that policy decisions and execution should occur at the lowest level appropriate to the decision—Hegel defends, for instance in VPR 3, 783, the "control from under" whose "authority" (*Berechtigung*) lies in "communities and corporations" (*Gemeinden und Corporationen*). Accordingly, when a higher-level community attempts to overreach its authority into a lower level, this lower-level community has a legal check it can assert and can call on the monarch's authority to support its veto. In this way, the associations preserve the individuality of their associations themselves, and hence, by extension, the individuality of this occupation. The mediating institution drives a wedge between the state and the individual, or, to use a different metaphor, it is a buffer zone between the two.[43] These associations play an important role, then, in marshalling group power to meet the encroachments of the state.[44]

At the same time, however, in resisting the encroachments of outside forces, these associations may claim too much power over individuals.

Accordingly, Hegel argues that individuals within these associations must be protected from the associations themselves by a court system that serves as a watchdog for liberal individual rights.[45] These associations must, furthermore, allow for free individual choice both to enter the association and to leave it, thus assuring each individual that he has free control over his destiny (PR 206). No one should be "born into" or fettered to these institutions. In this way, each association cannot squelch the distinctness of each individual within its boundaries, and hence dissolve individuality into universality within these subcommunities. Hegel's institutional design and strong "constitutionalism," then, is intended to protect the various differentiated parts of the whole from being swallowed up into an undifferentiated mass headed by a despot or a mob.

In addition to the negative tasks of the mediating institutions, which encourages individual independence, the positive task of these institutions fosters individual self-realization. As I said above, for Hegel, the individual only comes to achieve his autonomy by participating or investing himself in community. For Hegel, mediating institutions associations embody "the democratic principle, that the individual should share in the government of local communities, corporations, and guilds, which have within themselves the form of the universal" (VPR17 141A).[46] They embody this principle at the local and national level. At the local level, mediating institutions are assigned responsibility for the "particular concerns" of local communities (VPR17 141). These mediating institutions in turn divide the labor in taking care of these particular concerns among its members. Thus, my vocation as a member of this association involves not only performing my specific job, but also assisting in the effort of local communities to shape and satisfy local concerns from education, welfare, city maintenance and order, and so forth. In performing these additional tasks, the individual subject comes to realize himself in the world at a local level, where his own individual effort can make an important ethical difference.

At the same time, these mediating institutions constitute together the Estates Assembly (*Ständesversammlung*), the main legislative body for the nation as a whole. This assembly is a popular representative body, and hence involves the election of representatives most fit to act on behalf of every subject within the association.[47] The election of estates representatives is very different from the usual democratic election, however, in which candidates are selected based on a geographical basis (as in the United States) or some more or less vague ideology (as in European multiparty systems). In these democratic elections, an "undifferentiated" citizen body—one not rationally structured—ends up selecting candidates based on contingent characteristics (e.g., with whom you'd most like to have a beer), on particular, selfish desires, or ideological imperatives, rather than on rational or ethical considerations.[48] This is because an "undifferentiated" mass does not have the requisite internal rational division both to make intelligible and compelling to its members the common good towards which they are all tending. For Hegel, "if we hear any further talk of 'the people' as an unorganized whole, we know in advance that we can expect only generalities and one-sided declamations" (PR 303A). Thus, casting a vote involves choosing, as part of an "undifferentiated" mass, someone for whom I have no determinate, concrete ethical feelings and who does not bear my own subjective will in his activities. Consequently, for Hegel, it would be no surprise that voters in a democracy tend to view voting as a burden since this mode of election prompts them to see that their vote counts for next to nothing (PW 319). Further, it would also be no surprise that such voters tend to be extremely mistrustful of a government in whom they have no subjective ethical involvement.[49]

By contrast, the election of deputies in the Estates Assembly occurs within a structured, differentiated practice in which an ethical good has a history, a presence, and a character that binds all members together and guides their actions rationally. Hence, representatives would be selected based on their virtue, their "understanding" and capacity to fulfill the common good (PR 309). Casting a vote would furthermore be an ethical experience. That is, I would vote as part of a determinate common will finding its representative. Representation is, in Hegel's terms, not the "replacement of one individual by another; on the contrary, the interest itself is actually present in its representative, and the latter is there to represent the objective element he himself embodies" (PR 311A). Hence, the selection of this candidate would at once be a moment of individual ethical activity in which I vote for my representative, that representative in whom I can see myself and feel honor—my team captain, for instance (to follow up on the sports metaphor from the last chapter), rather than a distant, faceless bureaucrat.[50]

Finally, however, both local and national political participation would involve not just deeds, such as laboring and voting, but also speech—rational "deliberation" (PR 314). In order to decide how we as a community should act, we must deliberate about what the best thing to do is. Rational deliberation satisfies the individual subject in two ways. First of all, the collective decision arrived at based on reflection rather than feeling satisfies the fundamental demand of the human subject, that of absolute negativity. That is, the reason why a community acts in this or that way must be one the individual subject can endorse and legislate as his own, rather than one rooted in tradition, nature, or God, an "external" authority to the individual. Moreover, the subject assumes the highest form of self-realization in acting based on its reason rather than out of mere feeling, which is characteristic of familial relationships. Second, subjects can ascend above mere natural passion through the "education" in public deliberation to satisfy their absolute negativity in engaging in rational deliberation (PR 315Z). Since the rationality of any decision of a community is never immediately evident—universal norms must always be applied in particular, changing contexts—individuals are responsible for applying the right norm in the right place in the right way. Indeed, different individuals in the modern age occupy different perspectives, because they belong to many associations and hence are themselves crafting their unique identities. Thus, they offer different judgments as to what the right thing to do is. This deliberation in which citizens exchange one another's "perspectives" on the rational whole in itself would improve individual's capacity for rationality.[51] Furthermore, this deliberation pushes each individual to exercise his rational autonomy and see his will recognized and considered in the eyes of others. All these individual reasonings shape the collective will in small but nonetheless determinate ways that the individual subject can gain satisfaction in seeing his own will shape the whole.

The activity of communicatively transforming the whole through my interpretation is the crowning moment of my political freedom because it is the moment of my individual self-creation that is at once free from nature—from my particular desires and feelings—while also being free from society—from the alien assertion of the universal. I overcome my particular nature by acting based on my own interpretation of the good life, but I also avoid being enslaved to society by extending my subjectivity into the will of the whole, such that the whole then reflects back my own subjectivity to me. In this way, my active autonomy has been achieved through participation in public and political life, entering into an active, self-sufficient, and autonomous general will which I help shape and direct. As Hegel puts the point: "The principle of the modern world requires that whatever is to be recognized by everyone must be seen by everyone as entitled to such recognition. But in addition, each individual wishes to be consulted and to be given a hearing. Once he has fulfilled this responsibility and had his say, his subjectivity is satisfied and he will put up with a great deal" (PR 317Z).

The state and the mediating institutions within it promote such participation since the whole is not a static, hierarchical pyramid or artifact. Rather, it is more like an organism, internally dynamic, in which its whole is constantly being broken down and reconstituted by internal dissention and external threats. For Hegel, "living actuality consists in the continual self-generation and self-determination of substance." There is no final, static place at which the common good is finally established for good—rather, it is in "this moment of negativity [which] is the moment of freedom" (VPR17 130). As soon as the relationships among the whole and parts ossify—when they achieve a final resting place under a universally agreed upon view of the good—this is at the same time the death of the organism. Just as the state and institutions foster such individual participation, they receive an internal organic strength and dynamism from its individuals, who consistently engage in the activity of questioning and reinterpreting the central principles of the good. Accordingly, individuals avoid the same fate as the state, that of dying "as a result of habit." Individuals, like states, are "active only in so far as they have not yet attained something and wish to assert themselves and show what they can do in pursuit of it. Once this is accomplished, their activity and vitality disappear, and the loss of interest which ensues is mental or physical death" (PR 151Z).[52] As individuals participate in supporting the organically developing ethical institutions of public life, they sustain their own inner, subjective dynamism to extend themselves out into the world.[53]

At the same time, we should not think of Hegel as some kind of radical democrat. For all his democratic tendencies, Hegel argues that action and deliberation must be mediated through existing institutional structures that transcend individuals as wholes to individual parts. Only by encouraging individual reverence for these often deeply flawed ethical and political institutions can we stave off the excessive atomism of liberal theories of individualism.[54] These communal institutions cultivate citizen reverence for the institutions and common good, such that these can only be transformed very slowly. Hegel is no revolutionary thinker, but rather, like Burke, argues for incremental change. He argues, again like Burke, that the organic ethical and political system around us is the result of considerable effort of history. This system is an extremely complicated organism whose parts have emerged through the multitude of different exchanges within this nation's history. Each state has, then, a unique structure of whole and parts, such that what is appropriate for one country may not be for another, as Napoleon realized with the Spanish (PR 274Z). Furthermore, what may appear to the reflective individual to be inconsistent with an abstract sense of rationality may be wrong. Certain inequalities and differences among the legally enshrined estates and corporations may in fact be salutary for the health and flourishing of the whole, as these are constitutive elements in the organic totality that cannot simply be replaced.[55] This is not to say that change is impossible or undesirable, but only that it must move slowly and with prudence and restraint, as an all-too-radical treatment of any organic body can kill the patient before it cures him.

The distinguishing feature of his moderate politics, I argue, is the entrenched and powerful mediating institutions, which act much like the aristocracy of old, resisting the sweeping change coming either from an all-too-hasty democratic will or from the powerful authority of a central government.[56] This institutional system aims to shape citizens to defer to and identify ourselves with a rational order which transcends us and yet which we (as a community) have made slowly in history. In recognizing this rationality and participating in these institutions to maintain and improve its rationality, historical individuals come to craft their own identities and see themselves in the institutions of public life. Finally, this ethical participation and these institutions help stave off the dehumanizing effects of modern commercial society. Mediating institutions become a place for the individual to find an ethical home, in which he can become satisfied in the fellowship he shares with other members. These mediating institutions are of such importance because they provide for the "unity" and "fulfillment" of "subjectivity" that Hegel promises of the modern state (PR 260)—they cultivate individual particular desires and an attachment to the common good, all as mediated through the will of the individual subject.

5

Nietzsche's Defense of Individuality

Perhaps the most pervasive theme across Nietzsche's corpus is the problem and promise of individuality. In Nietzsche, unlike Hegel, one need not read too far before encountering his celebration of the individual and his tremendous fears of modern liberal democracy's tendency to squelch such individuality. However, even though this theme permeates Nietzsche's works, few have attempted to understand what Nietzsche means by individuality, and what his argument is for why individuality is good. Many readers have seen Nietzsche's celebration of individuality as a blind preference, as an atavistic longing for a bygone aristocratic era, or as the only desperate option left that will save us from the ghastly state of the "last men." Interpreters of Nietzsche also disagree as to what such individuality would actually look like—is the ideal individual a cruel, bloodthirsty "blond beast," or is he a refined and civilized nobleman?[1] Such confusions are to be expected, since Nietzsche's defense of individuality is scattered and adumbrated throughout his corpus. This chapter aims to piece together Nietzsche's arguments on the nature and goodness of individuality.[2]

Despite the confusions surrounding Nietzsche's view of the individual, an influential new interpretation has emerged in the wake of Nehamas's (1985) work. Interpreters from Nehamas to Ridley (2007) have argued that for Nietzsche the standard for the good individual life in Nietzsche is formal and aesthetic in nature. That is, Nietzsche does not offer a substantive blueprint for a certain end or function individuals ought to realize, but rather he argues that one's character must possess the formal virtues of a work of art, such as narrative coherence, self-reflexiveness, and creative harmony of whole and parts.[3] Furthermore,

as scholars such as Owen (2009) and Janaway (2009) have argued, the
very activity of aesthetic self-creation requires individual autonomy,
which, for these scholars, is Nietzsche's basic metaethical commitment.
This recent interpretation of Nietzsche's autonomous, aestheticized individual has influenced my own reading, as we will see below. What this
view fails to account for, however, is why such narrative coherence and
autonomous agency are valuable for the human being. What distinctive
and substantive human need do the formal virtues satisfy? I aim to defend this aesthetic conception by couching it in Nietzsche's more substantive notion of what it means to be a human being. In this chapter, I
couch Nietzsche's formal aesthetic criteria in Nietzsche's broader project of achieving a complete life for the human being as such. In chapter
6, I argue that the good life of individuality occurs not in the private
"life as literature," but rather is achieved through ethical activity performed in public. Finally, in chapter 7, I make the case that for Nietzsche in opposition to Hegel, individuality is distorted and enslaved by
political participation, and individuals can only lead complete lives at
the margins of politics in cultural communities.

In what follows, I make the case that Nietzsche owes a great deal to
Hegel's transformation of Kant's "Copernican Revolution" in philosophy. I understand Nietzsche's form of argument to be very similar to
that pursued by Hegel—the "natural law" that human subjectivity has
a distinctive longing to lead an individual life, and that human subjects
only come to be fulfilled through ethical participation in historical practices. Few scholars have pursued Nietzsche's debt to Hegel.[4] However,
that Nietzsche owed this debt should come as no surprise. Nietzsche's
Kantian commitments precluded him from stepping back to pre-Kantian metaphysics, and Nietzsche himself admits that Hegel put the
Kantian transcendental ego in motion by embedding it in history.[5]
Moreover, Nietzsche had to confront Hegel, who was a towering figure
in nineteenth-century philosophy, influencing figures from Strauss,
Feuerbach, and Marx on the left to the defenders of the Prussian state
on the right.[6] Though many "Left Hegelians" spent much of their ca-
reers pointing out where Hegel went wrong, they were still importantly
"Hegelians" in taking Hegel seriously and, most famously in the case of
Marx, retaining a similar dialectical scheme to Hegel's. Hegel's presence reached the public's attention, especially through the popular
texts of Strauss and Marx, and his views became an integral part of the
German *Zeitgeist*, to such a degree that Nietzsche would judge that the
"pupils of Hegel" were the "actual educators of the Germans of this
century" (AOM 170), and that the "Hegelian" philosophy's influence

was "enormous and still continuing" in young writers (UM 2.8).[7] The German education in Hegelian philosophy helped create, according to Nietzsche, the ideological defenses of the German state, which was taken to be the "absolutely complete ethical organism" (FEI 79) and "the highest goal of mankind. . . . A man has no higher duty than to serve the state" (UM 3.4; cf. UM 3.8).

At the same time, the young Nietzsche's most important philosophical influence, Schopenhauer, was locked in a lifelong battle against Hegelianism.[8] Yet Nietzsche engaged with Hegel independently of Schopenhauer, and came to see that they were "hostile brother geniuses in philosophy" (BGE 252). In short, from the beginning of his philosophical career in UM 2 (see especially section 8) to his mature career in GS book 5 (357) and BGE (204, 211), Nietzsche viewed Hegel as a fundamental interlocutor next to Plato, Kant, and Schopenhauer.[9] Nietzsche owed a lot more to Hegel than he gave Hegel credit for, as I hope to bring out in the next few chapters. Most importantly, under Hegel's influence, Nietzsche came to see that human beings are deeply and pervasively shaped by history, that what is "natural" or biological is always already informed by historical norms and customs.[10] For Nietzsche, human beings can never engage in "immediate self-observation," but rather we require "history [*Geschichte*], for the past continues to flow within us in a hundred waves" (AOM 223).

5.1   The Problem of Individuation in Nietzsche

Despite Nietzsche's professed support for individuality, some interpreters have argued that Nietzsche is best interpreted as a critic of individuality. These interpretations—I'll refer to them as the "metaphysical," "postmodern," and "naturalist" interpretations—must be addressed before we can move forward. Yet, as we will see, in examining these "anti-individual" interpretations of Nietzsche, I can bring my own view into sharper focus, since Nietzsche's debt to the German tradition of individual autonomy and practical reason represented by Kant, Fichte, and Hegel reveals clearly the errors of these alternative interpretations.

First, according to the metaphysical interpretation of Nietzsche, in his early work Nietzsche articulated a concept of the "Dionysian," the "primordial oneness" that is the chaotic passionate substratum on top of which the "Apollonian" principle of individuality casts its illusions. Only in certain cases is the "veil of Maya" is lifted, letting us see that the boundaries and categories we use to carve out differences between things are not actually real.[11] Similarly, in Nietzsche's late notebooks, he outlines a theory of passions and "quanta of power," which are the basic constituents of the universe. Human individuals and their "free will" are illusions, reducible without remainder to their natural, material drives and parts. These "drives" are engaged in a constant struggle for "mastery," which offers a better explanation for human behavior than some illusory appeal to an individual will (BGE 6; WP 488). Thus, what seems to be a conscious, uncaused free choice coming from "us" or from the "ego" is simply our identification with the winning "drive" among the tussle of the passions (BGE 19; WP 492).[12]

I do not deny that Nietzsche is engaged in a project of undermining what we typically understand to be "individuality" and "freedom" and of "translat[ing] humanity back into nature" (BGE 230). In fact, I consider this move to be integral to my account of Nietzsche's view of historical individuality. However, in this book I put Nietzsche's metaphysical views to one side, in part because it is difficult to impute a metaphysical view to Nietzsche given that much of the evidence comes from either Nietzsche's early "Romantic" phase or from his unpublished notebooks.[13] But more importantly, this view imputes to Nietzsche a pre-Kantian metaphysics of "substance," that the world is structured in such a fashion independent of the investigating subject. Yet Nietzsche follows Fichte and Hegel, who argue that the human subject is not a pure passive onlooker on the world as it is in itself; rather, the very categories we bring to bear in understanding the world are shaped by our practical activity and needs. As Nietzsche puts the point, "nothing else is 'given' [*gegeben*] but the world of our desires and passions, such that we cannot get down or up to any 'reality' except the reality of our drives" (BGE 36). The primary philosophical task for Nietzsche, then, is not to grasp the world as it is in itself and then seek to make individuality intelligible within it. Rather, the task is to trace the structure and aims of the practical needs that always already guide our knowledge of the world. Revealing his debt to the Kantian Copernican Revolution in philosophy, Nietzsche argues that this practical perspective gives rise to certain normative standards of human action and character (as we will see below) that we as practical beings must follow in order to lead a full human life.[14]

Second, the "naturalist" interpreters recognize that for Nietzsche human beings are shaped and driven by natural imperatives and desires. They are skeptical, though, that Nietzsche can defend "individuality" on this basis. In particular, the naturalist Nietzscheans Leiter (2002) and Acampora (2006c) have focused on Nietzsche's ideal of the "sovereign individual" of GM 2.2, and have argued that Nietzsche is not actually endorsing individuality in this passage.[15] Furthermore, they argue that his naturalism points human beings away from "individuality" as a much too traditional and baroque ideal. This ideal separates human beings as self-sufficient "monadic unitary entities," thereby denying our embodied social natures or our evolutionary urge to overcome humanity (Acampora 2006c, 149).

The main problem with the naturalist view is that for Nietzsche human beings are not entirely natural creatures. However, the naturalist interpretation suggests that the only alternative to "naturalism" is spooky supernaturalism (Acampora 2006a, 315). Rather, as we will see, human beings are those historical creatures who can call into question their natural urges and can cultivate through history a "second nature" that replaces the first and that responds to humanly created principles of the good. History is not a "supernatural" entity, nor are its effects reducible to natural psychophysical human behavior. Indeed, it is not at all clear why we should see "nature" as a normative authority binding upon us, nor is it clear that we can even access such a "first nature" anyway, buried as it is under tremendous layers of cultural meaning. In short, I think the central question Nietzsche asks is not what does nature dictate for human life? but what fulfills a distinctively human life?, where a human being is understood as a being whose embodied, natural needs have been thoroughly transformed by history.

Third, however, the postmodernists have already grasped the importance for Nietzsche of this deep historical conditioning of the human being.[16] They extend this historicism to argue that appeals to the "universal truth" of any norm are themselves forms of power that a historical community exerts upon its members in order to sustain the integrity and status quo of the community. Dissenting voices in these communities are squelched by what purports to be the "Truth" of things. In revealing the historical "contingency" of these claims, Nietzsche liberates the multiple different perspectives that always already exist in any human group. Yet this means that the notion of "individuality" as the good for human beings is itself an exertion of power that attempts to foist an artificial unity on a human subject who is constituted by many different capacities, drives, desires he is often unaware of.

To support their claims, the postmodernists appeal to some of the same passages in Nietzsche as the above interpreters, especially those passages in which Nietzsche seems to deny that human beings can exert free, autonomous agency over themselves and their lives. However, in the passages in which Nietzsche denies free will, he has a very specific target in mind—the Christian-Cartesian understanding of free will, which we have come to internalize and assume is the "Truth" about free will.[17] According to this "moral" conception of the will, our "true selves" exist separately from our desires and beliefs, indifferent to their influence, capable of exerting a sovereign free agency in selecting whatever course of action suits our whims of the moment.[18] According to this conception, we are always able "to do otherwise" no matter what our beliefs and desires urge upon us. Accordingly, Nietzsche argues, this view of free will made possible the practice of moral responsibility and punishment, a practice the slaves employed to overpower the masters (GM 1.13). This Christian-Cartesian conception of free will is not the only way of understanding human freedom for Nietzsche, and indeed it is a poor way of understanding it. If we think of ourselves as always already in full possession of our individuality and responsibility—as an atomistic agent always already free to "do otherwise"—then we fail to recognize the many ways in which we are not in sovereign control of our actions, the ways in which society or nature influences us without our knowing or consenting. It is an unrealistically high standard for freedom that ultimately masks our fundamental dependence on natural needs and social norms and hence fails to reveal how we can achieve individual freedom from a practical perspective "within" this fundamental dependence. For Nietzsche, as I will argue, the only way to avoid the unfreedom the postmodernists are concerned with is precisely to cultivate an individual life for oneself, a life that is free and good because it fulfills what it means to be a human being.

In other words, Nietzsche's critique of the Christian-Cartesian view of the self and his attendant naturalist emphasis—his remarks that we are little more than a bundle of competing passions—aims precisely to establish that human individuality cannot precede human action, that "there is no 'being' behind the deed," but the "deed is everything" (GM 1.13).[19] He sets this goal for himself to convince us, not that freedom is impossible, but that freedom and individuality are not "given" to some illusory soul-substance persisting within us. Rather, they are practical ends to be achieved through a series of actions that constitute a complete life.[20] In this, Nietzsche continues the Fichtean and Hegelian tradition of conceiving of the I not as a thing standing before the action, but as the structure emerging from a successful, human action—the great action is the one which "does not say 'I,' but does [*tut*] 'I'" (Z:1 "On the Despisers"), so as to live up to "this creating, willing, valuing I, which is the measure and value of things" (Z:1 "On the Afterworldly").[21] The task of realizing and satisfying the distinctively human is very difficult and rarely achieved. Indeed, he argues that "you are being acted upon! at every moment! Mankind has in all ages confused the active and the passive: it is their everlasting grammatical blunder" (D 120). Yet Nietzsche does not give up the task because of its difficulty but rather emphatically pursues it, claiming that he "base[s] ethics on the sharpest possible definition of self, and not on its vaporization" (L 78).

That Nietzsche holds this view should be no surprise. A casual reading of many of Nietzsche's major works reveals that he has a penchant for "big" individuals, like the "philosopher" (*Philosoph*) of the future in BGE, the overman (*Übermensch*) and higher men (*höhere Menschen*) in Z, the sovereign individual (*souveraine Individuum*) in GM 2.2, and the "knowers" (*Erkennenden*) of various works, among other ideals and exemplars.[22] One central feature of these "big" individuals that Nietzsche stresses time and again is precisely their individuality, that is, their uniqueness or distinctness from other human beings, and their freedom and responsibility to form a unified identity out of their passions. These "big" individuals were in no way "born" with such freedom, but had to strive to cultivate it over time, and in doing so they realized what is natural to human beings. As Nietzsche puts it, nature "is not really a going-back as much as a *coming towards* [Hinaufkommen]—towards a high, free [*freie*], even terrible nature and naturalness" (TI 9.48).

Since the distinctively human comes to be history, human beings are not ontologically distinct from nature. Nietzsche adheres to the "deadly truth" that there is no "cardinal difference" in the biology of "man and animal" (UM 2.9). At the same time, what has come to make humans distinct from the other animals is nonetheless crucial to understanding the good proper for human beings.[23] Consistent with Rousseau and Hegel, then, Nietzsche turns to the emergence of the human out of nature to pinpoint precisely what those distinctively human characteristics are. As we will see, the nature of human subjectivity will point toward individuality as the genuine fulfillment of what it means to be a human being.

5.2   Will to Power and the Development of the Distinctively Human

The Nature of Nature

As a modern thinker, Nietzsche claims that nature is "indifferent" to human affairs. Nature does not have as its aim the coming to be and eventual fulfillment of human beings. It is nonteleological, nonprovidential, seemingly chaotic and random. Nature is "profligate without measure, indifferent without measure, without purpose and regard, without mercy and justice, fertile and barren and uncertain at the same time" (BGE 9). It is like a blindfolded marksman, in Nietzsche's image, which generates ever new forms of life but "squanders" this life as it "takes no aim but hopes the arrow will stick somewhere" (UM 3.7). Nature is characterized by "sovereign becoming, of the fluidity of all concepts, types and species" (UM 2.9). Single entities and entire species emerge out of a generative nature, and at the same time whole species are destroyed, dissolving back into the stream of universal becoming. Nietzsche adapts an image from Heraclitus to describe the activity of nature, which, like a playful child, "builds up piles of sand only to knock them down again" (BT 24).

Yet if this is true, then, as Hegel would say, nature is "indifferent" or "external" to itself as well. Nature claims no right not to be manipulated by human effort, and, indeed, "nature lets itself be tyrannized as well" (BGE 9). Human beings hence can and do "wear away the earth" for all sorts of tasks, as Sophocles imagined, for their material well-being, for their entertainment, for war (*Antigone* l. 337). Yet the highest form of manipulation of nature is, Nietzsche argues, the transformation of nature into something purposive for the human individual. In particular, nature achieves its highest formation in the highest human life, in the life that submits nature to its own will. In this life, nature comes to be "redeemed" (*erlöst*) for its wastefulness, its indifference, its cruelty, since it has given rise to individuals who make nature into something meaningful (UM 3.5).

But why is this effort "higher" than any other? In a purposeless nature, how does one derive purposes which hence serve as a standard to adjudicate higher and lower, noble and base, good and evil? Such a standard cannot be wholly conventional or ineluctably rooted in particular human practices and psychology, since Nietzsche clearly wants to argue that nature illuminates a universal standard of better and worse human lives (TI 9.48).[24] On what basis does Nietzsche establish this standard? The second feature of nature, the will to power, serves as such a standard. There can be little doubt that Nietzsche came in his mature work to describe the "will to power" as the universal normative standard to adjudicate a better and worse human life (see, e.g., GM 2.12; BGE 19, 36). Yet this doctrine of the "will to power" is notoriously obscure, underdetermined, and possibly even incoherent. It is not immediately clear why we should believe it even if we think we know what Nietzsche means by it. There is considerable disagreement in the scholarly literature as to what this "doctrine" amounts to, and hence I will not attempt or even claim to settle the disputes here.

Instead, I want to build on a few sophisticated and well-developed interpretations of the will to power outlined by Richardson (1996) and Clark (1983). This interpretation can be bolstered by understanding Nietzsche's view in light of the post-Kantian emphasis on "organic" nature in opposition to Newtonian mechanistic nature. Let us begin by enlisting help from Richardson's sophisticated account of Nietzsche on nature. According to his account, nature is a system of competing wills or drives that each aim at some end and seek satisfaction for this end, such as sex, food, or shelter. At the same time, however, each will has a "second-order" desire to attain "power," understood as the ability to improve the capacity of the will to achieve these ends (23–24; cf. Clark 1983; BGE 6; AC 6).[25] Now we can describe these wills in terms of the content of their "first-order" desires or in terms of the "form" of their will, that is, in terms of its structure or capacity to fulfill its first-order desires.

The structural or second-order transformation of first-order aims occurs because these natural wills compete for the same scarce natural resources. Every natural being fights to stay alive. As the natural will of the lion sinks his teeth into his prey, for instance, it undermines the capacity of other natural wills—namely, the unsuspecting zebras in the vicinity of the lion—to satisfy their first-order aims. In order to stand a fighting chance, a will must incorporate other wills to form what Richardson calls a "synthetic" will (44). Previously independent wills are incorporated within a larger, more powerful will, subjected to its purposes.[26] Yet in the process of cooperating—or, more often, in being conquered by a larger will—each will becomes "sublimated," meaning that it pursues not its original first-order aim, but a new aim that it comes to assume as part of a whole, common will that it has formed with others.[27] When this cooperation becomes routine, the common will that is formed may appear to have autonomous agency over its parts, even though the common will is actually in fact just a well-structured organization of different parts. When single-celled organisms evolved to become multicellular organisms, for instance, those original single-celled "wills" no longer pursued the same first-order aims, but rather their wills had been changed fundamentally such that they acted as part of a larger whole which acted as a will itself.

Such a view of the nature of nature seems a far cry from Hegel's view. Yet I want to suggest that there are deep similarities. First of all, Nietzsche's view of the "will" is very similar to Hegel's view of the "subject." For both philosophers, a subject or will is a whole constructed out of otherwise conflicting parts. As Hegel puts it, the defining characteristic of a subject is the subject's capacity as a whole to "contain and endure" inner contradictions, to press its otherwise unruly desires into parts of the totality (EN 359A). Nietzsche argues similarly that the will is "something complicated" that involves a "plurality of feelings" and the ability to "command something inside himself that obeys" (BGE 19). The "strength" of a will consists in its ability to unify many different wills into a differentiated whole (see Richardson 1996, 49ff.). A whole is created and then subsequently maintained in both Hegel and Nietzsche by an internal structure of command and mutual recognition of each part. As Nietzsche points out, the properly constructed will is much like a "well-constructed and happy community." The will is a "society constructed out of many 'souls'" (BGE 19).[28] Nonetheless, as Nietzsche insists, the cooperation or harmony of the constituent parts of a will is not perfect, even in the best-constructed synthetic will. On the contrary, the different desires or "wills" that constitute us still vie for dominance within us, not in open battle but in a contained, "political" setting, in a "soul as a society constructed out of drives and affects" (BGE 12). Complex, synthetic wills strive constantly to unify their various parts into an ordered totality.

Nature is, then, a complicated and dynamic system of cooperation and antagonism, of love and strife. Yet for Nietzsche, as for Hegel, it is strife, or the desire to "negate" the other, that is the foundational motivating force of nature. The second-order desire to maintain and expand the will always precedes and shapes the specific first-order desires that any one will pursues. For Nietzsche and Hegel, we can distinguish the "higher" animals from the "lower" with this will-to-power standard. True power, for Nietzsche, is not blunt force, sharp teeth, big muscles, which merely rend and incorporates things of nature while leaving the subject and the world around it fundamentally unchanged. Rather, true power resides in one's capacity to transform oneself and one's environment. It is not the power to destroy, but the power to "negate," to use Hegel's terms, to negate the "otherness" of objects in the world and make them part of a subjective whole. Nietzsche argues that we "force" things of the world "to accept us, we violate them"—this "process," Nietzsche says, conjuring up the spirit of Hegel, "is called idealizing" (TI 9.8).[29] As the will negates the otherness of the other, incorporating some new part of the world, it itself changes, its set of first-order desires is transformed. Thus, the more expansive any one will gets, the more its structure becomes increasingly complicated without flying apart, incorporating wildly competing parts into itself, the more it achieves "power." Such a strong will has a tremendous "plastic power" (UM 2.1).

Accordingly, the best interpretations of Nietzsche's will to power, in scholars such as Kaufmann (1974), Richardson (1996), Clark (1983), and Reginster (2006), recognize that it is a formal or structural account of the will, not its substantive or first-order goal. Many readers of Nietzsche make this mistake, arguing that Nietzsche means by the will to power that we seek something very vague like "power" or more concrete and violent ends like "exploitation" or "cruelty."[30] Understanding the will to power as a second-order desire may sound somewhat puzzling, however, as if there were some metaphysical puppet master standing behind appearances directing first-order desires. Yet I think the basic point can be illustrated—imperfectly, as we will see—by comparing Nietzsche's view to the "selfish gene" theory of Richard Dawkins (1976).[31] The selfish gene seeks to reproduce and expand itself indefinitely, using an animal's first-order desires for self-preservation and reproduction as a vehicle for its second-order aims.

The Distinctively Human

In Nietzsche's view, human beings are not categorically different from all other organisms in the natural world. We are made up of the same basic natural material as all other organic beings. Like all organic beings—to use Hegelian language—all human "subjects" seek as a second-order desire to consolidate the divergent desires that make up their "substance" while at the same time expanding themselves into the world. In the primitive state of humanity, as in all animals, subject and substance are immediately unified within an organic whole—human beings act out of natural instinct, since there is not yet any "internalization of man" (GM 2.16). That is to say, our subjective will is simply the shape of our substantive desires—there is no gap between our natural desires and our subjective reasoning as there is in a distinctively human society. In our natural, barbaric state, we fight tenaciously to preserve ourselves and our offspring. Some of us make up a "conqueror and master race" and hence seek to dominate and rule over others (GM 2.17). These substantive, first-order aims are redescribable in formal, second-order terms as the will to expand and consolidate a genetic heritage. As embodied beings, human beings have genes, and these selfish genes construct human bodies as the vehicle for their transmission and proliferation.

At the same time, human subjectivity is distinctive in achieving a second, more radical form of the will to power, that is, a power over nature itself.[32] Human beings can turn away from our natural, genetic heritage, and hence can free ourselves from being enslaved to our natures. This "freedom" is the first distinctively human trait in Nietzsche's theory. Or rather, since Nietzsche does not use the term "freedom" for this trait eminently reminiscent of Hegel's view of autonomy, we should say the human being is the "esteeming" (*schätzen*) animal (Z:1 "On the Thousand"). As Nietzsche puts it, "Men gave themselves all their good and evil. Verily, they did not take it, they did not find it, nor did it come to them as a voice from heaven. Only man placed values in things to preserve himself—he alone created a meaning [*Sinn*] for things, a human meaning. Therefore he calls himself 'man,' which means: the esteemer" (Z:1 "On the Thousand"). That is, human beings give themselves a principle of the good, a "tablet of the good," in the form of a community. There is "no greater power on earth than good and evil," more powerful even than the impulses of nature (Z:1 "On the Thousand and One"). We "project" our values onto the world and hence light up the world with anthropomorphic purposes (Z:1 "On the Afterworldly").[33] Subsequently, we see ourselves in this world we have projected onto the "indifferent" nature, since what is most attractive to a people, Zarathustra states, is "whatever makes [us] rule and triumph and shine, to the awe and envy of [our] neighbors" (Z:1 "On the Thousand").

Nietzsche argues that the emergence of human esteeming and hence community is not something magical or mysterious that allows us to turn entirely away from our biological needs. On the contrary, our biological needs always make a claim on us. That our natural attachment to our family often damages our commitment to our community is one familiar example of nature's insurmountable power over us. Nietzsche refers to the internal conflict of human beings between our communal and natural needs as the "sickness of man." Yet in this way the human being becomes an "interesting animal" as a result of the conflict between its natural and communal attachments; the sickness is "like pregnancy" (GM 2.19). Nietzsche argues that the "prospect of an animal soul turning against itself, taking a part against itself, was something so new, profound . . . on earth that the whole character of the world changed in an essential way" (GM 2.16). The human being hence seeks ever more elaborate customs and institutions in order to resolve these conflicts, and, in doing so, creates an interesting and rich history of meaning around him.[34]

That is, the most effective tool a community has to rule the natural passions is to "sublimate" them. Culture redirects and hence transforms the natural passions so that they come under the employ of the good of the whole. This "shaping," the hammering of an otherwise recalcitrant nature into recognizably human shape, often takes a very violent form in Nietzsche's mind. For instance, to learn to fulfill a promise—the behavior that stands at the foundation of communal order—the "debtor" had to be physically pummeled by the "creditor" so as to learn to be responsible (GM 2.6–8). At other times, the sublimation is a much less forceful or artificial imposition, as when the Greeks sublimated their physical antagonism in the form of a cultural *agon* (HC 188). What human culture is taking advantage of here is a second distinctively human trait, what we called in chapter 2 "perfectibility." Our "first natures" can be shaped and added to such that eventually, through education, habituation to public norms, we can change our substance such that it becomes a "second nature" (UM 2.3; UUM 19.226). This second nature becomes so thoroughly embedded within us that we cease to have to reflect on how to act or to hold back our urges automatically. The community's aims and human passions are harmonized because the community's "tablet of the good" has been internalized in the second nature of its members.

Accordingly, Nietzsche's view of community is intelligible according to the very same will-to-power theory. For Nietzsche, society and nature are quite similar because they both are the structuring will, the second-order agent that shapes individual action and that seeks to expand itself in the world. Nature produces our bodies, but culture subsequently shapes our identities through education. This education internalizes a set of norms and a view of the good which we seek to realize in the world. The "evaluations and rankings" of the community's moral system "are always the expressions of the needs of a community and herd: that which benefits it the most" (GS 116). Thus, a member's actions are "above all directed at the preservation of a community, a people" (HH 96; cf. AOM 89). These actions have substantive or first-order ends—for instance, being a courageous Roman by winning this battle, becoming the next president of the United States by winning this election. Yet what shapes these first-order ends, makes them possible, and brings them into being in the first place—the whole to which they are a part—is the second-order aim of the preservation and promotion of the culture as a whole. The culture then is a collective subject, a "we," that comes to shape its parts—its human members—and expand itself into the outside world.

However, although there is a structural similarity between the will to power of nature and of culture, there is a crucial difference as well—the cultural human being is self-conscious or "free" in the post-Kantian sense we have been developing in the past few chapters. Culture has overcome nature in being the "true" wielder of the will to power. Our "selfish memes"—to use Dawkins's phrase—use our second nature and its first-order constructed social desires as vehicles for the preservation and promotion of our culture. Human beings are not simply drawn along in a natural stream of becoming, characterized by the endless pursuit of particular desires in concrete settings. We have the capacity to elevate ourselves out of this stream and "esteem" the natural world as communal beings, subsequently responding to the general norms of conduct we have given to ourselves in our esteeming.

Hence, this communal autonomy realizes human freedom in the world. Unlike nature, which churns out new individuals and species immersed "blindly" within a stream of "becoming," in society, human beings are internally divided, between our esteeming subjectivity, and the object that is to be esteemed.[35] The individual subject will act based only on a law that it esteems highly. And it will esteem highly that law that comes from itself. For this reason, the communal "world" that is produced in, say, ancient Greece is very powerful for Greek citizens. My esteeming subjectivity feels satisfied and whole in this artificial, objective "Greek" world, since this world permanently reflects back to me my own free nature. The Greek citizen in a Greek world is like one mirror placed in front of another mirror—both reflect and endorse the other, and hence assume an "infinite" mutual reflectivity (as two mirrors placed in front of one another do).[36] As Nietzsche puts it, the "history of his city becomes for him the history of himself . . . thus with the aid of this 'we' he looks beyond his own individual transitory life [*Einzelleben*] and feels himself to be the spirit [*Geist*] of his house, his race, his city" (UM 2.3).[37] The "Christian moral" world, for instance, "granted man an absolute value, as opposed to his smallness and accidental occurrence in the flux of becoming and passing away" (WP 4). In this way, as in Hegel, so for Nietzsche, nature becomes "self-aware" in the human being's reflection on and action within his own cultural world.[38]

I have suggested that for Nietzsche human community is a higher form of the will to power since it allows for the satisfaction of a subject within a community, rather than being an animal endlessly and fruitlessly seeking bodily forms of completeness. Yet the community also has another benefit. For all Nietzsche's criticism of the "ethical life of custom [*Sittlichkeit der Sitte*]," he thinks that communities are instrumentally good. They are a necessary preparation for the third and final step in the will to power, the individual. As Nietzsche puts it, the community's "ethical life of custom" has a "comprehensive meaning [*Sinn*] and justification [*Rechtfertigung*]" because it transforms the natural human being into the kind of being who can take responsibility for his promises (GM 2.2).[39] Indeed, Nietzsche argues that living up to one's promises is the "task which nature has set herself with regard to humankind" (GM 2.1), the completion of what is human as such. This claim might strike one as surprising until we understand "promising" in Kantian terms—what is distinctively human is the freedom to give myself a law, that "we *are able* to promise certain things and bind ourselves to perform them ('freedom of will')" (D 112). When I live up to my promises, my duties, my social station, I realize the freedom of the humanly created ethical laws of my community. Promising seems to be a mundane, humdrum characteristic of humanity, but it is in fact Nietzsche's shorthand for all forms of human, ethical activity that involve submitting oneself to duties, laws, customs.

The "ethical life of custom" makes human beings into promising animals, those responsive to human norms rather than acting out of instinct, by putting us in a "straitjacket" (GM 2.2). For Nietzsche, human beings had to submit our wills to what we took to be a transcendent power for a long while before we could submit our wills only to ourselves. As Hegel argued, the only way to get a natural being to become ethical is to be reborn in spirit. To be reborn in spirit is to submit one's natural will entirely to an ethical whole, to a general or universal self-consciousness, which is, in Nietzsche's terms, the "subordination to the will of another or to a comprehensive law and ritual" (HH 139).[40] For instance, Nietzsche argues that the creation of politics—the "setting up [of] a legal system"—is a necessary step in overcoming "reactive sentiment" (GM 2.11).[41] Religion, especially Christianity, "taught man to view himself from a distance and as something past and whole" by "describing eternal perspectives around him" (GS 78).[42] In other words, human beings must learn to recognize a "higher tendency" that possesses normative authority over one's natural will (BGE 60). Only by giving one's natural will up entirely to this ethical authority can one be sure that one's ethical claims will shape one's natural desires, and not the other way around. With a will mired in nature, one cannot simply will to be ethical, which would amount to a "*causa sui*" (BGE 21). The communal will "makes a man to a certain degree undeviating, uniform, a peer amongst peers, orderly and consequently predictable" (GM 2.2). Under the aegis of this communal will, the "reliable" human being becomes able to "promise" (GM 2.1). This "subordination is a powerful means of becoming master of oneself" (HH 139). We become able to, in other words, submit ourselves to a publicly accessible norm that we then are expected by others to live up to. In binding ourselves consistently to these norms of nobility and greatness, then, we actually become "something nobler, grander, goodlier, something 'divine'" (GS 352).

Individuality as the Completion of the Distinctively Human

However, Nietzsche insists that in positing God or tradition or community, rather than the individual, as the object of worship, this communal subordination has "flown astray" most fundamentally because individual human beings are expected to promote a community at the expense of themselves (BGE 60). The "freedom" of the community is the wrong sort of freedom. Others in society hold me answerable for my promises. But I have not yet held myself responsible for my own promises, for subjecting myself to my own law. For Nietzsche, individual subjectivity is not satisfied, as it does not see itself while being a fungible agent of the communal will.

However, the modern age allows us to correct our flight by providing the conditions for taking a third step in the evolution of the will to power. In the first step, nature was the subject that created and extended itself through human beings, who served as the vehicle for nature's self-promotion. In the second step, society helped human beings be reborn in spirit. Spirit or the communal will became the subject that created and extended itself through the vehicles of human beings. In the third step, we are reborn once again, now as beings who are free from both nature and community, who give ourselves our own laws as individuals, who can be "answerable for [our] own future" (GM 2.1). In other words, the third step consists of becoming an autonomous and whole subject exerting power over oneself, reproducing and extending oneself in the world. It is "to make of oneself a complete person, and in all that one does to have in view the highest good of this person [myself]" (HH 95). This "self-determination" or "self-mastery" or "responsibility for myself" Nietzsche refers to throughout his career as "freedom of the will."[43] Nietzsche understands this freedom explicitly in Kantian autonomy terms, as when he says freedom is "honoring the law which he himself has made" and "submitting only to the law which I myself have given, in great things and in small" (D 187). As Nietzsche puts it in his own categorization of the "three phases of morality hitherto," "at the highest stage of morality *hitherto,* [the individual] acts in accordance with *his own* standard with regard to men and things" (HH 94).[44]

The individual is the crowning achievement of the development of the will to power, the "end of history," as it were. Individuality is the result of the "deepening" of the human soul, brought about through the strong tension between our natural and social drives. Nietzsche argues that primitive human beings, naturally solitary and free, found themselves "imprisoned within the confines of society and peace." Social norms restricted the "external discharge of man's [natural] instincts." These natural instincts still sought an outlet and hence "turn inwards," leading to the "internalization of man," such that our "inner world . . . was expanded and extended . . . and gained depth, breadth and height in proportion to the degree that the external discharge of man's instincts was obstructed" (GM 2.16). Eventually, at the end point of this process, the long-term historical conflict between society and nature gives rise to deep human souls who can individually come to understand their development and hence control their destiny.

This historically developed ability is a towering exemplification of the will to power because the individual will is able to incorporate not just embodied, natural passions, but also his spiritual, ethical being as well. That is, the individual must weave together a tremendously diverse array of different determinations in order to maintain and reproduce himself. The individual's subjectivity must climb to the summit of his multifaceted identity, such that he can survey the different desires and inclinations that had come to constitute him. With such self-knowledge, the individual can then shape and master these many different determinations in accordance with his own law, his own view of the good. For instance, Nietzsche reverently recounts the "nature of iron" that Schopenhauer had to have in order to endure social pressure and to achieve a perspective of being a "stepchild of his age" (UM 3.3).

This development of the will to power is the "end of history," because there is no possible further "step" the will to power can take, as this configuration satisfies human subjectivity most deeply.[45] Nietzsche's second essay in the *Genealogy of Morality* makes such an "end of history" argument, as he claims that the individual is the "end of the immense process where the tree actually bears fruit, where society and its ethical life of custom finally reveal what they were simply the means to" (GM 2.2). The end point is the "sovereign individual," the one who has "freed itself from the ethical life of custom," the "man with his own independent, durable will, who *has the ability to promise*" (GM 2.2). This sovereign individual represents the final stage in the development of the will to power because in the sovereign individual, the logic of the will to power has arrived at what we may call an "equilibrium point." As we have seen, the logic of the will to power involves a super-subject that employs a subject's first-order desires to satisfy the super-subject's own second-order desires. With the sovereign individual, the individual becomes both super-subject and subject at once.

In other words—to put it in terms of Hegel's developmental logic of spirit—in the first step of the will to power, human beings were "immediately" immersed in nature. Nature served as the super-subject that employed living organisms' first-order desires for food and sex to satisfy their second-order "need" to promote and extend their genetic code. This "immediate" stage is in human beings the stage of "master morality," in which shallow, powerful "blond beasts" rule based on natural "instinct" (GM 2.17). This "immediate" unity of subject and substance in nature gave way to a second step of the will to power in which the distinctively human came on the stage. Here, there is a division between the social and natural needs of the human being. This second step is the melancholy "reflective moment" in the Hegelian logical scheme and the rise in the "sickly" animal in "slave morality," in which social norm and natural instinct are opposed to one another. Yet, as in Hegel, so too in Nietzsche, this moment involves an advancement, since the subject comes to recognize itself in the super-subject. A human community or culture inches human subjects closer to the point of completeness when the super-subject of the human community realizes its second-order goals, the human subject can find some satisfaction in the success of the super-subject, and individual souls are deepened through the process of social mastery over the passions. However, communities still employ their members as vehicles to carry out their will and to reproduce themselves.[46]

In the final, third step of the will to power, both super-subject and subject achieve reconciliation as one and the same in the individual himself. The individual reproduces himself in himself; he uses himself as his own vehicle, one could say, and hence the individual subject ceases to be a "vehicle" at all, but is rather the "true helmsman of his existence."[47] He is free from both nature and society in giving himself his own "law, the fundamental law of your own true self."[48] The individual subject is self-identical—"consistent in [his] uniqueness"—and hence assumes a position of "being" above the stream of "becoming" of both society and nature (UM 3.1).[49] He "imposes upon becoming the character of being," and this "is the supreme will to power" (WP 617). In being self-identical, the individual gains wholeness in reproducing himself in himself. He is a self-related circle, a mirror to his own mirror. This self-identical unity fulfills the distinctively human subject—as a free being, each human subject longs to "live according to our own laws and standards" and hence see his own law as the structuring, second-order need for his own first-order substantive desires (UM 3.1). The sovereign individual lives here according to his "conscience," which Nietzsche defines across nearly two decades as "being yourself," as having "freedom and power over himself" (UM 3.1; GM 2.2).

5.3 Individuality as a Narrative Unity

For Nietzsche, then, individuality is good because it is the completion of what the distinctively human will longs for. Individuality is not, however, an easy achievement. Like Hegel, Nietzsche argues that one's individuality does not exist as some pregiven substratum hidden within one—there is no "doer before the deed." Rather, individuality comes to be as a structural achievement of our will, the organization of our beliefs, desires, longings, capacities into a coherent whole that then bears the trace of our will. For Nietzsche, such individuality has a certain formal structure based on the underlying drive of the human will to externalize itself into the world.

In GS 290, Nietzsche outlines the basis and aim of individual character formation, and hence it is a good place to begin. He argues that one thing "is needful: that a human being should *attain* satisfaction with himself." That is, the human subject seeks to achieve satisfaction through the creation of a particular kind of life, and so we should heed this human subjectivity within us. The life our subjectivity longs for must reveal the "single taste [*selben Geschmack*] that ruled and shaped everything great and small," the "single taste" of an individual subject. One's character and history must resemble an "artistic plan" that is "perfected under [his] own law [*eigenen Gesetz*]," a law legislated by the human subject. The subjective artist achieves this individual character by "resist[ing] giving nature free rein" and rather organizing his own "strengths and weaknesses" into an "artistic plan." Furthermore, the "ugly that could not be removed is concealed" or else "it is reinterpreted into sublimity. Much that is vague and resisted shaping has been saved and employed for distant views—it is supposed to beckon toward the remote and immense." This artistic plan comes to be internalized as the individual's second nature, such that the individual desires, acts, and moves spontaneously in a way essentially consistent with the narrative history that has preceded him. In such an artistically constructed self, Nietzsche suggests, we onlookers can only understand this individual's actions according to the norms internal to the individual's own artistic plan for himself—that is, they are not reducible to the pursuit of social or political goods or natural pleasures. We all know personally and can point out "individuals," those persons who flout social customs in order to be "true to themselves." These "individuals" are often eccentric, flamboyant, unique. We cannot compare these individuals to anyone else but themselves. And in fact, when humdrum people we know act out of the ordinary, we tend to compare their surprising actions to those unique individuals we have come across.

Nietzsche argues, then, that the human subject achieves satisfaction within a character that is structured like an artistic object. As we saw in chapter 2, the logic of "individuality" demands such an artistic articulation of one's character. Nietzsche, like Hegel, wants to avoid two opposed yet equally dissatisfying forms of human life—that is, either giving oneself up to the "particular" natural passions in life and hence reducing oneself to an animal, or submitting oneself to the "universal" demands of the community. Rather, subjects can become individuals by weaving together particular desires and universal norms in my distinctive fashion. This fashion is not up to the whim of the moment, but is the accumulation of a series of previous actions in the past that cohere into an intelligible unified history guided by a single agent. Such a history, in being not a natural occurrence nor devoted to some higher cause but rather an artifice created by my will over time, closely resembles a piece of art. A good work of art is the work of a single hand that structures a series of particular events such that a general law or meaning emerges out of this series. Like Kant's view of the "aesthetic idea," this meaning is not subsumable under an abstract universal, nor is it reducible to its component parts; rather, it is an individual totality in which onlookers are invited to play among the whole and the parts.

Thus, not only is the individual life like a work of art, but the individual actor resembles the creative artist in continuing to produce this life. In this way, the individual engages in something like an improvisational art, being both character and author at the same time. The individual subject seeks to be the author of his own life, and so to do so must act creatively by judging what ought to come next given the artistic whole that precedes him. In UM 3.1, Nietzsche describes the process of how we should discern the meaningful whole or law that precedes us:

> What have you truly loved up to now, what has drawn your soul aloft, what has mastered it and at the same time blessed it? Set up these revered objects before you and perhaps their nature and their sequence will give you a law [*Gesetz*], the fundamental law of

your own true self. Compare these objects one with another, see how one completes, expands, surpasses, transfigures another, how they constitute a stepladder upon which you have clambered up to yourself as you are now; for your true nature lies, not concealed deep within you, but immeasurably high above you.

The result is an aesthetic "law," one not formulable in advance in rational terms, but only provisionally constructed from the past that points towards—but does not determine—some higher future self. As Ridley (2007) puts the point in the context of artistic creation, "When Beethoven saw, for example, how the coda to the finale of his C-minor symphony had to go, he was answerable to the demands of his material: he could have got it right, he could have got it wrong. But prior to his compositional act no one, himself included, could have stated a rule for arriving at what he arrived at. Rather, he 'strictly' and 'subtly' obeyed laws that emerged only in the course of his 'performance'—that were . . . internal to the exercise of his agency" (214).

In other words, there is a provisional relationship between the whole and parts of my individual identity that precedes the individual action. The individual is "answerable" to this relationship just as one is "answerable" for a promise one has made (GM 2.1)—he cannot "change the subject" and do something different without risking the loss of individual identity altogether. Yet this provisional relationship between whole and the parts does not dictate what is to come next, any more than the last line of *Hamlet*'s act 4 necessarily indicated to Shakespeare how he ought to have finished the play. Shakespeare may have had an idea of the events that would transpire in act 5; a few phrases may even have popped into his mind before its composition. But Nietzsche's point is that the activity of creation itself transforms the relationship between whole and parts. The creative activity brings into being a new set of parts, new actions, new experiences and the like.[50] Meanwhile, these new parts transform the nature of the whole in which they are embedded. The C-minor symphony was not what it is, a completed whole, before Beethoven completed the coda. The activity of completing the coda brought into focus what had been an inchoate "whole" or rather fuzzy relationship between whole and parts. If, for instance, whole and parts were complete and fully realized, then there would be no need for further aesthetic exploration. The fact that the law, the central narrative meaning of my life or my piece of artwork, is in question when I come to act necessitates individual action itself. Also, human action gives itself a law in the very process of acting, a law that is fundamentally consonant with what had come before, but that brings into sharper clarity than before what the totality of experiences, actions, musical movements that had come before all meant.

A good deal is packed in to this summary of the argument. Let us elaborate, then, on the components of an artistically structured individual life. Three are of crucial importance for Nietzsche: an individual life must display unity amidst diversity, self-determination, and uniqueness. First, an individual life must be extremely diverse yet at the same time must somehow be unified as a single character, not a series of partial characters arbitrarily set beside one another in the course of a life.[51] The basis of this criterion is that the individual subject longs to realize itself in the world, which means it must unify the results of its labors, as "our conception of the ego does not guarantee any actual unity" (WP 635). The unity of apperception is a practical achievement of subjectivity, not something given, in which the "'I' would be a synthesis that only gets produced through itself" (BGE 54).[52] It is very difficult to craft a self that testifies unmistakably to the "single taste that ruled and shaped everything great and small" (GS 290). Our bodies contain a swirling contradiction of desires, and in societies we have a multitude of different commitments and duties that often conflict with one another. We often participate in very different activities and communities within which we play different roles. As a consequence, we find ourselves torn between these different identities in some cases—which is the real me? How do we "organize the chaos" within us (UM 2.10)?

We achieve the unity of my character amidst the diversity of my commitments by telling a story about myself. Such a "story" is a meaningful narrative whole that draws connections among these different commitments and accords them a certain place or function within the whole. In giving this parade of different characteristics and commitments of my self a particular role, I make them my own, part of a single story of my life, rather than a random assortment of different lives existing alongside one another. Nietzsche himself seeks to tell such a story in his *Ecce Homo*, by, for instance, tracing out the two parts of his personality, one side stemming from his father and the other from his mother (EH Wise.1). Nietzsche envisions this aesthetic unity at the communal level as well, when he argues that a "culture" is characterized by a "unity of style," a historically evolving way of life collectively narrated by the culture's people (UM 1.1).

Just as my subjective will seeks a unity of individual character in the world such that it can see its own agency at work, it balks at excessive unification. One "must still have chaos in oneself to be able to give birth to a dancing star," Zarathustra says (Z P.5). The only way in which the subject can appear in the world is if it unifies those opposites that threaten to tear it apart—hence, in order for it to appear, there must be opposites. Fortunately, in the modern age all "races are mixed together" and "conflicting drives and value standards" constantly "fight with each other," such that the homogeneity of human character characteristic of premodern societies becomes impossible (BGE 200). In the modern world, each of us thinks of himself as belonging to many different communities with multiple competing identities and standards of ethical behavior. For many people, Nietzsche thinks, the result of such excessive diversification will result in an inability to unify one's personality and make oneself into an individual. Yet at the same time, this "age of disintegration" arouses a tremendous effort of narrative virtuosity on the part of "those amazing, incomprehensible, and unthinkable ones" who will outshine any individual the ancient world produced (BGE 200).[53]

Indeed, for Nietzsche, the relationship between unity and difference can be a salutary dialectical one. Every attempt on the part of the individual subject to fashion a unified meaning among its various determinations will inevitably fail, insufficiently taking account of other past beliefs or desires or inadequately accounting for ever new, surprising experiences that can change drastically the "meaning" of my life heretofore. We do not understand the depths of our own character, and hence we may unearth something in ourselves that we had never thought was there—we are "unknown to ourselves, we knowers" (GM P.1). Additionally, many of the components of my self will exist in an uneasy tension or outright contradiction with one another—such an inner struggle creates a tension of spirit (the "tension in the bow" image Nietzsche repeatedly uses) that prompts the subject to find a way to incorporate these tensions on a higher level of unity, to "sublate" them. The individual subject is moved to "self-overcoming" (*Selbstüberwindung*) in order to reconstitute his unity on the basis of a new and more comprehensive identity (BGE 257). Thus, the attempt to create a unity out of one's diversity is always provisional, since new experiences always come flooding in, upending the simple identity one has crafted for oneself up to that point. The identity one creates, then, is always incomplete. One is always on the way to individuating oneself, and one's act of self-unification always destroys itself and must be reconstituted again and again at a higher, more comprehensive level. For this reason, one's "true nature" lies "immeasurably high above you," always outside of every attempt one makes to impose unity on the plurality (UM 3.1).[54] If an individual self comes to "completion," if it unifies all its parts under one determinate meaning, the individual becomes dissatisfied. The subject becomes locked in what increasingly comes to be experienced as a rote routine, a mechanical habit, an ossified structure of life. The human subject, having the same formal structure and aim as a living organism, always seeks to expand and grow—stasis and contraction are the signs of declining life. "Life" in the human world is driven in large part through this dialectic of unity and diversity.

For a human subject, the greater the diversity, the greater the effort of unification required. But just as in a work of art, a strong unity amidst tremendous difference amounts to a greater or nobler individual character. The subject that can extend itself far and wide testifies to the enormous strength of its subjectivity to withstand contradiction the more it incorporates ever more divergent features. One's "freedom" in Nietzsche's terms is measured by "the resistance that needs to be overcome, by the effort that it costs to stay on top" and hence to unify one's individuality and satisfy subjectivity (TI 9.38). Nietzsche describes this ability of the subject as its "plastic power" (*plastische Kraft*). The plastic power of a culture, for instance, refers to how much a single culture can stretch without breaking in incorporating a multitude of different values and belief systems—its ability, in other words, to maintain and impose its internal hierarchical structure despite ever new challenges to this value system from the outside (UM 2.1). For Nietzsche, the Greeks were unparalleled in their formidable plastic power—they endured a "chaos of foreign, Semitic, Babylonian, Lydian, Egyptian forms and ideas," and "yet, thanks to that Apollonian oracle, Hellenic culture was no mere aggregate." The Greeks were able to "organize the chaos" and hence forge a unity out of this tremendous diversity, and hence are a "parable for each one of us" (UM 2.10).

Thus, individuality is indexed according to degrees of this same plastic power, the degree to which his unity can incorporate ever new diverse determinations and still maintain its coherence.[55] The human being who has no internal complexity is not much of an individual because he leads an empty life, one without passion or aim. Also, the human being with a complex inner chaos within him has little individuality as well because he is unable to harmonize these various competing characteristics into a whole—the individual's life seems to be haphazard in the way a sloppy piece of artwork is carelessly thrown together. On the other hand, the individual who is strong enough to unify a large number of competing determinations leads a life that resembles a complex and interesting work of art. The life is like a Melville novel or Beethoven sonata, in which parts and whole are harmonized in the action of individuals.

The second standard for individuality is the degree to which one's character appears self-determined. That is, this unity of self we have been describing must appear as *one's own* unity. The narrative coherence must not appear forced, imposed from some outside determination, otherwise the human subject will not be able to find itself in its own personality. We all know, for instance, those "individuals" who go out of their way to appear flamboyant and unique, and hence their style is forced, inauthentic, rooted in a pathological need to be socially liked, rather than a genuine self-determination. A genuine self-determination, by contrast, is one in which parts and whole seem made for one another. A true individual life appears as tailor-made for him; to take Nietzsche's favorite example, Goethe came into existence precisely to lead the sort of life that he led. Put otherwise, the individual life is a series of experiences and actions *necessarily* connected to one another as part of a total story. There is no contingency, no "and then this happened," since such contingencies would involve the imposition of some external agency on the internal workings of the narrative. In this way, there does not appear to be any external agency at work in doing the rough work of producing this self. As Nietzsche puts the point in reference to "artists": "Their feeling of freedom, finesse and authority, of creation, formation, and control only reaches its apex when they have stopped doing anything 'voluntarily' [*willkürlich*] and instead do everything necessarily,—in short, they know that inside themselves necessity and 'freedom of the will' [*Notwendigkeit und 'Freiheit des Willens'*] have become one" (BGE 213). The self-determination of the self accords with what we might expect—since the individual is producing himself, there is nothing "from the outside" molding the individual subject. The necessary unfolding of a life is accordingly a testament to a self-determined life. The self appears much like the result of an organic growth, or, better put, a seamless artistic whole.

Again, the self-determined life shares this characteristic with a good work of art. A true drama, for instance, will make the transitions from scene to scene, the transformation of character, the events of the denouement necessary rather than contingent. As one scene flows into another, the characters seem to come alive, and the end could not have been any different than it is. In all these cases, the artist's actual agency or "pen" recedes into the background and we as audience members "look on" as the necessity of the events unfold before us. At the thematic level of the whole, we cannot imagine this theme being explored in any other way than the way that the play itself explored it. This ideal is what Hegel has in mind when he speaks of the "Idea," in which the whole "differentiates itself" into its own parts (EL 237). The artist is successful, in Hegel's view, when the "shape itself lives and stands out," as when "Phidias has no mannerisms," when Phidias's constructive hand fades from view, when the thematic whole appears to be what makes these different parts necessary. It was not a matter of "particularity and arbitrariness" (*Willkür*) and artistic choice—and in BGE 13, Nietzsche's invocation of the Hegelian terms *willkürlich* versus *Freiheit* reveals their similarity—but the author was "inspired," we could say, by the internal logic of the work itself (PR 15Z).

Thus, Nietzsche claims, within the genuine individual character, "thinking and [one's] character stand in a relationship characterized by strictest necessity [*Notwendigkeit*]" (PTA 31). That is, in order for one's self to be self-determined, one's subjectivity or "thinking" and one's substance or "character" must come into a unity. The "law" of one's self must suffuse the different parts of oneself such that it comes to be "an instinct, [one's] dominant instinct" (GM 2.2). Consider, by contrast, what happens when an individual self or artwork is not characterized by such self-determination. In such a case, the dissatisfied subject must endure a strong distinction between his inner life and his outer action (UM 2.4; cf. GS 6). Hence, the subject has difficulty translating his thoughts into action, but rather suffers from *akrasia*, in which particular desires or social norms direct his actions.[56] Similarly, bad artwork appears clunky and contrived, having several scenes or a theme that does not seem to "belong" to it. Such an artwork bears the trace of many different "personalities" at work struggling to make the artistic whole their own. The artwork hence loses its unity and becomes, at best, three or four plays in one. An individual life, by the same token, can appear "forced" and affected as well. The life which contains many "contingent" happenings driven by many different competing drives or value systems reveals itself to be a life not entirely in control of itself. Several other external forces or drives, those nature or social determinations swirling within one, pierce the self-enclosed whole of individuality, undermining its wholeness by injecting contingency into its otherwise seamlessly unified narrative.

Now clearly, no actual individual can achieve such a seamlessly unified narrative for himself—all of us contain selves with many "contingent happenings." As in the case with unity and diversity, so too here, the norm of self-determination is a regulative ideal, one we constantly strive to realize by degrees but never quite attain fully. Some can have more individuality than others. However, Nietzsche asks us to respond to a different challenge on this point. In many points in an individual life, there are many "contingent happenings" that are deeply painful, shameful, even harrowing. For many, the temptation is to narrate a life that excludes this suffering, thereby painting an illusory rosy picture over the more dreadful things lying beneath. For Nietzsche, such a temptation should be resisted for a few reasons. First, suffering can augment our character by allowing our subjectivity to gain the capacity to overcome such obstacles independently. Papering over such painful parts of one's life makes one particularly unable to respond to such problems when they arise again. Second, these painful experiences cannot simply be narrated away. Suffering is more powerful than happiness in lodging itself into our memory (GM 2.3), and hence it makes an indelible mark on our character whether we like it or not. For Nietzsche, then, individuals can gain satisfaction through these ineradicable parts of their character by adopting an attitude of *amor fati*. This is not a metaphysical fatalism, but rather the affirmation of all parts of one's past, not just the good parts.[57] To be truly affirmed, I must weave even these elements of my character into an ongoing narrative, revealing them as a necessary part of the development of my personality. In taking what is "fragment and riddle and dreadful accident" and "will[ing]" it, the individual thereby "redeems" [*erlösen*] the suffering of his past—the only possible theodicy for Nietzsche, as we'll see in the next chapter (Z:2 "On Redemption"). In willing his saints and his demons, then, the individual does not take them "as is," but rather the very act of willing consists in affirming and transforming them into meaningful episodes in the history of his character.

The final standard of individuality is uniqueness, which Nietzsche stresses in UM 3.1. The self-determining unity of a life that the individual creates for himself is even greater if it is like nothing we have ever seen before or will see again. Even if the individual falls short of uniqueness, he nonetheless should achieve a certain degree of distinctness from others in order to claim those experiences and actions of his life as his own. That is, for an individual's actions to be his own, they must be intelligible as part of the individual's self-constructed personality, consistent with the other actions he performs and the idiosyncratic self he has constructed. A person's actions should not be intelligible simply based on social norms or biological imperatives. In such a case, he would be leading a life cobbled together from fragments of many other lives. In order to escape the gravitational pull of being "part" of the "whole" orbit of either society or nature, the individual has to display himself as distinct from these, as similar only to himself.

This uniqueness is not the singularity of, say, an extremely rare gem.

Rather, the unique individual self has made itself into such a singularity. In this way, its unique actions take on a peculiarly self-related character. All of the individual's actions point back to the individual himself as the originator and author of his deeds—"no one can construct for you the bridge upon which precisely you must cross the stream of life, no one but you yourself alone" (UM 3.1). The self-identical nature of uniqueness is important for human subjectivity because the human subject gains satisfaction in seeing itself reflected back at itself in the self it creates, in finding itself at the end of the "stepladder upon which you have clambered up to yourself" (UM 3.1). Thus, this uniqueness most fundamentally makes my subjectivity whole in unifying myself with myself, my subjectivity with the individuality it has created. Uniqueness is, in a sense, the crown of the formal virtues I have outlined thus far. It allows my subjectivity to claim this individuality as mine and mine alone. This individuality owes nothing to some social movements or political institutions; it is intelligible based on itself alone. It does not contain an echo of other individualities, nor am I simply a "one-trick pony," repeating my own unique insight over and over again. Rather, the totality of my life is the construction of my own subjectivity, and all my actions have as their aim the continuous construction of my free individuality. I "demonstrate" through my own unique life "why and to what end we came into existence now and at no other time" (UM 3.1). My actions are "justified" (*rechtfertigt*) as parts of my unique "whole." In this construction, one "ceases to be the toy [becoming] plays with," in which becoming "disperses the individual [*Individuum*] to the four winds," where the individual's actions are merely vehicles for some other will. Rather, the unique individual reflects back to himself the meaning of his own existence and becomes whole in his own, self-determined "being" (UM 3.4). I will have much more to say about this justificatory or redemptive character of individuality in the next chapter.

The above three normative criteria set the standard for what makes for a true individual, an individual life that will make the human subject whole. These criteria are similar to those we apply to aesthetic objects. However, for Nietzsche, the aesthetic model abstracts too much from the substantive goals of human individuals in particular historical communities. Nietzsche is no defender of "art for art's sake," since such artistic independence implies that the goal of life is ascetic, to be a self-enclosed world like a novel, insulated and removed from life with others, a curiosity to others, a life to be wondered at and appreciated from a distance, like the *Mona Lisa*.[58] This view of the human aesthetic, which Nehamas (1985) invokes, is not true to Nietzsche because it fails to take account of the human good in which these aesthetic criteria are embedded.[59] I have shown in this chapter that these characteristics are grounded for Nietzsche only on the basis of a more comprehensive project of living a full human life. Yet, as we will see in the next chapter, living an individual life requires ethical participation in human communities. Indeed, like Hegel, Nietzsche argues that not only are human beings thoroughly shaped by their historical communities, but individuals only come to be through a certain kind of participation in the public good. The crucial difference between the two, as we'll see, is that for Nietzsche, the human subject longs to be a founder of human communities, not simply a follower.

6

Nietzsche on the Redemptive Individual

In the previous chapter, I articulated and defended Nietzsche's view of individuality, while also bringing out how much Nietzsche's view shares in common with Hegel's. Though this self-narrating individual may seem to be a radically solitary character, emerging out of his own effort and discipline, Nietzsche claims that there are certain historical and political conditions that produce individuals. Nietzsche speaks again and again of various communities providing the right or wrong kinds of conditions for the cultivation of higher forms of humanity (see, e.g., BGE 211–12). We will explore several of these conditions in this chapter and the next. The more important and deeper case I want to make, however, is that Nietzsche defended an ethical connection between individuality and community. That is, for Nietzsche, leading an individual life requires that one "redeem" a community, that one incorporate and transform its experiences and traditions into a meaningful narrative. My view hence challenges two competing ethical views: that of the liberal Nietzsche, in which one's self-fashioning can occur in "private" separate from the community; and that of the radically aristocratic Nietzsche, in which individuals strive to remake community in their own image from the ground up.[1]

   In order to make this case, I argue that first, for Nietzsche, community or what Nietzsche calls "culture" plays a crucial function for human beings in providing meaning for human life and hence avoiding the paralyzing terror of "Silenus' truth." Human beings become individuals by enlivening and transforming this communal store of meaning, especially during times of crisis. Alternatively, we may become individuals by critiquing the communal tradition when it is overly narrow or repressive, and then by appealing to the wider fellowship of humanity as such.[2] In either case, individuals "become who they are" by making a community "their own," a process that is reciprocal—community is shaped by individuality, individuality is shaped by community. In this way, then, individuals cannot retreat from community (as the liberals assume), but must always already engage in it. However, individuals are rare and play an aristocratic role in society (as the aristocrats claim), but Nietzsche's "aristocracy" is one of "spirit," the transformation of culture through the activity of human excellence, not political, physical, brutish coercion.[3]

6.1   The Tension in the Bow and Human Community

In the preface to BGE, Nietzsche claims that the "struggle against Plato" and the subsequent struggle against Christianity, or dogmatic "Platonism for the people," by modern skepticism has "created a magnificent tension of spirit in Europe, the likes of which the earth has never known: with such a tension in our bow we can now shoot at the furthest goals" (BGE.P). This tension is, as we will see, a particularly powerful example of the universal tension that pervades all human societies. Nietzsche speaks of this broader tension in different forms—in UM 2.1, he speaks of the tension between justice and love, and in BGE 230, he discusses what Clark and Dudrick (2006) have called the "will to truth" and the "will to value." I will employ later the rather more colorful tension between *eris* and *eros*, Greek concepts that Nietzsche draws on heavily in his social theory. This tension lies at the center of Nietzsche's view of human community and is rooted in the basic internal division, incompleteness, or "sickness" of the distinctively human.

Let us examine this tension to understand its nature and why it is rooted in the general condition of being human. We will begin with the first part of the tension, with the side Nietzsche speaks about in various terms as "love," the will to "simplification, falsification," the "dogmatism" of philosophers. Nietzsche argues that human beings are living beings, similar to all other organic beings in that we desire to extend and consolidate our subjectivity (we discussed this activity of the subject as the "will to power" in the previous chapter). Human beings achieve mastery over nature and over ourselves most prominently in our social existence. We constitute communities by collectively "esteeming" the world in a certain way, by "assessing, preferring, being unfair, being limited" in relationship to nature and the other communities around us (BGE 9). We transform the world in our own image according to our "table of goods" such that we can live and act within this home we have made for ourselves (Z:1 "Thousand and One"). This "world" that we create for ourselves is a value-laden one—we give ourselves our own principle of the good, which binds us to living a certain way of life.

Yet such an "esteeming" nature involves a "closing [of] horizons," a willful "ignorance" about nature, a "falsification" of the complexities of nature and other cultures (BGE 230; UM 2.1). Without such "falsification," however, man "could not live" (BGE 24, 34). We are each of us finite in our capacity to grasp the plentiful nuances of the world, and hence we develop an innate psychological tendency to simplify the world by transforming it into something that bears our own image, something that appears more familiar and less threatening to us (GS 355). Nietzsche speaks of this "esteeming" drive as our tendency to "love," in the sense of loving what is one's own, what resembles, sustains, and extends our own subjectivity, even though what is one's own involves being "unjust towards what lies behind [us]" (UM 2.1). The "dogmatist" builds his philosophical systems precisely on these falsifications, on an "over-eager generalization from facts," a lack of attention to nuance and difference (BGE.P). In short, the demands of "life"—in the form of either our natural, biological desires or those of our community—overwhelm our due attention to truth.

The other part of the tension concerns the distinctively human qualities of "justice," the will to truth, to depth, to complexity, and the "skepticism" of philosophers. Whereas the first part of the tension concerned what human beings share in common with the animals, this part deals with the fact that human beings are unlike other living beings.[4] We can reflectively question the deliverances of both nature and of society. We can come to see our "horizons" for what they are, namely, limitations or illusory projections onto the world and others. Our reason allows us to escape from our parochial conventions and to reveal conventional norms as the falsifying imposition of the will of a collective subject, rather than as what is real and true in itself as these conventions purport to be. The "will to appearances, to simplification, to masks" hence "meets resistance" here, in this "sublime tendency of the knower, who treats and wants to treat things in a profound, multiple, and thorough manner" (BGE 230). Whereas the will to appearance involves "love," this will to know upholds "justice" as its highest value—the "demon of knowledge" does not manipulate and falsify things so that the world begins to resemble him, but rather he respects and treats each part of the world as it is (UM 2.6). Justice demands that our parochial love of our own be overcome so that we treat nature and other cultures as they are in themselves—the just man "holds the scales" and "sets weight upon weight with inexorable disregard of himself" (UM 2.6). "Absolute skepticism," for instance, does not take any claim for granted (as the dogmatist does), even if such a false presupposition would be edifying (WP 409; cf. BGE 209). Yet as a result, the drive for wisdom is in tension with the fundamental drives of life (Z:2 "Dancing Song").

The "absolute negativity" of human reason—to reflect, to question, to tear down "superstition" (BGE P)—creates this tension, but itself has its origins in natural drives. For Nietzsche, as for Hegel, reason is not a separate "faculty" of a disembodied mind.[5] On the contrary, reason emerged as a "rebellion," as it were, against our esteeming natures themselves. What we call "reason"—and the wisdom that it reveals—is the fundamental tendency of life, the extension of subjectivity, turned against itself.[6] Put otherwise, reason is the activity of esteeming of our capacity for esteeming. The rebellion of reason occurs in the slave "rebellion" against natural, master morality in Nietzsche's speculative human history. All human societies begin in a condition of natural inequality, in which stronger natural human beings oppress more peaceful natural beings, imposing their will on the latter (GM 2.17). The "slaves" are no longer able to exercise their subjective agency as the capacity to maintain and extend their will in the world.[7] Rather, they are subject to the alien agency of another—they see not themselves, but another's will reflected back at them, just as in Hegel's master-slave relationship. For Nietzsche, the slave's subjective desire to "esteem" does not cease (since esteeming is a basic condition of "life" as such), but rather finds a new outlet—the slave's subjectivity begins to find its agency in esteeming the masters' esteeming. Slaves responded to the brute strength of the masters by interpreting their strength as injustice. Instead of acting spontaneously and immediately from themselves as the masters did, the slaves reacted to their master's nature (and their own passions), by obeying a higher law, a law that they gave to themselves in the form of a god. According to this higher law, the masters are "evil" and will be punished in the long run, whereas the slaves are the "good" and empowered ones—they, the meek, will inherit the earth. The slaves hence subjected themselves to a collective, divine will opposed to the order of natural strength and domination (GM 1.13).

This "drive for knowledge," then, "can be traced back to a drive to appropriate and conquer" like any esteeming drive (WP 423). For the "war" against nature and the spontaneity of life to be successful, the slaves had to impose their rigorous spiritual, antinatural morality on themselves, their own desires, as well. This self-discipline led at once to the tremendous "internalization" of human beings (GM 2.16), a great "depth" of soul (GM 1.6), along with the capacity to promise (GM 2.1) and the possibility of human normativity in general (we explored this point, on the "straitjacketing" of humanity for its normative development, in the previous chapter). Under such discipline, passions were forced underground; they became internal, expanding and flowering in the inner self. The entire development of the rationalism of Socrates and the Enlightenment liberal democracy was an attempt to be "cruel" to nature by replacing its cruelty and harshness with justice (BGE 229).

My point here is not to trace the development of "slave morality," but rather to bring out what for Nietzsche is the source of the "sublime tendency of the knower" in the development of the distinctively human: the perennial tendency of the distinctively human to rebel against nature, to master the masters' natural will in society or in one's own body (insofar as each one of us is naturally dominated by natural passions). The slaves in all periods of human history learn the lesson of the priestly class as to what the best means to master nature is—that is, intellectualizing it, learning the "truth" about the world as it is (TI 9.8). Consequently, in achieving knowledge about the world, we endure a "fall" from our immediate immersion in nature—Nietzsche's Christian understanding here is unmistakable. Nietzsche says that "we knowers of today . . . still take our fire too from the flame lit by the thousand-year old faith, the Christian faith which was also Plato's faith, that God is truth, that truth is divine" (GS 344). Or, rather, we might say that the Hegelian influence is powerful—human beings begin immediately immersed in nature and then "fall" into a reflective state in which we distance ourselves from nature in our attempt to impose our will on it. Such a "fall" involves a tremendous tension between our natural desire to "esteem" the world in a simplified or falsified fashion, and hence to live within it, and our reflective desire to question these simplifications, and hence to upset the world that has come to oppress our own desire for agency.

Nietzsche rejects the Hegelian view that the tension between our fallen, reflective natures and our natural "immediacy" is finally reconcilable, however. For Nietzsche, the human being is the being torn internally by these two impulses, or two "wills," as he sometimes puts it—the "glance" that "plunges into the height" and the "will" that "clings to man" (Z:2 "Human Prudence"). For Nietzsche, our reason can never be reconciled with our esteeming nature, since all forms of esteeming are based on some unquestioned assumption that reason can reveal. Even the highly "rationalist" "table of goods," such as the one established by Socrates, rests on a dogmatic moral system, in which nature ought to be "corrected" (BT 13). The truth that Kant and Schopenhauer reveal is that the "will to truth," when turned against itself, reveals that there is no rational justification for such a rational pursuit (BT 18)—reason cannot even offer a justification as to why it should pursue truth rather than error, nor why nature should be corrected rather than let alone. In Nietzsche's terms, "logic curls up around itself at these limits and finally bites its own tail" (BT 15). The desire for knowledge is built on just as faulty a foundation as any other superstitious worldview, since every philosophy "creates the world in its own image"—in understanding the complex world in our own terms, we inevitably falsify and simplify the world (BGE 9). Thus, the development of the reflective drive leads inevitably to an unbridgeable standoff with life—reflection calls into question all principles that inform action, even the very impulses that lead to reflection in the first place.

Hence, the reflective nature of human beings always endangers our capacity to live. The danger is especially dire in times of social-political upheaval and the historical transition to a new culture, when a "table of goods" that a people had unreflectively embraced becomes increasingly an object of scrutiny until its authority erodes and it no longer motivates and consoles. Living in such times, these "latecomers" eventually adopt an "ironic self-consciousness" about their goods, hovering above life in a state of perpetual self-reflection (UM 2.8). Reflection, then, corrodes action. It tears us away from living in the world; it paralyzes us, and we live like Hamlet, perpetually in a state of indecision (BT 7). Reflection does this in two ways. First of all, it undermines all human standards of good or valuable action. Any principle of the good can be questioned or revealed as a parochial "preference," a "falsification." We can oppose any principle of action with another practical principle and stand unable to adjudicate the dispute rationally. Caught in an endless process of reflecting on how best to act, human agency becomes increasingly paralyzed, abstracting further and further away from the concrete, practical world with others, and hence human subjectivity fails to extend itself in the world and find wholeness. For Nietzsche, this problem is most dire in the modern age, when "all perspectives have been shifted back to the beginning of all becoming, back into infinity [*Unendliche*]," such that the "demands of life alone no longer reign and exercise constraint on knowledge" (UM 2.4).

Second, reflection imprisons us within our own endlessly questioning negativity, but it also corrodes the impetus for action by disenchanting the world out there. That is, even if we find a principle according to which we should exercise our agency, our reflection strips the world of any and all significance in which my action could find meaning. This is the fate of Hamlet, for whom action is "repulsive, for their actions can do nothing to change the eternal essence of things; they regard it as laughable or shameful that they should be expected to set to rights a world so out of joint" (BT 7). For Nietzsche, reason reveals all human worlds as poetically created worlds, conventions that simplify and falsify the nature they purport to reveal. Reason unveils these conventions as little more than fairy tales in which this community can glorify itself in its deeds and stories. Yet once these conventions are revealed as conventions, as falsifying impositions of meaning, actions performed according to or within these conventions lose significance. Our subjectivity no longer finds satisfaction in this life when reason intervenes, because reason pierces through these conventions, turning what was solid into air. What had reflected the subject's identity back to him and made him whole now leaves him incomplete and dissatisfied.

6.2   Silenus' Truth

In dissolving all human conventions, the reflective subject bottoms out in coming face to face with nature, yet a nature that is not a welcoming home to his longing for meaning, but rather a nature that is cruel and indifferent—the subject learns the "terrible truth" that nature is meaningless in itself (BT 7).[8] A wholly disenchanted world leaves the subject in the melancholy state of longing for meaning while finding all socially constructed forms of meaning illusory and nature a realm of chance and indifference. In such a disenchanted world, suffering and death—those evils that had been rendered meaningful within a human community—become pressing problems for the human soul. Religion, for instance, tells a story about human life and nature that renders both the toils of life and the inevitability of death significant. The suffering we endure is important—even desirable—as, for instance, a test of our devotion to a deity. If we endure particularly bad suffering with virtuous activity, we will be rewarded. It is not easy to endure nor to witness pain, but it is possible when man considers himself to have "*meaning* [Sinn], from now on he was no longer like a leaf in the breeze, the plaything of the absurd, of 'non-sense'; from now on he could *will* something" (GM 3.28). Yet it is infinitely more difficult to endure and witness pain when this suffering is not made intelligible as part of some kind of human convention or religion, but rather is a random, meaningless event in nature. Animals, for instance, endure constant torment, and nature is entirely indifferent to their plight: "No harder fate can be thought of than that of the beast of prey pursued through the wilderness by the most gnawing torment, rarely satisfied and even then in such a way that satisfaction is purchased only with the pain of lacerating combat with other animals. . . . To hang on to life madly and blindly, with no higher aim than to hang on to it . . . that is what it means to be an animal" (UM 3.5). Similarly, the random natural "evils," such as hurricanes, tsunamis, and earthquakes, claim the lives of thousands of human beings every year. There is a certain torment for the human subject who cannot master nature and thus find a meaningful home in it, but rather is faced with a harsh and alien world.

Yet even if one can escape the random suffering and death nature causes, no organic being can escape death finally. The fact of death confronts all organic life eventually with the complete dissolution of the body (AC 40). The fear of death does not haunt animals, who live moment to moment, but it does haunt human beings, who recognize that all their efforts, their striving, will come to nothing at the end of their life. Each of us will recede back into the stream of becoming, our uniqueness consumed, never to be seen again. Such a fear of death may make us wonder what is the point of constant striving, of the incessant worries of our day-to-day lives. If our constant strivings "do nothing to change the eternal essence of things," then what is the point (BT 7)? By contrast, within a human convention, death is rendered significant because, for the Greeks for instance, a beautiful death will be remembered and hence will be meaningful within that community. Yet when reflection is fully aroused, such conventions appear as mere fairy tales with no consoling force.

"Tragic knowledge" is for Nietzsche the knowledge of the falsity of all human conventions and the meaninglessness of nature.[9] It is the "truth" of the whole, and it is a paralyzing truth, one that undermines our capacity to "esteem" and hence to act—"it could even be part of the fundamental character of existence that people with complete knowledge get destroyed" (BGE 39).[10] For Nietzsche, such "tragic knowledge" creates a tortured subjectivity, one who longs for meaning and finds it nowhere, and in continuing to live must endure evils which are completely senseless.[11] This is the extremity of the reflective drive of human beings, when the tortured subjectivity confronts Silenus' truth, which states that it is better for human beings "never to have been born," second best to "die soon," to return to the stream of becoming

(BT 3). That is, it is better for the distinctively human never to have come into existence and experience this horrific realization of the "wound" at the center of existence, that is, the wound within human beings, their perpetually frustrated longing for meaning.[12] Human subjectivity makes us worse off than animals when coming to this realization of the senselessness of existence. When we come to recognize that our reflection, our memory, brings with it the knowledge of loss, regret, trepidation, we even "envy" the cow's "happiness" (UM 2.1). In other words, for Nietzsche, the human being most fundamentally is not naturally attracted to life. The human being is the only being who can commit suicide. The fundamental experience of human freedom, then, is one of personal horror in the face of the irrationality of existence. For Nietzsche, human beings must possess some kind of artificial reason to stay in existence. To put the point in another way, Nietzsche encourages us to affirm life. Yet his enjoining us to affirm life presupposes that the value of life is somehow in question. Nietzsche imagines what would happen if such deadly knowledge were to spread to the general public—when

> man's instinctive lust for life would probably have been so weakened amidst general wars of extinction and unceasing migrations that, with suicide having become habitual, the individual would be bound to feel the last remnant of a sense of duty when . . . he throttles his parents as their son . . . a practical pessimism which could generate a horrifying ethic of genocide . . . a pessimism, incidentally, which exists, and has existed, throughout the entire world, whenever art has not appeared in one form or other, especially as religion or science, to heal and to ward off the breath of that pestilence. (BT 15)

The unleashing of this knowledge is a particular problem for the modern age, as we have seen, in which "God is dead" and all "horizons" of meaning have been extended to infinity. The modern age, then, is particularly susceptible to such a "practical pessimism."[13] At the same time, Nietzsche worries that the confrontation with this nihilism will lead modern human beings simply to give up the pursuit of meaning in the first place and hence become immersed in our bodily pleasures and become animals, as he recounts in the haunting "last man" speech of Zarathustra's (Z.P.5). Accordingly, for Nietzsche, the "coming generations" will be faced with this "terrible" dilemma: "either abolish your venerations" through increased skepticism or "yourselves" as distinctively human beings. Both, Nietzsche claims, are forms of "nihilism" that we moderns must avoid (GS 346).[14] In this context, Nietzsche seeks to engage in a "critique of knowledge," to trace the limits of where the human subject ought to stop pursuing knowledge and put that "knowledge in the service of the best life" by justifying a community aesthetically (UUM 19.35).[15]

6.3   The Aesthetic Justification of Existence

Nietzsche argues that the foundational task of human community—especially in the form of artistic cultures—is to overcome Silenus' truth, and thereby save us from losing our "esteeming" desires entirely. We overcome Silenus' truth by providing for ourselves a "justification" (*Rechtfertigung*) for the irrationalities of human life (BT.Attempt.5). Nietzsche understands such a "justification" in the tradition of his German predecessors such as Leibniz as a "theodicy," an attempt to show why seemingly meaningless forms of evil are actually justified as necessary parts in a divine plan (BT 3). Silenus' truth is a particularly thorny version of the problem of evil—one that paralyzes our practical lives in addition to establishing the incomplete rationality of the cosmos—and hence Nietzsche argues that we must justify this apparent evil. However, we are "justifying" existence not for the sake of an illusory divinity, but rather so that it can appear to us as a home worthy of human habitation, rather than a cruel and indifferent nature. Also unlike his German predecessors, Nietzsche rejects a rationalist approach to the justification of existence. We cannot reason our way out of Silenus' truth, since reason is what got us into trouble in the first place. Reason is ultimately corrosive, not constructive. But neither can we jettison our tortured subjectivity and embrace a state of unreflective "last man" animality without giving up on the distinctively human.

As we saw in the previous chapter, so too here, Nietzsche invokes the category of the "aesthetic" to solve the problem of Silenus. As Nietzsche puts it, "life is made possible and worth living" as a result of art (BT 1). We "possess art lest we perish of the truth" (WP 822). The artist shows the "desirability of life," such that art "is the great stimulus to life"; it reveals "fearlessness in the face of the fearful and questionable" (TI 9.24). Or, in Nietzsche's famous phrase, existence is "justified" (*rechtfertigt*) only as an "aesthetic phenomenon" (BT Attempt.5; BT 5). Such a claim, that the aesthetic is the route to the justification of existence—rather than the rational, which one might assume, given Nietzsche's invocation of the traditional term "justification"—has puzzled inter-preters. Just what does Nietzsche mean?

Nietzsche interpreters generally agree that the "aesthetic justifica-tion of existence" is directed at the problem of the meaning of human existence. Yet they are divided about both the nature and function of an aesthetic justification. Interpreters tend to read Nietzsche's view of the function of beauty naturalistically. That is, they read Nietzsche's remarks about beauty as Apollonian "appearance" (*Schein*) as a kind of pleasurable distraction from the horrors of human existence.[16] Beauty dazzles our eye with shapes and colors that bring us pleasure and make us forget our tragic woe. According to this reading, Nietzschean art could be similar to Hume's backgammon, a consistent source of plea-sure that outweighs pain and keeps the human animal in existence.[17] However, this view fails to account for Nietzsche's view of the function of the aesthetic in the distinctively human community. That is, it fails to take seriously Nietzsche's insistence on the normative or justifica-tory character of art—that it satisfies our tortured subjectivity, our dis-tinctively human selves. This view "changes the subject" whenever the question of Silenus' truth comes up, indulging our whims and treat-ing us as animals by causing our attention to shift in one way or another rather than treating us with the "dignity" that Nietzsche insists upon (BT 9).[18]

A better reading of the "aesthetic justification of existence" stems from Heidegger's reading of the "poetic" or "sophistic" Nietzsche (vol. 1, lecture 12). According to this reading, the function of the beautiful is not just to provide an occasional distraction when attending theater or reading poetry. Rather, the beautiful is much more fundamental than any actual piece of artwork being produced—the artist "creates and gives form," while the "artist-philosopher . . . gives form to beings as a whole, beginning there where they reveal themselves, i.e., in man" (vol. 1, lecture 12). The beautiful forms the foundation of a historical culture and hence pervades all our interactions and our self-understanding, as Nietzsche discusses in his account of the struggle of "tragic" and "So-cratic cultures" in BT 16–19. For example, Nietzsche, like many others, points to Homer as a foundational figure in constructing the Greek community (HH 262; UUM 19.278). Homer's beautiful poetry and sto-ries created a world of meaning that the Greeks realized in their politics and society and hence internalized as a "second nature." Homer re-counted tales of Greek gods and heroes who suffered and toiled yet demonstrated courage and fortitude, virtues that citizens are uplifted by and attempt to emulate. It is a story of human excellence in the face of the abyss that appeals to the human subject at bottom, not sententious moralizing.

This reading is true to Nietzsche because it connects up nicely with Nietzsche's view of the "esteeming" nature of human beings and the self-legislative character of our societies that we saw in the previous chapter. The aesthetic "justifies" the "table of goods" enshrined within a culture by reflecting back to that culture those features of it that made it possible in the first place—"only man placed values in things to preserve himself" (Z:1 "On the Thousand"). The members of the culture respond so well to this poetry because it reflects their own deeply felt sentiments while delighting their senses and thereby protecting this convention from the corrosive gaze of reason. The "beauty" of this poetry stems from the fact that "human beings posit themselves as the measure of perfection; in select cases, they worship themselves in it" (TI 9.19). However, this view nonetheless fails in once again treating the aesthetic as a distracting pleasure, or, as the sophist Gorgias describes his art in the *Encomium of Helen,* something like "witchcraft." The verse and meter of poetry so enchant the ear, the color and structure of a painting enthrall the eye, that we stand unable to escape from beauty's spell. Though this view of the aesthetic gets right the connection to the esteeming nature of human beings, it does not reveal why the aesthetic is a "justification" at all, rather than simply a natural distraction and a pleasurable self-reflection that keeps us from asking too many questions.

The source of the problem with these views is that they misunderstand the nature of the aesthetic in Nietzsche. They understand Nietzsche's view of the "aesthetic" to be primarily associated with representational or mimetic forms of artwork or art objects. It is easy to make such an error, since Nietzsche talks extensively in BT about artwork—lyric poetry, dithyrambs, tragic drama, and so forth. The problem with treating art objects as the primary justificatory forces is that we are led to emphasize the falsifying, representational qualities of art objects.[19] For instance, the content of the Homeric myth gives to the people a habitable human world that falsifies and yet covers over the horrors of nature in itself, and the form of the myth is expressed in such a style as to enchant generations of Greeks into paying no attention to their tortured subjectivity. In short, the aesthetic is supposed to do for we moderns what is impossible—to get us to believe in something we know to be an illusion.

Is this true? Does Nietzsche ask modern human beings to believe the illusory, as Hussain (2007) and Nehamas (1985, 61) have argued?[20] I agree that Nietzsche argues that man lives poetically—that is, culture provides the foundation for our ethical lives. Rarely does any one of us actually take the trouble to reflect on the deepest foundations of our cultural life, and much of this has to do with the beautifying illusions at the center of culture. But regardless of whether anyone actually does reflect on these foundations, there is still, Nietzsche argues, a standing need for a justification. The *quid iuris* should not be mistaken for a mere *quid facti*. Indeed, in times of spiritual crisis, this apparently abstract demand takes on dire practical implications. Fortunately, Nietzsche has a deeper understanding of the nature of such an aesthetic experience, such that the aesthetic in his view ceases to be a mere (factual) distraction and becomes instead a (normative) justification. To use contemporary philosophical language, Nietzsche is not a "global antirealist" about value, but rather he has one objective "metaethical" commitment, that of the redemptive individual life.[21]

For Nietzsche, the justificatory aesthetic experience is not primarily of art objects, but rather of individual lives—"nothing is beautiful, only people are beautiful" (TI 9.20). Nietzsche states that the Greeks "knew and felt the terrors and horrors of existence; in order to live at all they had to place in front of these things the resplendent, dream-born figures of the Olympians" (BT 3). The gods provided the aesthetic justification sorely needed by the Greeks. The gods "justify [*rechtfertigen*] the life of men by living it themselves—the only satisfactory theodicy" (BT 3).[22] For Nietzsche, as human history proceeds, human beings begin to replace these illusory divinities with actual individuals, patterned on the same model.[23] In particular, Nietzsche singles out the "genius," those rare human individuals who forge a culture based on their own lives and in so doing "justify [*rechtfertigen*] life as such" (UM 3.3).[24] They justify a community's life by living nobly or beautifully (*kalos*) despite the horrors of nature. Hence for these individuals and those who are aroused by them, the "wisdom of Silenus" is reversed: "the very worst thing for them was to die soon, the second worst ever to die at all" (BT 3).[25] Other human beings recognize in these individuals their own tortured subjectivity, as well as their ability to overcome such horror. It is the self-justifying, aesthetic life that draws individuals out of their personal paralysis with Silenus' truth and into a community of attachment to this individual exemplar. Nietzsche sees in these individuals the object of human *eros*. According to the Platonic view of *eros* that Nietzsche draws on, the beautiful draws human beings out of themselves and turns them toward the good.[26]

That the aesthetic is connected most deeply with the individual, beautiful life should come as no surprise given our reflections in the previous chapter about the "individual" and the "aesthetic" as mediating figures between universal norms and the particular natural desires. Furthermore, in the previous chapter, we saw that the individual's beautiful life is self-justifying. The individual "demonstrates why and to what end we came into existence now and at no other time" (UM 3.1) by making himself into a self-enclosed normative system, the "self-propelled wheel," in Nietzsche's terms (Z:1 "Way of Creator"). The pains and toils he endured are justified in light of the narrative he tells about himself.[27] Accordingly, the beautiful individual is not a "representation" of anything at all. He is not a falsification of the world or of culture. Rather, he reveals a beautiful world of his own self that he invites members of the community around him to inhabit.

In the preface to *Philosophy in the Tragic Age of the Greeks*, Nietzsche argues that Greek philosophical systems have long ago been demolished from the perspective of human reason, but what is still valuable is the "personal element" in the philosopher. This personal element "alone is what is forever irrefutable" (PTA 25). The drive of the "sublime knower" can never undermine the "great individual human being" and his "personality," because, as we have seen, individuality forms itself into its own self-enclosed normative system, such that the individual "lives according to [his] own laws and standards" (UM 3.1). Even if the general claims he makes fail to hold according to some general standard, his "personality" is irrefutable, because the standard binding on this personality is the self-legislated law internal to the personality itself. The individual "personality" thus reveals the limitation of reason that Nietzsche had been looking for in his Kantian-inspired "critique of knowledge" (UUM 19.35). Nietzsche's task, then, "is to bring to light what we must ever love and honor and what no subsequent enlightenment can take away: great individual human beings" (PTA 24).

For Nietzsche, then, a good community is one that fosters and houses these individual personalities. Indeed, further, the very fabric of human interaction should be mediated by the presence of individuality. Nietzsche observes that no community can be entirely impersonal, without a history of great individual lives, solely committed to universal norms or to particular desires. Without the element of unique individuality to mediate universal and particular, Nietzsche contends, the community and its members will cease to believe in the justification of human existence. When, in particular, a community "undermines continuing and especially higher life, when the historical sense no longer conserves life but mummifies it, then the tree gradually dies." Life loses its substance and vivacity, universal ideals become hollow husks, and we tend to "rotate in egoistic self-satisfaction around [our] own axis" (UM 2.3). As we will see in the next chapter, many human associations in the modern world, such as the modern state, mass society, and the modern market, fail to live up to this condition of being a genuine human community.

6.4   The Individual's Redemption

As in Hegel, so too in Nietzsche, true community and genuine individuality are interdependent and mutually reinforcing, rather than in tension with one another. Community points toward individuality, just as individuality has community as its end. This is not to say that all empirical communities foster individuality and all individuals help redeem communities—far from it. Nietzsche argues that the vast majority of human associations are antithetical to the production of individuals, and most human beings fail to be genuine individuals. Nonetheless, he argues that subjects can only become genuine individuals—and hence satisfy their subjective will—through ethical activity intended to redeem the community, to demonstrate why the community is worth fighting for. In what follows, I argue that Nietzsche's theory of community is an inegalitarian one, but not radically so—redemptive individuals exist in a reciprocal relationship with community, and hence do not view community as an instrument of their wills.

For Nietzsche, human beings must redeem community in order to become whole individuals. His argument is as follows. For Nietzsche, we are all of us children of our communities as historically conditioned beings. Our community's past is our past. Nietzsche adopts Hegel's view of the historical nature of human identity—"the past continues to flow within us in a hundred waves" (AOM 223), constituting the "very body" or even "essence" of a person or thing (GS 58). The "resonance and remnants" of one's history "ultimately constitute our existence, no matter how much the individual tends to see himself as something wholly new and unique" (UUM 26.13).[28] Thus, our identity is shaped deeply by the history of the struggle for the good in this community, and the community's crisis of meaning in the face of Silenus' truth is at once this individual's own crisis. He cannot, then, curl up within himself and provide a private answer to this crisis of meaning, because the very principles he draws upon to weave a story of his own life are communal in character (nor can he create *ex nihilo* such principles [BGE 21], and even if he could, such principles would be unintelligible to others).

Without a public in which to perform his actions and reveal his identity, he can never be sure whether or not he gets the principles right in adopting them. In order to make intelligible to himself the good and the meaning of his own life, he must draw on the history of his community, which is his own and others' history. But that means the success of his own self-creation of identity, his own redemption of his own past, is at once inextricable from the community's redemption. Just as we saw in the previous chapter, an individual cannot suppress parts of the community's history of suffering and victory any more than he can eliminate features of his own past.[29]

Thus, to be a genuine individual, a subject must confront the crisis of his community, which is at once the crisis of his own fragmented identity. The individual renders the history of suffering meaningful by embedding it within the narrative that he tells about himself. That is, the individual makes the communal history his own history by performing a series of actions that affirms the past history of himself and his community while at once rendering coherent their shared history as part of a successful narrative leading to the present and into the future. The irrational suffering of the community's history is redescribed by the individual not as horrific, meaningless moments, but as necessary stages on the way to the creation of a whole community led by this whole individual. In incorporating the community's past as part of his own past, the individual essentially founds or refounds the community, transforming this aggregate of human beings into a whole, in which the members of this community come to think of themselves as belonging to this whole common self established by the individual. In short, the individual redeems the community by making it part of his self-justified narrative. The redemptive man Schopenhauer, for instance, "voluntarily takes upon himself the suffering involved in being truthful," and thereby helps modern human beings from enduring the meaningless suffering by facing the truth that "all that exists that can be denied deserves to be denied" (UM 3.4).

Nietzsche discusses these matters most clearly in Zarathustra's speech "On Redemption." For Zarathustra, the modern community's reaction to the meaninglessness of nature is horror and resentment, exclaiming, "alas, where is redemption [*Erlösung*] from the flux of things and from the punishment called existence?" Zarathustra himself "walks among men as among the fragments and limbs of men," so that human society appears as nothing but a "dreadful accident" of becoming. The individual's task— Zarathustra's task—is to found a new community by transforming communal self-understanding such that its members see themselves as part of a whole, justified history, focused in the founder's will. Zarathustra hence "walks among men as among the fragments of the future—that future which I envisage. And this is all my creating [*Dichten*] and striving, that I create and carry together into One what is fragment and riddle and dreadful accident." For Zarathustra, this activity of taking on the "punishment" and suffering and fragmentation of a community is that community's "redemption," to "recreate all 'it was' into a 'thus I willed it.'"[30] Just as the individual wills and transforms his own past as part of a coherent self-narrated self, so too does the individual will the community's past as the part of this same self. As a result, his past and the history of the community gain meaning and is justified in light of the role it plays in the narrative whole. This "redemption" in Nietzsche's mind is a "reconciliation" (*Versöhnung*) of past contradictions. In invoking Hegel's term "reconciliation," Nietzsche in fact announces his central disagreement with Hegel (Z:1 "On Redemption"). While for Hegel, reconciliation occurs through the ever progressing rationality of political community, for Nietzsche, reconciliation is effected through the personality of an individual exemplar.[31]

The individual must therefore demonstrate why this history of injustices or suffering is worthwhile in order to redeem a community. We may think here of examples in the oratorical tradition of Pericles to Cicero (and even including figures like Martin Luther King Jr.) who sought to narrate the goodness and worthiness of a community's history of trial and glory. Yet at the same time, for Nietzsche, mere oratory with a good narrative is not enough. The individual also must act in public, fashioning a "beautiful" or "noble" life in order to be the object of *eros*. Nietzsche draws primarily not on modern notions of beauty, but on the Greek notion of *kalos* here, which means both "beautiful" and "noble," part of a desirable life they called *kalos k'agathos*.[32] Nietzsche is here drawing on this meaning of *kalos* primarily, the *kalos* of an individual life with integrity and virtue, a term that only derivatively means what we moderns understand by "beauty," as a pleasing appearance. As Nietzsche describes such a life, the noble or beautiful person "has enough fullness to enrich everything . . . someone in this state transforms things until they reflect his own power, until they are the reflexes of his perfection" (TI Skirmishes.9). This Greek notion can help us see how the beautiful, self-narrating life we described in the previous chapter can at the same time be a noble life, that is, a life that brings meaning to a community.

Let us take up, then, the three characteristics we discussed in the previous chapter, self-determination, uniqueness, and unity amidst diversity, and see how each of these characteristics expresses the "beauty" or "nobility" (*kalos*) of the individual, and hence how this beauty can help the community to overcome Silenus' truth. First, for Nietzsche, there is a certain beauty or nobility in willfully overcoming nature and hence displaying one's self-determining freedom from it. Animals cannot stake their lives for an abstract ideal, but human beings can. The Greek gods, one of Nietzsche's examples of founding "individuals," staked their lives "to overthrow the realm of the Titans and slay monsters" (BT 3)—the representation of lawful human civilization against natural chaos and strength—hence revealing their freedom from the most basic natural impulse of self-preservation.[33] They are not selfish animalistic beings, but rather they stake their lives for an ideal of the good or the just that itself becomes the founding notion of the good for a community. The individual acts with "fearlessness in the face of the fearful and questionable"; he has the "courage and freedom of affect in the face of a powerful enemy, in the face of a sublime hardship, in the face of a horrible problem" (TI 9.24). The striving individual does not "cling to [life] so desperately" but rather "has no respect for existence," regarding it "with Olympian laughter" (UM 2.2). Indeed, the more powerful the adversary, the more strength of will the individual must muster to meet the challenge, and hence the nobler the display. The "degree of resistance that must be continually overcome in order to remain on top is the measure of freedom" (WP 770). Individuals in this sense are noble because they challenge the notion that suffering is without meaning or irrational, but rather that it is a condition for their achievements and a constant test of their dedication to a self-determined life.

Second, the individual leads a life that no one before has led and no one after will lead. Such a life is noble or beautiful because it is extremely difficult to achieve. We have tremendous natural impulses to conform to custom of mass society out of "fear" of our "neighbor's" recognition, or to give in to our immediate natural passions out of temptation (UM 3.1). Being truly unique and hence self-consistent over time takes enormous discipline. It requires becoming someone partially estranged from his home, someone singular, a single, unified organization of a diversity of parts that has never been put together in just this order. This beautifully unique life erotically draws human beings out of their concern with the irrationality of death. Death, the perpetual passing away of what is and the coming to be of something new, is given meaning as part of this unique life. "Eternal becoming is a lying puppet-play in beholding which man forgets himself, the actual distraction which disperses the individual to the four winds," whereas the unique life "ceases to be the toy it plays with" in attaining a measure of "being" in being self-related and self-sufficient (UM 3.4). This life cannot be compared to anything but itself, and hence it stands apart with its shining appearance from the rest of becoming, which produces copies in the form of social man or natural member of a species. The unique, self-identical life is represented in the immortal gods, the very exemplification of perpetual "being." Indeed, for Nietzsche, when such unique, mortal individuals like "Raphael" pass out of existence, it is a tremendous "injustice" that nature commits in not allowing these geniuses to live longer (UM 2.8).[34]

The third way in which individuals are *kalos* is that they combine the formal harmony or "measure" with the substantive superabundance of life; they are unified amidst their own diversity (BT 4). The order and "moderation" required by such harmonious unity reveal the individual as a rational totality—the individual possesses a remarkable harmony of whole and parts containing no excess, no contingency in a "classical" ideal of beautiful order (BT 4). Such rational harmony satisfies the subject's aversion to the irrational disorder of nature, and hence draws the subject to the rational harmonious "world" of this individual. It pleases our eye in its beautiful harmony. At the same time, however, the individual cannot appear as an abstract lifeless harmony etched in stone. This divine individual must "live" in the hearts and minds of community members as one with "overbrimming" life (BT 3). Such superabundance is alluring because no one can ever be sure what to expect next out of the unique individual. The living superabundance of this individual reminds each of us of our own unique and powerful potential; it reminds us of our capacity to extend our subjectivity far into the world in a new and unique way. The superabundance is a "wasteful and extravagant" gesture of the individual—he gives himself away and encompasses a new people because "people praise . . . a hero's indifference to his own well-being, his devotion to an idea, a great cause, a fatherland" (TI 9.44). The "gift-giving virtue" of "becoming sacrifices and gifts yourselves" is the "highest virtue and useless" because it forms a new culture, a "chosen people," inflaming the desires of a new generation (Z:1 "Gift-Giving").

For Nietzsche, then, the community is founded and refounded by individuals. It is "formed following the example set by powerful individual [*einzelner*] personalities" (UUM 19.39). Accordingly, not just one but a series of individual "geniuses" shape the self-understanding and the good of the community. These important individuals—Achilles and Socrates in the ancient world, Rousseau, Goethe, and Schopenhauer in the modern world—are "founders" of a sort. They are not, like Solon or Lycurgus, founders of codes of law. Rather, they are "founders" of a culture or way of life, an ethical value system that grounds and makes sense of subsequent and derivative political foundings—the "ethical strengths of a nation . . . are exhibited in its geniuses" (UUM 19.1). Socrates' influence, for instance, "has spread out across all posterity to this very day, and indeed into the whole future, like a shadow growing ever longer in the evening sun" (BT 15). Rousseau, Goethe, and Schopenhauer "set up the image of man when all men . . . have thus declined from that image to the level of the animals or even of automata" (UM 3.4). These founding individuals come to frame our self-understanding so thoroughly that we cannot conceive of ourselves apart from them.[35] Goethe, for instance, represents the life of the German "contemplative man in the grand style"—his own self-narration shapes and arouses all subsequent German contemplative lives (UM 3.4).

These individuals lead exemplary lives—they embody meaningful lives which others strive to emulate.[36] In emulating this life, each member of a community finds a degree of wholeness in realizing the character of the exemplar within himself. Without a whole community, we have, Nietzsche says, an "immeasurable longing to become whole" (UM 3.6), given that we find ourselves as a "dreadful accident." We seek to overcome our immersion in the stream of becoming by reduplicating the individual's "redemption" by seeking redemption from our incompleteness. Through the "fire of the brightest and greatest love in whose light we cease to understand the word 'I'" we follow the exemplar by seeing that "there lies something beyond [*jenseits*] our being . . . and we are thus possessed of a heartfelt longing for bridges between here and there." The individual exemplar "draws us aloft" from our natural selves in the project of imitating the exemplar's character (UM 3.5).

For Nietzsche, in our moments of "animality" we "hasten to give our heart to the state, to money-making, to sociability or science" (UM 3.5), but by contrast, we embrace what is distinctively human in us when we "consecrate" ourselves to "culture," when we recognize one another based on our common longing for these exemplars (UM 3.6), or, simply put, we all belong to the same "culture" produced by these individuals. The human being who "believes in culture is thereby saying: 'I see above me something higher and more human than I am; let everyone help me to attain it, as I will help everyone who knows and suffers as I do: so that at last the man may appear who feels himself perfect [*voll*] and infinite [*unendlich*] in knowledge and love, perception and power, and who in his completeness is at one with nature" (UM 3.6). Or rather, as Nietzsche puts the point in his later work, the desire to "make perfect [*Vollkommne*] is—art," and hence one "finds inherent pleasure in things that he himself is not; in art, people enjoy themselves as perfection" (TI 9.9).

This view of the satisfaction of individuals in a community contrasts sharply with Hegel's ontology of community, which is based on an Aristotelian account of parts and whole. For Hegel, subjects achieve wholeness in seeing themselves as parts of a common whole, of fulfilling a particular, necessary role or task which takes on meaning as part of the common good. By contrast, Nietzsche's ontology of community is based on an updated Platonism, as he says explicitly at UM 3.5: one's own individuality is "that ideal man who, as his Platonic ideal as it were, holds sway in and around him." The good, the source of human meaning, is not a whole to which we belong as parts. Rather, the good is a pattern, a form, or an idea that transcends empirical instantiations. In Plato, the empirical world consists of false "images" or imperfect representations of the ideal pattern—they are the "archetypes of things themselves" in Kant's description (CPR B370).[37]

Nietzsche updates this Platonism in the same way that Hegel updates his Aristotelianism—by filtering it through Kant. In Nietzsche's hands, the good becomes not an eternal pattern in heaven, but a living pattern of a good human life. The individual narrative becomes the self-understanding of a people, the basis of their "table of goods." Thus, each member of the community views his own self as a false "image" of the individual self that stands at the heart of the community, just as for Plato empirical objects are false images that participate in archetypal forms.[38] For Nietzsche, the "entire life of a people reflects in an impure and confused manner the image presented by its highest geniuses: they are not the product of the masses, but the masses exhibit their aftereffect" (UUM 19.1).[39] Each feels a sense of shame at his own self in light of his higher self as represented in the exemplar. We see that we are driven by greed or by power—we have not been able to incorporate our animal desires into a coherent individuality. Yet each of us has a "profound kinship and involvement with the genius" since he gave us a sense of who we are in our best moments (UM 3.6). Thus, we are aroused to action, to strive to make ourselves like this individual. In patterning ourselves in light of his example, we create for ourselves a life that takes on meaning to the degree to which we realize this example. The individual is the good that we erotically strive to attain in our own lives, "for it is love alone that can bestow on the soul not only a clear, discriminating and self-contemptuous view of itself, but also the desire [*Begierde*] to look beyond itself and seek with all its might for a higher self as yet still concealed from it" (UM 3.6). He is our own better self that we seek to imitate—the "individual [*einzelne*], morally outstanding human being radiates a power of imitation" (UUM 19.113).

Thus, when Nietzsche argues that we should not live "for the good of the majority," but rather "for the good of the rarest and most valuable exemplars," he is offering an account of what will satisfy our own agency, not just the desires of the few (UM 3.6). That is, given that individual and community are interdependent, working for the individual exemplar just is working for my own humanity.

At the same time, the genuine individual founder is not to be thought of as some kind of god to be slavishly followed. Indeed, there are many empirical examples of such a relationship in which an individual establishes such a cult in which members blindly follow his example. Yet for Nietzsche, subjects can only attain full individuality when there is a reciprocal interaction between individual and community. We already discussed in chapter 3 how for Hegel individuals require the recognition of others in order to witness their own subjectivity in the world. A similar kind of claim is at work in Nietzsche's view. For Nietzsche, as we have seen, the very notion of an "aesthetic justification" requires that the individual treat those he justifies as human, that is, as potential agents to whom justifications are appropriate, as opposed to the appeal to the senses appropriate to animals.

In order to grasp the reciprocal activity involved in this aesthetic relationship, recall that Nietzsche is adopting in his notion of the individual narrative life Kant's notion of the "aesthetic idea."[40] The "aesthetic idea" in Kant is a work of art that arouses both our understanding and our sensual imagination—it pleases our senses while also making us think, yet it cannot be reduced simply to particular sensual pleasure nor subsumed under universal, conceptual claims.[41] Milton's description of Hell, for instance, in *Paradise Lost*, is an aesthetic idea in that it has a unique character—it is not reducible to the mere concept of hell (a place where unrepentant sinners go), nor is it simply an eloquent, dazzling image (the result of interesting word choice and rhythm).[42] Milton creates a unique world populated with unique characters in which readers are invited into the "free play" (*freie Spiel*) of the "imagination" and our "understanding" (CJ 26–27; UUM 19.285, 23.30). That is, the beauty of artwork appeals to human freedom as our capacity to be free from the mere sensual desires of nature and the conceptual claims of nature, to break both chains by engaging in the interplay between passion and reason. Our whole being, both our passions and our reason, is aroused and satisfied in engaging with this "idea." We are invited as readers of *Paradise Lost*, for instance, to "play" between whole and parts, between the thematic "meaning" of the work and the events, description, and presentation of the work, and how the author accomplishes both by harmonizing whole and parts, by allowing the "meaning" of the work to shine forth from the parts as we read. The work of art confronts us with the fact of our freedom, because in order to fully appreciate the work of art, we must play with different themes, echoes of other works, motifs that emerge in the work, and with how these themes are underlined and challenged in the formal structure of the work itself.[43] The individual life is hence like Milton's classic work in sensuously embodying an artistic whole that invites onlookers to engage in the free play between the individual's whole and parts.[44] In addition to the formal elements of the work, the viewer engages with its substantive themes, as the individual's narrative story contains within itself a transformed version of the community's story as well—this individual life has been embodied as the "fundamental *idea* [*Grundgedanke*] of culture" that holds together a "mighty community" (UM 3.5, my emphasis). Yet since the genius's life is an idea, the genius invites freedom of participation on the part of the community.

Indeed, Nietzsche argues that in inviting the community to play within the contours of his idea, he also invites and arouses competitors to counter and transform his own narrative of the community. Each member of this community, in bringing to the common experience his own particular history, will inevitably have a slightly different understanding of the significance of some events.[45] Moreover, new events and experiences will arise that will force a reconsideration of the individual's previous narrative. An individual gains recognition for his own successful redemption—and hence inclusion in the "republic of geniuses"—when it is deemed worthy of challenge, when the individual's narrative itself is taken up as part of the community's past and stands in need of interpretation itself.[46] Thus, Nietzsche emphasizes the importance of rivals as part of the process of the individual's self-fashioning—"in a friend one should have one's best enemy" (Z 1.Friend). The aesthetic relationship to community is very different from the command-structure relationship of reason to the community—whereas the first commands acceptance according to iron-clad rules of reason, the former arouses free hermeneutic engagement.[47]

6.5   *Eros* and *Eris* of Community

One final way to defend the "reciprocity" point in Nietzsche is to note that total "reverence" for an individual saps community members of their distinctive humanity. Human beings are "reverent" animals, but we are also "mistrustful," both esteeming and skeptical (GS 346).[48]

Some mistrust is crucial to keep the spark of humanity alive in any community, and hence to provide conditions for a future individual who will challenge or transform his predecessor. However, a community should ensure that such mistrust does not extend so far that no individual lives and no common goods are honored above any other, a threat in modern Enlightenment society that may end in "nihilism" (GS 346). Instead, a community must maintain the tension between reverence and mistrust as it establishes the very tense condition for the cultivation of individuals, the tense bow that can "shoot at the furthest goals" (BGE.P). Such a balance is difficult, and Nietzsche relies on the Greek social model, which held together *eros* and *eris*, or love and strife. These two concepts were central to Nietzsche's early work—the concept of *eros* or "love" Nietzsche found in his *Lieblingsdichtung*, Plato's *Symposium*, and he associated it with the "true" and "great eroticist" Socrates (UM 3.5, BT 13, TI Socrates.8); by contrast, he investigated the concept of *eris* through the agon in his essay "Homer's Contest."[49]

Nietzsche cites Plato's *Symposium* extensively in his early career, and was deeply influenced by Plato's notions of "begetting" in the beautiful and the "ladder" to the beautiful (see, e.g., UUM 19.10). Nietzsche is particularly taken with the discussion between Socrates and Diotima on the nature of the beautiful, a discussion that informs Nietzsche's own view of the role of love in human community.[50] Consider Socrates' argument that human love or *eros* is characterized by inherent incompleteness or want. We would not love if we did not lack the object of our love (200aff.). Love, then, is characterized by the desire for perpetual wholeness—it "wants the good to be theirs for ever" (206a). Socrates' account of *eros* here reflects Nietzsche's own notion of the desiring subject, that subject that seeks to extend and indeed immortalize itself in the outside world.

Yet Nietzsche cites directly a further point made by Diotima as recounted by Socrates. Our desire, she contends, is aroused only in particular contexts, namely, when we are in the presence of beauty. The beautiful draws us out of ourselves and prompts us to extend ourselves in the world, to "beget in the presence of beauty" (206b). A young man is aroused by the beauty of a woman and seeks to beget a child and, indeed, to immortalize himself, in her presence. Nietzsche employs this language in claiming that the genius "procreates" in the "beautiful" (TI 9.22; cf. UUM 19.53, 19.152). As we saw already above, the beautiful draws human beings out of what for Nietzsche is their most personal, their horror at an irrational existence. But the beautiful also carries us out of and beyond ourselves, in creating children with a beautiful woman, in helping found a new social or political community, in participating in a philosophical dispute across the ages, which are all forms of the extension of subjectivity out into the world with the ultimate aim of immortalizing oneself. As Nietzsche puts the point, as we feel the "fire of love" in the presence of the beautiful individual, we "cease to understand the word 'I,'" recognizing "something beyond our being which at these moments move across into it, and we are thus possessed of a heartfelt longing for bridges between here and there" (UM 3.5).

Furthermore, this "begetting" in the beautiful assumes different shapes, Diotima claims, depending on one's level of self-development.[51] At the lowest level—the level we share with the animals—we "procreate" and extend ourselves in physical reproduction (206b). For Diotima, this urge for physical procreation can be elevated to procreating ourselves as master or statesman or general. Others look up to us and may recount our stories through the ages. This is a higher stage of "begetting" because it consists in a mental, human procreation here—others obey our actions because they obey norms of human creation (208c–d). The "beautiful" that we are in the presence of is not a beautiful body, but a beautiful city or community, one in which all members of the community resemble or strive to resemble individual exemplars. We ourselves try to be the best of the best, the best instantiation of an Achilles or a Pericles—we are "pregnant with virtue," in Diotima's description (209a–b).

The final rung on the "ladder" of the beautiful is the encounter with the "beautiful" itself (211a–b). Since Nietzsche follows Kant's "Copernican Revolution," he rejects the idea that the "beautiful" is a category structuring the cosmos itself. The beautiful that arouses us here is not the idea of beauty, but humanity as such, represented by its highest exemplars. We are aroused by the beauty of the individuals who structure human worlds, who give sense to the human notion of the beautiful by living a beautiful life. The striving individual obeys the "rule over him" that "that which in the past was able to expand the concept 'man' and make it more beautiful must exist everlastingly [*ewig*], so as to be able to accomplish this everlastingly" (UM 2.2). These beautiful individuals together constitute the universal notion of the beautiful by uniting humanity as such in the common pursuit or "chain" of individual greatness (UUM 19.16; UM 2.2). It is here, Nietzsche insists, "where Plato's procreating in the realm of the beautiful belongs—thus, the overcoming of history is necessary for the birth of genius, history must be immersed in beauty and made eternal" (UUM 19.10). That is, to become a true individual, one must also be able to overcome the narrowness and ugliness of one's time and engage in the community of the beautiful exemplars that have come to constitute the chain of humanity before one. The ladder of love eventually drives the individual beyond the narrow confines of his political community to the community of humanity as such.[52]

For Nietzsche, then, following Plato, the human subject has a distinctive erotic drive to participate in something higher than ourselves—whether in a family, a state, or the cultural and intellectual accumulation of humanity as such—as it is the opportunity for us to witness our own subjectivity in the world. We "see above [us] something higher and more human than [we are]" (UM 3.6). We seek to extend ourselves in these higher entities, while recognizing that to love them involves giving up sovereign control over them, participating in them and thereby changing their character, while also submitting oneself to the judgments of others and of future generations. We constantly must be "ashamed of [ourselves] without any accompanying feeling of distress" (UM 3.6), constantly preparing the way for future incarnations of individuality.[53] Individuals treat their predecessors with respect rather than rejecting them, because each individual recognizes himself as part of a long chain of humanity rather than a self-created man, and each recognizes that he contributes to this chain by marking another high point in its development, one that will make possible future individuals.

Eros hence plays an important role in supporting the "reverence" or "esteem" for a community. However, *eris* is also required to allow individuals to make their distinctive mark on history and community.[54] For the Greeks, *eris* is the basic, brutal condition of nature, that "night and horror" of the "pre-Homeric" world (HC 188).[55] It is the barbaric state, the state of warfare, the state in which might makes right and all forms of human order are constantly being torn apart by physical struggle. Eris is the relative of Ares, who in the *Iliad* helps enrage the characters, inflaming their lust for destruction. For *eris*, "combat is salvation and deliverance, the cruelty of the victory is the pinnacle of life's jubilation" (HC 188). It loves combat and cannot endure defeat—it is the flat-footed refusal of the subject to accept any order encompassing it. The subject will fight if necessary to free itself from such domination. *Eris*, then, is the condition of fragmentation, of atomism, of "every man for himself." It is reflected and sublimated in the tortured subjectivity of the reflective ego, that ego that cruelly rejects every social and natural determination, finding itself ultimately alone and paralyzed like Hamlet.

The Greeks were afraid of such violent struggle in nature, but they also saw great potential in it if it were harnessed properly. There developed a "good" form of *eris* that placed this form "amongst men" so that "neighbor competes with neighbor for prosperity" and everyone benefits from the hard work (HC 189–90). The struggle or agon was brought within the city walls and made part of athletic and rhetorical contests; the struggle was sublimated, the combatants disciplined, primarily through the rules and procedures circumscribing the contest. But more importantly, the contest ceases to be about physical mastery of others, but rather about our mastery of the physical as such—that is, how well we can discipline our natures and bring these transformed natures to bear in contest with others. If participants fail to play by the rules, they are "ostracized" so that "a new contest of powers can be awakened" (HC 191). Yet, most fundamentally, *eris* is tamed and sublimated by beauty. It is the presence of a beautiful, striving individual who obeys the rules that fundamentally keeps the struggle in order. Our erotic connection to beauty and nobility encourages us to submit ourselves to the civilized discipline of the contest.

But it is our *eris* that sets us in opposition to others, that seeks to break the order and shared self my companion and I had. In the contest, we are adversaries, rather than friends. *Eris* is still circumscribed by a higher order, that of common citizenship, but our friendship is set aside for the duration of the contest. We are no longer friends because *eris* arouses a "mistrust" among selves. It puts us on guard against the machinations of others. The controlled struggle ensues, and the struggle is salutary, because it forces each member of the community to strive his hardest to create a self that will win the contest. Each participant must work and train harder, practice longer, innovate new techniques, in order not to lose and hence submit to the will of another. Emerging victorious, then, is extremely satisfying because my subjectivity and mine alone is reflected back at me in the winner's circle. The adoring crowds recognize *my* individuality, not the glory of Athens. *Eris* hence helps my subjectivity achieve the wholeness it so longs for in its own individuality. My subjectivity does not have to settle for being one among the crowd, but the crowd recognizes my distinctness in winning the contest. After the contest, finally, I return to my friendship with my adversary, returning to my *eros*, which is a necessary moment to maintain the satisfaction of the victory of the contest, since I must see the recognition of the Athenians, for instance, as something erotically desirable, for the victory of *eris* to be lastingly satisfying. "Love for one's native city contains and controls the agonal drive" (UUM 21.14), for otherwise *eris* would tear the human from all forms of human connection, all human societies and forms of recognition, infinitely transcending one's erotic bonds with others, as, for instance, in the fate of Penthesilea as dramatized by Kleist.[56] The animalistic *eris*, chaotic and destructive, displays no human virtues, no beauty or nobility.

We can see, then, the kind of balancing that is required in the community to unleash the force of *eris* without letting it dissolve and fragment community as such. The erotic drive connects all people, including aspiring individuals, to their community and hence to the community's individual exemplars. All people understand themselves in light of the exemplars' characters. They strive to imitate and hence participate in the communal good shaped by these exemplars. Yet aspiring individuals need an element of "mistrust" of their community, its ideals, and the individuals who stand behind them. Aspiring individuals cannot slavishly "revere" previous individuals, because they will never escape from under their shadow. Thus, Nietzsche criticizes the "exclusivity of genius in the modern sense," claiming instead that there must be "several geniuses to incite each other to action, just as they keep each other within certain limits too" (HC 191–92). Only by mistrusting others can we aspiring individuals craft for ourselves a self that stands apart in its distinctness and uniqueness. The eristic drive prompts us to be creative or generative, first by distinguishing ourselves from the other individuals who have shaped our identities. Yet, second, the eristic drive propels each individual to "victory," in this case being the individual self that encompasses and redeems the community. Each individual strives to assume the mantle of founding a "new mode and order," as Machiavelli puts it, by incorporating previous individual identities within his own larger identity, and hence by crafting a community in which all members recognize this individual as the "genius" that they should imitate. Each wants to "embed [himself] in great communities; [he] wants to give a single form to the multifarious and disordered; chaos stimulates [him]" (WP 964). The contest among individuals, then, is a contest of mutual incorporation.[57] Each attempts to destabilize the narrative order of the other by incorporating the other into one's own narrative, so that the other ceases to be the genius figure who redeems the irrationalities of a community and projects a notion of the good. Yet at the same time, individuals must possess a reverence for the communal tradition that has existed before them—they cannot simply destroy the tradition and start again, which amounts to a loss of freedom for all and a return to relationships of animalistic brute force. *Eros* and *eris* are both conditions for individuality, and their dialectical tension preserved by the community drives individuals on an endless quest of self-overcoming.

The American presidency involves an example of this contest of mutual incorporation. Mansfield (1993) has argued that modern constitutionalism has attempted to "tame the prince," that is, to circumscribe and sublimate the tyrannical urges of a founding prince to impose a new mode and order on the world. Modern constitutions redirect these individualistic energies toward the preservation of order, rather than to its destruction and a new founding. Yet the destructive, eristic desire of the prince still exists, even if it is suitably tamed or disciplined within a constitutional order. Therefore, each new president attempts to claim the U.S. identity and agenda as his own through the inaugural speech. The inaugural speech is the perfect opportunity for individual action, to display to the world who the individual is. It is also the opportunity both for continuity and for change, for the individual to show how he as a new president and the country as a whole owe a great debt to all individual presidents and the community that has come before. Yet it is also a time for the new individual president to show how he will change the direction of the country by putting his own particular narrative twist on the future story of the nation. In the inaugural speech, as Skowronek (1993) has argued, the president is most effective in getting across his unique narrative twist precisely by incorporating the past history within the story of his own approach. That is, the president redescribes the history of the nation and of its individual presidents as a story that leads up to him as its redeemer. Previous individual presidents have led their countries with courage and intelligence, but were not quite able to grasp the contours of the problems they faced, since they were "within" the problem itself. Later presidents hence are able to achieve a more synoptic vision, and, if they are good presidents, can craft a narrative identity synoptic in scope to bring together the history of the suffering of the nation and focus it in this one world-historical moment.

I use the American presidency as an example of how communities foster both *eris* and *eros*, and how individuals themselves maintain the delicate balance between these two drives—the erotic drive attaching the inaugural president to the nation, and the eristic drive motivating him to distinguish himself from all others by incorporating that very nation's past and hence his own past. In understanding individuality in this way—as arising out of and promoting the fundamental human interactions constituted by *eros* and *eris*—I have argued that individuality and community are interdependent and reciprocal. The individual can no more destroy or force a community to bend to his will than a community can eliminate its individual exemplars. Individuals require a communal aesthetic experience to reflect back to them their own aesthetically created identity, which involves respecting and redeeming the community. Community requires individuality in order to provide it with its lifeblood, with the justificatory reason for it to embody a form of life rather than simply fade out of existence. We will see in the next chapter, however, that there are modern historical forces that militate against this harmony, but there are others that provide the modern world with a unique opportunity for such harmonization never seen before.

7

Nietzsche on the Antipolitical Individual

In the previous chapter, we saw that for Nietzsche human beings become individuals through ethical activity, through the redemption of community. The task of this chapter is to investigate the historical and political conditions for the right kinds of individuals and communities. Initially, the prospects of healthy individuality and community in the modern age seem dim. Nietzsche is an outspoken critic of modern liberal democracy, which, in Nietzsche's mind, diminishes human ambition and freedom by "unbending the bow," the tension constitutive of the human being that fuels our progress and creativity (BGE P). Diminishing the tension within the human heart means dissolving the relationships shared among us that aim to render this tension meaningful and salutary for some further communal purpose. Hence, for Nietzsche, "everything that once bound human beings together is becoming more abstract" (UUM 29.141). Nietzsche regards modernity as a moment of danger or crisis, in which social and political conditions are growing increasingly inhospitable to the production of individual geniuses. Yet in contrast to Hegel, for whom the hedonism of modern civil society is self-defeating, Nietzsche argues that the great danger of modern historical conditions is that we will lose our humanity and never get it back.

At the same time, however, Nietzsche regards the modern world as a moment of stupendous opportunity for individual creativity, a point often overlooked in standard readings of Nietzsche as a critic of the modern world and a harbinger of "postmodernism" and a new revolutionary age. As we will see, according to Nietzsche, the very same conditions that render individuality difficult to achieve also afford the aspiring individual conditions for unprecedented greatness. Accordingly, my view challenges those readers of Nietzsche who see him as a radical critic of modern political order or as an "aristocratic" fanatic.[1] For Nietzsche, it is only by adapting and transforming the institutions of the modern political order that we may hope to stave off the slide into the animalistic "last men" of the liberal democratic movement while avoiding the opposite extreme of a return to subhuman relationships of force and violence characteristic of a new "aristocratic age." The modern state in particular plays an important role in maintaining the difficult balance between danger and opportunity. Yet at the same time, criticizing Hegel, Nietzsche rejects the view that the state is the "destiny" of human beings. Rather, "a state has no purpose [*Zweck*]: it is only we who attribute to it this or that purpose" (UUM 29.72). The state has a mere instrumental purpose for the maintenance of human culture, which is transpolitical.

As I read Nietzsche, he is attempting to adopt a quite nuanced political view despite his piercingly loud denunciations of modern political orders. Nietzsche resists the "progressive" tendencies of modern politics because these indicate for him a decline, yet he seeks to retain existing institutions and the historical accumulation of meaning around them because these represent ripe conditions for the creation of individuality. Accordingly, this discussion aims to push the scholarly discussion beyond the debates between the "Right" and the "Left" Nietzscheans into discussion about Nietzsche's ambivalence about modern politics. In so doing, then, we can compare Nietzsche's ambivalence about modern life to Hegel's own. In order to make this case, I will draw on Nietzsche's view of history and community in the previous chapter and apply it to his historical reflections on the nature and development of the state in antiquity and modernity.

7.1   Historical Development of State and Culture in Modernity

Nietzsche, like Hegel, claims that the ancient world was very different from the modern world. History effects a deep and profound transformation in the human soul. As Nietzsche says, "in comparison with the mode of life of whole millennia of mankind we present-day men live in a very immoral age" (D 9). Nietzsche regards these ancient communities as having a certain advantage and a disadvantage, very similar to that in Hegel's view. Ancient communities are problematic because ancient "peoples" upheld their "table of goods," their tradition, their community as authoritative and sovereign above individuality (Z:1 "On the

Thousand"). All human beings were educated to fulfill some role within this tradition and to understand themselves as part of the whole, and any attempt to think for oneself or act based on one's own notions of right and wrong was summarily punished. Hence, "in all the original conditions of mankind, 'evil' signifies the same as 'individual' [*individuell*]" (D 9). Individuality was a threat, a sign of corruption of the smooth hierarchical unity of a community (GS 23). The "ancient way" was to "think under the spell of ethical life [*Sittlichkeit*], for which there was nothing but established judgments, established causes, and no other reasons than those of authority" (D 544).[2] It was none other than "Socrates who discovered the antithetical magic" of a reflective individuality (D 544). For Socrates and for his modern individualist heirs, ethical life must be submitted to his sovereign judgment (D 9).

At the same time, the ancients' pervasive reliance on custom was advantageous, as represented most clearly by the Greeks. The Greeks realized what Hegel called "substantial freedom," or rather, as Nietzsche puts it, the Greeks community exerted a high degree of "plastic power" (UM 2.1, 2.10). The Greeks proved able to "organize the chaos" of the different cultures within their territory and take "possession of themselves" so as to perform great deeds as Greeks (UM 2.10). The Greek community possessed the rare ability to submit many different and conflicting drives and values to a harmonious and hierarchical value standard without this standard being undermined in its members' behavior. This Greek standard of the good was so powerful for Greek citizens that their actions were animated by a "burning wish to be an instrument of the salvation of his city in the contest of the cities" (HC 89). Since the community strongly asserted its ethical law in the world, the members of such a community gained meaning and wholeness as part of this rigid and exclusive whole. In this nonalienated relationship to community, human subjectivity comes to see itself reflected back at itself in the norms and activities of the communal will.

How was such harmony possible? If we examine the institutional structure of the "Greek state," we see that, for Nietzsche, the strong unity of the Greek community kept the apparatus of governing human passions—the state—and the space for spiritual self-cultivation and artistic activity—culture—closely allied. Nietzsche argues that the Greek state "leads by the hand the gloriously blooming woman, Greek society" (GrS 52). Greek culture "grew up so luxuriantly precisely under the careful and wise guard of [the state's] institutions . . . the [Greek] state was not a border guard, regulator, or overseer for his culture; rather the robust, muscular comrade, ready for battle, and companion on the way" (FEI 77).³ In fact, Nietzsche argues in *The Birth of Tragedy* that the poets' works and the Greeks' political activities were not only intertwined, but also helped the other achieve its own distinctive forms of excellence. Nietzsche describes the audience experience of tragic drama as the necessary consolation for the horrors experienced during war—they needed "tragedy, of necessity, as a restorative draught" (BT 21).⁴ Though the unity of state and culture maintained a harmony between the bodily and spiritual needs of human beings, Nietzsche argues that this unity also stunted the growth of individuality in culture. The state, for instance, employed its coercion to police individual attachment to cultural norms.⁵ Socrates, for instance, was put on trial because of his questioning of Homeric religion and its moral code, a system of beliefs that maintained citizen devotion to the state.

Yet the modern world does not immediately claim a clear victory over the ancient world, as it too has its advantages and disadvantages. However, ultimately, Nietzsche agrees with Hegel and many other modern thinkers that it is on the whole better than the ancient world. Nietzsche lauds the modern liberation of the individual from the "power of custom [*Sitte*]," which has become "astonishingly enfeebled and the feeling for ethical life [*Sittlichkeit*] so rarefied and lofty it may be described as having more or less evaporated" (D 9). Nietzsche argues that it is impossible to turn back the clock to a more traditional form of communal existence anyway, since "after Socrates it is no longer possible to preserve the common good, hence the individualizing ethics that seeks to preserve *individuals* [Einzelnen]" (UUM 19.20). The modern world has trained us moderns to think for ourselves and be mistrustful of what are essentially parochial and "falsifying" claims of particular traditions. At the same time, the "historical sense" affords us moderns with the knowledge and ability to appreciate a breathtaking array of different cultural works both past and present (BGE 224). The individual is then free to cultivate for himself his own identity out of the myriad possibilities on offer, and hence the modern age points toward the realization of what Hegel calls "subjective freedom." In short, human beings are free to become individuals in the sense we have been exploring in the last few chapters. Hence, for Nietzsche, "the individual himself [*der Einzelne selber*] is still the youngest creation," the creation of the modern age (Z:1 "On the Thousand").

The disadvantage of the modern age, however, throws into doubt the hope that such subjective freedom can be possible for the majority of human beings, or even possible at all. Here Nietzsche parts ways with Hegel's analysis of modern life. The disadvantage is that modern skepticism of communal traditions and practices leaves us with no source of meaning within which to exert our agency. Modern science debunks the moral world around us, revealing the principle of the good to be the quixotic creation of a poet's imagination, thereby dissolving our attachment to this moral world. Consequently, all our moral "perspectives" have "been shifted back to the beginning of all becoming, back to infinity," and we feel as if we can no longer get any traction in this frictionless moral void (UM 2.4). We have no ethical standards of the good life, no individual exemplars, by which to regulate our lives.[6] At the same time, even if we could cobble together a provisional community in which we could act, the "historical sense" burdens such a community with a tremendous influx of different moral systems, further undermining the unity of "taste" that once existed in traditional cultures (BGE 224). With the decline and dissolution of moral worlds, human beings lose the "meaning" that their lives had within these communities. With the "death of God," for instance, Nietzsche argues, comes the loss of the cosmic significance of human beings and our recognition that we are ourselves part of a cruel and alien universe where right and wrong are not enshrined in the nature of things and we ourselves are "straying as though through an infinite [*unendliches*] nothing" (GS 125). Religion "quietens the heart of the individual in times of loss, deprivation, fear, distrust" with a comforting myth about a providential universe in which one's suffering has meaning (HH 472). Yet without such meaning, suffering and toil become increasingly difficult to endure.

Accordingly, in these conditions, it is very tempting for modern human beings to throw ourselves blindly and wholly on atavistic, traditional forms of community, as if we are trying to turn back the clock to before the emergence of modern skepticism.[7] Nietzsche worries that the modern human beings will in fear fall back on the comforting agency of either society or nature. Nietzsche sees in modern life a rise in the "fanaticism" of "faith," even when one's faith has been "refuted to him a thousand times" (GS 347). The impassioned attachment to religion or to nationalism testifies in Nietzsche's mind to the unconscious awareness of the essential fragility of these communities in the modern age, to the "need for faith, a foothold, backbone, support" (GS 347). Modern human beings seek meaning and must cast themselves ever more completely into a society in order to work "as little as possible with their heads," lest their modern reflective drive question their attachment to these parochial, nationalist societies (HH 480). It is because the participants realize that their communities—and indeed community as such—

are always under threat that they have to compensate and become ever more vociferous and fanatical about their devotion to it.

Nietzsche does not think the great danger of modernity lies here, however. Such fervent communitarianism will always be held in check by the dominant trend of the modern age, that of the reflective drive for truth. Nietzsche's main worry is instead that human beings will give themselves over to the agency of nature. He offers two reasons for this worry. First, the loss of communal meaning undermines our attachment to one another, casting us all back upon ourselves. The most pressing desires we find when we return to ourselves are our natural desires. Natural desires are private, subjective, internal—they do not rely on the judgments or recognition of others for their creation and fulfillment. Nietzsche argues that as "a people . . . perishes" as a result of the rise of "petty egoism, ossification and greed," then "in its place systems of individualist egoism, brotherhoods for the rapacious exploitation of the non-brothers, and similar creations of utilitarian vulgarity may perhaps appear in the arena of the future" (UM 2.9). Second, pursuing our natural desires can masquerade as individual autonomy, that bedrock good of the modern age. That is, giving ourselves over to our most internal drives appears to be an act of individual self-sovereignty against oppressive custom. It appears as such because these desires come from within "me." By acting based on them, then, it seems as if I have exercised my freedom. Yet for Nietzsche, such a return to our given natural desires is not a moment of freedom, but a step back in the development of the will to power, as we saw in chapter 5. Human community controls natural desire precisely for the purpose of realizing human freedom, and so if we simply let go of the reins of community, natural desire strips us of freedom, submitting our will entirely to our chaotic and debasing appetites.[8]

Nietzsche argues that the great disadvantage of this "return to nature" is that it will lead to a "prudent practical egoism" (UM 2.5), a hedonism in which we cease to pursue human meaning and give ourselves over to our selfish bodily desires. Initially, Nietzsche thinks, such egoism creates a problem of order. Egoism can lead to "absolutely fundamental convulsions," since "we live in the age of atoms, of atomistic chaos," without any principles to order human communities (UM 3.4). The appearance of egoism marks, then, "the hour of a great peril" (UM 2.9). Yet egoism is perilous according to Nietzsche not for the reason that its atomism may undermine communal order and lead to tumult and instability. Rather, Nietzsche sees that human communities are structured around a principle or "table of goods," so we are constantly hungry for a foundational principle which can bring meaning to our actions and a direction to our agency. What is so perilous, then, is that human beings will uphold egoism itself as the new principle of communal order. In this context, Nietzsche describes egoism as the tempting "devil"—the Mephistopheles who indulges every one of Faust's desires—since egoism is sadly appearing to be the "regent of this world and the lord of success and progress" (UM 2.9).[9] Human beings thus no longer strive to be self-creating individuals, but rather strive to be "money-makers and the military despots," whose "egoism . . . hold[s] sway over almost everything on earth" (UM 3.4).

In other words, "communities" in the modern age obviate the slide into political disorder by making the problem worse. Since retrieving any traditional sort of "culture," based on ethical principles gleaned from tradition, nature, and religion, becomes increasingly impossible, modern human beings require a different sort of ethical order. Modern human beings turn to the "state" for the "founding of the world-system of egoism," because the state is already equipped with the institutional instruments to channel selfish desire. Through its institutional checks and balances, the state promulgates that principle of "egoism which imposes certain restraints upon itself so as to ensure its endurance" (UM 2.9). The "state certainly makes an attempt to organize everything anew out of itself and to bind and constrain all those mutually hostile forces" (UM 3.4).

The modern state is so successful in enshrining this new principle of order because it itself is organized following this same principle, the principle of a "hundred appetites" (Z:1 "New Idol"). The state's institutions are designed with the very expectation of corruption of society and of government officials. Hence, the state successfully enshrines this principle of order because it can efficiently fulfill it through its regulation of a well-designed civil society. As Hegel noted, the main modern advancement of political science has occurred in political economy and the creation of commercial society. The state regulates a properly designed civil society of market exchange. Individuals thus can enter the market and satisfy whatever egoistic desire they happen to have. When many individuals engage in the satisfaction of their given desires—even quite vicious and grasping desires—civil society as a whole benefits. As Bernard Mandeville argued, the more grasping, acquisitive behavior unleashed into the market, the more these desires are satisfied as a result. Production must keep up with this hungry demand, which opens up many more jobs and allows more and more human beings to satisfy their needs. In this way, the system of civil society is self-perpetuating—not only does it satisfy needs and hence placate human beings, but it also creates the very desires it aims to satisfy. Individuals come to "determine the value of a thing . . . according to the needs of the consumer," and this "becomes the character of an entire culture" (D 175). These institutions are, after all, the source of the individual's "education" or self-formation.

Not only does the state replace the function of culture, it also puts culture to rest, settling for "barbarism" (UM 1.1). It does this by taking the place once occupied by culture in human self-consciousness. The state "wants men to render it the same idolatry they formerly rendered the church" (UM 3.4). Even though human beings have witnessed the self-destruction of all traditional cultural principles, they still long for institutions and political individuals that would focus and embody the unifying principles of the community in the way that their cultural institutions did.[10] Perhaps not surprisingly, Nietzsche thinks that none other than G. W. F. Hegel has provided the ideological statement of the state's supremacy.[11]

The state assumes culture's place in three ways: first, it becomes the "absolutely complete ethical organism" as "Hegel . . . designates it" (FEI 79). The state positions itself no longer as an artificial, instrumental mechanism serving culture, but as an organic outgrowth of a people. For Nietzsche, culture had always occupied the position of being this organic outgrowth, as when he suggests that the "unconsciousness of the people" have as their "motherly vocation . . . the begetting of genius" (FEI 67). When the state claims for itself the position of autochthony within the mythology of a people's genesis, there is no escape from the state's comprehensive reach. Thus, whenever "culture" may appear within a people, the state co-opts it and releases "the spiritual energies of a generation to the extent that will serve the interests of existing institutions" (UM 3.6).[12] Any striving beyond egoism, any other activities of free self-determination, will be immediately co-opted by the state's task of promoting itself or the egoistic desires of its citizens. Second, the state also replaces culture's traditional role by asserting itself as its own end and the end of human beings. Nietzsche states that this "doctrine" has been "lately preached from all the rooftops" (UM 3.4), undoubtedly an allusion to the Hegelian view, which has had an "enormous and still continuing influence" (UM 2.8): the state "is the highest goal [*Ziel*] of mankind . . . [and] a man has no higher duty than to serve the state" (UM 3.4). Not the individual and his culture, but the state becomes the end of human beings. Finally, the state inscribes itself in the habits and everyday lives of its people. It creates bureaucracies, systems of discipline and control, a scholarly apparatus, all intended to regulate the behavior of individuals. In the premodern era, the community had promulgated a "table of goods," and this moral system animated and circumscribed human action. By contrast, the modern state replaces an ethically based system with a thorough habituation to bureaucratic norms.[13] For Nietzsche, this latter transformation is a deeply problematic trend because the state's lack of ethical norms prevents the appearance of free human behavior, which arises out of ethical norms—instead, it lulls human beings into a smooth, mechanical, subhuman feeling of contentment with the pleasures of natural desire, which marks, for Nietzsche, the "slow suicide of all is called 'life'" (Z:1 "New Idol").[14] Nietzsche claims that the state treats human beings as animals to be mastered in the machinery of the state, that is, as natural beings responsive to the pain of the "sword" and the pleasures of "a hundred appetites" (Z:1 "New Idol"). In being treated as animals, human beings are more likely to become so by embracing the principle of egoism lying at the heart of the state's dominance.

The promulgation of egoism can lead in two very different directions. On the one hand, egoism can result in a nihilistic community Nietzsche envisions, like the "last men," who have their "little pleasures" and seek merely to prolong their lives, but instill their lives with no meaning beyond what nature breathes into their desires (Z.P.5). On the other hand, the apotheosis of the state can herald a resurgence of a power politics, yet on a scale never before seen in human history, given the kind of total control the very large nation-state commands over human beings. Nietzsche offers undisguised contempt every time he speaks of the new *Reich* (founded in 1871).[15] In fact, Nietzsche sees the rise of the power politics of the new *Reich* under Bismarck as an outgrowth also of Hegel's political philosophy,[16] in which the "state is the highest goal of mankind . . . [and] a man has no higher duty than to serve the state" (UM 3.4). For Nietzsche, the state's claim that "there is nothing greater than I: the ordering finger of God am I" (Z:1 "New Idol") and that the state is the result of "God's sojourn on earth" (UM 2.8, an even clearer allusion to Hegel) give unprecedented freedom of activity to an all-powerful state.

Bergmann (1987) is thus correct to interpret Nietzsche as fearing the state as an "all-enveloping force which threatened to engulf both the religious and the cultural" (4). As Nietzsche puts the point, if the state is "completed and perfected too far it will in the end enfeeble the individual [*Individuum*] and, indeed, dissolve him" (HH 235). Yet Nietzsche does not think this is a necessary outcome of modern history. Nietzsche still holds out the hope that we can return to the original division at the onset of modern life between state and culture. Comprehensiveness is the goal of the political institutions of the state, but they have not yet attained it. That individuals such as Schopenhauer are able to extricate themselves from its grasp and live at the margins of the state testifies to a last gasp of an independent culture. Nietzsche recognizes that in order to create the conditions for the appearance of more individuals like Schopenhauer, state and culture must first be separated; second, Nietzsche's task is to reverse the priority of state over culture.[17] The state must be decentered, dethroned from its position as the apotheosis of modern individual freedom. As we will see, Nietzsche envisions quite a different role for the state.

7.2   On the Nature and Function of the Modern State

How does Nietzsche think we ought to navigate this doleful condition of modern politics and culture? For Nietzsche, the rise of the modern state has threatened the possibility of genuine culture, so we must investigate Nietzsche's assessment of it. First, we must ask, what is the normative status of the state? Does it have a value, or is it justified at all? Nietzsche claims that the state is justified as an instrument to culture and to genius. This argument contradicts the "antipolitical" reading put forward in a recent and sophisticated form by Tamsin Shaw (2007). Second, assuming that the normative function of the state is to provide the conditions for culture and the genius, how should we organize the state such that it produces these ends? I argue that Nietzsche defends a "weak" understanding of the power the state should wield, that the state should be primarily conservative in nature, preserving the present legal order, rather than engaged in actively transforming human cultural interactions. Radical changes in the nature of the political order will either cause rampant violence and chaos (and hence the impossibility of culture) or accelerate the immanent development of modernity toward the "last man" (and hence the defeat of culture). This interpretation contradicts the "aristocratic radical" interpretation of Nietzsche, in which Nietzsche adopts a "strong" understanding of the power of the state in regulating and transforming human behavior in accordance with a monstrous or fascistic ideal, or even in reconstructing the political community with aristocratic institutions and norms.

Despite the drawbacks of the modern state, Nietzsche does not reject it in particular or politics in general. He does not counsel a retreat from politics and society into solitude. Every time Zarathustra returns to the solitude in his mountains, for instance, he is impelled to return, to "go down," to humanity. But perhaps Nietzsche "rejects" politics in a different sense. That is, perhaps Nietzsche argues that no modern political order can be normatively justified. Shaw (2007) has argued that for Nietzsche the secularization of the modern age has led to the view that "reason is the only legitimate guide to belief and value" (8). Since a state has coercive power over all individuals within its borders, it must attain a rational consensus as to its normative authority. But, Shaw's Nietzsche argues, attaining such a normative consensus is unlikely, since many individuals are unable to grasp the arcane truths about norms discerned by philosophers. Also, this consensus is most likely impossible, since all "moral realist" claims grounding state rule are problematic.[18] As a result, no modern political order can be normatively justified, even though states continuously create the appearance of legitimate rule through their exertion of power.

Shaw sets up the problem very well—she is right to point out that modern politics poses problems unknown to previous epochs. She correctly brings out Nietzsche's worries about the manufactured legitimacy of the modern state, as we can see from his reflections about the toady scholars who use their argumentative clout to support the Bismarckian state, and from his view that the modern state is the "coldest of all cold monsters," which creates the illusion of legitimacy by gratifying our appetites (UM 3.8; Z:1 "New Idol"). Shaw fails, however, to account for the moments in Nietzsche's text when he sees a positive role for the modern state. Her failure is rooted in a philosophical misunderstanding of what would count as a justification of the modern state for Nietzsche. Shaw's assumption that for Nietzsche the state must be rationally grounded is the wrong requirement for the legitimacy of state action. Indeed, Nietzsche insists that reason cannot establish any normative truths about the world on its own—Nietzsche understands Kant's distinctive contribution precisely to be the critique of the "limits" of rational knowledge (BT 19) and that all we can know are the categories and values that we create. Fortunately, there is, for Nietzsche, an alternative, nonrational, instrumental justification for the state. The state is justified as an instrument to the most basic form of "justification" (*Rechtfertigung*) of communal human life, the aesthetic justification we spoke of in the previous chapter. The aesthetic justification does not rely on a "moral realist" or "antirealist" "metaethics," but rather is a post-Kantian justification, a law that we recognize as valid and impose on ourselves. Shaw is right, then, that the state and its actions have no intrinsic legitimacy for Nietzsche, but she is wrong to think it can have no legitimacy at all. Her interpretation fails because she overlooks the essential role culture plays in Nietzsche's view of the justification of the state.[19] Accordingly, Nietzsche's view does not jettison reason nor the modern state, but rather these are displaced from their traditional, foundational role.[20]

In his text as well, Nietzsche is clear as to the function of the state, and hence the source of its justification. The state's "task is to furnish the basis of a *culture*. In short, a nobler humanity is the goal of the state. Its goal lies outside itself. The state is a means."[21] Nietzsche argues in UM 3.4 that the "teleology" of the "species of man" is "independent of the welfare of a state, that of culture." Culture is indeed the "teleology" of the "species of man," because the "goal of all culture" is the "procreation of genius," or genuine individuality (UM 3.3). In short, Nietzsche justifies state and culture with a kind of chain of justifications: the individual justifies himself; culture is justified by giving rise to individuality; the state is justified by preparing the way for culture.

How, then, can the state fulfill this function best? Some scholars think that the means that the state must employ are oppressive. Scholars such as Detwiler (1990) and Appel (1999) put forth what I call a "strong" view of the state, that the state achieves the promotion of individual genius by openly and actively disciplining human behavior and thereby "breeding" ever greater forms of human character.[22] The proponents of the strong view of the state put forth two different claims—that the state must be consciously led by the very same individuals Nietzsche is trying to promote in culture, and that the institutions that promote such individuality require the many to sacrifice their freedom and happiness for the few (Hurka's maximax principle).[23]

In support of the first claim, Appel (1999) argues that for Nietzsche, the overman, who is concerned with the "discipline and breeding" of a new class of human beings, should employ political laws in order to carry out his program. Certainly a good deal of Nietzsche's rhetoric makes one think that the overman will take on such oppressive duties—the "breeding of tyrants" (BGE 242), the "true philosophers" who are "commanders and legislators" (BGE 211), and the "conscious breeding of the opposite type" to the "herd animal," such as the "Caesarian spirits" who would produce a "new and sublime development of slavery" (WP 954).[24] Nonetheless, Nietzsche does not think that the individual should wrest the helm of the state from the democrats and use it in conscious service of cultural goals. There are three reasons we can marshal in support of this claim.

First, the "breeding" programs of moral systems such as the "law of

Manu" celebrated by Nietzsche (TI 7.3; AC 57) are firmly part of the ancient world. As we have seen, in the ancient world human beings accepted and indeed embraced such a hierarchically designed community intended to benefit the few. Yet the modern world explodes all such codes of morality and forces them to address and receive endorsement from each individual. As Nietzsche puts the point, "there will never again be a life and culture bounded by a religiously determined horizon" (HH 234). History circumscribes the types of communities possible for human beings, and modern life will not accept such traditional forms of association. Yet furthermore, for Nietzsche, this is a desirable development, because individuals strive to treat one another as human beings so as to be recognized in return as such, rather than struggle with one another as "beasts of prey." In the modern age, we have reached a point "when an extraordinary, long accumulated energy of will exceptionally transferred itself through inheritance to *spiritual* [geistige] goals." This "high point of intelligence" allows us to struggle and develop ourselves spiritually, rather than physically (HH 234). Nietzsche reveals himself at his most Hegelian when he argues that the "will to power" is at its height in "thought," which "becomes powerful and demanding, and in the long run it tyrannizes over all other forces. Finally, it becomes 'passion-in-itself'" (WP 611; cf. BGE 9).[25]

Second, since we must assume that modern, democratic citizens would not take too kindly to such physically oppressive codes of conduct such as the one enshrined in the law of Manu, then the overman would have to impose stiff physical punishment to regulate human behavior. Yet Nietzsche claims that human beings have developed as a race such that we no longer desire to master one another physically. The use of physical intimidation and force is an indication of a previous epoch of humanity, in which our natural desires mastered us (GM 2.17). By contrast, the spiritualization of human beings "weaken[ed] covetousness, draw[ing] much of the available energy to themselves for the promotion of spiritual objectives" (HH 464). Nietzsche argues that the "spiritualization of hostility" involves a "deep appreciation of the value of having enemies; basically it means acting and reasoning in ways totally at odds with how people used to act and reason" (TI 5.3). Struggling with "enemies" for the new modern soul hence becomes less about besting them in physical combat, and more about besting them in argument. A good indication of "spiritual" power is precisely to sublimate and put to ethical use our own animalistic brutish instincts.[26] The best indication of "spiritual" power is, for Nietzsche, when a philosopher is able to found a new community simply based on his own individual presence and narrative, that is, without physically forcing anyone to believe, like the "unarmed prophet" Jesus. In order to promulgate one's own individuality, one must learn to master oneself.[27] Individuals hence become less interested in mastering others and more interested in mastering the labyrinths of spiritual thought. The latter activity is not accomplished through politics, especially not through a bloodthirsty power politics.

Indeed, the textual evidence also cuts against the strong state theory. If we read the important passages in Nietzsche marshaled in service of the strong state theory, we see that again and again Nietzsche employs "great politics" as a *metaphor* for spiritual legislation, not physical enforcement. Jesus' great politics is Nietzsche's example of how power can be much more pervasively wielded than by actual, physical polities, that is, through the preaching of a spiritual way of life (GM 1.8).[28] Nietzsche's "true philosophers" who are "commanders and legislators" are so only metaphorically (BGE 211). Nietzsche explains that the philosopher's "legislation" is the activity of "legislating greatness"—that is, determining what is "most worth knowing" and doing (PTA 43). One cannot simply declare what is "most worth knowing" and really expect anyone simply to accept it, even and especially if one backs up one's proclamation with force.[29] Nietzsche is using "legislation" here in the Kantian sense that I have been developing in the past few chapters—that is, that the philosopher determines for himself what is the "law" of his own being (see UUM 19.83 on the "legislation of morality"). The philosopher's character then becomes the foundation for a new culture, as in, for instance, Socrates and the development of the Socratic culture (BT 15). Nietzsche argues that the new "masters of the earth" will indeed be a "tremendous aristocracy," but they will be a "new aristocracy," one created out of the "severest self-legislation." This "higher kind of man" owes his influence to this self-legislation and hence to his "superiority in will, knowledge, riches, and influence," but not to his strength or his marauding instinct (WP 960).[30]

The third reason militating against the strong state theory is that spiritual activity and political activity actually run at cross-purposes with one another, so the overman would be ill-advised to enter into politics anyway. In UM 3.4, Nietzsche speaks of those Hegelians who "lately preached from all the rooftops, that the state is the highest goal of mankind and that a man has no higher duty than to serve the state." This duty is incompatible, Nietzsche claims, with the "world which is again fairly independent of the welfare of a state, that of culture." In his late work TI 8.4, Nietzsche argues that "culture and the state—let us be honest with ourselves here—these are adversaries: '*Kultur-Staat*' is just a modern idea. The one lives off the other, the one flourishes at the expense of the other. All the great ages of culture have been ages of political decline: anything great in the cultural sense is apolitical, even *anti-political.*" According to Nietzsche, in most ages of human community, either the demands of culture reign over politics or politics directs the "energies" of culture. Either individuals expend themselves in the pursuit of external and material goods—those of maximizing the economic, military, or political clout of the nation while outmaneuvering other nations—or they seek to develop internally, by cultivating artistic and philosophical accounts of the world in a cultural community with other individuals.[31] Nietzsche explicitly states in his middle-period work that "political and economic affairs are not worthy of being the enforced concern of society's most gifted spirits," because when individuals engage in politics, "it squanders the most precious thing there is, the spirit [*Geist*]" (D 179).

Politics, for Nietzsche, is very mechanical and complex, requiring one to concern oneself with many petty details of public opinion and majority interest, so as to conceive of laws that will maintain peace and stability. Politics, in Nietzsche's view, tends by and large to traffic in what is subhuman—satisfying "interests," pursuing naked power, arousing unreflective patriotic dispositions. As a result, Nietzsche thinks, "it will probably be increasingly the sign of spiritual superiority from now on if a man takes the state and his duties towards it lightly; for he who has the *furor philosophicus* within him will already no longer have time for the *furor politicus* and will wisely refrain from reading the newspapers every day, let alone working for a political party. . . . Every state in which anyone other than the statesman has to concern himself with politics is ill organized and deserves to perish by all these politicians" (UM 3.7). However, this is not to say that the spiritual individuals remove themselves utterly from political life: the individual "will not hesitate for a moment to be at his place when his fatherland experiences a real emergency" (UM 3.7). But Nietzsche does indeed seek to separate the spheres of culture and politics in the modern age. In fact, he argues that if the state is properly doing its job, then it is justified. Nietzsche emphasizes that if a physically coercive overman were to come along and threaten the state, the state would be "justified [*im Recht*] in expelling such a man and treating him as an enemy" (UM 3.8).[32]

Let us turn now to the second part of the strong view of the state interpretation. The point is expressed in Hurka's (1999) maximax principle—the end of politics for Nietzsche is the production of the "rarest and most valuable exemplars." The task of politics is the task of culture, to provide the conditions and cultivate the good for the wisest, best individuals. But in order to "live for [their] good," Hurka argues, we must live at the expense of our own happiness (UM 3.6). We must redistribute primary goods from the many to the few. However, *contra* Hurka, it does not follow from such an end of politics that the means we must employ involve burdening the many with unhappiness and unfreedom to benefit the few. Such a calculus would involve computing the good in quantitative terms, when in fact Nietzsche defends a qualitative understanding of the good, in terms of what satisfies the distinctively human. Pleasures, comforts, and the array of primary goods do not satisfy our subjectivity. In fact, in terms of such bodily, material goods, Nietzsche argues that the few "is the more capable of suffering and suffers more, its enjoyment of existence is less, its task heavier" than the many (HH 439; cf. HH 462). This is because, for Nietzsche, the individual has the "most comprehensive responsibility, whose conscience bears the weight of the overall development of humanity" (BGE 61). For Nietzsche, the individual is devoted to realizing the happiness of the many, because the individual sees that his happiness is required so that he can continue his activity of self-creation. Therefore, the truth of the situation is precisely the opposite of the maximax principle—in terms of happiness and primary goods, the many enjoy much more than the few.

Furthermore, as we saw in the previous chapter, human beings only become individuals when they are able to draw human beings out of the horror of their existence and form a community. In particular, as Nietzsche continues at the beginning of his essay "The Greek State," "only those individuals can emerge from this horrifying struggle for existence who are then immediately preoccupied with the fine illusions of artistic culture, so that they do not arrive at that practical pessimism which nature abhors as truly unnatural" (GrS 176). Or, as Nietzsche puts it in BGE 61, the individual must be concerned with the "contentment with [the] situation and type" of the many. The individual must "provide something of a justification [*Rechtfertigung*] for everything commonplace, for all the lowliness, for the whole half-bestial poverty of their souls." For Nietzsche, it is the prevailing "religion" of the time that the individual will invoke, just as "he will make use of the prevailing political and economic situation" in order to benefit the lot of the many. Religion supplies the members of the community with a "meaning" (*Bedeutsamkeit*) for their lives, a human world in which they can make their suffering intelligible and meaningful, in which they can endure their trials and take pride in their successes. Rather than the many sacrificing their happiness for the few, Nietzsche claims the opposite—the few sacrifice themselves for humanity as a whole, a task that requires ensuring the happiness of the many.

Especially in his early and middle-period works, Nietzsche is reluctant to claim that the state should have a "strong" agency; rather, it should take on a "weaker" role, deferring in many ways to culture. If "change" is to occur, Nietzsche argues, it "must be given in the smallest doses but unremittingly over long periods of time." This is because we cannot "exchange the state of morality to which we [have been] accustomed" since the ancient world "for a new evaluation of things head over heels and amid acts of violence." Such "impatience" is "dangerous" because, for Nietzsche, it takes a long time for human beings to develop a civilized culture, and this culture is extremely fragile (D 534). It is all too easy for human beings to regress back into the chaos of our natural desires where we began, since "political society" is based on a "firm agreement" about the "customary use of metaphors"—hence the decline in customs, traditions, and habits, or the creation and imposition of new ones, can very easily destroy the fragile order that has been accumulated over time (UUM 19.229). Any attempt to create something new and "great" cannot occur with a "single stroke"—indeed, such attempts have been "nothing more than a pathetic and bloody piece of quackery"—but rather must be internalized over long periods of time (D 534).

Instead, Nietzsche argues that the primary focus of politics should be on conserving the order of the passions, as it is a "prudent institution for the protection of individuals [*Individuen*] against one another" (HH 235). Nietzsche seeks to make use of the state both to restrain the excesses of the passions and to indulge many of the desires of democratic citizens. Nietzsche argues in FEI 78 that the "great majority" of human beings "are boundlessly egoistic, unjust, unfair, dishonest, envious, wicked, and thereby very limited and queer in the head." Culture is utterly impossible under these conditions, in what Nietzsche calls, following in the tradition of modern political thought, the "state of nature." Without a strong government to regulate the behavior of mostly egoistic human beings, a "communality collapses completely and everything dissolves into anarchy, [and] then there at once breaks through that condition of unreflecting, ruthless inequality that constitutes the state of nature [*Naturzustand*]" (WS 31). Without "the state," Nietzsche argues, "in a natural *bellum omnium contra omnes*, society generally cannot take root in a greater measure and out beyond the domain of the family" (GrS 52–53, quoting Hobbes). Nietzsche recognizes, like all the great political thinkers of the past, that a political community is a necessary means to secure any distinctively human end.

The dangers of the state of nature direct us to the necessary function of the state. Nietzsche states in FEI 78 how difficult it is for a state to govern human beings, given the "boundlessly egoistic" majority, "greedy neighbors," and "malicious robbers," whom Nietzsche seems to identify as corrupt state officials. The state thus needs to "govern human beings" by "preserv[ing] upright law, order, quiet, and peace among many millions."[33] As Nietzsche argues in WS 26, the "rule of law" must be employed as a "means" to ensure peace and eliminate corruption not just of the majority, but also of the governing officials themselves. Thus, we can see that Nietzsche endorses Schopenhauer's view when he describes the latter in the following way: the "purpose of the state [is] to provide protection against forces from without, protection against forces from within, and protection against the protectors" (UM 3.7). Nietzsche thus claims that the function of the state must be the protection of external goods or rights: the state protects citizens from foreign invasions, protects citizens from the oppressions of factious majorities, and protects its citizens from the corruption of its own officials. Such order is increasingly important to maintain in the modern age, when moral principles are ever more unable to regulate the behavior of citizens.

In Nietzsche's middle-period works, as others have pointed out, Nietzsche reveals himself to be friendly to democracy, and hence not an advocate of revolutionary aristocratism.[34] Yet he is no friend to democracy for its own sake, but rather as the best modern instrument for the promotion of culture. Nietzsche upholds democracy in part because he regards it as inevitable—"since [the democratic revolution] has happened one has to accommodate oneself to the new conditions" (HH 438). Instead of a battle of the few against the many (which the few will lose), the best means to mitigate the oppressive effects of the many on the few is to gratify the basic needs of the many such that they will give the few free rein. As Nietzsche puts it, the "purpose of politics" is to "make life endurable for as many as possible" (HH 438). In the modern age, life can only be made endurable in a condition of political equality and "self-determination" (HH 438), such that "government" is understood as "nothing but an organ of the people and not a provident, venerable 'above' in relation to a diffident 'below'" (HH 450). The modern *demos* enjoins the state to satisfy basic bodily desires. The satisfaction of the people's egoistic desires "renders their life so pleasant to them they are happy to bear the calamitous consequences of their narrow-mindedness"

(HH 438). When their basic egoistic passions are satisfied, Nietzsche argues, they are less likely to control the thought and behavior of individuals in culture—they cease to think that "everyone should live and work according to such a standard" (HH 438). They become less outraged when individuals escape from the grasp of public opinion and live in the margins of society—a "few must first of all be allowed, now more than ever, to refrain from politics and to step a little aside" (HH 438).

One final point on Nietzsche's view of the "weak" role of the state: Nietzsche argues in TI 9.39 that "our institutions are no good any more," but "this is our fault, not the fault of the institutions." For Nietzsche, it is not that the modern state is hopelessly corrupt or debasing—at least not yet. The institutional apparatus of the modern state can be salvaged so long as we resist the early modern "liberal" impulse towards egoism, which tears community apart and subjects us to domination by our natural desires. Nietzsche hence agrees with Hegel that we must transform what we moderns call "freedom," which for us means "living for today" and hence "despising, hating, rejecting" our institutions because of the duties they impose upon us. Despite Nietzsche's similarity to the classical liberals institutionally, he departs from them normatively. For Nietzsche, modern liberals like to think of themselves as free beings existing apart from all institutions and practices, regarding "authority" as a "new sort of slavery." Instead, Nietzsche argues, we must offset the egoism of the modern age by upholding the "will to tradition, to authority, to a responsibility that spans the centuries, to solidarity in the chain that links the generations forwards and backwards ad infinitum."[35] We must come to understand ourselves as part of a community that we have built for ourselves over time, since we ourselves are "ultimately constituted" by this past, "no matter how much the individual [*Individuum*] tends to see himself as something wholly new and unique" (UUM 26.13). A "nation that preserves itself best is the one in which most men have, as a consequence of sharing habitual and undiscussable principles . . . a living sense of community [*Gemeinsinn*]" (HH 224). Hence, Nietzsche asks members of the state to recognize the historical basis for their identity, that who they are is the creation of historical interactions and labor that stretch back many centuries and that provides the very context in which they can further create themselves.[36] Rather than seeking to promote some ideological or material agenda, the state, for Nietzsche, must uphold and defer to its cultural history in which genuine humanity appears.

Indeed, for Nietzsche, culture "can endure" if the "sound sleeping of the people" continues—their slumber brought on by the satisfaction of their basic needs (FEI 67). A "high culture can stand only upon a broad base, upon a strong and healthy consolidated mediocrity . . . [and] the honorable term for mediocre is, of course, the word 'liberal'" (WP 864). Hence Nietzsche does not think state institutions should redistribute goods from the many to the few, but rather he strives to keep politics from interfering in culture. The separation of politics and culture in the modern age can hence be a salutary development as long as the forces of politics are restrained from their tendency to overreach into the domain of culture. The separation of politics from culture is not just a cease-fire such that culture can go its own way; this separation also affords culture that "pathos of distance" that Nietzsche insists is a condition for the creation of a higher order of the soul.[37] Culture needs the state as something separate from it, and indeed, Nietzsche argues, as something recognized as *beneath* it, in order to ascend to its own heights. By understanding what it is not—namely, the state's maintenance of bodily order—cultural individuals can better guide their own positive goals, that of the development of a spiritual, personal identity. The political life, in Nietzsche's mind, consists in the animal life of human beings—hence, it is only by overcoming the political life and creating oneself within culture that we can achieve what is distinctively human. This is not to say that the two spheres of culture and state do not interact. On the one hand, the state is the origin of the individual, since every individual always stands under laws. No human individual can wholly overcome his bodily nature (nor is this desirable), and hence the interactions among individuals must always require a neutral arbiter in the state's laws to adjudicate possible conflict. On the other hand, members of the state are not entirely motivated by bodily desires. They are, as we saw in the last chapter, uplifted by the personalities of individuals whom they witness in culture.[38]

The argument for the weak theory of the state, then, is this: the state is naturally powerful in the modern age, expanding and overreaching its territory. Hence, we must resist its expansion, which will turn everyone into "egoists" or last men. The notion that aspiring individuals should wield political power in service of individualistic goals—aside from its sheer logistical difficulties—is bad from Nietzsche's perspective because it would eliminate the sources of friction and the "pathos of distance" created by structural differences. It would, moreover, cease to treat potential human beings as human beings, as beings responsive to the beautiful allure of the individual, but treat them rather as animals who are "trained" to act in this or that way. Instead, Nietzsche thinks, the state must be weakened, by its members being satisfied and understanding themselves to be part of an ongoing political and cultural tradition that cannot be thrust aside. Thus, the weakening of the state allows for the reinstatement of the separation of culture and state inaugurated in the modern age. It is in the sphere of culture, a sphere that transcends political borders, that the struggle among individual human beings takes place.

7.3   The Possibilities of Modern Culture

Nietzsche is ambivalent about the modern age, for "the same conditions that hasten the evolution of the herd animal also hasten the evolution of the leader animal" (WP 956). On the one hand, as we have seen, Nietzsche criticizes modernity for setting us on a path toward the "last man" or to nihilism. On the other hand, however, Nietzsche argues that modern life affords human beings an unprecedented opportunity for the satisfaction of individuality in a form the likes of which the world has never seen. In this section, I want to explore why Nietzsche thinks the same modern conditions he fears can at the same time supply individuals with a tremendous opportunity. Nietzsche's answer, in brief, is that the dissolution of particular "peoples" in the modern age allows for the possibility of a creation of a universal "humanity." The aim of subjectivity is human freedom, and a universal cultural community devoted to human freedom is what is most satisfying to the individual subject. In defending a cosmopolitan, nonpolitical community, Nietzsche disagrees vehemently with Hegel's political solution.

Why does the modern age provide us with conditions ripe for the satisfaction of individuality? For Nietzsche, the right kind of condition for the production of "genius" is one in which the genius is challenged, in which the genius must rise to the occasion to overcome adversity and rise to the difficulty of the occasion. The greater the difficulty, the greater the heights to which the individual must aspire to in order to overcome it. The genius must "lose his way in a forest but strive with uncommon energy to get out of it again," and thus he will "discover a new path which no one knows" (HH 231). Challenging conditions have been available to many past geniuses. There are two features distinctive to the modern age that make the challenge particularly acute.

First, Nietzsche argues that modernity is the "age of disintegration," in which all cultures and peoples and "races are mixed together" such that a "person will have the legacy of multiple lineages in his body, which means conflicting . . . drives and value standards . . . fight with each other and rarely leave each other alone" (BGE 200). The challenge of incorporating these conflicting, diverse strands into a unified personality is difficult for many, and hence most desire simply to "end the war that he is." Furthermore, Nietzsche fears that the "notion of happiness" for the modern human being—the notion of happiness of the last man—"corresponds to that of a medicine and mentality of pacification." It is "a notion of happiness as primarily rest, lack of disturbance, repletion, unity at last" (BGE 200). In other words, the first challenge of the modern age is that modern peoples try to ease the "tension of the bow," to give up on the conflict between our "esteeming" and our "skeptical" natures (BGE.P; GS 346). There is a strong pressure in the modern age to jettison our humanity and live in accordance with mere animal desires. The "ideology" of liberal democracy thus exerts a kind of "spiritual" oppression, tempting one to give up the task of creating oneself. This kind of ideological challenge is different in kind from all previous forms of control, in which "ethical life" or "tradition" would co-opt individual greatness for its own spiritual purposes (D 9). In the modern age, all "spiritual purposes" are looked upon with skepticism.

Second, even if one overcomes the devilish temptation to bodily pleasure of liberal democracy, one is still dogged by the "war that he is" (BGE 200). How do we organize the chaos of our inner selves without a communal standard of the good? How can we guide our lives when "God is dead," and hence no Christian culture can determine the relative goodness we assign to different values flowing through us as part of an eclectic and cosmopolitan modern age? Without such a standard of the good, and by being forced to grapple with a multitude of values, the modern age tasks the individual with a particularly daunting effort. Yet the successful creation of individuality involves "those amazing, incomprehensible, and unthinkable ones, those human riddles destined for victory and for seduction" (BGE 200). These individuals contain and organize "powerful and irreconcilable drives" and hence reveal themselves to have a sublime depth of self and a beautiful harmonization of these drives (BGE 200).

However, the genius would not be able to arise if the whole deck were stacked against him. He would have no encouragement to proceed in the first place. Three features of the modern age provide good conditions for the cultivation of individuality. First, as I have claimed already, Nietzsche does not think that liberal democracy is bad full stop. Rather, he argues that the aim of the liberal democratic movement is bad (the "easing" of the tension in the bow), but the institutions can be salutary. In particular, Nietzsche applauds the "pride" in the "feeling of self-determination [*Selbstbestimmung*]" encouraged by democratic institutions. The "few" who come to "step aside" from politics are "prompted to this by pleasure in self-determination [*Selbstbestimmung*]" (HH 438).[39] Furthermore, liberal "institutions . . . are actually powerful promoters of freedom" (TI 9.38). Nietzsche argues that it is only when liberal institutions are "being fought for" that they have the effect of encouraging individuals to strive for freedom. Yet one of the enduring features of liberalism has been that its cause is ever ongoing—defenders of liberalism continue to strive for economic, social, and political rights for many individuals across the globe. Thus, Nietzsche thinks that liberal democratic institutions can have a salutary side effect in cultivating the desire on the part of the individual to transcend his time and craft a unique self for himself.

For Nietzsche, however, education is the most important institution for the development of individuality. He uses the term "education" (*Erziehung*) in its literal sense, that is, to "draw out" (*er-ziehen*) individuals from their social and political surroundings. In his early work, Nietzsche confessed that Schopenhauer was one of the individuals who drew Nietzsche out of being a "child of his age" such that he became a "stepchild of his age" (UM 3.3).[40] For Nietzsche, "your educators can be only your liberators." The activity of education is "liberation [*Befreiung*], the removal of all the weeds, rubble and vermin that want to attack the tender buds of the plant, an outstreaming of light and warmth" (UM 3.1). Similarly, Zarathustra teaches and thereby seeks to liberate individuals from mass society, "luring many away from the herd" (Z P 9). This liberation occurs most prominently through one's erotic attraction to individual exemplars, dramatized in Zarathustra's sermons and deeds—a relationship we explored in the last chapter.

The second feature of the modern age that can help generate individuality, then, is a substantive feature of modern education, its cultivation of the "historical sense." Nietzsche describes the "historical sense" from his early work to his late as distinctive of modernity and as the source of creative possibilities. Nietzsche traces the development of the "historical sense" to "that enchanting and crazy *half-barbarism* into which Europe has been plunged through the democratic mixing of classes and races," the mixture we spoke of above that is introduced in BGE 200. As a result of this mixing of class and race, we moderns are thrust above the fray, forced to examine and assess the various different value systems that "radiate into us, we 'modern souls.'" Thus, we cultivate a sense to "guess the rank order of the valuations that a people, a society, an individual has lived by, the 'divinatory instinct' for the connections between these valuations, for the relationship between the authority of values and the authority of effective forces" (BGE 224). We can read our way into Homer once again—we can research Greek culture, read a multitude of historical texts about Homer, do anthropological research about the Greek world—all in the project of understanding this culture. Yet with understanding comes a flagging of our instincts— our "instincts are running back everywhere and we ourselves are a type of chaos" (BGE 224). We become "walking encyclopedias" whose inner life is a chaos of accumulated knowledge unable to manifest itself in external action (UM 2.3). We become less and less able to act within a value system or table of goods, since all particular value systems have been exploded, revealed to be parochial judgments resting on historical contexts and needs. We can only hover above them and appreciate the "noble" or rather hierarchical "taste" they lived by, while we ourselves are "crossed by infinity" (HC 192) in Nietzsche's terms. We have many different standards or tastes swirling within us, threatening to paralyze the very possibility of distinctively human agency.

However, Nietzsche argues that "spirit . . . eventually finds that this is to its own advantage." For Nietzsche, the historical sense affords us "secret entrances everywhere, like no noble age has ever had, and, above all, access to the labyrinths of unfinished cultures and to every half-barbarism that has ever existed on earth" (BGE 224). The modern age educates human beings to think for themselves. Part of this project of education is to acquire a historical sense and with it a knowledge of a multitude of cultures, along with an attenuated attachment to all of them, including those closest to us. This experience is paralyzing for some, but it also affords the possibility of engaging in a higher form of life, that of the self-conscious appropriation of past historical cultures in our own individual self-creation. That is, human beings can delve deeply into historical cultures and appropriate features of these cultures that are healthy and powerful, features that can rejuvenate an increasingly herdlike modern age. Nietzsche's project of retrieving Greek tragedy, for instance, is an effort of self-conscious appropriation for a cultural renewal. I have argued elsewhere that Nietzsche seeks to retrieve a kind of Aristotelian magnanimity, marrying it to Christian and modern features to produce a new brand of individuality.[41]

For Nietzsche, the most promising feature of the modern age is its historical sense, since it contains a bottomless source of knowledge that can fuel the endless appropriation and transformation of past forms of meaning—that is, so long as "historical knowledge" is guided toward the project of producing individuality, rather than pursued as an end in itself, which, as Nietzsche worries in UM 2.4, leads to the undermining

of life. Yet once we realize that we can produce individualities endlessly and in different variations—the possibilities are "boundless and
limitless"—we begin to enjoy an "abundance of subtle pleasures in suddenly harnessing and fossilizing, in settling down and establishing [our-
selves] on ground that is still shaking." We love the freedom of being
"crossed by the infinite"—it is no longer paralyzing when we appropriate the multitude of different cultures as part of ourselves. Hence,
Nietzsche argues that for us moderns, "Moderation is foreign to us, let
us admit this to ourselves; our thrill is precisely the thrill of the infinite, the unmeasured. Like the rider on a steed snorting to go further
onward, we let the reins drop before the infinite, we modern men, we
half-barbarians—and *we* feel supremely happy only when we are in the
most—*danger*" (BGE 224). Nietzsche argues that infinity is something
eminently dangerous and possibility paralyzing, but when harnessed as
part of the project of producing individuality, it can be tantalizing. We
are riders in "danger" because the very project of self-cultivation could
go horribly awry at any moment and we could be lost in the infinite
chaos of historical knowledge. Yet we nonetheless "let the reins drop"—
that is, we do not allow any of our particular culture to determine the
ranking and meaning of these different values within ourselves. By contrast, it is we ourselves who produce our individuality. The "infinite,"
moreover, constantly beckons us to "self-overcoming," to a constant
revision and incorporation of ever new forms of meaning into ourselves
without end.

Not only does the historical sense goad the individual to ever greater
heights of self-overcoming and self-creation, but also it provides the
conditions for universal redemption of human community. Thus, it
makes real the goals we spoke of in chapters 5 and 6. It helps create, we
could say, an "end of history" that complements the end of history we
discussed in chapter 5.[42] All previous moments of history, Nietzsche
suggests in "On the Thousand and One Goals," were ones in which
human beings strove to realize the "table of values" implicit in their
community. Yet Nietzsche argues that such pursuits do not actually answer the question nagging every individual's subjectivity—what justifies my existence? How can I lead the best human life? Why did I come
into being at this point and at no other (UM 3.1)? All these previous
moments employed the individual as just another "pawn" in the "founding of cities and states, their wars, their restless assembling and scatter-
ing again, their confused mingling, mutual imitation" (UM 3.1, 3.5).
Every "culture," by contrast, "seeks to lift the individual [*einzelnen*] human being out of the pushing, shoving, and crushing of the historical

stream and makes him understand that he is not merely a historically limited being [*historisch begrenztes*], but also an absolutely extrahistorical and infinite being [*ausserhistorisch-unendliches Wesen*] with whom all existence began and will end" (UUM 35.12)

Consequently, when we come face to face with "infinity"—that is, with the reflection on the "Thousand Goals" of history, rather than being part of any one of them—we are freed from living under any one of these parochial goals. In this condition, we come to see that the "yoke for the thousand necks is still lacking: the one goal is lacking. Humanity still has no goal" (Z:1 "On the Thousand").[43] That is, universal humanity as such becomes the standard for the only possible human community to which we can give ourselves heart and soul—the universal community of humanity as such is the only community that can measure up and hence make whole the infinite longing of subjectivity, my "absolutely extrahistorical and infinite being." All other communities appear as parochial and falsifying. But since humanity has no goal as of yet, the people of the modern age lose a sense of the meaning in their life, a sense of a belonging to human community. They feel as if they are the product of the meaningless historical development with no aim, no redeeming telos, no theodicy for the suffering and agony of their country and the "thousand" peoples of the past. The "terrible truth" of the "wound" at the center of existence confronts modern peoples most profoundly. The individual, then, is tasked with the project of "redemption," of setting the single goal of humanity that will give meaning to each human community in light of how it forms part of the story of universal humanity.[44] For instance, America's founding was hailed by its founding individuals as an example, a "city on a hill," that would help bring light to a benighted humanity. The founders articulated the narrative of the United States as the completion of the narrative of the development of humanity as such.

As we saw in the previous chapter, the activity of redemption involves incorporating all "it was" into the narrative of one's own self—one must especially show why the moments of great agony and suffering were a necessary component in the creation of this individual self (Z:1 "On Redemption"). But in order to will the "it was," we must know what happened in the past. The future individual must be a "skeptic" of past value systems but also a "historian" of them (BGE 211). For Nietzsche, the historical sense supplies the individual with the capacity to know the past, to know the "thousand goals" of the past and hence to show why these thousand goals are actually necessary conditions for the creation of the one goal that encompasses them all, the one goal enshrined in the individual's self. The historical sense, in other words, equips the individual with the capacity to understand the past and hence appropriate it as part of his activity of self-creation and redemption.[45] With this historical knowledge, the individual can become the "synthetic, summarizing, justifying man" of humanity (WP 866).

The third and final feature of the modern world that prepares the way for modern individuality and for universal human redemption is the education in Kantian philosophy. With Kantian and Hegelian philosophy, we come to discern the limits of "scientific Socratism's" optimistic rationalism (BT 19). The endless pursuit of knowledge through science will not result in truth, happiness, and order. Furthermore, with Kant and Hegel, we discover that concepts and values are human creations, not implicit features of nature as such.[46] It is this activity of "legislation" of what is valuable or "great" that "elevates man over the blind unrestrained greed of his drive for knowledge" (PTA 43). We understand that human beings assign value to our own lives, and we must assess what is the best or highest end in light of our nature as value assigners. In coming to this knowledge, we learn about the possibility of human freedom.[47] If concepts and values are our creations, we can continue to create them well into the future. This time, we can create concepts and values with an aim for the betterment of the species, in order to, as I have suggested, make whole the human subject. For Nietzsche, the creation of values is in no way an arbitrary or radically voluntaristic activity—the *causa sui*, Nietzsche claims, is the "best self-contradiction that has ever been conceived" (BGE 21). This self-creation involves giving oneself the law of one's own being, an activity constrained by one's own past narrative history (as we discussed in chapter 6) and by the past events and actions that constitute the community in which one has gained one's identity and in which one's individuality will exert its influence (as we discussed in chapter 7).

Human values may indeed be "illusory" impositions of human beings onto nature, but this does not make them any less real nor unjustified, any more than the institution of promising can simply be willed away or declared unjustified. For Nietzsche, we have come to be inescapably normative beings, that is, beings who "promise," who exchange and respond to reasons, and who, above all, create for ourselves a narrative personality. These "values" are the necessary structural outcome of the development of human subjectivity out of nature and out of society and politics. Kantian philosophy reveals to human beings that human subjectivity is an achievement, yet it is an achievement that we cannot will away. The very activity of thinking ourselves out of normativity involves the use of subjectivity. We are inescapably the creatures who assign value to the world. In attempting to understand the value of our nature, we are thrust back in upon it. Thus, Nietzsche grounds his own ethical theory in this Kantian discovery of the nature of subjectivity, that we assign value to the world. To achieve fulfillment, the subject longs to extend itself into the world and transform the world in its own image, such that the subject can reflect on itself and see that it has lived up to its nature as a value-assigner. This fulfillment, Nietzsche suggests, can only occur in the context of spiritual engagement with other individuals who shape my identity and can indicate to me the success or failure of my activity. Such self-reflection or self-knowledge through the eyes of others is the embodiment of the infinite self-regard so prized by Hegel. In this way, Nietzsche thinks that the discoveries of Kant can help us recognize that this task of self-creation is the highest human task, the task most needful to our nature as distinctively human beings. We hence can become reconciled to a cultural community that seeks to achieve these ends, and we ourselves long to create for ourselves an individuality that will redeem humanity as such.[48]

This condition is one, however, that must be transpolitical, one not connected to the "common good" of the state, as Hegel envisioned all his communities would be. We come then to the central disagreement between Nietzsche and Hegel on the satisfaction of human individuality. For Hegel, the individual finds fulfillment in participating in the institutions of the modern state. For Nietzsche, by contrast, the individual finds fulfillment only by participating in a culture radically distinct from the modern state. For Nietzsche, submitting one's will to the will of the state involves giving up importantly on the universal nature of human beings. A state is always a parochial community, falsifying the world in order to appear to curry attachment to its cause. The state represents an ideal that is not one's own, since it uses each individual for the promotion of its own purposes. Individuals lose their freedom as self-creating beings when their actions are the result of the agency of some higher will, rather than their own will. In order to be a center of self-determining subjectivity, individuals still need states—we cannot live like angels without laws—but individuals must submit the state to their own identities as universal beings detached from belonging to any one state. Association with one political will clips the wings of a free subjectivity that yearns to ascend to the level of universal culture to be free.[49]

Despite his rather harsh criticisms of political participation and identification, I think Nietzsche's view can help us think through some contemporary political and cultural problems. Let me conclude this chapter with an example. Nietzsche's view of culture offers an implicit defense of the idea of a liberal arts education.[50] Now, of course there are many ways in which universities arouse Nietzsche's ire, especially when scholars become slavishly attached to a political regime or cause, or when the institution itself becomes "houses of correction for disciplinants," to produce not whole human beings, but half-formed soldiers for the modern state. Nonetheless, Nietzsche looks to "those ancient schools," which were "educational institutions for pupils" in the genuine sense (UUM 29.126). This "genuine" education involves an engagement with the great works of the past, a staple of a liberal arts education. Such an engagement requires a deep reverence for and erotic attachment to the past high points of human civilization, as, for instance, Nietzsche thought that Germany had for ancient Greece. Nietzsche argued that there was a "band which is tied between the innermost German essence and the Greek genius" (FEI 60). As we have seen, this engagement also requires a rejection of state involvement in education, as well as a resistance to what Nietzsche sees as the Enlightenment's task of universalizing access to education, which amounts to dumbing it down (FEI 66–67). Finally, such an education ideally would involve for Nietzsche a mistrust balanced against the reverence for these works of the past, a mistrust that affords the worthy individual the possibility of engaging in humanity's self-narration, not just being an audience for it.

CONCLUSION

This book has been an effort to articulate and defend the strand of modern individuality developed by the German philosophers Hegel and Nietzsche. This task is important for a number of reasons. First, Western liberalism is at bottom justified by the value of individuality, and every liberal state professes to defend individuality. Yet this liberal ideal of individuality stands in tension today with defenders of what I have called a "premodern" understanding of religious and communal authority—namely, that community is the source of individual identity, the sovereign authority over individuals, and sets the aim towards which individuals ought to strive. A good deal of social tension and political conflict stems from this deep disagreement about the value of individuality. Furthermore, Okin (1999) has argued that liberalism must confront this tension within itself. Should liberalism, she asks, grant group rights to communities that uphold a premodern understanding of individuality, one that stands as a challenge to liberalism's foundations of the equal rights of all individuals? Her answer is no, liberalism's commitment to modern individuality should trump premodern views in cases of conflict. Part of the task of this book has been to defend modern individuality against the premodern understanding, which is still in ascendance today. However, Hegel's and Nietzsche's critique of the premodern, or in their terms, "ancient," view is not categorical. They both employ the ancient model as a challenge to the moderns, yet ultimately claim that modern life can incorporate the advantages of the ancient on the basis of individuality.

This task of defending individuality is important for a second reason. Within contemporary political theory there is confusion about what individuality is and whether it is valuable. Conservatives, communitarians, postmodernists, progressive and classical liberals all have different conceptions of what the individual is and what the nature of community is that flows from such a value. At the same time, several theorists critique individuality as a desideratum. In this book, I have aimed to clarify the confusion surrounding this concept by tracing its historical development in the modern age, and I have made a case for one particular strand of modern individuality, the historical individual, over its predecessors.

Thus, the critical part of my argument, developed in chapter 1, elicited the insights and drawbacks of these previous understandings of individuality, the "natural" and "formal" individual. The positive part of my argument, developed in chapters 2–7, has been to elucidate and defend Hegel's and Nietzsche's shared notion of the "historical individual." In eliciting their commonalities on this concept, this project has also contributed to our historical understanding of these two important philosophers. They are not philosophical opposites as so many have thought; rather, they share a deep kinship concerning this basic notion of individuality, a kinship that has ramifications throughout the development of their thinking. For Hegel and Nietzsche, the human self is a historically embedded self, and hence one that requires human community to elevate it out of brute nature and shape it into an autonomous, self-determining, independent agent. Individuality is not something given, but an ethical goal to be achieved in our communal living together. In short, then, Hegel and Nietzsche make the case that individuality perfects our distinctively human nature. Leading a complete human life means becoming an individual, which requires two conditions—the autonomy of individual agency and the ethical meaning of individual action.

For Hegel and Nietzsche, however, the problem is that the modern age renders the realization of these two components extremely difficult and hence threatens human beings with incomplete, fragmented, or distorted lives and characters. I have articulated in chapters 2 and 5 Hegel's and Nietzsche's strategies for realizing individual autonomy, and in chapters 3 and 6 their strategies for realizing ethical meaning. In chapters 4 and 7, I addressed their concrete social and political proposals for restoring both autonomy and meaning. In these concluding remarks, I want to suggest that these problems the philosophers were addressing are our very own, and the solutions implicit in realizing the "historical individual" can help illuminate our own situation.

Autonomous, individual agency faces two obstacles in the contemporary world. First, the contemporary individual has been gradually losing power over his individual character and his political surroundings, as multinational corporations or bloated bureaucratic governments treat him as a fungible, malleable demographic statistic for the purpose of regularizing and satisfying desire in an ever more targeted way. These forces wield great power, but they also transform our social and political character. As our desires become fulfilled in these sophisticated and varied ways, our desire for independence and our capacity for self-government erode.[1] Second, advances in neurobiology and the philosophy of mind cast doubt on whether the notion of a self-initiated action of the "free will" is possible or even coherent. Social scientists now readily employ brain-imaging techniques in order to determine what natural processes and evolutionary genetic behavior are working through us to produce behavior. Based on these and other considerations, some postmodern thinkers have argued that individuality as an ideal is a myth. We are all more multifarious and mysterious to ourselves than can be so pridefully subsumed under my own self-determined autarchic will. It is a pernicious myth at that. The demand for independence and singleness of purpose can damage our relationships with others and force us into psychological self-harm by denying the plurality of selves that constitute each one of us.

Hegel and Nietzsche anticipate both of these concerns and nonetheless assert that autonomous agency is both possible and desirable, so long as we understand autonomous agency as a feature of a properly formed human character. Their argument, in brief, is this. They uphold the notion of what I have called the "historical individual," whose behavior is deeply shaped by the social practices, psychological traits, and genetic heritage from which he arose. Nonetheless, they argue that individual subjectivity is infinite in that it has the theoretical capacity to transcend any and all social pressure and natural impulse. The only thing that can satisfy the infinite individual subject is that norm the individual freely imposes upon himself. This does not mean that there is a "doer behind the deed," as Nietzsche puts it (GM 1.13). Rather, following Fichte, Hegel and Nietzsche argue that the free individual agent can only appear in (a particular kind of) action itself, not before it, issuing from some miraculous Cartesian ego. Accordingly, individuality is not something pregiven to human beings, but a character or "soul" always imperfectly created through action in public, a perfectible ideal in the ancient tradition of the "care of the self" that we are always already on the way to realizing.

Hegel and Nietzsche understand this formation of character according to a literary model. Individual actions are not discrete units with no relationship to one another, nor is the individual agent conceived as some all-self-knowing sovereign agent, as the Cartesian individualist tradition would have it. On the contrary, human beings see that actions (a) will satisfy my desire to conform to my social surroundings or will indulge in my natural appetites or whims, or (b) help make consistent or develop the narrative of my own unique personality. For Hegel and Nietzsche, most human beings accept reasons from category (a) for most of their lives—it is comforting to fit in with others and it feels good to satisfy my appetites. Yet Hegel and Nietzsche argue that category (b) represents the distinctively human form of individual agency. We should each of us develop an ongoing meaningful story of ourselves, in which we are the main character, we have a certain set of character traits that distinguish our hero from others, we make decisions with others that are consistent with these traits, that further shape and fulfill my identity and narrative goals. The human individual has an "immeasurable longing to become whole" (UM 3.6), in Nietzsche's phrase; there is a longing in all of us to make our present actions consistent with that narrative self that exists not just in my head but also and primarily with others—to, in short, render meaningful these actions by fitting them in to larger purposes. We desire to see our subjective agency realized in these larger purposes and hence reflected back at us in the eyes of others. I desire to show them that this action I am performing right now fits in to the ongoing story of me, this story that you and I know and share, and hence reveal that this action comes from me, from my free agency.

Hegel's and Nietzsche's narrative understanding of individual self-creation helps us contemporaries address the problem of individual autonomous agency in at least three ways. First, the narrative understanding of individuality assumes that individual agency is not something we are automatically blessed with or given. In fact, we as a community can actively and conscientiously cultivate the capacity to become an individual as a public good, through political means (in the case of Hegel)—through, for instance, supporting groups of autonomous agents and denigrating oppressive groups, or reforming public educational curricula to foster this aim. Second, narratives of ourselves are constructed in public—that is, with family, friends, co-workers, and so forth. Unless we respect these others and share our narrative with them, encouraging them to validate and correct my narrative, this narrative can begin to seem unimportant, or can fly into incoherence without any external will helping me resist my own excesses. Accordingly, the narrative conception of individual agency can help forge needed communal bonds and build "social capital," thereby avoiding the slide into individual powerlessness. Third, narrating my self involves developing a certain creativity and exploring spiritual matters. Creative spiritual matters expand my horizons and the scope of my will while benefitting all those who engage with me. Such a notion of the self helps combat material desires and the majority will that stunt our development, regularize our will, stifle the plurality implicit in every interesting narrative.

The second problem of the modern age, however, renders problematic the very possibility of my forming a story about myself. Modern life systematically tends to destroy ethical communities, communities in which human beings recognize one another based on shared standards of the good life, replacing them with attenuated and abstract relationships of economic exchange, disembodied Internet chatting, or sheer force and brutality. Traditions and religions lose their ability to confer meaning on human life as modern science erodes religious conviction and liberalism envisions the individual as self-sovereign and divorced from an essential lived connection to ethical practice. Late modern capitalism ravages local communities by buying out local businesses that bring a familiarity, intimacy, substance to living together in a small community. Advanced "information" economies divide and specialize labor to such a degree that rarely can two workers understand the other's task in order to recognize one another based on a common understanding of good work and its connection to the good life. Global technology stifles our desire for tangible, visceral connections, rendering all human attachments ever more abstract and insubstantial. These developments are highly unfortunate because only within ethical communities can we make intelligible the difference between a life well and poorly led. They supply examples of such lives in history and in the present by which we can pattern ourselves. Without a community in which to share, embody, and aspire to these principles, we begin to feel as if our actions lose a sense of direction or purpose. Our characters cease to fit in with general ethical purposes within shared practices. There is nobody with the communal resources to cheer me on with recognition for a life well led, devoted to some calling higher than myself, nor one to critique me for going astray. Rootless, I cannot begin to understand how to piece together a story about my own life; I have no shared ethical meaning with which to cobble together my own story. It is in this context, Hegel and Nietzsche see, that the longing for a return to ancient forms of community and virtue begins to seem attractive.

Hegel and Nietzsche do not think it possible or desirable to return to the ancient priority of community, yet they seek to resuscitate ancient forms of community and virtue on the basis of modern individualism and modern institutional design. Hegel and Nietzsche disagree considerably about the kinds of community that would suit individuality, though both philosophers' suggestions are, I think, relevant to contemporary politics. On the one hand, Hegel argues that our economic associations should be bolstered socially and politically so as to mediate the individual's relationship with the state. Economic associations are foundational to the modern project, as revealed in the influential writings of Locke, Hume, and Smith, for whom commerce is the means to spread freedom and prosperity. Modern political and commercial society is premised on the notion that human beings are most fundamentally driven by a desire to lead a commodious and even luxurious life. For Hegel, this commercial society tends toward a pathological excess of greedy self-interestedness, in which efficiency, quantity, and the almighty dollar become the sole standards for leading a good individual life in business. "Interest" satisfaction begins to erode our longing to lead a free, self-determined life. However, Hegel sees another path for modern commercial society. So long as we bolster and encourage the sentiments of honor and respect for one's profession, individuals will come to find meaning at very local and concrete levels among their business associations, each of whom recognizes all the others as fellow members in the pursuit of leading a good life in this business, by producing high-quality goods for the aim of garnering recognition, rather than producing high volume for maximal profit.

Hegel's view of mediating institutions can help contribute to our normative understanding of civil society in three ways. First, Hegel makes a strong case for bringing economic associations back into our discussion about civil society. Discussions recently have focused on noneconomic voluntary associations, which Hegel would regard as rather "free-floating" and without a solid foundation in our economic lives, which occupy us for most of our day. Noneconomic voluntary associations may therefore have a certain salutary effect in civil society, but they ultimately would be unable to steer our economic desires away from greedy and grasping material excess. Second, Hegel encourages us to think about our economic lives very differently than we do now. In the contemporary world, we tend to think about economic associations, their relationships with one another in the market and with the government in lobbying groups, in terms of interests and incentives. Such an understanding has the tendency to be expanded to encompass all of political reality, as in Dahl's vision of "pluralism," in which political activity is the result of innumerable groups from society, the economy, and government jostling and bargaining to maximize their self-interest. Hegel would bemoan such a development, along with its widespread consequences for American politics, such as in engorged federal legislative bills hardly concerned with caring for the "common good," but rather stuffed with "pork" distributed to a thousand different mouths.

For Hegel, when we begin to think of our economic associations in terms of the common good and the good life, our interactions can finally take on meaning and our goals substance. Finally, by giving each worker a stake in the activity of the whole and by educating workers to understand their particular function within the whole, these economic associations can help form autonomous civic character, personalities concerned not with one's selfish interest, but rather with democratically participating and bettering the whole.

On the other hand, Nietzsche views economic activity as debasing and political participation as alienating. For him, culture is distinctively human; culture individuates. Unlike Hegel, who defends a broadly Aristotelian social ontology, in which individuals long to be parts of an ethical whole, Nietzsche defends a Platonic social ontology. That is, human beings gain meaning in their actions by imitating or by being imitated aesthetically—by approximating the archetypal "idea" or by living an ideal, exemplary life oneself. For Nietzsche, these exemplary lives are led in culture and thus are most fundamentally aesthetic in nature. This is not to say that these individuals are all flash and no substance. On the contrary, individuals can only lead compelling, attractive lives if they embody in word and deed a story about the historical community that heals the wounds of this community and brings vivacity and fullness to the community's striving. Martin Luther King Jr., for instance, never ran for public office, never fought in a war, but in his many public speeches and appearances he transformed the self-understanding of an entire community. Such an individual "refounds" his community by embodying its virtues while transforming it in accordance with the individual's own unique personality.

Nietzsche's understanding of the meaningful community speaks directly to contemporary identity politics and multiculturalism, where the problem at stake is precisely how to "empower" the life and meaningfulness of a shared identity or culture. Nietzsche offers us an alternative way to understand the nature of our attachment to culture. Good cultures should not regard themselves as the victims of identity formation from some external, oppressive force. Rather, culture is and should be regarded as something created and transformed by exemplary individuals who suffer and seek deliverance for the community, who lead arduous lives with grace and dignity, who offer unique patterns of speech, outlooks, and practical possibilities that construct the culture. Human beings hence should embody and defend a culture because of their erotic attachment to these exemplars, because of our longing to imitate the great deeds and dedication and wit of these men and women. Nietzsche offers us reasons to doubt that the goals of cultural protection, mutual recognition, or equality of identity are the right kinds of goals for this kind of politics. The goal of legal protection for and mutual recognition among cultures may lead to cultural stagnation, since cultures may become essentialized and recognized only as an enumerable system of beliefs and practices, rather than a fluid space of meaning in which individual exemplars struggle with one another to make sense of the cultural heritage. But neither should we understand the task of identity politics to be the erasing of difference of identity. For Nietzsche, it is a certain cultural heritage of meaningful experiences, hopes, and individual actions that provides the basis for future individual creativity. In forgetting the past or in treating individuals as beyond their culture or gender, we lose the repository of meaning and standards of the good life that make individual lives possible in the first place. For Nietzsche, by contrast, we must understand culture agonistically—the meaning and practices of culture are open to creative revision and transformation by individual exemplars. Accordingly, individuals cannot radically transform these cultures, nor understand them in any way the individual wants. Rather, for individuals even to be able to disagree about what a culture is, there must be some shared agreement, basis for shared respect, and set of norms upon which individuals act and within which individuals craft their identity. In this way, Nietzsche marks out a moderate political space in democratic theory, between the rationalist trend of "mutual recognition" among groups and the movement to "agonistic" confrontation among groups. For Nietzsche, both approaches are important in satisfying the tension-ridden longings of the distinctively human, *eros* and *eris*.

For Hegel and Nietzsche, an individual life is a complete human life, and individuality requires both autonomy and ethically meaningful actions. However, as we have seen, Hegel and Nietzsche diverge sharply on the concrete conditions for cultivating an individual life. In fact, we could say that their two solutions contradict one another. Developing Rousseau's "citizen" model of individuality, Hegel argues that individuals can only achieve wholeness through participation in politics. Adopting Rousseau's "solitary dreamer" portrait of individuality, Nietzsche claims that politics obstructs human fulfillment, and satisfaction lies beyond the boundaries of politics.

What explains this sudden divergence? The fundamental source of disagreement between the two concerns the place of rationality in the distinctively human subject. For Hegel, human history consists of the progressive rationalization of human community. The distinctively human subject, Hegel argues, longs for, and can only be satisfied by, finding its own distinctively human rationality reflected back at it in the modern world. For Nietzsche, too, history contains a progress of rationality of a sort, though it is a history that ends with reason's recognition of its own limits. Reason cannot provide a complete ordering principle of human community, as it fails to grasp the affective, creative element of human beings. Rather, individual exemplars—whose lives are structured not according to the canons of rationality but according to aesthetic, narrative norms—supply a living "justification" of the design of this community. Rational states cannot provide such living justifications, and hence the human subject gains satisfaction only in finding itself as part of an aesthetically designed order.

We can see a similar disagreement between the contemporary camps of "deliberative democracy" and "agonistic democracy." On the one hand, the deliberative democrats prize ethical relationships of mutual respect and recognition, transparency, and rational discussion. For them, politics is about coming together and considering what is the best course of action, what law or policy best promotes the common good. As the agonists tirelessly point out, the deliberative democrats aim for "consensus" as the purpose of politics, for a rational formation of the general will. On the other hand, the agonistic democrats argue that all this debate and this emphatic need for closure, consensus, and uniformity are wrongheaded at best and oppressive at worst. For them, any attempt to come to consensus will threaten to destroy the distinctness of these identities by submitting them to a general principle that abstracts from individual differences. By contrast, the agonists call for the proliferation of debate, criticism, openness, plurality, and so forth. The purpose of politics—to put it in Nietzsche's terms—is to provide a space for exploration of human self-creation.

My view is that this disagreement between Hegel and Nietzsche comes from a "wound" in the nature of human subjectivity. After Kant and Fichte exploded the old rationalist and empiricist approaches to the nature of the human mind, philosophers grappled with how to conceptualize the human subject as distinguished from both natural desires and social norms. What remains after we "subtract" nature and society from the human subject? We certainly cannot examine the subject upon introspection—when we turn inward, all we find are our desires, beliefs, hopes, and dreams, those characteristics that make up my identity, but that are not the I. We can never catch our I by turning inward, since it is our I precisely that does the turning inward. Rather, we can only grasp the nature of the I in the act, as it were, by examining the actions and labor of human beings that bear the trace of human subjectivity. This action was performed by "me," that house is "mine," and so forth.

For Hegel, what we find is that the human subject longs for rational order, a harmonization among wholes and parts, among universals and particulars. The subject longs for this order because disorder and conflict involve parts and wholes inexplicable to the human subject and hence a challenge to his infinite negativity. He strives, then, to "negate" the otherness of a conflicting position and incorporate it into an historically evolving rational general structure of intelligibility. By contrast, Nietzsche argues that infinite human subjects are also dissatisfied by rational structures and orders. Such orders fail to capture the ineffable uniqueness of individuals, and rather falsify this uniqueness by forcing it into some category or structure which establishes sameness with other individuals. For this reason, human subjects are satisfied not by rational structures, but by the beautiful, embodied lives of individuals who bring order to community but nonetheless sustain the generative, affective creativity impenetrable to reason. Subjectivity, in other words, responds most deeply to the vivacity of human presence, human stories and life, not to rationally organized practices and communities.

My claim, then, is that the historical individual rests on an internally divided notion of human subjectivity. It bears a wound that cannot be healed, an internal bifurcation already seen by Rousseau and incapable of being reconciled in theory. The immanent structure of this historical subjectivity offers us two different paths—one toward a rational self-grounding and another toward a creative, affective self-grounding. Neither offers a decisive criticism of the other without begging the question as to whether reason can indeed offer a satisfactory structure to render unique human individuality intelligible.

Accordingly, then, neither Hegel nor Nietzsche is entirely right about the distinctively human, but neither are they entirely wrong. What appears to be a deep problem with this concept, however, could be advantageous. What is contradictory in theory, in brief, can become complementary in practice. By keeping in mind the limitations of the arguments of both Hegel and Nietzsche, we could weaken our demands for those contradictory conditions Hegel and Nietzsche call for. Accordingly, we could jettison the strong claims that (a) the human being can only be fulfilled in politics and (b) the human being finds enslavement in politics. In place of these claims, we could follow both Hegel and Nietzsche with a weaker claim, namely, that human beings may find fulfillment in politics or may find it outside of politics (or both). This moderation of our theoretical views might help quell the kinds of contemporary disputes such as the one I mentioned above between the deliberative and the agonistic democrats (that consensus can be good but so can contestation, depending on the circumstance). That is, each party might come to see that it possesses only a one-sided view of the truth, which must be balanced by the other party's view.

This reconciliation in theory could be matched by one in practice. Based on the weaker theoretical claim, we could cultivate both ideals at once without threatening to tear the community apart. The community could encourage belonging to political groups while also fostering space for cultural exploration and identity formation. The state might encourage attachment to itself and to its mediating institutions, while also seeing that it promote a robust form of the right to "exit" from this political participation in an independent culture. These two options could even be reconcilable within a single individual—an individual might practice cultural self-determination at certain times, while participating in the common good of the community at others. Each individual, in other words, might be able to wear two hats, one as citizen, one as member of culture. Most contemporary liberal democracies contain both tendencies already anyway, though they tend to emphasize one over the other.

There are obviously difficulties with reconciling these two tendencies in practice, since they naturally seem to come apart from one another. Aesthetic cultures thrive in the absence of political regulation and are threatened by being subsumed under political demands. Accordingly, the desire for cultural self-determination leads to the demand to limit our duties and attachments to the political order. By contrast, political communities are more than mere aggregates of individuals and groups seeking their self-interest. Political community is founded on the pursuit of the good life. In order to foster citizen attachment to the ethical aims of this comprehensive community, politics naturally limits the claims and shapes the identities of the groups within it. Indeed, what these two tendencies share in common—that they are both concerned with our highest, ethical vocations as opposed to our mere interests or material needs—may be the source of their most intractable conflict. We can compromise about material interest, but it is difficult to do so when honor and spiritual fulfillment are on the line.

However, the greatest loss in the transition to the "weaker" claim about historical individuality is that we must give up on the hope for infinite autonomy. For both Hegel and Nietzsche, infinite autonomy consists in being self-sufficient, obeying a law that I have made for myself, or, as Hegel puts it, being at "home with oneself in one's other" (EL 24Z2). Yet Hegel and Nietzsche offer two very different "infinites" that face the individual. Suspended between them, the individual in my pragmatic sketch can achieve neither. This is not only because in such a pragmatic community the individual cannot give himself heart and soul to either strand of historical individuality. It is also because one's human subjectivity is divided between these two longings. Human self-sufficiency hence appears impossible for divided beings such as we are.

NOTES

Introduction

1. See, e.g., Sandel (1982), Taylor (1985).
2. See, e.g., Wolfe (2006).
3. See, e.g., Marx, "On the Jewish Question," and, more recently, Cohen (1995).
4. See, e.g., Taylor (1994), Parekh (2000).
5. See, e.g., Connolly (1991), Shanahan (1992), Mouffe (1996).
6. My project, then, shares in common with Crittenden (1992) an aim to reconstruct and defend the liberal individual between the atomistic and communitarian models. It also shares with Kateb (1992), Cavell (1990), and Zakaras (2009) the defense of individuality not just as a legal political unit, but also as an ethical ideal to be achieved, an ideal that meets resistance from various forces of the modern age.
7. See Löwith (1964), Deleuze (2006).
8. See Houlgate (1986), Dudley (2002), and Jurist (2000) for important explorations of the Hegel-Nietzsche connection. None of these scholars explores the foundational premises Hegel and Nietzsche share; rather, they establish their convergences on the themes of metaphysics (Houlgate), philosophy (Dudley), or culture (Jurist). Jurist's insightful book helpfully brings out the similarities between Hegel and Nietzsche on the historical problems of modern Cartesianism and the solutions in a non-atomistic agency and culture to resolve these problems. I differ from Jurist on the characteristics of an "integrated agency"—his are "narcissism, the body, affects, and the past" (225). See chapter 5 on my view of Nietzsche's view of the requirements of autonomy and chapter 6 on the ethical components of successful agency.

Chapter 1

1. Cf. Strauss (1950, 323): "the quarrel between the ancients and the moderns concerns eventually, and perhaps even from the beginning, the status of 'individuality.'"
2. Qtd. in Riedel (1984, 13). For the moderns, Hegel continues, the "individual [is] the first and highest principle."
3. Cf. VPR21 Preface, 34: what is called the "Enlightenment" is the "tendency that the validity of everything is to be justified in and through thought and that there is no higher authority than my knowledge. . . . This spirit of inquiry turned also into political form. Man brought out of himself universal principles and tested them and discarded them." Cf. 38: "The state no longer depends on faith, trust, or authority, but rather, on the contrary, the demand of knowledge through thought comes on the scene."
4. See Locke, *Second Treatise*, chaps. 2, 9.

5. A further problem concerns the content of the natural individual's identity, that the individual by nature has a certain set of passions. As Rousseau first argued, Hobbes and Locke have "transferred to the state of nature the ideas they acquired in society. They spoke about savage man, and it was civil man they depicted" (SD 38). The empiricist thinkers purportedly begin with natural givens—with raw sense data or with raw, natural human passions. Yet they fail to recognize that these "givens" are not given at all, but rather the result of the historical development of the human understanding and of a society in which material accumulation is favored over nobility and excellence. This blindness to the historical basis of natural "givens" becomes important when it comes to historically persisting inequalities that advantage some and disadvantage others out of the starting gate. Smith (1989, 65–70) offers a good explication of Hegel's treatment of this critique.

6. Hobbes, *Leviathan*, chap. 7; Hume, *Treatise of Human Nature*, bk. 2, pt. 3, sec. 3.

7. See Bacon, *The Great Instauration*, in Bacon (1980): Bacon's project is to create the conditions so that the "mind may exercise over the nature of things the authority which properly belongs to it" (7), so that we can "lay the foundation" for "human utility and power" (16).

8. See Machiavelli, *Prince*, chap. 15; Mandeville, introduction to *An Enquiry into the Origin of Moral Virtue:* "most writers are always teaching men what they should be, and hardly ever trouble their heads with telling them what they really are."

9. See Hobbes, *Leviathan*, chap. 13: "To this warre of every man against every man, this also is consequent; that nothing can be unjust. The notions of right and wrong, justice and injustice have there no place."

10. Hegel's critique of "happiness" as the highest good is related to this criticism of the early modern empiricists insofar as "the universality of happiness takes its content from the stuff of drives, and thus does not determine itself. This is the unfreedom of this final end" (VPR21 21).

11. Hume, *Treatise of Human Nature*, bk. 1, pt. 3, sec. 6.

12. Ibid., bk. 1, pt. 4, sec. 7.

13. Hegel's relationship to his predecessors in the early modern period is much more complicated than this short critique can convey. See Church (forthcoming a) for a more nuanced view of Hegel's critique of Locke.

14. Patten (2001) helpfully raises this point: "Hegel's most interesting objection to social contract theory, then, is that it operates with an excessively instrumental view of state and society" (173). However, Patten does not differentiate between the two different forms of "atomism" in Hegel's view of social contract theory, that of the "naturalists" and the "formalists."

15. Cf. VPR.1.232: "In Germany there are especially those whose first concern is their private right, and last comes the right of the state."

16. In PR 75, Hegel describes how his contemporaries transplant the "determinations of private property" and economic exchange to "a sphere of a totally different and higher nature," that of the state. For Hegel, this social contract thinking is the "result of superficial thinking," since the "arbitrary will of individuals is not in a position to break away from the state, because the individual is already by nature a citizen of it."

17. Crime negates "right" as such with a "negatively infinite judgment" because unanswered crime renders the existence of right impossible (PR 95).

18. See also Fichte's *Addresses to the German Nation*, in which Fichte radicalizes Kant's imperative to transform our empirical characters. Fichte argues that political education should have this task (Fichte 2008, 22–46).

19. For a further exploration of Hegel's critique of Kant's practical philosophy, see Wood (1990), Sedgwick (2000a), Geiger (2007); on Hegel's critique of Kant's theoretical philosophy, see Williams (2006–7), Bristow (2007). On Hegel's relationship and debt to Fichte, see Pippin (1989, chap. 3).

20. See Norton (1995) for an informative history and fuller explication of the critiques of the beautiful soul.

21. This criticism is particularly damaging to Kant's position, since Kant draws a strong distinction between freedom and nature. Since the formal will cannot transform contentful nature, one can never find oneself in one's inclinations or desires one engages in. Most of human life is lived, according to Kant, in a state of unfreedom. Realizing this unfreedom prompts the individual obsessed with his autonomy or his self-sufficiency into a stance of irony or a state of being a "beautiful soul." See Sedgwick (2000a) for helpful explication of Hegel's concern with drawing this strong distinction.

22. On Hegel's critique of the modern problem of "homogenization," see Taylor (1975) and Kolb (1986).

23. See, e.g., Aristotle, *Politics*, bk. 7, chap. 1.

24. See Schiller (2005) for the origin of this "ethical" critique of Kant (pp. 150–54).

25. See Neuhouser (2008) for a fuller account of Rousseau's project of the redemption of the modern age and his transformation of *amour-propre*. See also Velkley (2002) for an illuminating account of Rousseau's attempt to redeem modernity by recovering "a human sense of wholeness and of belonging to a whole" (4). My thesis in this book is also influenced by Velkley's account of Rousseau's profound influence on the tradition of German philosophy.

26. Shklar (1969) expresses these two paths as "two utopias" which "were meant to stand in polar opposition to each other" (3). She concludes that according to Rousseau, it is tragic that we must choose "between the two models, between man and the citizen" (5). Shklar's two ideals—the man of the family and the citizen of the state—approximate but are not exactly the two ideals I describe. Our point of disagreement is with the former ideal, that of the "man." I stress Rousseau's Romantic, solitary individualist side, whereas Shklar examines the familial aspect—both of these aspects are part of Rousseau's project to retrieve nature in civilized context. See Todorov (2001), who interprets the two ideals as citizen and solitary individual, a conclusion that I endorse. I disagree with Todorov in his belief that Rousseau describes these ideals but maintains a critical distance from them. Instead, Todorov speaks of a "middle way" between these two extremes (see chap. 4). Other Rousseau scholars who speak of a "middle way" between the extremes I have mapped out include Marks (2005, 52), who argues that natural disharmony points toward the need for perfection (Rousseau's "problem is to find a place in a life for those [disharmonious] goods without setting himself in contradiction"), and Cooper (1999, 50), who claims that denatured individuals can order their souls so they can live in accordance with nature in society ("nature and society . . . are not such utter contraries").

27. The path of influence here was rather direct; we know that Hegel was an avid reader of Rousseau and he attributed to Rousseau the invention of the "will" (PR 258, HP 3.401–2), the concept which serves as the foundation of Hegel's PR (PR 4). See Neuhouser (2000, 296n2) on Hegel's personal interest in reading Rousseau's *Social Contract* and *Emile*. Also, the *Social Contract* model of "moral" or "civil freedom" clearly influenced Kant (see KPW 77 and 139 on Kant's appropriation of the "general will"). Hegel detected in Kant and Fichte problems that stemmed from Rousseau as he was developing his political philosophy in the PR. See PR 258 on Rousseau's connection to the French Revolution, PW 211–12 on Kant's expression of the principles of the French Revolution, and PR 6, 15 on *Willkür* and its connection to formalism and the thought of Kant and Fichte.

28. Unlike Hegel, Nietzsche openly derided Rousseau (see, e.g., WP 98–99), though he was much more charitable and openly engaged with him in his early (cf. UM 3.4) and middle periods (cf. AOM 408). See, however, Ansell-Pearson's (1991) insightful study, in which he claims that Rousseau was crucially influential on Nietzsche's conception of the problem of modernity. The path of influence on the matter of solitary

individuality from Rousseau to Nietzsche is indirect, by way of Rousseau's influence on a number of thinkers of early German and French Romanticism. See Del Caro (1989) and Behler (1991, 90ff.) on the connection between Romanticism and Nietzsche. Despite his open critique of Romanticism at GS 370, Nietzsche learned from these thinkers the value of individual creativity and the obstacles to individuality posed by modern society.

Chapter 2

1. This claim particularly aroused Marx's ire. See his *Critique of the Philosophy of Right*, remarks to PR 287–97.

2. See Hardimon (1994, chap. 5) and D. James (2007) for important articulations of Hegel's commitment to individuality. Hardimon (1994) offers the most helpful and persuasive reading of Hegel's view of "individuality" in the literature. He argues that, first, Hegel defends a "weak" and a "strong" sense of individuality: in the "weak" sense, we are all individuals understood as separate beings with separate bodies, and in the "strong," modern sense, Hegel puts forth a perfectible account of individuality that involves crafting a self, bearing particular interests and rights, and upholding one's unique conscience (147–49). Second, Hegel claims that individuality can only come to be within society, yet though the "central social institutions shape the fundamental needs and values of modern people, [they do not] uniquely fix them" (156). Third, for Hardimon, individuality and community are compatible because communal institutions promote the aim of the qualities of "strong" individuality described above. I agree with much of Hardimon's view, though he omits a discussion of why individuality in a strong sense is *valuable* to pursue—on my account, because it satisfies infinite subjectivity and hence amounts to a complete human life.

3. See, e.g., Neuhouser (2000), Wood (1990); for exceptions, see Losurdo (2004), who helpfully distinguishes Hegel's political views from the British liberal position and displays their similarities to the continental republican position, and Patten (1999), who defends a "civic humanist" understanding of Hegel's politics.

4. See recently, for instance, Steinberger (1988), Franco (1999), Dudley (2002), Lewis (2005); but cf. Neuhouser (2000) as an exception, and the exchange between Neuhouser (2004–5) and Dudley (2004–5) on the question of the logic in reading Hegel.

5. See Beiser's (2008, introduction) recent defense of the metaphysical interpretation of Hegel, in which he puts the question in these very terms. Beiser tries ingeniously to attack the Kantian, nonmetaphysical interpreters of Hegel like Pippin by charging them with the same problem Hegel himself brought to Kant: that the latter was a "subjective idealist." See especially in Hegel EL 40ff, PhG 73ff.

6. The metaphysicians are wrong to read Hegel's "spirit" as a metaphysical "entity," or a godlike being independent of its parts. As Kolb (1986) has argued, Hegel himself sees this metaphysical view as a thought-determination that is overcome in the progression of human thinking.

7. See, e.g., Pippin (2008a), for a clear statement of what Brandom (2002) has called Hegel's "pragmatism": "Hegel has what could be considered a historicized or social or pragmatic conception of practical reason" (7). Yet this "pragmatism" is unable to supply the justification "in itself" of an historical practice, since, according to this pragmatism, all inferences are justified based on other inferences to norms within the practice— there is no foundational claim, as I am arguing here. Pippin seems also to oscillate between defending a Hegel who seeks to justify modern life "in itself" (see, e.g., 240, "we can be said to be getting better at the process of . . . justification," 243, 247), and rejecting what I take to be the necessary claim Hegel must make in order to justify modern

life "in itself," that is, that our collective human "self-making has an underlying fixed teleological direction [that] . . . is beginning to be achieved in Western modernity" (229–30). Pinkard (1996) offers a somewhat different though nonetheless "pragmatic" account of Hegel's "Spirit." His view of the *Phenomenology* is that it is a "dialectical-historical narrative of how the European community has come to take what it does as authoritative and definitive for itself," the result of a series of "forms of life" whose internal contradictions have forced new forms of life to rise and then fall until we reach the present (12–13). Yet Hegel seeks to offer not only a "narrative" of the "European community," but also an account of *human* self-consciousness and its development, in order to achieve a justification that is not only "for itself," but also "in itself."

8. See Hegel's adherence to Aristotle's thesis that man is a political animal in PW 159–60. Schiller seeks to redeem modern institutions based on the wholeness of the human being in *Letters on the Aesthetic Education of Man*. See Hegel on Schiller's contribution at EL 55A.

9. According to the "premodern" natural law, human beings derived their function and hence the notion of what a good life is from a teleologically structured natural whole and their nature within it. According to the "modern" natural law that Hegel defends, human beings transcend nature, and their function and good life is derived from a teleologically structured free subjectivity embedded in certain historical practices.

10. Hegel admires Kant for overcoming the Cartesian-rationalist view of mind as substance in his "Paralogisms" (see EL 47). Yet for Hegel, Kant's synthetic subject remains insufficiently grounded in the "noumenal" realm.

11. See D. James (2007, chap. 1) for a good case to examine Hegel's notion of subjectivity historically. See section 3 of EN on organic beings for the biological basis of human history, especially EN 369ff. on the force of natural instinct and its "defect" (EN 359Z). Cf. also Hegel's remarks about the "primal state of innocence" in which spirit is submerged in nature (EN 246Z). See, however, Hegel's claim that human beings were nonetheless different "from animality proper" since human freedom "is present in the beginning" (PHI 133).

12. At SL 115, Hegel speaks of the "beginning of the subject" precisely here, in the "negative of the negative," that is, in the negation of the various negating determinations within the subject and hence the "negative unity with itself." See Stone (2005) for a helpful and exhaustive analysis of Hegel's *Philosophy of Nature*.

13. Biological nature is hence not intelligible for Hegel apart from investigating what Daniel Dennett (2004) calls the "design" level as opposed to the "physical" level. To investigate why this male gorilla is engaging in this fight here, for instance, it is not helpful to look to some basic physical state that makes up the gorilla's body. Rather, one must be attuned to the social structure in which gorillas live so as to understand why this gorilla is active in just this way.

14. See PHI 44: "after the creation of the natural universe, man appears on the scene as the antithesis of nature; he is the being who raises himself up into a second world. . . . The province of spirit is created by man himself."

15. Nature is, according to Hegel, "other in its own self" (SL 118), which means that nature is not self-conscious, but various natural beings exist "indifferently" alongside one another. By contrast, spirit is at home with itself, self-knowing, since the various beings that constitute it—human beings—do not exist indifferently toward one another, but exist in an ethical, self-regarding relationship to each other.

16. Cf. ES 381Z: "the transition from nature to spirit is not a transition to an out-and-out Other, but is only a coming-to-itself of spirit out of its self-externality in nature."

17. See helpful articulations of Hegel's view of freedom in Franco (1999, chap. 5) and Tunick (1992, chap. 3). Allen (2006) offers a compelling adaptation of Hegel's view of freedom to contemporary expressivist and nondomination theories.

18. It is no surprise, Hegel might point out, that the child's development of what is distinctively human involves incessant questioning as to the "why" of things—why the sky is blue, why the child ought not have cookies whenever he wants, etc.

19. Cf. VPR21 5: "In the human being there is the possibility to jettison everything particular."

20. At the same time, it must be said that it is not a prerequisite of our free subjectivity that we *explicitly* call these determinations before our mind's eye to call them into question. Rather, the human subject is always the "self-conscious" basis of his actions—by "self-consciousness," Hegel means that human subjects act for reasons that have in some sense already been shaped by their subjectivity and could be recognized as their own, rather than immediately based on impulses.

21. Hegel asserts that "it is only the moment of individuality that posits the moments of the concept" (EL 165). The "individual, the subject" is the only means to "posit" the determinations binding on it as a "totality," rather than simply an assertion of force (EL 163A). The individual, then, is in this sense the "ground" of the universal, self-"identical" norms and particular, "distinct" desires that it "posits" (EL 164A). On Socratic philosophy as justifying itself through the process of critique, see Stern (2008).

22. Cf. a further development of the will in PR 14: Hegel speaks of the "finite will, purely with regard to its form, is the self-reflecting *infinite I* [unendliches Ich] (see PR 5) which is with itself." This will "*stands above* its content" and has the "*possibility* of determining myself to this or to something else." Hegel declares this development to be the "arbitrary will," and it is a false development if one arrests the individual's development here (see PR 15).

23. Without the synthetic unity of the subject, "I would have as multicolored, diverse a self as I have representations of which I am conscious," and hence no intelligible experience (CPR B134).

24. See CPR B157n: "The I think expresses the act of determining my existence. . . . I do not have yet another self-intuition, which would give the determining in me . . . even before the act of determination."

25. See Neuhouser's (2009) clear statement of Hegel's difference from Kant on subjectivity: "In contrast to his predecessor, Hegel sees a self-conscious subject as characterized by a goal—that of demonstrating its sovereignty and self-identity by overcoming the opposition between itself and its other—and the subject's drive to realize this goal accounts for its practical nature" (38).

26. The turn from the epistemological passive ego to the active ego is made by Fichte—see, for instance, part 3 of *The Vocation of Man*. See Wood (2000) and Neuhouser (1990) for helpful analyses of the "primacy of practical reason" in post-Kantian German philosophy.

27. See Locke, *Second Treatise*, chap. 5 on this. See my piece (forthcoming a) on Hegel's debt to Locke on this view of the laboring subject.

28. I am indebted to Zuckert (1994) for introducing me to this conceptualization. See also W. James (1985) and Mead (1934) for previous attempts to systematize the I-Me-Mine. See PR 44 on Hegel's discussion of the I's externalization of itself into its possessions as the creation of what is "mine."

29. See Brandom (2002), who understands this move to be a kind of "pragmatism"—"Hegel places the sort of inferential/causal *process* central to [Kant's] functionalism in the larger frame of *historically* extended *social practice*" (47, emphasis in original). I disagree that Hegel's view is a "pragmatism" if we mean by that something akin to Richard Rorty's (1989) pragmatism, in which there is no final justification for the our conventional norms (see 73–74). Hegel seeks to justify this "pragmatic" move based on the natural right of the subject to achieve satisfaction, and hence he would disagree with Rorty's (1998) statement (describing his and Brandom's pragmatism): "philosophy

can never be anything more than a discussion of utility and compatibility of beliefs. . . . There is no authority outside of convenience for human purposes that can be appealed to in order to legitimize the use of a vocabulary" (127).

30. Hegel often uses this example because "language is the work of thought" (EL 20A).

31. Hegel remarks often on this peculiarity of the "I," that it refers both this particular subjectivity—me—and inevitably to subjectivity in general (PhG 102, EL 24Z1). In SL, Hegel states that the "I" refers, first, as a "pure self-related unity," or "universality," and, second, the "I as self-related negativity" or as "individuality" and "individual personality" (583). For Hegel, the "I" is the proper place to begin because it dialectically moves within itself between a normative universal self-consciousness and my own particular individuality. In other words, I can think for myself and use my reason to guide my own life and select the occupation that best suits me (PR 206), but at the same time, "when we think rationally . . . we think not only subjectively, but also the rationality of the thing is active, and I as a particular subject only look on" (VPR21 2). Human subjectivity exists between the purity of abstract rational thought and the embodied, particular perspective.

32. "Spirit" has many different forms, from the spirit of a people (*Volksgeist*) to the spirit of humanity (*der absolute Geist*) as a whole (see PHI 51–52). For Hegel, spirit consists in the combination of universal subject and substance, or rather the general will and the set of institutions, norms, and dispositions in which this general will has reality. I will elaborate at greater length on the notions of universal subject and substance in chapter 3. See Pinkard (1996, chap. 1) for a good, succinct account of the view of spirit as a "space of reasons" that I am broadly following here.

33. See Steinberger (2004) for a further elaboration of the state as a "structure of intelligibility."

34. As Hegel puts it, the "I is thinking as the subject" (EL 20A). See DeVries's (1988) insightful discussion of Hegel's identification of the I and "thinking" (95ff.).

35. Hegel argues that the "individual" is the "ground" of its determinations, harmonizing and hence giving sense to otherwise senseless general norms and particular desires (EL 164A). For Hegel, then, individuality is the realized result of the immanent aims of the "absolute negativity" of subjectivity. See SL 437 ("Light essentially possesses in its infinite expansion and in its power to promote growth and to animate, the nature of absolute negativity"); SL 571 (the "self-identical negativity" is "the individual"); and VPR.3.118 (the "self-determination of the I" is "individuality" [*Einzelheit*]).

36. As Hegel puts it, the decline of traditional ethical life frees individual self-determination and hence makes "infinite subjectivity" and autonomy possible (PH 238).

37. Cf. also PR 124: "what the subject is, is the series of its actions."

38. Hegel follows Rousseau on the matter of perfectibility at PHI 124: "historical change in the abstract sense has long been interpreted in general terms as embodying some kind of progress towards a better and more perfect condition. Changes in the natural world, no matter how great their variety, exhibit only an eternally recurring cycle. . . . In short, [the human being] possesses an impulse of perfectibility." Perfectibility for Hegel, as for Rousseau, does not have a set teleological purpose, but rather it "is without aim or purpose, and the better or more perfect condition to which it supposedly tends is of a completely indefinite nature."

39. See PHI 86 on Hegel's critique of Kant's ontology of reason and passion—"passion is usually regarded as something contrary to right and more or less base in nature, and man is expected not to have any passions. . . . [However,] the particular content of such personal ends is so much a part of the individual's will that it determines it completely and is inseparable from it, and it is this which makes the individual what he is. For the individual exists as a determinate being, unlike man in general, who has no existence as such."

40. For a helpful discussion of habit in Hegel's philosophy of spirit, see Lewis (2005, chap. 2).

41. See PR 19 on the transformation of natural desire into a rational self-determined system of my identity. As Hegel puts the point in the context of "deciding," the "I is the oneness [*Eine*] in opposition to the many [desires]," and it "makes itself identical to itself . . . in this content" (VPR.3.129).

42. For Hegel, the activity of investing one's ego into one's character when one "determines oneself" is the best expression of "absolute negativity" as the idealization (or making-into-ego) of everything concerning one's character, and hence the "infinite" [*Unendlichen*] (VPR 4.122).

43. The term "ennormed" is mine, as I am attempting to express the way in which Hegel aims to harmonize yet keep distinct mind and body, reason and passion. Hegel himself uses the terms "ensouled" and "embodied" to capture the intimate relationship between mind and body: "Concept ensouls the real existence which embodies it, and therefore is free and at home with itself in this objectivity" (Aesthetics 112).

44. Patten's (1999) illuminating account of Hegel's view of "rational self-determination" fails because of its overly static and formal account of what freedom consists in for Hegel. Patten does not take account of the moment of "individuality" and the task of narrative self-understanding.

45. See Hegel's dialectical account of the nature of judgment, which always already includes universal, individual, and particular elements (EL 166–80).

46. See Kolb (1986, chap. 4) for a further elaboration on Hegel's views of individual, particular, and universal. Dudley (2002) helpfully analyzes the movements in the *Philosophy of Right* with the three elements of the concept.

47. See PH 333: the human being is the "image of God and a source of infinity in himself. He is an end to himself [*Selbstzweck*], and has in himself an infinite [*unendlichen*] value, an eternal destiny [*Bestimmung*]"; also PR 185A: "The principle of the self-sufficient and inherently infinite personality of the individual . . . arose in an inward form in the Christian religion."

48. Hegel speaks about the "individual" in his *Logic* in similar terms of self-creation. The task of the "individual" is precisely to "posit" the other moments of universality and particularity, and to posit them as a unity (EL 165). In positing universal norms and particular desires, for instance, the individual acts as the "*inward* reflection of the determinacies of universality and particularity" (EL 163, my emphasis). The individual is the "negative inward reflection of the concept"; it is "free distinguishing, as the first negation" (EL 165). In other words, in confronting the world, the individual must make the world meaningful to himself. But in applying universal norms to particular desires and hence rendering the world meaningful, the subject also realizes and unifies *himself* as the kind of being who looks at and acts in the world in just this way.

49. See also Hegel's reflections in *On the Positivity of Christian Religion*, in which Hegel criticizes the Christian church when it imposes a "law whose yoke he [the 'pious' man] bore was not given by himself, by his reason, since he could not regard his reason as free, as a master, but only as a servant" (ETW 80). For Hegel, the example of Jesus is one of autonomy, of obeying the "free virtue springing from man's own being" (ETW 71). "Every man," Hegel argues, "has the right to develop his faculties, i.e. to become a man" (ETW 114).

50. See Redding (1996) for an illuminating "hermeneutic" reading of Hegel. See especially his chapter 7 for an account of the "hermeneutic" nature of the relationship among universal, individual, and particular moments, an analysis I am indebted to here. See also Lewis (2005) on the hermeneutic relationship between theoretical and practical reason in Hegel (111ff.).

51. There has been considerable recent interest in the concept of the narrative individual, though—see especially MacIntyre (1984), Taylor (1989), Schechtman (1996).

Hegel and Nietzsche's contribution to this discussion, I think, is to argue that (a) narratives can be better and worse depending on the individual, and (b) a properly constructed narrative is an integral part to leading a good life.

52. Hegel does not explicitly employ the narrative or literary metaphor in reference to the creation of the individual self, but he suggests it at a couple important moments (see PR 15Z and EL 133Z). Consider, however, his account of modern art at Aesthetics 602ff., in which he argues that now "Humanus" is the new "holy of holies," that what has become salient for art—and hence for individual development in general—is the "depths and heights of the human heart as such, mankind in its joys and sorrows, its strivings, deeds, and fates. Herewith the artist acquires his subject-matter in himself and is the human spirit actually self-determining and considering, meditating, and expressing the infinity of its feelings and situations" (Aesthetics 607). Cf. also his discussion of "character" at Aesthetics 236ff., which is the moment in which the "self-related subjective individuality" must embody universal principles and particular circumstances in a narratively constructed "richness of character." Moreover, Speight (2001) has drawn out in detail Hegel's explicit connections between the production of literature and the agential production of a self in the Jena *Phenomenology*.

53. See Taylor (1985, chap. 5) for a nice account of how others can point out flaws in my own self-conception.

54. For a development of the social or intersubjective conception of agency, see especially Arendt (1998), Honneth (1995), Pinkard (2003) and Pippin (2008a).

55. See Hegel's fuller description of the "ages of man" in ES 396.

56. See also Pippin (2008b) on the developmental, never completable element of "Absolute Knowing" in Hegel's *Phenomenology*.

57. See Hegel's critique of the Romantic post-Fichteans in PR 140 as hypocritical, self-ironic, and ultimately self-destructive. See also Hegel's critique of Fries in PR Preface as advocating irrationality through the "hatred of law." On Hegel's critique of the Romantics, see Pöggeler (1999).

Chapter 3

1. See Neuhouser (2000), who discusses the subjective and objective preconditions for "social freedom" (see chaps. 3, 5), and Honneth (2000), who discusses ethical life in terms of its "(pre-)conditions for the actualization of autonomy" (42).

2. I use "common good" rather than "intersubjectively held norms" because I am uncomfortable with the increasingly popular use of the term "intersubjective" to reconstruct Hegel's view. First, it is awkward and fails to indicate Hegel's connection to his historical predecessors who speak regularly about common goods. Second, I think the "inter" prefix fails to account for Hegel's view that the common good should transcend individual wills, not just exist between them. Finally, my term "common good" does not fall into the worry that I think animated the use of "intersubjectivity," which is that the former implies an "external," very often premodern, authority grounding the norm. The common good is not "external" to its individuals, but rather common to them. See Pinkard (2000) for such a misunderstanding—that the "common good" must refer to premodern societies—but also a useful qualification, which I endorse: "Although the state must embody the collective aspiration for the free life of a 'people,' nowhere does Hegel say that it ought to prescribe some one way of life or set of virtues that would be common to all" (487).

3. Readers of Hegel either attempt, like Taylor (1975), to see Hegel's communitarian reflections as assertions of the state's using individuality as a "vehicle" for its own will, or, like Wood (1990) and Neuhouser (2000), see Hegel's state as one community among others in which the individual can autonomously determine his identity. Many

contemporary readers, in other words, fail to take Hegel's reflections as to the comprehensive ethical wholeness of the state seriously, something I would like to remedy in what follows. One exception is Steinberger's (2004) Hegelian reflections on the comprehensiveness of the state.

4. Hegel is in this way drawing on Aristotle's view of the naturalness of politics for human beings, understood as shared deliberation and sentiment about good and evil, just and unjust. Aristotle, like Hegel, argues that it is the natural telos of human beings to lead a political life, and when human beings enter in to the polis, the polis reveals itself as "by nature clearly prior to the family and to the individual, since the whole is of necessity prior to the part" (Aristotle 1996, 14). See Hegel's citation of this section of the *Politics* at PW 159–60; the "Ethical Life" section of his PR can be read as a transformation of Aristotle's natural history of human beings. The crucial difference between Aristotle and Hegel, however, is that Hegel refers to the nature of free human subjectivity, whereas Aristotle rests his view on the biological nature of human beings.

5. See, e.g., Knowles (2002, 221–23) on ethical life as "our station and its duties" as a response to Kantian abstraction.

6. Hegel argues that particular kinds of communities condition such action; modern civil society cultivates selfish individuals (PR 184, 185A), whereas the Roman empire demanded slavish conformism to a distant tyrant (PhG 482–83).

7. Many readers understand Hegel's master-slave dialectic to be an "epistemological" account of the conditions for the possibility of individual "self-sufficient agency." See especially Pinkard (1996, chap. 3) and Bernstein's (1984) excellent analyses of the transcendental requirement of community for self-consciousness. My historical-phenomenological reading of Hegel's account is justified by Hegel's later lectures on Africa in the *Philosophy of History,* in which the master-slave relationship appears at the dawn of human history (PHI 173ff.).

8. See Redding (2008) on the animalistic or naturalistic valence of Hegel's term "Begierde" as opposed to more spiritual or civilized terms he could have used (98).

9. See Hobbes, *Leviathan*, chap. 11: human beings have a "a perpetual and restless desire of power after power, that ceaseth only in death."

10. In denying that there is a "desire for recognition," Redding (1996) misses key claims of Hegel's such as this one, that we have an "impulse" (*Trieb*) for recognition which supervenes on our natural desires (see ES 425, 430 on the spiritual "impulse" for recognition).

11. See Stern (2002) for a careful analysis of the argument spanning "desire" to the "struggle for recognition" (75–83).

12. See Honneth's (2008) helpful connection to empirical child developmental psychology, on coming to recognize the other as human through the unpredictability of the other (85–86).

13. See Redding (1996) on an account of the master-slave dialectic that turns on the mutual recognition of the other as an "object." In emphasizing our mutual recognition of the other as an object (rather than in emphasizing our recognition of our similarity or identity), however, Redding fails to account for why Hegel thinks this relationship is of the "highest contradiction."

14. Alexander Kojève (1969), who more than any other commentator made Hegel's view of recognition central to understanding the basis of Hegel's social theory, understood the desire for recognition in terms of a natural desire for glory, in something of a Hobbesian spirit. Commentators since Kojève, such as Gadamer (1976) and Redding (1996), have rightly criticized Kojève's naturalistic interpretation of Hegel's "desire for recognition," pointing out that recognition is a need of self-consciousness, not of our natural bodies. Redding points out that "the phrase, 'desire for recognition' does not appear anywhere in the section on the struggle and its resolution" (121). However, Kojève has a better account than his critics give him credit for. As we have seen already,

Hegel refuses to draw a strong ontological distinction between consciousness and body—indeed, the former is simply a more complicated organization of the latter. In this way, we can expect that the desire for recognition has a naturalistic basis—indeed, as I have argued, the desire to expand subjectivity into the world is at work both on the natural and on the spiritual level. See, in this regard, Hyppolite (1974) on the desire in recognition: "we should recall that this being [of man] is not the being of nature but the being of desire, the disquiet of the self" (167). Yet what Gadamer and Redding get right is the fact that the "desire for recognition" is fueled and satisfied cognitively or rationally, rather than through the satisfaction of given appetites.

15. See Tobias's (2006–7) illuminating distinction—similar to the one I make here—between the master's "recognition" and the slave's "self-determination," which are two parts of "autonomy" (109). Tobias is concerned here with critiquing the use of Hegel's view of recognition by identity politics, which shirks the necessary accompanying, "self-determining" element of human autonomy.

16. On this point, see especially Russon (2004, chap. 4).

17. For Hegel, the "universal self-consciousness" of human community is the answer to a recurring problem in German Idealism first posed by Fichte, who took it to be the dire problem of the modern age—if the individual subject is infinite in its normative sovereignty, then what limits its infinity? Why aren't the limitations from societal rules always oppressive and limiting? Why aren't all natural desires to be denied? For Hegel, the answer comes in the common creation of a universal self-consciousness through mutual recognition. Such a universal self-consciousness is, according to Hegel, my own consciousness. I, along with the others, brought it into being through a common act of self-legislation, and I can only understand myself as a result through my activity within my creation. Thus, in participating and obeying communal rules, I limit the legitimate scope of my own action. In limiting myself, I achieve true "infinite" freedom, rather than being unduly constrained by a social "master."

18. See Neuhouser's (2009) helpful gloss on these points: "the problem of self-consciousness's dependence on an alien other will be solved not by retreating from the ideal of self-sufficiency, nor by eschewing all dependence on others, but instead by an identification with the object depended on [the 'we'] that abolished not the object itself but only its otherness" (46).

19. See Hegel's remarks about the training of the feelings in ES 472Z. He argues that "thought" is "received into the feeling will," by which he means that the normative system or way of life implicit in the community comes to structure our affective relationships with one another. While we have a natural affection for our species, which results in copulation and in the natural family (EN 368), this natural affection can be harnessed into social virtues like benevolence, honor, and friendship. See also Rousseau on the natural affective relationship of pity, which, he thinks, can form the foundation for genuine solidarity in society—a good kind of *amour-propre* to replace the destructive and envy-ridden bad kind: "from [pity] alone flow all the social virtues. . . . what are generosity, mercy, and humanity, if not pity applied to the weak. . . . Benevolence and even friendship are, properly understood, the products of a constant pity fixed on a particular object" (SD 54). Honneth (1996) makes the affective character of recognition central to his account of why human beings are due recognition—we need the recognition of others so that we can feel toward ourselves the emotions of self-respect, self-esteem, and self-trust, necessary components for subsequently leading an autonomous life.

20. A *Stand* (estate) is a core ethical association for Hegel, and plays a large role in Hegel's defense of the modern state, which we will discuss in the next chapter. See VPR 4.622 on the corporation as an "organic" association, VPR 3.726 on the state as an "organic" community.

21. Hegel makes this point often with the example of "honor" that can satisfy the desire for "recognition [*Anerkennung*] in his own eyes and in the eyes of others" (PR 207).

22. See, e.g., PR 201 on the "differentiation" of society into "universal masses." These different "masses" emerge as different "estates" with distinctive forms of ethical life and views of the good. In chapter 5, I will examine Hegel's view of the division of labor and its potential for supporting ethical communities in the modern age.

23. In part, this is because the great diversity of different ways of life in the modern age resists immersive identification with any one way of life (as in premodern regimes) and hence promotes a rational reflectiveness required for a genuinely rational—as opposed to purely affective—ethical disposition on the part of individuals.

24. Aristotle (1996, bk. 1, chap. 2).

25. See Ferrarin (2001) for an erudite and exhaustive account of Hegel's debt to Aristotle.

26. See, e.g., PR 263Z, in which Hegel compares the constitution of the state to the "nervous system" of an organism.

27. An organism's members are converted into "means" so that "each member is reciprocally end and means [as it] maintains itself through the other members and in opposition to them" (EN 356).

28. For Hegel, the individual is hence held responsible if he fails to live up to the norms embedded in this community, because, argues Hegel, the individual has "posited" (*gesetzt*) the "right" of the community in his "action" (*Handlung*). For Hegel, human action—as opposed to "animal" instinct—has the "concept of the universal in it," or rather, a "law" is "represented" in it (VPR.3.315).

29. See Hegel's discussion at VPR17 134 on "by whom is the constitution of a people to be made?" Hegel's answer is that the constitution should be regarded as the "foundation of a people's life," not something "made and subjectively posited." This does not mean change should not happen, but that it should happen only through slow "development."

30. See VPR 4.659–60 for Hegel's rejection of the "contemporary" approach to changing political constitutions with "abstract thought" (*abstrakten Gedanken*), but yet his embrace of organic change according to the internal developmental principles of a "nation's spirit"; for Hegel, a "constitution, especially in the West where subjective freedom rules, never stands still, but is constantly changing, always being revolutionized."

31. Markell (2003) argues that Hegel's "diagnostic and critical account of the struggle for recognition" in the master-slave dialectic "stands at odds with his own vision of a community of mutual recognition" (92). The first kind of recognition admits that there are plural and incommensurable perspectives on human community, while the second kind upholds a unitary normative system structuring human community and apparently eliminating human plurality. Markell, however, is wrong to think these are two different forms of recognition in Hegel, and wrong to argue that the second "kind" of recognition is as oppressive as he claims. On the one hand, for Hegel, the physical struggle for recognition can only be resolved through a mutual subsumption of one another's will under a general normative system. On the other hand, such a subsumption does not mean that these wills are "bound" to this normative system without escape—first of all, Hegel argues that plurality and difference are only possible and intelligible as part of a shared structure of intelligibility; second, the normative system itself is not static and unchanging, but on the contrary constantly revised through deliberation.

32. As Hegel puts the point, the political "disposition takes its particularly determined content from the various aspects of the state. This organism is the development of the Idea in its differences and their objective actuality" (PR 269).

33. See Pinkard's (2008) excellent description of Hegel's view of the Greek life and how Hegel employed the concept of the community of Leibnizian monads to understand Greek ethical life (115–16). For Hegel, the harmony of community and individual-

ity is a vision of "beauty." The Greek city in particular exemplifies such "beautiful freedom" (PHI 202). Each Greek city-state was small enough such that every citizen of this city recognized every other as "identical" or fellow pursuers of the common good. Additionally, the city-state was differentiated into several classes, from the rulers to the gentlemen to the artisans (and the slaves), each of whom had its own practices with its own rules and aims. These different classes were themselves divided into particular stations, each occupied by a single individual. Finally, and most important, these stations, classes, and communal whole were all woven together in one beautiful, organically interdependent union, a "truly harmonious . . . kingdom" (PHI 202).

34. For Hegel, marriage is the only form of romantic relationship that constitutes a genuine "ethical love, so that the transient, capricious, and purely subjective aspects of love are excluded from it" (PR 161Z). This is because, as we will see in the next chapter, communities must have an immanent connection to the comprehensive political community in order to be ethical, so that human beings can achieve wholeness as all their communities that they belong to are themselves part of one political whole. For Hegel, the subjective passion in contemporary relationships has a certain "contingency" and selfishness associated with it, as if this relationship has no bearing to their family, their local community, their business, and the state to which they belong (PR 162A).

35. In this way, I disagree with Rorty (1998) and Brandom (2002). Here is Rorty: "In Brandom's preferred terms of 'social practices,' decisions about truth and falsity are always a matter of rendering practices more coherent or developing new practices. They never require us to check practices against a norm that is not implicit in some alternative practice, real or imagined" (129).

36. See PHI 130: "during the first . . . stage in the process, the spirit . . . is still immersed in nature, in which it exists in a state of unfree particularity (only One is free). But during the second stage it emerges into an awareness of its own freedom. The first departure from nature is, however, imperfect and partial—only Some are free."

37. See, however, Siep (2006) for an exception, who offers an illuminating parallel between Hegel's rational development and structure of the modern state and Aristotle's view of the polis. Siep rightly brings out that Hegel retrieves Aristotle's claim that human beings are political animals.

38. See Franco's (1999) helpful analysis of Hegel's argument as to the "destiny" of individuals to lead a universal life in politics, and his connection of Hegel's view to Aristotle's (284ff.). See Aristotle's *Politics* bk. 1, chap. 2 for Aristotle's account of the "political" nature of human beings in connection to our rational natures.

39. See Aesthetics 181 for a clear statement of the autonomy condition for public institutions: "the ideal individual must be self-contained [and hence] what is objective must still be his own and it must not be separated from the individuality of men. . . . thus in this regard the universal must indeed be actual in the individual as his own . . . as his character and heart."

40. Hegel cites this portion of the Funeral Oration at PH 261: "'we love the beautiful' he says, 'but without ostentation or extravagance; we philosophize without being seduced thereby into effeminacy and inactivity."

41. Thucydides (1993, 44).

Chapter 4

1. See Yack (1992) for a thorough review of the role of the ancients in arousing "longing and social discontent" among eighteenth- and nineteenth-century social and political philosophers.

2. See Wolff (2004) for an illuminating account of the logical underpinnings of Hegel's view of the state.

3. See also PHI 202: the Greek life is "not yet morality, but merely unreflecting ethical existence; for the individual will of the subject intuitively adopts the customs and habits laid down by justice and the laws. The individual is therefore unconsciously united with the universal end. Accordingly, this kingdom is truly harmonious."

4. See PR 185A for a clear account of the deficiency of Greek ethical life, the lack of the "principle of subjective freedom," which, for Hegel, "arose in an inward form in the Christian religion and in an external form . . . in the Roman world."

5. Cf. Ross (2008), who helpfully shows that in Hegel's early Jena writings, he was already committed to maintaining the "mechanistic" element of modern commercial society, while still incorporating this mechanism within a larger modern organic whole. However, Ross emphasizes too heavily the state's intervention in civil society in cultivating an ethical politics. See, e.g., VPR17 132A: "the universal must be accomplished . . . in such a way that the individual, in accomplishing the universal, is working for himself. The particularity of the individual will must be maintained in the universal will."

6. Cited in Neuhouser (2000, 296n2).

7. In particular, scholars have focused on (a) Hegel's critique of Rousseau's social and political ontology, and (b) Hegel's indebtedness to Rousseau's view of the free will. Taylor (1975, 185–86) details Hegel's critique of Rousseau's political philosophy. Franco (1999, chap. 7) details Hegel's critique of Rousseau's criticism of liberalism, and in chapter 1 he brings out Rousseau's sweeping influence on the concept of the will. Neuhouser has elicited Hegel's debt to Rousseau's analysis of the ground of rational or moral freedom (2000) and Hegel's debt to Rousseau's account of the source of moral norms requisite for rational recognition and individual right (2003). Ripstein (1994) offers a helpful analysis of Hegel's critique of the "arbitrariness" at the heart of Rousseau's general will, and what Hegel learns from Rousseau as to how to avoid such arbitrariness in politics. Pelczynski (1984a) has highlighted Hegel's appropriation of Rousseau's view of conscience. Fulda (1991) has revealed Rousseau's importance for Hegel's early philosophical development. Duso (1991) has brought out Hegel's complex relationship with Rousseau on the issue of representation.

8. No one has examined Hegel's response to Rousseau's critique of modern civil society in the "System of Needs" section in the *Philosophy of Right*. Some, like Siep (2006), argue that Hegel disagrees with Rousseau on the effects of commercial society (156). Neuhouser (2000, chap. 2) touches on some of the issues I discuss here. Neuhouser discusses Hegel's conceptual debt to Rousseau's view of freedom, which has two parts, "objective" and "subjective" freedom. "Objective" freedom is the freedom of the Social Contract, in which rational beings "freely" will the general will because it is, in some sense, their true will. "Subjective" freedom, by contrast, is the freedom of "independence," in which one "self-sufficient with respect to the satisfaction of one's needs" (64). Neuhouser is certainly correct in his account of both forms of freedom and their origin in Rousseau. Neuhouser does not, however, detail Rousseau's critique of modern commercial society on the issue of the expansion of desire (the mechanism which makes self-sufficiency impossible), nor does he detail Hegel's specific response to Rousseau's argument.

9. See also VPR 4.477: "we find the terrifying description of the misery which is brought forth by the satisfaction of needs [*Bedürfnisse*], especially in Rousseau and several others. These men deeply grasp the misery of their time, their people; they deeply grasp and vividly portray the evil will [*bösen Willen*] that springs from this related ethical corruption, from the fury, the disgust of men about their misery and about the contradiction between what they demand and the state in which they find themselves, their exasperation, the mockery about this state and the inner bitterness."

10. See Hegel's outline of his response to Rousseau's critique of civil society at VPR21 185: "Rousseau saw the misery of civil society, and told human beings to go into the woods and throw away everything else. He came to this thought in deep pain over

this corruption. He wanted to tear away this whole edifice, on which everything rested, on which particularity develops itself. . . . But it is a higher reconciliation, which allows the principle to be true in itself, that elevates this freedom to the freedom of the universal." Cf. VPR18 91Z.

11. This critique is ultimately ancient in origin—see Socrates' famous metaphor of the "leaky jar" in Plato's *Gorgias* 493bff.

12. See VPR17 93: Through the division of labor, desires undergo a process of "division and differentiation into single parts and aspects, which in this way become different needs, more particularized and at the same time less concrete, more abstract."

13. Rousseau describes a similar origin to these social desires at SD 63–64: individuals gather in societies for the mutual satisfaction of need and hence become dependent on one another, individually weaker and yet collectively more productive. Yet their leisure time allowed for the development of our "comparison" of one to another and hence the replacement of natural desires with these social "comparative" ones.

14. See PR 193 on the desire for "equality" or "sameness" (*Gleichheit*), and VPR17 95 for the desire to be "recognized [*anerkannt*] by the other as his equal."

15. Cf. VPR 4.491: "We imitate, this is the origin of styles, so that we want to have what the other has, we want to achieve this, such that we are not satisfied until we have this particular thing, until we imitate the other. Thus it goes endlessly [*Unendliche*] this way."

16. See SL 412ff. on the dialectical relationship between identity and difference.

17. Hegel more clearly distinguishes the two normative demands in VPR17 95–96.

18. See Hegel's approval of the "invisible hand" theory of modern political economy, that, as Hegel puts it, "in the very act of developing itself independently to totality, the principle of particularity passes over into universality" (PR 186). See Waszek (1988) for an exhaustive account of Hegel's debt to the Scottish Enlightenment in his discussion of "Civil Society," and Church (forthcoming a) for an analysis of Locke's influence on Hegel's thinking on this point.

19. This self-enslavement is exacerbated and maintained at a material or structural level for Rousseau and Hegel, in the sense that the division of labor and social comparisons lead to the inequality of property, which causes many problems of its own. Hegel argues that the expansion of a capitalist economy necessarily disenfranchises a group of workers.—on this matter, see especially Taylor's (1975, 436) and Avineri's (1972, 148–49) accounts of the cause of poverty. Hegel at the same time attempts to solve this difficulty through a few institutional means of state intervention in the economy. This topic is too large to discuss here, and is treated at length in, for instance, Dudley (1997), Hardimon (1994), Anderson (2001), and several articles in Maker (1987). Williams (1997) helpfully bridges the gap between the psychic harm caused by "atomism" and the systematic tendency toward capitalist overproduction (242ff.).

20. See Rousseau's reflections on the imagination as the source of human unhappiness in E 219.

21. Hegel's worry about the deleterious effects of money can be inferred from a few passages: Hegel worries about the issue of "selfishness." Hegel does employ selfishness as Mandeville does, as when "subjective selfishness turns into a contribution towards the satisfaction of the needs of everyone else" (PR 199), but he also sees this selfishness as having deleterious effects as a result of the introduction of money and the accumulation of wealth, coupled with the abstract equalizing of and thus dissolving of the bonds among individuals (Hegel's Rousseau-inspired worry). In VPR.3.791, Hegel remarks that in the "modern world," everything is "reduced to money," which means to "what is abstract . . . what is spiritless [*Gemütlose*]." In PR 201Z, he suggests that the introduction of mediating institutions can ameliorate the turn to selfishness. In PR 236A, Hegel worries about the blind immersion in "selfish ends" and suggests the intervention of the police power. Further, Hegel suggests that those left outside the corporations and

estates will engage in precisely what I have been describing: the vain attempt to "gain *recognition* [*Anerkennung*] through the external manifestations of success in his trade, and these are without limit. . . . his of his trade" (PR 253A; cf. VPR17 121A). Cf. also Hegel's discussion of luxury [*Luxus*] in VPR21 195, especially "Luxury . . . is for its part an expansion of dependence and need." One should, however, always keep in mind that for all its disadvantages, Hegel argues that money is a positive, rational development, which makes possible trade among people and nations, see PR 299A.

22. Cf. PR 253A on Hegel's remark about joining an illegal corporation, thus being outside of the legally recognized communal life.: "If the individual is not a member of a legally recognized corporation . . . he is without the *honor of belonging to an estate* [*Standesehre*], his isolation reduces him to the selfish aspect of his trade, and his livelihood and satisfaction lack *stability*. He will accordingly try to gain *recognition* [*Anerkennung*] through the external manifestations of success in his trade, and these are without limit [*unbegrenzt*]."

23. See Dudley (1997) for a further development of this point.

24. See Villa's (2005) comparison of Hegel and Tocqueville as thinkers who both combat the individualizing tendencies of liberal thought with the integrative institutions of civil society. Cf. also Dallmayr (1993), who argues that the "central significance of the estates resides in their integrative function" (131), and Franco (1999) on the educative function of the estates and corporations.

25. Cf. VPR.3.624: through the estates, individual "selfishness [*Selbstsucht*] becomes knotted up with the common good of the state."

26. That is, Hegel seeks to avoid excessive state regulation, which has the effect of alienating citizens from the state as something imposed upon them rather than, as in the system of mediating institutions, sustaining a free civil society such that particular desires "flow into" the good of the whole state (VPR17 128).

27. See Pinkard's (2000) account that Hegel's key concern in the 1820s was "how the various mediating bodies of the emerging German civil society were to be regulated and organized so as to harmonize with the aims of the modern state" (606).

28. Though the precise character of Hegel's institutions may be outmoded, his insights into the origin, nature, and function of these institutions are still valuable. See Harris (1983) on this point. Harris argues that Hegel's view is in fact consistent with the possibility of institutional change: "every customary structure must be submitted to criticism, and the necessary process of justification is one of communal justification" (56)—not only will economic structures change, but they ought to be submitted to deliberative assessment and justification. No arrangement of institutions, for Hegel, is justified simply by tradition, by nature, or by God; it must be justified by the canons of rationality.

29. See VPR17 132A: "if individuals vest their aptitude in a particular sphere of action, they must defend this status and view it as their own. A universal spirit of patriotism is formed by the fact that universal freedom comes about through particularization." See also Cohen and Rogers (1995) for a more extended argument as to the importance of rooting associations in economic institutions.

30. See Chambers and Kopstein (2006), Putnam (2000).

31. See Luther (2009, 5–10, 165–90) for helpful reflections on Hegel's project to make modern commercial society ethical.

32. Qtd. in Avineri (1972, 107).

33. See Prosch's (1997) clear explication of the differences between Hegel's corporations and contemporary corporations.

34. In his *Critique of Hegel's Philosophy of Right*, Marx attacked Hegel particularly for the undue trust that Hegel places in the bureaucracy for protecting public interest. Yet Hegel has, I think, built-in institutional means to make the bureaucracy better: first, it contains a system of education and incentives so that the most qualified individuals will

enter office. Second, the executive bureaucracy is checked by the monarch on the one hand and the corporations and estates on the other from overreaching or from bureaucratic indifference and inefficiency.

35. See Hegel's concerns about the excessive power of the corporations in Germany at VPR17 121A, 125A, and PW 10–12.

36. See Heiman (1971) for helpful background on Hegel's sources for these institutions. Cullen (1979, 91–94, 100–102) and (1988, 22–41) clearly analyzes the economic and educational support the corporations provide. Hardimon (1994, 197–202) discusses the formation of individual identity and the representative and participatory activity of the corporations. Scholars such as Neuhouser (2000, 205ff.) and Lewis (2005) argue that Hegel's theory of associational life is both unnecessary and a blemish on Hegel's otherwise good liberal view. Lewis and Neuhouser go too far in their criticisms with statements such as this: Hegel's view "assigns different rights of political participation to different classes of individuals" (Neuhouser 2000, 206). Contrary to Neuhouser, though, Hegel thinks that all individuals have the same right of self-determination within their respective classes. These classes replace parties, for instance, in being a mechanism for translating the individual vote into a coherent political preference.

37. Hegel points to the success of British mediating institutions "because . . . the state, as universal will, is their will, the people's own will" (VPR17 129A).

38. See Tocqueville's (2000) analysis of the New England townships for a similar view of the interlocking chains of autonomy created by different levels of administrative authority. As he puts it, this individual is "glorified in the glory of the nation; in the success that it obtains he believes he recognizes his own work, and he is uplifted by it; he rejoices in the general prosperity from which he profits" (90).

39. Hegel would not go so far as Rousseau in claiming that "the better constituted the State, the more public business takes precedence over private business in the minds of citizens." Rather, for Hegel, a citizen's public "disposition" must combine public and private business—that is, we must always see the public implications of the private activity we engage in most of the time. Accordingly, Hegel would agree with Rousseau when the latter claims, "Once someone says what do I care? about the affairs of state, the state should be considered lost." (SC 74, emphasis in original). See PR 324 on the need for war to reveal "the vanity of temporal things and temporal goods . . . [as taking] on serious significance."

40. See PR preface, 11, "comprehending" the "truth concerning rights, ethics, and the state." Understanding the rationality of the whole can help otherwise alienated individuals come to tolerate the authority of the state. But to get citizens involved, they must have a practical stake in the whole, which means they must invest themselves in it.

41. As Hegel puts it, in the corporation, the individual "is himself a moment [of the whole], not merely a part" (VPR18 113Z).

42. See Hartmann (1984) for an analysis of the principle of subsidiarity at work in Hegel. In VPR.4.690–91, Hegel is explicitly concerned with balancing "rule from above" with rule by the corporations; his solution is one of subsidiarity. The "universal" concerns are to be handled by the general government, while the "particular interests" (*besonderen Interessen*) are to be overseen by the corporations. Cf. qtd. in Avineri (1972, 47): "we also regard these people as fortunate to which the state gives a free hand in subordinate general activities."

43. PR 288, 295: "the protection of the state and the governed against the misuse of power on the part of the official bodies and their members is . . . [the responsibility of] communities and corporations, for this prevents subjective arbitrariness from interfering on its own account . . . and supplements from below that control from above which does not extend as far as individual conduct." See also PR 297.

44. I disagree with Arato's (1991) critique of Hegel as not reconciling two series of authority in civil society, that of the bureaucratic, governmental, coercive power and

that of the participatory mediating institutions. In addition to the corporation's direct check on the executive branch, they can turn either to the monarch or to the estates assembly to redress grievances. See VPR17 145, 157. Thus, I disagree with Arato's assessment that "unfortunately for Hegel the public freedom possible in the corporation, involving relatively high level of participation, cannot be primary in society as a whole" (317). Cf. Horstmann's (2004) argument that Hegel's view contains an irreconcilable contradiction between a liberal civil society and an omnipotent state to which civil society must answer. Theunissen (1991) also argues that "the theory of the state erases every trace of intersubjectivity in it," especially that produced by civil society (56–57).

45. The court system is technically part of civil society, though the appointment of judges belongs to the tasks of government, since government is the objective authority enshrining the law of the community. The government achieves this objective status through an internal system of institutional checks and balances familiar to students of Montesquieu.

46. See Dahl (1989, 324–32) for an a defense of the "democratization" of economic associations. While Hegel would approve of the spirit of Dahl's suggestions, he would not be quite as radical in according procedural equality regardless of institutional status.

47. See PR 301A: legislative delegates should have "extra insight . . . first of all into the activities of those officials who are less visible to their superiors, and in particular into the more urgent and specialized needs and deficiencies which they see in concrete form before their eyes; and secondly, it lies in the effect which the expectation of criticism, indeed of public criticism, at the hands of the many has in compelling the officials to apply their best insights, even before they start, to their functions and to the plans they intend to submit, and to put these into effect only in accordance with the purest of motives."

48. For Hegel, the bigger problem of the "crowd or aggregate, unorganized in their opinions and volition" is that it can be easily coopted by forces of irrationality and hence "become a massive power in opposition to the organic state" (PR 302). Mass elections may seem to be the fairer mechanism, but in fact "an institution of this kind achieves the opposite of its intended purpose, and the election comes under the control of a few people, of a faction, and hence of that particular and contingent interest which it was specifically designed to neutralize" (PR 311A).

49. See Hegel's remarks in the "Proceedings of the Estates Assembly" on this critique of democracy: "The citizens come to the scene as isolated atoms, and the electoral assemblies as unordered inorganic aggregates; the peoples as a whole are dissolved into a heap. This is a form in which the community should never have appeared at all in undertaking any enterprise; it is a form most unworthy of the community and most in contradiction with its concepts as a spiritual order. Age and property are qualities affecting only the individual himself, not characteristically constituting his worth in the civil order. Such worth he has only on the strength of his office, his position, his skill in craftsmanship which, recognized by his fellow citizens, entitles him accordingly to be described as a master of his craft" (qtd. in Rawls 2000, 357n).

50. Since there is bound to be disagreement between the estates and the government, between particular interests and common good, Hegel argues that this "opposition" should become a "rational relation" in the form of a competitive party system (PR 304, VPR17 156).

51. Hegel's institutional design of dividing the estates (PR 313) and of having deliberation in public (PR 315) also, for him, augments the rationality of the deliberation.

52. Accordingly, Hegel argues, the state must avoid excessive centralization of power: "how dull and spiritless a life is engendered in a modern state where everything is regulated from the top downwards, where nothing with any general implications is left to the management and execution of interested parties of the people" (qtd. in Avineri 1972, 49).

53. See Goldstein (2004) for a fine development of this point in terms of Hegel's desire to avoid the "enervation" of "habit" (483).

54. See Villa (2008, chap. 3). For Hegel, Villa rightly points out, a "strong identification with society's basic institutions and norms [is] the only real counter to the alienation" of a liberal polity (80).

55. Accordingly, I agree in large part with Losurdo's (2004) erudite study of Hegel's putative "liberalism." Losurdo's rich account of Hegel's political views aligns him in part with the liberal tradition of England, but much more closely with the Rousseauan republican tradition. Losurdo rightly brings out Hegel's distance from Burke's parochial pragmatism (see chap. 10), but he overstates their distance. The main way that Hegel differs from Rousseau, we might say, is by injecting a Burkean sentiment of moderation and organicism in his view of historically evolving practices.

56. See Tocqueville (2000) on the function of the mediating institutions of civil society to serve this double-checking function: "in democratic peoples, associations must take the place of the powerful particular persons whom equality of conditions has made disappear" (492).

Chapter 5

1. See MacIntyre (1984) for the "cruelty" reading of Nietzsche, and Kaufmann (1974) for the civilized, sublimated understanding of Nietzsche's individual.

2. I challenge here, then, Williams's (1993) claim that Nietzsche's texts are "booby trapped, not only against recovering theory from it, but, in many cases, against any systematic exegesis that assimilates it to theory" (4). My interpretation here is a reconstruction of what I take to be a coherent theory of individuality expressed in scattered fragments by Nietzsche.

3. See, e.g., Nehamas (1985, chap. 6); Ridley (2007), Janaway (2007), Owen (2007).

4. There are a few important exceptions. Kaufmann (1974) argues that Nietzsche's "sublimation" thesis is indebted to Hegel's "dialectic," a view I am very much indebted to. Houlgate (1986) has offered the most helpful documentation of Nietzsche's personal knowledge of Hegel's philosophy. He also usefully compares Hegel and Nietzsche's contributions to critiques of "metaphysics." Jurist (2000) argues correctly that Hegel and Nietzsche's philosophical positions are not as opposed as they have been usually taken to be, and he substantiates this claim by turning to their shared views on culture and agency.

5. Nietzsche identifies the "astonishing move [*Griff*]" Hegel makes and the profound effects it had on nineteenth-century German philosophy. Nietzsche argues that "we Germans are Hegelians . . . insofar as we . . . instinctively attribute a deeper meaning [*Sinn*] and greater value to becoming and development than to what 'is'" (GS 357). Nietzsche repeats this fundamental finding of Hegel elsewhere in his corpus (see, e.g., BGE 204 and KSA 11.34.73).

6. This claim hence directly contradicts Leiter and Clark's (1997) view that Hegel's "influence was waning seriously" by the mid-nineteenth century, and that Kant had begun his resurgence (ix). The rise in historical studies, the continued interest in hermeneutics leading up to Dilthey, the emphasis on the centrality of the state in the ethical life of a people—all these issues ensured that Hegel remained a powerful intellectual force after the middle of the nineteenth century, especially given the fact that he was constantly a target of criticism. On the other hand, the history of Kant's reception is complex, though Kant's influence was largely relegated to Schopenhauer and to the universities. See Köhnke (1991) on the history of neo-Kantianism. As Leiter and Clark point out, "materialism" as a philosophical movement was very influential on Nietzsche's thought. This is certainly correct, though Nietzsche only accepted materialism as, one

might say, a "metaphysical" position, that only material bodies exist. As an "ethical" thinker, Nietzsche rejected those like Marx who reduced the human good to materiality. Rather, Nietzsche's ethical good is far closer to Hegel's idealist position, that human freedom consists in the creation and maintenance of an artificial human world.

7. Cf. KSA 8.23.126: "the highest power of Hegel over the German mind appeared . . . in many philosophical writings over the last fifteen years."

8. For one example of Schopenhauer's slurs against Hegel, see "[there is no] grosser nonsense [than] the ponderous and witless Hegel" (1969, 419). Nietzsche chastises Schopenhauer for being "impoverished" precisely on the issue Hegel introduced to the German world, the "historical sense" (BGE 204).

9. See the following as some evidence for Nietzsche's extensive concern with Hegel (a good deal more evidence could be marshaled):—Nietzsche's extensive interest with Hegel in Summer–Autumn 1873 (see UUM 29.38–74; Hill 2003, 13n21, who claims that UM 2 is targeted at "Hegelianism"). See Warren's (1988) explication of Nietzsche's criticism of Hegel in UM 2.8 (87–88). It is hard to deny that Nietzsche had Hegel himself in mind when he called history "das Wandeln Gottes auf der Erde" (UM 2.8); Hegel had referred to the state as the "der Gang Gottes auf der Erde" (PR 258Z). Also, Nietzsche quotes Hegel's *Philosophy of History* directly (and approvingly!) in UM 2.9. Nietzsche also may have Hegel in his sights in Z,"On Redemption," as Strong (2000, 225–26) argues. See Nietzsche's concern with and quotations from Hegel's *Philosophy of History* at KSA 7.29.72–74. Nietzsche also correctly attributes to Hegel the critique of the Romantics and his turn to justification based on reason and the state. See KSA 12.9.178: "Since Hegel's success against the 'emotionalism' and the romantic idealism was rooted in the fatalism of his path of thought, which, according to him, amounts to the greater rationality on the side of the victors—such is his justification of the actual [*wirklichen*] 'state.'" Nietzsche also demonstrates in this journal entry a knowledge of the *Spinozastreit* and its connection to Goethe and Hegel. Hegel is the ninth–most cited philosopher in Nietzsche's corpus (see Hill 2003, 5n8).

10. See especially Nietzsche's remark that the British genealogists lack a "historical spirit" (GM 1.2). Pippin (2010) expresses the point nicely: Nietzsche's view "is that views of the soul and its capacities vary with beliefs about and commitments to norms; normative commitments are subject to radical historical change; and so what counts as soul or psyche or mind and thus psychology also changes. The 'soul' is merely the name for a collective historical achievement, a mode of self-understanding, of one sort or another, what we have made ourselves into at one point or another in the service of some ideal or other" (3).

11. See, however, GS 99 for a clear statement of Nietzsche's rejection of Schopenhauer's metaphysics on the ground that it implies the "denial of the individual [*Individuum*]."

12. See Nietzsche's criticisms of the unity of the "ego" at WP 485. There and elsewhere, Nietzsche repeats the criticisms of the Cartesian "substance" view of the mind found initially in Kant's "Paralogisms of Pure Reason" (CPR 406Bff.). On BGE 19, see Leiter (2009) for a "naturalist" reading, and Clark and Dudrick (2009) for a challenge.

13. I also set aside the metaphysical approach to individuality because this problem has been treated very well in both White (1997) and Nabais (2006). Gardner (2009) offers a penetrating analysis of the "disunity" of theoretical and practical reason in Nietzsche's thought. For Gardner, Nietzsche maintained both the theoretical dissolution of the self and the practical defense of the self, and ultimately concluded that the tension between these is an "antinomy" of human reason. Responding to Gardner's impressive work would take us too far afield, but I think (a) Nietzsche's metaphysical views underwent a greater change than his practical or ethical views over his career, and (b) in the case of his deflationary theoretical views, Nietzsche almost always targets Platonist-Christian dogmatism, to clear the way for his practical project. In this way, I

think of Nietzsche as the mirror image of Kant—instead of combating materialism to make room for the truths of practical reason à la Kant, Nietzsche is attacking dogmatic idealism to make room for practical reason.

14. Nietzsche's debt to Kant has been well documented recently. See Hill (2003), Green (2002), Sokoloff (2006), Doyle (2004).

15. See Acampora (2006a) and Leiter (2002) for strong defenses of Nietzsche's naturalism. This naturalist interpretation is clearly an advance in Nietzsche scholarship beyond the "postmodern" interpretation, which understood Nietzsche to question the claims of science. In uncovering Nietzsche's deep admiration and commitment to the scientific method and scientific discoveries, these naturalists are following in the influential footsteps of Clark's (1990) text, which argued that Nietzsche should be read as a kind of neo-Kantian. Although this naturalist interpretation (with its neo-Kantian comrades-in-arms) gives us a truer (or at least more sophisticated) Nietzsche, it also overlooks some crucial elements of the "normative" or "practical" Nietzsche which I am defending here, which takes a different standpoint as primary: the first-person agent point of view, as opposed to the third-person scientific observer point of view. In particular, Leiter (2002) defends the "higher man" interpretation of Nietzsche, but grounds Nietzsche's defense of the "higher man" on natural "type facts" that distinguish the higher man from the lower. However, it is not clear on Leiter's account then why we should follow these natural "type facts" at all—Leiter even admits that Nietzsche's admiration for the "type" rests on his "subjective preference." See also Janaway's (2006), Clark and Dudrick's (2006), and Gardner's (2009) arguments on the limitations of ascribing a naturalist position to Nietzsche.

A focal point of the debate between the naturalists and their critics has been Nietzsche's "sovereign individual." Both Leiter and Acampora have, in particular, denied that Nietzsche means the "sovereign individual" as a serious ethical ideal. First, Leiter (2008) pokes fun at the thought that the "sovereign individual" may be Nietzsche's ideal, since the individual merely develops the ability to make promises. Yet since the ability to make promises is what Nietzsche identifies as the task of nature for the distinctively human (GM 2.1) and stands as the cornerstone for human civilization, it is hard to see why "promising" would be such an insignificant ideal. Furthermore, Leiter also concludes from the fact that Nietzsche uses the Latin phrase *souveraine Individuum* that he does not mean the ideal seriously. Even if we grant Leiter this claim, however, Leiter still owes us an explanation for the rest of Nietzsche's description, which is quite serious in tone, as Nietzsche outlines what seems to be an ideal that shares many characteristics with other individual ideals Leiter recognizes as such (such as the "awareness of power," the feeling of superiority, the "self-mastery," his "standard of value," his "honor," his cruel treatment of the "febrile whippets" below him, his good "conscience," and so forth). Second, Acampora worries that Nietzsche's view of the sovereign individual involves too much sovereignty, an escape from social and political conditions entirely—hence Nietzsche could not accept this ideal. However, though Nietzsche thinks that autonomous individuals are opposed to *Sittlichkeit*, he nonetheless argues that they must be "responsible"—and hence one must be responsible to another human being, which always already involves human community.

16. The "postmodern" reading of Nietzsche tends to claim that Nietzsche was a critic of unity, individuality, freedom, and all traditional philosophical categories. For classic statements, see De Man (1982) and Hatab (1995). In particular, Hatab, like Acampora and Leiter, argues that Nietzsche could not defend the "sovereign individual" (GM 2.2) as his ideal. Hatab argues that this sovereign individual attributes to Nietzsche a goal foreign to him, that is, an attempt to constrain contingency and difference, subjecting it to the human will. Yet Nietzsche argues that for differences to be possible at all—for us to distinguish between me and you—an individual cannot be a complete chaos of conflicting impulses, but must actually harness these impulses into an over-

arching plan, in order to "shoot toward the most distant goals," as Nietzsche puts it in BGE preface. Furthermore, elsewhere Nietzsche upholds "sovereignty" as the "highest form of individual freedom" (WP 770).

17. See Nietzsche's sustained critique of the Christian-Cartesian notion of freedom—philosophers call it the "libertarian" notion of freedom, the ability "to do otherwise"—at GM 1.13, TI 6.7; shorter discussions at HH 1.39, 70, 105, 107; D 13, 116, 236, 252. A characteristic account is at WS 23 on the need to punish and hence to impose the fantasy of the Christian "free will" to allow for punishment. For Nietzsche, this abstract view of freedom came to be a necessary feature of the moralizing strategy of the "slaves" against the "masters" (see GM 1.13 and Williams (1993). Scholars such as Leiter (2002) argue that Nietzsche rejects human free will as such, though Leiter makes this claim because he himself remains broadly within the ambit of conceptualizing the "free will" in terms of contemporary philosophy of action, rather than in the terms of the Kantian "autonomy" tradition to which Nietzsche belongs (see esp. 87–88, where Leiter assumes that "conscious states would have to figure in the causation of *autonomous* action"—neither Hegel nor Nietzsche share this assumption, while nonetheless upholding freedom as autonomy). According to the latter tradition, "freedom" and "necessity" are not only compatible, they necessitate one another. See Gemes (2007) for a critique of Leiter on this point and a helpful distinction between two kinds of freedom and responsibility, the "desert responsibility" with its Christian notion of guilt and punishment, and the "agent responsibility" of giving oneself the law.

18. We have inherited this conception of ourselves as the "doer [*Täter*] behind the deed [*Tun*]," Nietzsche argues, from the Christian view of the self, which had been taken up by Descartes in the modern age. See GM 1.13, where Nietzsche describes the slave revolt as defending the following view: "just as the common people separates lightning from its flash and takes the latter to be a *deed*, an action [*Wirkung*] taken up by a subject . . . popular morality separates strength from the manifestations of strength, as though there were an indifferent substratum behind the strong person which had the *freedom* [*freistünde*] to manifest strength or not. But there is no such substratum; there is no 'being' behind the deed . . . the 'doer' is invented as an afterthought,—the deed is everything." Cf. BGE 16–17 on Descartes's error, rooted in the same Christian "atomism" introduced by the slave revolt (BGE 12).

19. See, e.g., Pippin (2006) for a Hegelian reading of GM 1.13.

20. Gerhardt (1992, 35) has persuasively argued that the self-conscious agential elements of human life are ineliminable: "consciousness and will, intention and self-knowledge remain hence a reality in the life of human beings." Gerhardt's article charts Nietzsche's use of moral terms that refer to individual responsibility, duties, and promising throughout his corpus, including the free spirit, sovereign individual, and overman. Gerhardt helpfully highlights that even Nietzsche's emphasis on the body over the soul reveals Nietzsche's deeper commitment to a view of free agency, as opposed to a simple repudiation of moral ideals (he provides further evidence for this claim in Gerhardt 2006). Gerhardt puts forward an interesting view of the ground of Nietzsche's moral system in the "claim of the individual from himself" (40). My view of the ground of Nietzsche's system differs from Gerhardt's in that I argue the individual is not entirely self-grounding in Gerhardt's Fichtean interpretation of Nietzsche, but always already arises within a cultural and political setting. Nonetheless, Nietzsche does follow in the Fichtean tradition of thinking about the self-legislating individual through action. In BGE 44, for instance, Nietzsche argues that the coming philosophers will have an "excess of 'free will' [*freiem Willen*]" and they will be "inventive in schemata [*erfinderisch in Schematen*], sometimes proud of tables of categories [*stolz auf Kategorien-Tafeln*]." Far from destructive of the German tradition, Nietzsche embraces its schemata and categories, but forces it to take the practical turn Fichte had initiated.

21. In other words, Nietzsche is not trying to jettison human agency entirely, but trying to reconceive the problems of attaining it, and the preconditions for attaining it. Just because there is no doer behind the deed does not mean free human agency as such is impossible. For instance, in WP 675, Nietzsche argues that one "should take the doer back into the deed after having removed the doer and thus emptied the deed; that one should take doing *something*, the 'aim,' the 'intention,' the 'purpose,' back into the deed after having artificially removed all this and thus emptied the deed." Similarly, in GM 3.4, Nietzsche argues that one should "separate an artist sufficiently far from his work [*Werke*] as not immediately to take the man as seriously as his work." In other words, one can separate the doer from the deed.

22. Excellent discussions of Nietzsche's particular ideal types can be found in the following works: on the "philosopher of the future" from BGE, see Lampert (2001); on the overman, see Lampert (1986), Gillespie (2005), and Rosen (1995); on the sovereign individual, see Gemes (2007).

23. See Zuckert (1983) for an elaboration of the notion of the "distinctively human" in Nietzsche and a defense of the philosopher as the perfection of our humanity.

24. I find Guay's (2002) interpretation of Nietzsche as putting forward a "practice theory" of truth and goodness very persuasive, yet it is not persuasive on this fundamental point—contrary to Guay's claim, Nietzsche argues that his view of the good transcends any and all human conventions.

25. Clark (1990) is right to argue that the will to power describes the second-order structure of agents, but she is wrong to think that "he does not regard this as a truth or a matter of knowledge, but as a construction of the world from the viewpoint of his values" (227). On the contrary, Nietzsche is attempting to trace the structure of human subjectivity as such in order to benefit humankind as a whole.

26. Nietzsche offers an account of such sublimation at the human level, for instance, in the creation of "slave morality," in which human wills associate in the form of "herds" in order to accomplish their victory over the "masters."

27. See Richardson (1996, 23) and Kaufmann (1974, 220ff.) for similar accounts of the will's sublimation. It seems to me that Nietzsche's view of the will to power is not very far from contemporary evolutionary biology. See Dennett (2004) for an overview and Richardson (2004) for an elaboration.

28. For instance, the mitochondria of our cells cannot decide to go on strike, since they themselves depend for their very existence on the other parts of our cells, even though they were once independent organisms in their own right. See Clark and Dudrick (2009) for a close analysis of BGE 19.

29. Cf. also Nietzsche's many reflections on the "possessing" and greedy ego, a set of reflections I take to be essentially consistent with a Fichtean understanding of the "positing" of the ego. The "sole purpose of human action is possession," because the "ego wants everything" (D 281). The "ego's desire for appropriation is without limit [*keine Gränzen*]" (D 285). It seeks to expand itself endlessly, and finds satisfaction when he finds himself in his possessions (the meaning of Nietzsche's term *Aneignungslust*), when he can say "all this am I" (D 285). In GS 14, Nietzsche argues that "possession means . . . changing something new into ourselves." The ego "subdues and kills: it operates like an organic cell: it is a robber and violent. It wants to regenerate itself—pregnancy. It wants to give birth to its god and see all mankind at its feet" (WP 768).

30. Reginster (2006, 126) insightfully brings out that in BGE 259, Nietzsche claims that "exploitation . . . belongs to the essence of what lives" and is a "*consequence* of the will to power," not the nature of the will to power as such (my emphasis). In other words, exploitation could be one substantive "first-order" result of the will to power, but there could be others.

31. I will continue to use the example of genes in the rest of the chapter, though I recognize that Nietzsche took himself to be a critic of Darwin on the grounds that Darwin thought natural beings sought to preserve themselves, while Nietzsche argued that natural beings long to expand themselves. In my limited understanding, contemporary biology attempts to do justice to both views—animals seek to preserve themselves while expanding their gene pool as far as possible. See also Richardson (2004) and Nietzsche's claim about "Darwinism, which, by the way, I consider to be correct" (UUM 19.132). See, however, Johnson (2010) on Nietzsche's "anti-Darwinism."

32. For Nietzsche, individuality requires "cutting down and pruning" one's natural instincts, emphatically not giving in to them. Only by controlling nature does the individual have the possibility of becoming "*complete* [ganz]" (TI 9.41). The communal control of the natural human being is the first step toward this goal.

33. Despite Nietzsche's repeated attacks on the problems of Christianity, it nonetheless has allowed human beings to emerge from nature by "taming the beast in man" (D 60). See also Nietzsche's remark that the "institution of marriage" is contrary to nature and a "pia fraus," but nonetheless it is justified because it has "bestowed upon love a higher nobility" (D 27).

34. See Nietzsche's remarks about the ascetic priest, who, in "deepening" the human soul by making it social, established "man's superiority, hitherto, over other animals" (GM 1.6).

35. The division between subject and object, the rise of self-consciousness and value systems, all create the possibility of the "*infinite value* [unendlich wichtig]" of the individual [*einzelne Individuum*]" (UUM 19.50), impossible in the state of nature.

36. For Nietzsche, the Kantian activity of "constructing concepts, species, forms, purposes, laws" that make a "world for ourselves" does not reveal the "real world," but rather a "world for ourselves in which our existence is made possible—we thereby create a world which is calculable, simplified, comprehensible, etc, for us" (WP 521).

37. Cf. UUM 35.14: in the human being "existence holds before itself a mirror in which life no longer appears meaningless [*sinnlos*] but appears, rather, in its metaphysical meaningfulness [*Bedeutsamkeit*]."

38. Nietzsche accounts for the transition from nature to community in various places. For Nietzsche, a human world is formed when a people project their own virtue, their own selves, onto nature in the form of gods who reflect their own deepest commitments (AC 16). This cultural "world" replaces nature with stories and myths about how nature itself is structured in human, purposive terms—a lightning bolt is not an indifferent natural phenomenon, for instance, but Zeus's judgment of human activity. The creation of a world gives us mastery over nature by transforming it in accordance with our own purposes—the "instinct of fear bids us to know" nature, that is, trace the "unfamiliar" in nature back to what is familiar to us (GS 355, cf. WP 135). This new, second "nature" reflects back to me a purposive world in which I have a home, rather than appearing as an indifferent, alien, purposeless world.

39. Or, as Nietzsche puts it more strikingly, "Slavery is . . . the indispensable means of spiritual discipline and cultivation" (BGE 188). Cf., of course, Hegel, PhG 194–96.

40. Cf. GS 14 on the origin of the higher ideal in friendship, a "shared higher thirst for an ideal above [the friends]."

41. Cf. GS 76 on Nietzsche's respect for law, which allowed us to "reach agreement about very many things and to lay down a law of agreement."

42. Nietzsche's point about the value of the "eternal perspective" of the Christian God is echoed later in GM 3.12: "let us not be ungrateful towards such resolute reversals of familiar perspectives and valuations with which the mind has raged against itself for far too long."

43. Nietzsche connects "self-determination" or "self-mastery" or "responsibility" for oneself with "freedom" at GS 347, GM 2.2, D 112, TI 9.38. The entity that fuses

these, the "individual," is "something quite new which creates new things, something absolute; all his acts are entirely his own. Ultimately, the individual derives the values of his acts from himself; because he has to interpret in a quite individual way even the words he has inherited. His interpretation of a formula at least is personal, even if he does not create a formula: as an interpreter he is still creative" (WP 767).

44. Nietzsche argues in a quite Fichtean vein that we cannot conceive of "what things 'in themselves' may be like," because we cannot get around the "activity" or "positing" of the "subject." The "subject alone is demonstrable," and "only subjects exist" (WP 569). If this is true, then subjectivity, not nature or society, should be the source of the individual's norms.

45. This is not to say that upon becoming an individual, one's will to power has reached an end point. Rather, the activity of becoming an individual is endless, described well by Conant (2001) as a process rather than a telos.

46. See especially Nietzsche's remarks about "consciousness" and its "origin" in GS 354. What we take to be "consciousness" "actually belongs not to man's existence as an individual [*Individual*] but rather to the community." For Nietzsche, "at bottom, all our actions [*Handlungen*] are incomparably and utterly personal, unique [*einzig*], and boundlessly individual [*unbegrenzt-individuell*]," yet every time we attempt to express ourselves to others we must be "translated back into the herd perspective." The ethics of the herd does not satisfy the "utterly personal" subjectivity of each individual—what is required is a movement beyond herd morality. See also, for another example of communal appropriation of individuality, Nietzsche's view of the state and its employment of its academic scholars as ideological vehicles and "pawns" to "legitimize" its own power in the eyes of the people (UM 3.1, 3.8). For Nietzsche, there is a standing "demand that one overcome [*überwinden*] oneself, that is, overcome the secular, the spirit of the age" (UUM 19.7)—just as, for instance, Kant argued that one must overcome one's natural self to realize one's freedom in a rational self, Nietzsche sees the Kantian rational self as the social self, as a second step that must be overcome on the way to the individual self.

47. Nietzsche reveals his debt to—and critique of—Hegel in this regard when he employs the characteristically Hegelian term *aufheben* to refer to the tendency of "ethical life" to "sublate itself" [*Selbstaufhebung*] (GM 3.27).

48. See also Nietzsche's Kantian autonomy formulation: individuals who "give themselves laws [*Gesetz*], who create themselves" (GS 335). Cf. Zarathustra's connection between communal autonomy and individual autonomy: just as a "tablet of the good hangs over every people" in communal agency, now, here, one must "give yourself your own evil and your own good and hang your own will over yourself as a law [*Gesetz*]" (Z:1 "On the Thousand," "Way of the Creator").

49. See UM 3.4 on the "lesson set" to one "by existence," which is that "eternal becoming is a lying puppet-play in beholding which man forgets himself. . . . That heroism of truthfulness consists in one day ceasing to be the toy it plays with. . . . He can resolve [this] only in being, in being thus and not otherwise, in the imperishable."

50. See Owen (2009) for a further exploration of the notion of agency that stands behind this view of self-creation, in which "one's deeds are seen as criteria of one's intentions, beliefs, desires, etc." (207).

51. The Schrift (2000)–Dombowsky (2002) debate reveals that in the literature, scholars oscillate back and forth between focusing on Nietzsche's concern for unity and on his concern for difference. Nietzsche, however, clearly longs for "unity in multiplicity," as he puts it in his late work BGE 212, or as he puts it in the early work UM 2.1 (the most powerful nature "would draw to itself and incorporate into itself all the past, its own and that most foreign to it"), or as he states in WP 259, "The wisest man would be the one richest in contradictions, who has, as it were, antennae for all types of men—as well as his great moments of grand harmony—a rare accident even in us!"

52. See Hill (2003, chap. 5) on Nietzsche's reading of Kant's Transcendental Deduction.

53. Nietzsche's celebration of the "discipline of suffering, of great suffering" aims to establish precisely this point. Suffering—the endurance of "contradictions" within oneself—is not intrinsically good, but instrumentally good as the "sole cause of every enhancement in humanity so far" (BGE 225).

54. This is the meaning of Nietzsche's famous and puzzling phrase, "become who you are" (GS 270). Nietzsche implies that there is a self that exists in "being"—who you "are," truly—and a self that exists in "becoming." Nietzsche seems to be putting forth a familiar two-world view, a noumenal and phenomenal self view. However, what he is actually talking about is the idea of an imagined, perfectible self projected as the completion of the subject's longing and its rough empirical imitation. The "being" here refers to the "being" that is the object of the subject's longing, a complete justification for its own existence. The "becoming" is the ever ongoing activity of the subject in leading toward this ideal that it cannot in the end achieve.

55. In this context of "plastic power" and "will to power," Nietzsche invokes the language of "strong" and "weak" wills to describe human beings (BGE 21). Nietzsche uses "power" and "strength" here metaphorically, as we have seen, but they are useful metaphors because they admit of degrees just as individuality does. A higher degree of the will to power means a greater control of the subject's law over its internal determinations—as Nietzsche puts it, for example, the "strength of a spirit" is one who does not need the diversity of the world "to be thinned out, veiled over, sweetened up, dumbed down, and lied about" (BGE 39). Nietzsche argues that the expansion of the self makes us "become more beautiful," which is a "consequence of enhanced strength" (WP 800).

56. See WP 46: "The multitude and disgregation of impulses and the lack of any systematic order among them result in a 'weak will'; their coordination under a single predominant impulse results in a 'strong will.'"

57. See Dove (2008, chap. 3) for a helpful and elaborate defense of this claim.

58. For Nietzsche, artistic objects do not provide the model by which we can lead our lives. On the contrary, leading an artistic life provides the model for an artistic object. Artistic objects themselves derive their pattern and significance from the model of individual lives. For Nietzsche, to be tautologous, the individual aesthetic life is to be lived. That is, I must determine for myself my own "law" and then internalize it in my own flesh, making it my own second nature. It is when these laws of my own making animate my activity without reflective thought, when they are "quivering in my muscles," that I have truly achieved a self-creation, where there is no distance between creator and created, but a self-identical being acts from himself (GM 2.2). Nietzsche again and again applauds the ancient model of a philosophical life, in which the philosophers "lived philosophically." Such a philosophical or aesthetic life is foreign to us moderns, who are used to conceiving of philosophy as "political, policed by governments" and art as an object to be reflected upon (PTA 37–38). But it is significant because only by living my self-constructed life do I fully realize the "law" that I have created for myself. If I created my life simply to reflect upon and aesthetically appreciate, we would have to wonder what social need or natural desire brought this apparent self-constitution on—in other words, my aesthetically self-created life would not be "mine," after all.

59. My main disagreement with Nehamas (1985) emerges here—namely, that Nehamas does not pay sufficient attention to how the aesthetic conception of the human individual is connected to human freedom. My disagreement with Nehamas is similar to that of Reginster (2006), who argues that Nehamas's view does not "provide a clear account for the necessity of a revaluation" and the possibility of redemption (220).

Chapter 6

1. See Rorty (1989) and Nehamas (1985) for good statements of the Nietzschean liberal, "private" self-actualization view. See Detwiler (1990) and Appel (1999) for the Nietzschean radically aristocratic view. I engage with the latter camp at greater length in the next chapter.

2. I do not explore this second, cosmopolitan option at length in this chapter; see Church (forthcoming b) for an elaboration.

3. R. W. Emerson, who influenced Nietzsche heavily on this point, expressed the power of the individual genius in this way: "nor he is great who can alter matter, but he who can alter my state of mind. They are the kings of the world who give the color of their present thought to all nature and all art, and persuade men by the cheerful seren-ity of their carrying the matter, that this thing which they do, is the apple which the ages have desired to pluck, now at last ripe, and inviting nations to the harvest. The great man makes the great thing" (Emerson 1983, 65). Accordingly, for Nietzsche and Emerson, the inequality of human beings is not a natural, biological inequality, but an inequality of merit, an inequality of our excellence as human beings. See Owen (2002), who helpfully clarifies Nietzsche's view of inequality and its relationship to "self-re-spect" and individual character.

4. As I stated in the previous chapter, however, the development of human "es-teeming" does mark an advance beyond the animalistic state in the sense that we can find meaning in the worlds we create—yet at the same time, esteeming resembles ani-mal behavior in its service to the needs of "life."

5. For Nietzsche, "in reality there is no such separation [between the natural and the human]: 'natural' characteristics and those called specifically 'human' have grown together inextricably. Man, in his highest, finest powers, is all nature and carries na-ture's uncanny dual character in himself" (HC 187).

6. That our reflective natures arose out of our more immediate esteeming natures helps us make sense of Nietzsche's claim that the "will to know [rose] up on the founda-tion of a much more powerful will, the will to not know, to uncertainty, to untruth! Not as its opposite, but rather—as its refinement!" (BGE 24).

7. See Warren (1988) for a further development of the claim that slave morality is built on the desire to realize one's agency.

8. See also GS 346: "the world is not at all divine—even by human standards it is not rational, merciful, or just. We know it: the world we live in is ungodly, immoral, 'inhuman.'"

9. See BT 7 on the "terrible truth" of the meaninglessness of nature, and BT 15 on the "tragic knowledge" that nature is not wholly rational. Few scholars focus on the terrible truth of existence. For an exception, see Kain (2007), who makes a strong case that Nietzsche was concerned with this problem throughout his career.

10. See also PTA 54: "The everlasting and exclusive becoming, the impermanence of everything actual [*Wirklichen*], which constantly acts and comes-to-be but never is . . . is a terrible, paralyzing thought. Its impact on men can most nearly be likened to the sensation during an earthquake when one loses one's familiar confidence in a firmly grounded earth." The confusion and terror brought on by this "terrible truth" is one repeated by the madman in Nietzsche's famous GS 125: "What were we doing when we unchained this earth from its sun? Where is it moving to now? Where are we moving to? Away from all suns? Are we not continually falling? And backwards, sidewards, for-wards, in all directions?"

11. The tortured subjectivity is reached in the modern age "when we have sought a 'meaning' in all events that is not there: so the seeker eventually becomes discour-aged . . . becoming aims at nothing and achieves nothing" (WP 12). The desire for

meaning arose, Nietzsche argues, from the "teachers of the purposes [*Zwecke*] of existence," the slave moralists who insisted that the world assume some kind of justification. Nietzsche argues that we have irrevocably become such beings, so that we have "acquired one additional need. . . . [He] must from time to time believe he knows why he exists; his race cannot thrive without a periodic trust in life—without faith in *the reason in life* [Vernunft im Leben]" (GS 1).

12. Goethe's *Faust* dramatizes the tortured human subjectivity, that "human beings torment themselves" with endless searching and not being satisfied with their knowledge. Goethe's play is an attempt to answer Mephistopheles' charge that man "would have an easier time of it had you not let him glimpse celestial light" (Goethe 1985, 19). Nietzsche argues that "Faust, who storms unsatisfied through all the faculties, who has devoted himself to magic and the devil out of the drive for knowledge; we only have to compare him with Socrates to realize that modern man is beginning to sense the limits of the Socratic lust for knowledge" (BT 18).

13. See also Nietzsche's claim that the ancients did not endure as acute a tension as the moderns, because the ancient Greek philosophers "had life itself before and around them in luxuriant perfection and because, unlike us, their minds were not confused by the discord between the desire for freedom, beauty, abundance of life on the one hand and on the other the drive to truth, which asks only: what is existence worth as such?" (UM 3.3). Furthermore, Nietzsche claims that the "homogenization" of modern peoples calls out for a "justification" (WP 898).

14. For helpful explications of Nietzsche's concept of nihilism, see Strong (2000, chap. 3), Gillespie (1995), Reginster (2006, chap. 1). Although Reginster speaks of the "death of God" as a reason for the emergence of nihilism, he fails to discuss Nietzsche's broader worry about the unconstrained accumulation of knowledge, the paralysis of the will and the horror at the meaninglessness of existence that results. Reginster also fails does not take seriously Nietzsche's claim to offer a "justification" of human existence, in arguing that "perspectives are inescapable" for rational human judgment (84). Yet Nietzsche's "justifications" are not rational in nature, but aesthetic.

15. The Kantian allusion (*Kritik des Wissens*) here is unmistakable, as Nietzsche makes explicit in WP 448; for Nietzsche, as for Kant, the rational impulse turns upon itself and destroys itself. The difference between the two is that for Kant, the problem with reason is that it creates illusory metaphysical worlds, whereas for Nietzsche, reason destroys these very same metaphysical worlds, leaving the human subject with no impulse to act, not even an impulse to continue to reason. In other words, Nietzsche is not asking us to jettison reason or science or the pursuit of knowledge; on the contrary, the reflective drive is an integral component of leading a human life and must be retained. Rather, Nietzsche argues that reason is itself a second-order or reflective form of "esteeming." The pursuit of knowledge itself necessitates a first-order estimation that such a pursuit is good. Yet the pursuit of knowledge ends in the knowledge that no pursuit can be proven good through reason, not even the pursuit of knowledge. In the end, then, the rational reflective drive of human beings "bites its own tail" and provides an opening for human beings to harness the drive for knowledge in new and unexpected aesthetic directions (BT 15).

16. See, e.g., McGinn (1975): Nietzsche's "grim romantic-pessimistic view of the human condition . . . serves to activate a psycho-physical survival impulse which, in turn, calls art and other forms of culture into being to combat the agony of this state of affairs" (80). Also, the "'eternal wound of existence' . . . cannot in fact be healed but rather only disguised, cosmetically treated, or periodically lanced" (81).

17. See Hume's *Treatise*, bk. 1, pt. 4, sec. 6. I think it is tempting to read Nietzsche in this way, given the kinds of bodily adjectives he uses about art and its tendency to "heal and ward off the breath of that pestilence" (BT 15); he uses often a medical

metaphor as when "tragic knowledge, which, simply to be endured, needs art for protection and as medicine" (BT 15); finally, our relationship to art is one of "intense inward pleasure" from the dream-image of art (BT 4).

18. Nietzsche clearly distinguishes between the normative and the empirical at WP 254, where he anticipates a charge of the "genetic fallacy" often leveled against him. Nietzsche claims that "the inquiry into the origin of our evaluations . . . is in absolutely no way identical with a critique of them." In other words, uncovering the origin of values simply brings out their empirical or factual development. It in no way has to do with their normative "value." Nonetheless, the activity of revealing the origin of value has the causal effect of a "feeling of a diminution in value of the thing that originated thus and prepares the way to a critical mood and attitude toward it." This distinction between the normative and empirical—as well as Nietzsche's view of the causal, psychological effects of the empirical revelation of morality's origin—is also emphasized in GM P.3, 6. See also Church (forthcoming b) on an analysis of Nietzsche's use of the Kantian term "dignity" in BT 9.

19. See Plato, *Republic*, bk. 10 for the first critique of representational art.

20. There is an extensive disagreement in the literature about Nietzsche's "meta-ethics," that is, on the question of the basis of Nietzsche's justification for his own "positive" values. This debate has become quite extensive in part because the interlocutors import contemporary philosophical oppositions such as "objectivism" and "subjectivism" or "realism" and "antirealism" unjustifiably (in my view) into their reading of Nietzsche. On the one hand, there are a few, such as Shaw (2007), who defend a "realist" claim about Nietzsche's view of values, that moral values exist "out there" in the world. On the other hand, many scholars, such as Hussain (2007), Reginster (2006), and Leiter (2002), argue that Nietzsche rejects the notion that moral values are objective descriptions of the world, and that he holds an "error theory" about moral value, that moral value "falsifies" the world. Hence, no value—including Nietzsche's—is justified "objectively." But the consequence of this view is that the "subjectivist" or "fictionalist" Nietzsche cannot engage in the project of justification, but rather merely attempts to cause (or perhaps force?) other human beings to adopt his beliefs. See Shaw's (2007) critique of this "fictionalist" view (88ff.). However, the problem with both of these camps is that they assume that Nietzsche must supply a rationally grounded defense of moral value. This is precisely what he denies, and he replaces rational justification with "aesthetic justification." Yet this "aesthetic justification" is to be distinguished from "fictionalism" in that, as we will see, Nietzsche's foundational aesthetic justification is not a representational artwork (which fictionalizes the world) but rather an individual life (which represents nothing but simply is).

21. Nietzsche does, then, have an "epistemic privilege" in his metaethics, contra Leiter's (2000) argument. Leiter does not take up the metaethical possibility I outline here.

22. Cf. GS 1: "Every time 'the hero' appeared on stage, something new was attained: the gruesome counterpart of laughter, that profound shock that many individuals feel at the thought: 'Yes, living is worth it! Yes, I am worthy of living.'" See Berkowitz (1995), who argues that Nietzsche's view of the best life is "making oneself a god" (15).

23. See Nietzsche's reflections in GS 143 on the role of the gods in polytheism to represent the ideal of the "individual [*Einzelnen*]" who can "posit his own ideal" and "derive from it his own law, joys and rights." The activity of the gods was "the invaluable preliminary exercise for the justification of the selfishness and sovereignty of the individual." Religion, for Nietzsche, as he goes on to say in GS 300, makes "it possible one day for a few individuals [*einzelne Menschen*] to enjoy the whole self-sufficiency of a god and all his power of self-redemption [*Selbsterlösung*]." With religion, man learned to "feel hunger for himself and to find satisfaction and fullness in himself."

24. Nietzsche also connects the issue of "justification [*rechtfertigen*]" with the task of "demonstrating why and how the philosopher is not a chance random wanderer, exiled to this place or to that" (PTA 33).

25. As Nietzsche puts it, "it is a measure of the degree of strength of will to what extent one can do without meaning in things, to what extend one can endure to live in a meaningless world because one organizes a small portion of it oneself" (WP 585)—enduring a meaningless world by crafting one's individuality as a moment of being to spurn becoming reveals one's strength of will.

26. See especially *Phaedrus* 250d–252b. See Cooper (2008) for an illuminating reading of the phenomenon of eros, along with Plato and Rousseau's influence on Nietzsche on this point.

27. See TI 9.32, in which Nietzsche argues that no "ideal" can ever justify a human life—rather, "people are justified [*rechtfertigt*] by their reality,—it will justify them for ever."

28. Both Guay (2002) and Ridley (2007) have helpfully shown that for Nietzsche human cultural practices are necessary conditions for the possibility of distinctively human actions. These cultural practices—from the institution of language to marriage to law and politics—are structured according to certain general rules. Actions must abide by these rules in order to count as human. In BGE 188, for instance, Nietzsche speaks of the "limited horizons" in which human beings must act, the "obedience" to certain laws they must display in order to develop their humanity. This discussion in BGE 188 is a continuation of Nietzsche's more elaborate discussion of the necessity of "horizons" to make human action intelligible and meaningful in UM 2.1. Otherwise, an action that willfully flouts cultural rules is meaningless, as if, for instance, I "act" within a chess game by moving my rook diagonally.

However, Nietzsche is making a more radical, ethical argument than this Wittgensteinian point emphasized by Guay and Ridley. It is not enough to talk about the lawlike nature of human practices; for Nietzsche, it is essential to understand why human beings follow these norms. That is, human beings take up and follow certain laws because they implicitly take these laws to be good (Z:1 "On the Thousand"). Hence, culture requires that human action take on a particularly self-related character, that the individual implicitly endorses the good at which human practices aim in acting based on its laws. For Nietzsche, as for Hegel, it is only in light of this communal good that one's action takes on significance as "belonging" to this community. Thus, actions that are performed for the common good—in fighting and falling for one's country, for instance—gain significance in light of the part or role they play in realizing the common good.

29. See in this regard Gardner (2009), who defends the need for a "public" or objective self to make sense of the practical transcendental ego: "Just as the 'I think' as a condition of judgment does not make the I into a topic of judgment, so the Nietzschean I will does not mean that all that is ever valued is oneself, as per practical egoism; to the contrary, an element of self-transcendence—a moment of relating to something other, by means of which a relation to self is constituted—is built into Nietzsche's picture" (9). My view stands in contrast to readers such as Jurist (2000) who argue that unlike Hegel, Nietzsche has no view of the constitutive character of intersubjective recognition.

30. See Mulhall (2005) for an interesting interpretation of Nietzsche's desire to be redeemed from Christian redemption and the kind of self-reflexive problems involved in this project. I argue here that Nietzsche is not trying to escape from slave moral thinking entirely, especially on the matter of redemption—he even says that "genius" is the "cross-bearer of humanity" (UUM 24.6).

31. Cf. Nietzsche's remarks at UUM 19.16, where he claims that the "individual" [*Individuum*] makes "what is specific in this people" into something "universal . . . applied to solving the riddle of the universe." The individual elevates the people

above themselves, puts them in contact with the being of his personality, and thereby is a "means for coming to rest in the rushing current."

32. See BT 9 on the "noble human being," TI.2.5 on the noble and beautiful undermined by Socratic dialectic, and TI.19–20, 24 on the beautiful as a spur to noble action. For further exploration of the Greek and Kantian elements of Nietzsche's view of the beautiful individual, see Church (forthcoming b).

33. See also Nietzsche's approving remark about Schiller's "infinitely more valuable insight" about the origin of the chorus as a moment of "poetic freedom" against nature (BT 7).

34. That Nietzsche includes the lives of individuals within the calculation of "justice" means that individual lives really do supply a real "justification" of human existence. Otherwise, no human life would be "worth" more from the perspective of "justice," only from the perspective of "love." Thus, Came (2006) is wrong to argue that the aesthetic "justification" is "epistemologically neutral." Rather, as Nietzsche argues, human beings can come to know which justifications are true and which are not.

35. See Nietzsche's reflections on "monumental history" in UM 2.2, in which he claims that the "path" to immortality "leads through human brains," the creation of a new order based on the individual's life.

36. Nietzsche's ideas of individual exemplars and the attendant ethic of "perfectionism" have received attention in the works of Cavell (1990) and Conant (2001). Cavell and Conant interpret Nietzsche, however, to be putting forth a personal, individualistic ethic of intra-psychic self-development. Conant's claim is that one can read Nietzsche's discussions of perfectionism as referring to the "exemplar" or the "genius" of one's own self, and being calling out to one's true self from one's "conscience" (UM 3.1). While they are absolutely correct to see Nietzsche's "perfectionism"—the realization of individuality, in my terms—as his ethical good, they fail to appreciate the ways in which such self-development occurs within a historical or cultural context, and how difficult it is for this ideal to be realized democratically.

37. Cf. Nietzsche, UUM 23.27: "All archetypes partake of the idea of the good, the beautiful, and hence are also existent (just as the soul partakes of the idea of life)."

38. See *Republic* bk. 10.596a.

39. It should be noted that for Nietzsche, although the "masses are only to be regarded as 1) faded copies of great men on poor paper and printed with wornout plates," they also can offer "2) resistance to the great" (UUM 29.40), the relationship between the few and the many is not one-way (the few imposing their will on the many). Rather, there is a reciprocal relationship between them.

40. It is with this "idea" that we get to the heart of the updating of Plato's notion of the idea. See Kant's remarks on his notion of the "idea" as a better "understanding" of Plato "than he understood himself." CPR B370.

41. See Kant's definitions at CJ 192 and 194.

42. CJ 192: "the poet ventures to make sensible rational ideas of invisible beings, the kingdom of the blessed, the kingdom of hell, eternity, creation."

43. Kant claims that we exhibit "autonomy" in judging artwork, since we do not follow a law cognitively nor follow nature's pleasures and pains, but rather direct both in their "reciprocally expeditious" mutual influence (CJ 26–27).

44. As we saw in the previous chapter, the individual life is very similar to Hegel's notion of the "Idea," in the sense that the individual life appears to differentiate itself into a self-enclosed normative system. It is the self-enclosed normative system that holds together Plato, Hegel, and Nietzsche—the individual, for Nietzsche, can legislate a new community by setting his own life as the pattern for a new age.

45. See Nietzsche's remarks about "perspectivism" at BGE.P and GS 374. See Strong (1985) for an insightful view of the implications of Nietzsche's view.

46. See UM 2.9 on the task of "history to be the mediator" among the great individuals of history who "form a kind of bridge across the turbulent stream of becoming" in the "republic of genius." In becoming a "great moment in the struggle of the human individual," one becomes a link in the "chain" that "unites mankind across the millennia" (UM 2.2).

47. This is all to say that an individual cannot think of himself as separable from the community, nor can he think of the community as a mechanistic instrument to satisfy pregiven desires, because the very fabric of his own identity is wrapped up in this community. Thus, the individual is answerable to history and components of the community, just as he is answerable to his own narrative history. The individual can no more whimsically destroy or distort a part or whole of the community than he can whimsically alter his own life story. Indeed, if he were to do so, he would cease to be an individual, given the fact that individuality requires the creation of coherence out of one's history. Trying to make oneself out of nothing is tantamount to radically changing the plot, characters, and theme of a novel—that is, it ceases to be a (good) novel. In this way, the individual is not "burdened" by this history of the community, but in fact liberated through his engagement within it.

48. Nietzsche identifies "mistrust" and "reverence" as two fundamental passions of human beings at GS 346, but at UM 2.2, Nietzsche identifies a third passion—the human is a "being who suffers and seeks deliverance." Whereas mistrust and reverence are passions characteristic of community, deliverance is the passion characteristic of the escape from an unworkable, oppressive society.

49. For an investigation of the connection between Nietzsche's view of the erotic and Socrates, see Church (2006).

50. Nietzsche was, however, also impressed by Aristophanes' speech, which he understands as the "longing for oneness" in opposition to the "agonal" drive for difference: "The symbolism of sexual love. Here, as in Plato's fable, the longing for oneness is expressed, as is the fact that at one time a greater unity already existed. . . . Everything was connected only by love, hence supremely purposive. It was torn asunder and split by hatred" (UUM 23.34).

51. See Nietzsche's agreement with the ascending character of love: "beauty stands in the service of love: the steadily increasing transfiguration, as described by Plato. Procreation in the realm of the beautiful genuinely Hellenic. The growth of eros must be depicted—marriage family state" (UUM 21.14).

52. In other words, individuals are erotically drawn up by the "republic of geniuses," that group of individuals who constitute the personalities that have come to shape Western civilization—Socrates, Jesus, Rousseau, Goethe, Schopenhauer (UM 2.9). Each individual has reverence for the other across the span of generations, thus forming a "spirit-dialogue," one that is not constituted by accident and becoming, but a "bridge" of being over the "turbulent stream of becoming" (UM 2.9) New individuals may be added over time, but fundamentally, this "spirit-dialogue" does not change—it still consists of disagreements as to how human beings should live their lives and how community ought to be structured so as to promote this good. The "spirit-dialogue" is itself the crowning example of human freedom made manifest—no natural or social determination is dogmatically followed, but rather individuals engage in the perpetual activity of incorporating the others' claims.

53. I read Nietzsche's descriptions of the *Übermensch* in this way, that the *Übermensch* is a regulative ideal in the Kantian sense—we are always on the way to realizing such a redemptive figure, but can never complete the task. See Schrift (2000), who has offered a well-developed argument along these lines.

54. See UUM 23.34: "Dualistic nature—the agonal and the loving."

55. Eris is the "cosmic principle" of becoming in Heraclitus's universe, and this meaningless "contest" constituting an indifferent nature is the "terrible truth" Nietzsche reveals to the moderns (PTA 54–55).

56. Several "agonistic" democrats have appropriated Nietzsche's discussion of eris in "Homer's Contest," such as Honig (1993, 69ff.) and Hatab (1995, 62–63). However, these authors insufficiently acknowledge the role of eros and reverence for the law in the process of what Honig calls "self-discipline" or "self-limitation" (72). See, however, Hatab's helpful discussion of love and community on (185–93), though ultimately Hatab argues that "an agonistic model of politics . . . may suffice for political relations" (192). As we will see at greater length in the next chapter, however, for Nietzsche there cannot be a strong distinction between cultural and political relations, and indeed a certain erotic relationship is necessary for healthy "political relations," even if based on agonistic respect.

57. Nietzsche discusses the "erotic contest" introduced by Plato's philosophy, which I take to be a model for Nietzsche's own view of the sublimated physical contest (TI 9.23).

Chapter 7

1. The postmodern and agonistic interpretation of Nietzsche is best expressed by Connolly (1991), Hatab (2008), and Honig (1993), while the aristocratic radical interpretation is defended by Detwiler (1990) and Appel (1999).

2. Cf. GrS 183: "Citizens are in the dark about what nature intends for them with their state instinct, and follow blindly."

3. Nietzsche employs the term *Staat* more expansively than simply to refer to the modern state, as when he discusses the "Greek state." In the latter case, Nietzsche recognizes that the Greek state incorporates both political and cultural approaches into one organic unity. As we will see below, Nietzsche sees that such an organic unity is impossible to retrieve—*pace* Hegel—due to the division that modern life has effected between state and culture, or what we might call now the right and the good. However, as Ottmann (1999) brings out, Nietzsche did, like many German thinkers before him, celebrate the Greek ideal of the polis. Nietzsche went even further and considered suggesting Plato's *Republic* as an aspirational ideal, though Ottmann states that it is open to question whether Nietzsche supported Plato's design seriously or not (see 44–48). However, we can see by the end of GrS that Nietzsche does not suggest Plato's design be taken literally. Rather, what Nietzsche derives from Plato is that the state can have a distinct purpose, that of producing genius: Nietzsche interprets the "secret teaching" of the *Republic* to reveal the "connection between state and genius" (GrS 186). This connection requires a class system, including a class of warriors and slaves. Yet as Nietzsche states at the beginning of the text, he does not think that modern life literally can have slaves, but that modern human beings now think and act "slavishly." Thus, even though the modern many are not literally slaves, they still fulfill the function as such. All this is to say that I agree with Ottmann's suggestion that Nietzsche celebrated Plato's ideal, but not as a kind of utopian project Ottmann has in mind. Nietzsche admired Plato's *Republic* rather as a lesson about the nature, limitations, and possibilities of politics.

4. Nietzsche claims that the Dionysiac "fervor" for the "liberation" from politics is perfectly balanced against the "state-founding Apollo" in the Greek community. Nietzsche contrasts the Greeks' balance with the Buddhist withdrawal from the world into Dionysiac fervor and with the Roman all-too-worldly "greedy urge for this existence" (BT 21). See also Zumbrunnen (2002) and Gambino (1996) for illuminating takes on Nietzsche's appropriation of the Greeks.

5. See Nietzsche's reflections on the "corruption" of a people at GS 23. When "morals decay," Nietzsche argues, "individuals" [*Individuen*] begin to arise who are the "spiritual [*geistigen*] colonizers and shapers of new states and communities." Yet in the meantime, communities seek to clamp down on individual difference by asserting the "necessity" of "sacrifice" for the community's moral code and hence for the community itself (GS 21).

6. Nietzsche holds that there must be some kind of publicly held "standard" in order to claim knowledge: "without a standard, that is, without any limitation, there can be no knowledge" of right and wrong, true and false, noble and base (UUM 19.155). Unless we possess a standard of true and false, we cannot test whether or not our claims are false. If we cannot know whether our claims are false, we cannot know whether they are true.

7. See WP 20: "Having unlearned faith" in God, human beings "still follow the old habit and seek another authority that can speak unconditionally and command goals and tasks," such as the "authority of reason. Or the social instinct (the herd). Or history." One wants, in other words, "to get around the will, the willing of a goal, the risk of positing a goal for oneself; one wants to rid oneself of the responsibility." Cf. WP 716–17 on the state as the locus of the shirking of responsibility: "only individuals feel themselves responsible. Multiplicities are invented in order to do things for which the individual lacks the courage" (716).

8. Cf. TI 9.41: "in times like these, giving in to your instincts is just one more disaster. The instincts contradict, disturb, destroy each other. . . . Today the individual [*Individuum*] would first need to be made possible by being cut down and pruned. . . . And the opposite is what happens: the people who make the most passionate demands for independence, free development, and laissez aller are the very ones for whom no reins would be too firm. . . . Our modern concept of 'freedom' is one more proof of the degeneration of the instincts."

9. See Goethe's *Faust* (1985, 11): Mephistopheles: "Leave off your ruminations, and go with me into the teeming world."

10. This account of the origin of the "veneration" for the state differs markedly from Taylor's (1997) otherwise very illuminating account. Taylor sees the individual's veneration for the state stemming from a "purposive nature," what Taylor characterizes as Nietzsche's "metaphysical" account (32). In general, Nietzsche's "metaphysical" statements are holdovers from his debt to Schopenhauer and the German Romantics and should be demythologized in light of Nietzsche's professed naturalism.

11. See Taylor's (1997) helpful discussion of Hegel's philosophy as part of the modern state's aim "at omnipotence" (20). Taylor clearly shows that Nietzsche had Hegel in mind as an important target in overcoming the supremacy of the state in the modern age.

12. At the same time, Nietzsche suggests, the state will not release many cultural energies, because its agents "hated . . . the dominating genius and the tyranny of the real demands of culture" (UM 1.2). They will not risk allowing the resurgence of culture, but rather rely on Hegel's ideological justifications of the "apotheosis of the commonplace" based on the "rationality of the actual [*Vernünftigkeit alles Wirklichen*]," an allusion, of course, to Hegel's famous statement in PR Preface of the rationality of the actual and the actuality of the rational (UM 1.2).

13. See Nietzsche's critique of the "greed of the state" at UM 3.6, where he argues that the state "unchains" the "spiritual energies of a generation to the extend that will serve the interests of existing institutions." Nietzsche argues that the state employs the language of "good and evil" of premodern communities in order to legitimate its rules, but the "state tells lies in all the tongues of good and evil" (Z:1 "New Idol"). For a helpful exploration of the modern state's falsifying activity of "self-justification," see Shaw (2007).

14. Nietzsche is claiming, then, that the modern age is on a terrible course toward a nefarious reconciliation of state and culture and hence an ersatz return to the unity witnessed by the Greeks. This "reconciliation" is in fact simply the comprehensive assertion of control by the state. Nietzsche does not mince words in discussing the state's new form of control when it overruns culture in Zarathustra's speech "On the New Idol." The state is the "coldest of all cold monsters." It "signifies the will to death" (Z:1 "New Idol"). It is a cold "monster" because it devours "peoples." It heralds the "death of peoples" because it prevents new forms of "esteeming," new "tables of values," which are perennially characteristic of "peoples" (Z:1 "On the Thousand"). Instead, the state falsely declares that it is "the people" (Z:1 "New Idol"), which forecloses the source of new values, new creations, new life.

15. See Taylor's (1997, 21–27) illuminating discussion of Nietzsche's critique of the *Reich*; see also Bergmann (1987) on Nietzsche's evolving relationship to the *Reich*.

16. See FEI 76 for a clear statement: "it would perhaps not overstate to maintain that in the subordination of all educational endeavors under the purposes of the state Prussia has appropriated the practical, usable heirloom of the Hegelian philosophy with success."

17. See Ottmann's (1999, 23–25, 44–51) helpful explication on Nietzsche's overturning of the priority of state to culture..

18. Aside from the criticism against Shaw I will level below, I find that her use of contemporary metaethical terms obscures rather than reveal the issues in Nietzsche, since they import concepts that are foreign to Nietzsche's own views. Furthermore, even if we allow contemporary metaethical categories into the discussion, Shaw overlooks what seems to me to be a neglected third alternative between realism and antirealism central to the whole post-Kantian tradition, that of the self-legislation of norms. Self-legislation involves neither the "discovery" (realism) nor the arbitrary "creation" (anti-realism) of norms.

19. The closest Shaw gets to the "artistic justification of existence" is in her quite good critique of Hussain's "fictionalist" reading of the "artistic justification" (88–95). But the problem is that both Shaw and Hussain assume that Nietzsche's "justification" must be in the form of "fictionalist simulacra," instead of reading Nietzsche's justification as a nonrepresentational justification based on an embodied way of living.

20. See Taylor's (1997) discussion of the early Nietzsche's view of the need to maintain a certain role for the state (27ff.). Taylor offers the very sensible interpretation of Nietzsche's early political theory that "in practical terms, the state should seek out and facilitate those social conditions which foster the continuous emergence of exceptional individuals and permit these exceptions to live and create at a height" (35). Taylor infers that for Nietzsche, the state itself should be designed to benefit the few. However, I think it is a better interpretation of Nietzsche and a better philosophical argument to see the state as to be separated from culture. The state "prepares the way for culture" by ensuring peace and order—culture autonomously benefits itself from there. The "laissez-faire" understanding of the state fits, I think, with a number of explicit statements Nietzsche makes (the separation of the political and cultural drives), but it also fits with Nietzsche's understanding of the rise of democracies in Europe (democracy is on the rise, and the "few" have to make do at the margins of society).

21. Qtd. in Taylor (1997, 34).

22. Both Detwiler and Appel focus on Nietzsche's use of the term "breeding," concluding that Nietzsche considers the "many" to have the same normative status as dogs or some such breed-worthy animal. See Kaufmann's note to bk. 4 of WP on Nietzsche's infrequent use of breeding. Nietzsche employs the term "breeding" (also *Züchtung*, cultivation) in a much more expansive and metaphorical way than these authors suggest. See WP 980 for a characteristic discussion of Nietzsche's "educator."

23. See Church (forthcoming b) for a critique of Hurka's maximax principle and a reading of Nietzsche's notorious statement that your life takes on the "highest value" by "living for the good of the rarest and most valuable exemplars" (UM 3.6).

24. But cf. Nietzsche's "main consideration," which is "not to see the task of the higher species in leading the lower . . . but the lower as a base upon which higher species performs its own tasks—upon which alone it can stand" (WP 901). For Nietzsche, "state and society" should serve "as foundation," not as the aim of the individual's task.

25. Cf. WP 614: "to 'humanize' the world" is to "feel ourselves more and more masters within it." WP 928: "a higher stage is . . . to perform a heroic act not on impulse—but coldly, *raisonnable*, without being overwhelmed by stormy feelings of pleasure."

26. See Owen (2002, 122ff.) for a helpful elaboration along these lines of the sublimation of the animal instincts and the need for a brutal, political "pathos of distance."

27. Korsgaard (1996, 158–60) helpfully brings out this point.

28. See especially Young (2006), who also recognizes the historical, sublimated character of Nietzsche's "great politics." However, Young interprets Nietzsche as a defender of religious communitarianism, which is inconsistent, I have argued, with Nietzsche's views about the reflective nature of the modern age.

29. Cf. Rousseau's critique of the "might makes right" view at SC 143.

30. This passage from WP helps illuminate Nietzsche's much-cited quote that "every enhancement so far in the type 'man' has been the work of an aristocratic society" (BGE 257). As with many of Nietzsche's claims, he enjoins us to understand it in its historical context. In BGE 257, Nietzsche is mostly concerned with how "aristocratic societies" have enhanced humanity in the past, leading up to a sublimated "aristocratic society" of the soul that Nietzsche discusses in BGE 257 and WP 960. Indeed, Nietzsche argues that this aristocratic society "*in some sense* needs slavery" (my emphasis)—it does not need legally recognized slaves, because, as Nietzsche argues, "we moderns have the advantage over the Greeks with two concepts given as consolation, as it were, to a world which behaves in a thoroughly slave-like manner whilst anxiously avoiding the word 'slave': we speak of the 'dignity of man' and the 'dignity of work.' We struggle wretchedly to perpetuate a wretched life" (GrS 176). In other words, for Nietzsche, many modern human beings already play the role of "slaves" without actually performing such a legal function. An aristocratic society can still be created, in other words, within modern, democratic politics without resorting to openly aristocratic politics.

31. Cf. also GrS 182: only "in the intervals between" political expansion and war, "the concentrated effect of that *bellum*, turned inwards, gives society time to germinate and turn green everywhere, so that it can let the radiant blossoms of genius sprout forth as soon as warmer days come." Cf. Nietzsche's critique of war at UUM 32.62.

32. Taylor (1997) misreads this passage in proposing it can be read in two ways: either (a) Nietzsche meant this phrase ironically, adopting the "logic of Leviathan" to poke fun at any justification the state can provide, or (b) Nietzsche means it seriously, so that he actually calls on states to persecute philosophers for the benefit of philosophy, because such persecution "would perhaps strengthen philosophy and enhance the significance of the philosophic life, just as the Roman persecutions (inadvertently) strengthened and enhanced early Christianity" (25). Yet Nietzsche offers no indication that this passage should be read ironically, since Nietzsche follows up the state's justified (*im Recht*) persecution with a comparison to the state's right to "expel and treat as an enemy a religion which sets itself above the state and desires to be its judge." That Nietzsche aligns philosophy and religion here is an indication that Nietzsche is concerned to maintain the rule of law so that philosophy can be maintained within it. But Taylor's suggestion (b) is also not warranted by the text, since Nietzsche gives no indication that the philosopher would benefit by political critique: indeed, Nietzsche indicates that the philosopher's engaging in political critique actually takes him away from

his philosophical activity and, furthermore, undermines the needed "pathos of distance" from politics to sustain individual self-overcoming.

33. In FEI 78–79, Nietzsche continues on to say that it is only when we begin to see the state "as this Hegel did, as the 'absolutely complete ethical organism'" that the state oversteps its boundaries and co-opts the direction of culture.

34. See Abbey (2000) and Villa (2001, chap. 3).

35. This discussion in Nietzsche's late TI echoes an earlier discussion at HH 472, in which Nietzsche worries about the "disregard for and the decline and death of the state, the liberation of the private person." The liberation of the private person will not liberate the "individual," but rather the "chaos" of natural desires. Thus, Nietzsche upholds a conservatism of the "'prudence and self-interest of men' to preserve the existence of the state for some time yet and to repulse the destructive experiments of the precipitate and the over-zealous."

36. Echoing Hegel, Nietzsche argues that even the "idea that is overcome is not annihilated, only driven back or subordinated. There is no annihilation in the sphere of spirit" (WP 588). Thus, each one of us owes our identity to the accumulated wisdom of centuries. We cannot simply know ourselves or act based on our true self by "immediate self-observation"—rather, we require "history [*Geschichte*], for the past continues to flow within us in a hundred waves" (AOM 223).

37. Nietzsche worries that this "pathos of distance" is "getting smaller and smaller these days," but argues that we must be the counterweight against this movement in upholding the pathos of distance, that "rift between people, between classes, the myriad number of types, the will to be yourself, to stand out" (TI 9.37).

38. Nietzsche argues that the "giants" of the "republic of geniuses" transcend particular states, but the "dwarfs" of the states "struggle with the things that the giants have dropped, proclaim heroes, who themselves are dwarfs," and hence gain meaning in light of these cultural goods. Meanwhile, "those giants spirits are not disturbed by any of this, but simply carry on their lofty dialogue between spirits" (UUM 24.4).

39. See Siemens (2008) for a helpful and illuminating analysis of the shifting target that is Nietzsche's view of democracy. Siemens enumerates four different views that Nietzsche adopted over the course of his career—that democracy and "enhancement" are incompatible, that democracy provides some conditions for enhancement and prevents it in other ways, that democracy and enhancement are compatible, that they are mutually reinforcing. Siemens's final category, that of the mutual reinforcement of democracy and enhancement, appears here in Nietzsche's thought, in which the spirit of self-determination of democracy can inform the spirit of self-determination in culture.

40. Nietzsche here implicitly criticizes Hegel's famous remark that an individual is a "child [*Sohn*] of his age" (PR Preface) in arguing that "in the end the supposed child of his time proves to be only its stepchild [*Stiefkind*]" (UM 3.3).

41. See Church and Zuckert (2008).

42. Nietzsche, in a surprisingly Hegelian moment, argues that the "history of culture" can be understood as the "ever increasing self-revelation of [the] god." It is "not all a blind mechanism, a senseless, purposeless, confused play of forces" (HH 238). Yet the difference between Hegel and Nietzsche on this matter is that for Nietzsche, it is the individual's task to embody the "self-revelation of the god," whereas for Hegel, the state is responsible for the task of theodicy.

43. Cf. GS 34, in which Nietzsche points to the individual for whom a "thousand secrets of the past crawl out of their hiding places" and "for his sake all of history is put on the scale again."

44. Nietzsche argues that "most men represent pieces and fragments of man," such that "one has to add them up for a complete man to appear." Even "whole ages" reveal themselves to be "fragmentary," and it might have been necessary that "man should evolve piece by piece." Yet Nietzsche insists that the aim of individual and community

is the "production of the synthetic man," the man that reconciles, synthesizes, and hence redeems all the fragments of the past (WP 881).

45. Cf. GS 337 on the historical sense which affords us with a "horizon [which] stretches millennia before and behind him." The historical sense makes one the "first of a new nobility the likes of which no age has ever seen or dreamt: to take this upon one's soul—the oldest, the newest, loses, hopes, conquests, victories of humanity. . . . To finally take all this in one soul and compress it into one feeling—this would surely have to produce a happiness unknown to humanity so far."

46. Nietzsche argues that "we can comprehend only a world that we ourselves have made," echoing a similar claim made by Kant at CPR Bxiii: "reason has insight into what it itself produces according to its own design."

47. See Zuckert (1976) on Nietzsche's locating the "destruction of both knowledge and morality" as a result of "modern philosophy" (80).

48. See Lemm (2009), Franco (2007), and Church (forthcoming b) for further explorations of Nietzsche's view of culture.

49. See Nietzsche's metaphor, derived from Plato's *Phaedrus*, of the human erotic encounter with the beautiful as cultivating the growth of "wings," while the state cages our eros and stunts the growth of our wings (FEI 55, 98).

50. See Heilke (1998) and Church (2006) for further reflection on Nietzsche's view of education.

Conclusion

1. See Sandel (1996, 3): we "fear that, individually and collectively, we are losing control of the forces that govern our lives."

REFERENCES

Abbey, Ruth. 2000. *Nietzsche's Middle Period*. Oxford: Oxford University Press.

Acampora, Christa Davis. 2006a. "Naturalism and Nietzsche's Moral Psychology." In Ansell-Pearson 2006, 314–33.

———, ed. 2006b. *Nietzsche's "On the Genealogy of Morals: Critical Essays."* Lanham, Md.: Rowman and Littlefield.

———. 2006c. "On Sovereignty and Overhumanity: Why It Matters How We Read Nietzsche's *Genealogy* II:2." In Acampora 2006b, 147–62.

Allen, Michael. 2006. "Hegel Between Non-domination and Expressive Freedom: Capabilities, Perspectives, Democracy." *Philosophy and Social Criticism* 32 (4): 493–512.

Anderson, Joel. 2001. "Hegel's Implicit View on How to Solve the Problem of Poverty: The Responsible Consumer and the Return of the Ethical to Civil Society." In R. Williams 2001, 185–206.

Ansell-Pearson, Keith. 1991. *Nietzsche Contra Rousseau: A Study of Nietzsche's Moral and Political Thought*. Cambridge: Cambridge University Press.

———, ed. 2006. *A Companion to Nietzsche*. Malden, Mass.: Blackwell.

Appel, Fredrick. 1999. *Nietzsche Contra Democracy*. Ithaca: Cornell University Press.

Arato, Andrew. 1991. "A Reconstruction of Hegel's Theory of Civil Society." In Cornell, Rosenfeld, and Carlson 1991, 301–20.

Arendt, Hannah. 1998. *The Human Condition*. Chicago: University of Chicago Press.

Aristotle. 1996. *The Politics and the Constitution of Athens*. Edited by Stephen Everson. Translated by Benjamin Jowett. Cambridge: Cambridge University Press.

Avineri, Shlomo. 1972. *Hegel's Theory of the Modern State*. Cambridge: Cambridge University Press.

Bacon, Francis. 1980. *New Atlantis and The Great Instauration*. Wheeling, Ill.: Harlan Davidson.

Behler, Ernst. 1991. *Confrontations: Derrida/Heidegger/Nietzsche*. Stanford: Stanford University Press.

Beiser, Frederick C. 2005. *Hegel*. New York: Routledge.

———, ed. 2008. *The Cambridge Companion to Hegel and Nineteenth-Century Philosophy*. Cambridge: Cambridge University Press.

Bergmann, Peter. 1987. *Nietzsche, "the Last Anti-political German."* Bloomington: Indiana University Press.

Berkowitz, Peter. 1995. *Nietzsche: The Ethics of an Immoralist*. Cambridge: Harvard University Press.

Bernstein, J. M. 1984. "From Self-Consciousness to Community: Act and Recognition in the Master-Slave Relationship." In Pelczynski 1984b, 14–39.

Brandom, Robert. 2002. *Tales of the Mighty Dead: Historical Essays in the Metaphysics of Intentionality*. Cambridge, Mass.: Harvard University Press.

Bristow, William F. 2007. *Hegel and the Transformation of Philosophical Critique*. Oxford: Oxford University Press.

Came, Daniel. 2006. "The Aesthetic Justification of Existence." In Ansell-Pearson, *Companion to Nietzsche*, 41–57.

Cavell, Stanley. 1990. *Conditions Handsome and Unhandsome: The Constitution of Emersonian Perfectionism*. Chicago: University of Chicago Press.

Chambers, Simone, and Jeffrey Kopstein. 2006. "Civil Society and the State." In *The Oxford Handbook of Political Theory*, edited by John S. Dryzek, Bonnie Honig, and Anne Phillips, 363–81. Oxford: Oxford University Press.

Church, Jeffrey. 2006. "Dreaming of the True Erotic: Nietzsche's Socrates and the Reform of Modern Education." *History of Political Thought* 27 (4): 685–710.

——. 2010. "The Freedom of Desire: Hegel's Response to Rousseau on the Problem of Civil Society." *AJPS* 54 (1): 125–39.

——. Forthcoming a. "Personhood and Ethical Commercial Life: Hegel's Transformation of Locke." In *Natural Right and Political Philosophy: Essays in Honor of Catherine and Michael Zuckert*. Notre Dame: University of Notre Dame Press.

——. Forthcoming b. "Two Concepts of Culture in the Early Nietzsche." *European Journal of Political Theory*.

Church, Jeffrey, and Catherine H. Zuckert. 2008. "The Magnanimous Overman: On Nietzsche's Transformation of Aristotle's Greatness of Soul." In *Magnanimity and Statesmanship*, edited by Carson Holloway, 109–29. Lanham, Md.: Lexington Books.

Clark, Maudemarie. 1983. "Nietzsche's Doctrines of the Will to Power." *Nietzsche Studien* 12:458–68.

——. 1990. *Nietzsche on Truth and Philosophy*. Cambridge: Cambridge University Press.

Clark, Maudemarie, and David Dudrick. 2006. "The Naturalisms of *Beyond Good and Evil*." In Ansell-Pearson 2006, 148–68.

——. 2009. "Nietzsche on the Will: An Analysis of BGE 19." In Gemes and May 2009, 247–68.

Cohen, G. A. 1995. *Self-Ownership, Freedom, and Equality*. Cambridge: Cambridge University Press.

Cohen, Joshua, and Joel Rogers. 1995. *Associations and Democracy*. London: Verso.

Conant, James. 2001. "Nietzsche's Perfectionism: A Reading of *Schopenhauer as Educator*." In *Nietzsche's Postmoralism: Essays on Nietzsche's Prelude to Philosophy's Future*, edited by Richard Schacht, 181–257. Cambridge: Cambridge University Press.

Connolly, William. 1991. *Identity/Difference: Democratic Negotiations of Political Paradox*. Ithaca: Cornell University Press.

Cooper, Laurence D. 1999. *Rousseau, Nature, and the Problem of the Good Life*. University Park: Pennsylvania State University Press.

——. 2008. *Eros in Plato, Rousseau, and Nietzsche: The Politics of Infinity*. University Park: Pennsylvania State University Press.

Cornell, Drucilla, Michel Rosenfeld, and David Gray Carlson, eds. 1991. *Hegel and Legal Theory*. New York: Routledge.

Crittenden, Jack. 1992. *Beyond Individualism: Reconstituting the Liberal Self*. Oxford: Oxford University Press.

Cullen, Bernard. 1979. *Hegel's Social and Political Thought: An Introduction*. New York: St. Martin's Press.

——. 1988. "The Mediating Role of Estates and Corporations in Hegel's Theory of Political Representation." In *Hegel Today*, edited by Bernard Cullen, 22–41. Aldershot, Hants, England: Avebury.

Dahl, Robert. 1989. *Democracy and Its Critics*. New Haven: Yale University Press.

Dallmayr, Fred R. 1993. *G. W. F. Hegel: Modernity and Politics.* Lanham, Md.: Rowman and Littlefield.

Dawkins, Richard. 1976. *The Selfish Gene.* New York: Oxford University Press.

Del Caro, Adrian. 1989. *Nietzsche Contra Nietzsche: Creativity and the Anti-Romantic.* Baton Rouge: Louisiana State University Press.

Deleuze, Gilles. 2006. *Nietzsche and Philosophy.* New York: Columbia University Press.

De Man, Paul. 1982. *Allegories of Reading: Figural Language in Rousseau, Nietzsche, Rilke, and Proust.* New Haven: Yale University Press.

Dennett, Daniel C. 2004. *Freedom Evolves.* London: Allen Lane.

Detwiler, Bruce. 1990. *Nietzsche and the Politics of Aristocratic Radicalism.* Chicago: University of Chicago Press.

DeVries, Willem. 1988. *Hegel's Theory of Mental Activity: An Introduction to Theoretical Spirit.* Ithaca: Cornell University Press.

Dombowsky, Don. 2002. "A Response to Alan D. Schrift's 'Nietzsche for Democracy?'" *Nietzsche-Studien* 31:278–90.

Dove, Craig M. 2008. *Nietzsche's Ethical Theory: Mind, Self, and Responsibility.* New York: Continuum.

Doyle, Tsarina. 2004. "Nietzsche's Appropriation of Kant." *Nietzsche-Studien* 33:180–204.

Dudley, Will. 1997. "Freedom and the Need for Protection from Myself." *Owl of Minerva* 29 (1): 39–69.

———. 2002. *Hegel, Nietzsche, and Philosophy.* Cambridge: Cambridge University Press.

———. 2004–5. "The Systematic Context and Structure of Hegel's Social Theory: A Response to Frederick Neuhouser." *Owl of Minerva* 36 (1): 3–14.

Duso, Giuseppe. 1991. "Freiheit, politisches Handeln und Repräsentation beim jungen Hegel." In Fulda and Horstmann 1991, 242–78.

Emerson, Ralph Waldo. 1983. *Essays and Poems.* New York: Library of America.

Ferrarin, Alfredo. 2001. *Hegel and Aristotle.* Cambridge: Cambridge University Press.

Fichte, Johann Gottlieb. 2008. *Addresses to the German Nation.* Translated by Gregory Moore. Cambridge: Cambridge University Press.

Franco, Paul. 1999. *Hegel's Philosophy of Freedom.* New Haven: Yale University Press.

———. 2007. "Nietzsche's *Human, All Too Human* and the Problem of Culture." *Review of Politics* 69 (2): 215–43.

Fulda, Hans Friedrich. 1991. "Rousseausche Probleme in Hegels Entwicklung." In Fulda and Horstmann 1991, 41–73.

Fulda, Hans Friedrich, and Rolf-Peter Horstmann, eds. 1991. *Rousseau, die Revolution und der junge Hegel.* Stuttgart: Klett-Cotta.

Gadamer, Hans-Georg. 1976. *Hegel's Dialectic: Five Hermeneutical Studies.* Translated by P. Christopher Smith. New Haven: Yale University Press.

Gambino, Giacomo. 1996. "Nietzsche and the Greeks: Identity, Politics, and Tragedy." *Polity* 28 (4): 415–44.

Gardner, Sebastian. 2009. "Nietzsche, the Self, and the Disunity of Philosophical Reason." In Gemes and May, *Nietzsche on Freedom and Autonomy,* 1–32.

Geiger, Ido. 2007. *The Founding Act of Modern Ethical Life: Hegel's Critique of Kant's Moral and Political Philosophy.* Stanford University Press.

Gemes, Ken. 2007. "Nietzsche on Free Will, Autonomy, and the Sovereign Individual." *Proceedings of the Aristotelian Society* 80:321–28.

Gemes, Ken, and Simon May, eds. 2009. *Nietzsche on Freedom and Autonomy.* Oxford: Oxford University Press.

Gerhardt, Volker. 1992. "Selbstbegründung: Nietzsches Moral der Individualität." *Nietzsche-Studien* 21:28–49.

———. 2006. "The Body, the Self, and the Ego." In Ansell-Pearson 2006, 273–98.

Gillespie, Michael. 1995. *Nihilism Before Nietzsche.* Chicago: University of Chicago Press.

————. 2005. "Slouching Towards Bethlehem to Be Born: On the Nature and Meaning of Nietzsche's Superman." *Journal of Nietzsche Studies* 30:49–69.

Goethe, Johann Wolfgang von. 1985. *Faust: First Part.* Translated by Peter Salm. New York: Bantam Books.

Goldstein, Joshua D. 2004. "The 'Bees Problem' in Hegel's Political Philosophy: Habit, Phronesis, and Experience of the Good." *History of Political Thought* 25 (3): 481–507.

Green, Michael Steven. 2002. *Nietzsche and the Transcendental Tradition.* Urbana: University of Illinois Press.

Guay, Robert. 2002. "Nietzsche on Freedom." *European Journal of Philosophy* 10 (3): 302–27.

Hardimon, Michael O. 1994. *Hegel's Social Philosophy: The Project of Reconciliation.* Cambridge: Cambridge University Press.

Harris, H. S. 1983. "The Social Ideal of Hegel's Economic Theory." In *Hegel's Philosophy of Action,* edited by Lawrence S. Stepelevich and David Lamb, 49–74. Atlantic Highlands, N.J.: Humanities Press.

Hartmann, Klaus. 1984. "Towards a New Systematic Reading of Hegel's Philosophy of Right." In Pelczynski 1984b, 114–36.

Hatab, Laurence. 1995. *A Nietzschean Defense of Democracy: An Experiment in Postmodern Politics.* Chicago: Open Court Press.

————. 2008. "Breaking the Contract Theory: The Individual and the Law in Nietzsche's *Genealogy.*" In Siemens and Roodt 2008, 161–90.

Heidegger, Martin. 1979. *Nietzsche.* Translated by David Farrel Krell. New York: Harper and Row.

Heilke, Thomas. 1998. *Nietzsche's Tragic Regime: Culture, Aesthetics, and Political Education.* DeKalb: Northern Illinois University Press.

Heiman, G. 1971. "The Sources and Significance of Hegel's Corporate Doctrine." In *Hegel's Political Philosophy: Problems and Perspectives,* ed. Z. A. Pelczynski, 111–35. Cambridge: Cambridge University Press.

Hill, R. Kevin. 2003. *Nietzsche's Critiques: The Kantian Foundations of His Thought.* Oxford: Clarendon Press.

Honig, Bonnie. 1993. *Political Theory and the Displacement of Politics.* Ithaca: Cornell University Press.

Honneth, Axel. 1995. *The Struggle for Recognition: The Moral Grammar of Social Conflicts.* Translated by Joel Anderson. Cambridge, Mass.: MIT Press.

————. 2000. *Suffering from Indeterminacy: An Attempt at a Reactualization of Hegel's Philosophy of Right.* Assen: Van Gorcum.

————. 2008. "From Desire to Recognition: Hegel's Account of Human Sociality." In Moyar and Quante 2008, 76–90.

Horstmann, Rolf-Peter. 2004. "The Role of Civil Society in Hegel's Political Philosophy." In Pippin and Höffe 2004, 208–38.

Houlgate, Stephen. 1986. *Hegel, Nietzsche, and the Criticism of Metaphysics.* Cambridge: Cambridge University Press.

Hurka, Thomas. 1999. *Perfectionism.* Oxford: Oxford University Press.

Hussain, Nadeem. 2007. "Honest Illusion: Valuing for Nietzsche's Free Spirits." In *Nietzsche and Morality,* edited by Brian Leiter and Neil Sinhababu, 157–91. Oxford: Oxford University Press.

Hyppolite, Jean. 1974. *Genesis and Structure of Hegel's "Phenomenology of Spirit."* Translated by Samuel Cherniak and John Heckman. Evanston: Northwestern University Press.

James, David. 2007. *Hegel's Philosophy of Right: Subjectivity and Ethical Life.* New York: Continuum.

James, William. 1985. *Psychology: The Briefer Course.* Notre Dame: University of Notre Dame Press.

Janaway, Christopher. 2006. "Naturalism and Genealogy." In Ansell-Pearson 2006, 58–75.

———. 2007. *Beyond Selflessness: Reading Nietzsche's Genealogy.* Oxford: Oxford University Press.

———. 2009. "Autonomy, Affect, and the Self in Nietzsche's Project of Genealogy." In Gemes and May 2009, 51–68.

Johnson, Dirk. 2010. *Nietzsche's Anti-Darwinism.* Cambridge: Cambridge University Press.

Jurist, Elliot L. 2000. *Beyond Hegel and Nietzsche: Philosophy, Culture, and Agency.* Cambridge, Mass.: MIT Press.

Kain, Philip J. 2007. "Nietzsche, Eternal Recurrence, and the Horror of Existence." *Journal of Nietzsche Studies* 33:49–63.

Kateb, George. 1992. *The Inner Ocean: Individualism and Democratic Culture.* Ithaca: Cornell University Press.

Kaufmann, Walter. 1974. *Nietzsche: Philosopher, Psychologist, Antichrist.* Princeton: Princeton University Press.

Knowles, Dudley. 2002. *Hegel and the Philosophy of Right.* New York: Routledge.

Köhnke, Klaus Christian. 1991. *The Rise of Neo-Kantianism: German Academic Philosophy Between Idealism and Positivism.* Cambridge: Cambridge University Press.

Kojève, Alexandre. 1969. *Introduction to the Reading of Hegel: Lectures on the Phenomenology of Spirit.* Edited by Allan Bloom. Translated by James H. Nichols Jr. Ithaca: Cornell University Press.

Kolb, David. 1986. *The Critique of Pure Modernity: Hegel, Heidegger, and After.* Chicago: University of Chicago Press.

Korsgaard, Christine. 1996. *The Sources of Normanivity.* Cambridge: Cambridge University Press.

Lampert, Laurence. 1986. *Nietzsche's Teaching: An Interpretation of "Thus Spoke Zarathustra."* New Haven: Yale University Press.

———. 2001. *Nietzsche's Task: An Interpretation of "Beyond Good and Evil."* New Haven: Yale University Press.

Leiter, Brian. 2000. "Nietzsche's Metaethics: Against the Privilege Readings." *European Journal of Philosophy* 8 (3):277–97.

———. 2002. *Nietzsche on Morality.* London: Routledge.

———. 2008. Review of Janaway, *Beyond Selflessness. Notre Dame Philosophical Reviews,* June 3.

———. 2009. "Nietzsche's Freedom of the Will." In Gemes and May, *Nietzsche on Freedom and Autonomy,* 107–26.

Leiter, Brian, and Maudemarie Clark. 1997. Introduction to *Daybreak.* Cambridge: Cambridge University Press.

Lemm, Vanessa. 2009. *Nietzsche's Animal Philosophy: Culture, Politics, and the Animality of the Human Being.* New York: Fordham University Press.

Lewis, Thomas A. 2005. *Freedom and Tradition in Hegel: Reconsidering Anthropology, Ethics, and Religion.* Notre Dame: University of Notre Dame Press.

Losurdo, Dominic. 2004. *Hegel and the Freedom of Moderns.* Durham: Duke University Press.

Löwith, Karl. 1964. *From Hegel to Nietzsche: The Revolution in Nineteenth-Century Thought.* Translated by David E. Green. New York: Columbia University Press.

Lukes, Steven. 1973. *Individualism.* Oxford: Blackwell.

Luther, Timothy. 2009. *Hegel's Critique of Modernity: Reconciling Individual Freedom and the Community.* Lanham, Md.: Lexington Books.

Machiavelli, Niccolò. 1995. *The Prince.* Translated by David Wootton. Indianapolis: Hackett.

MacIntyre, Alasdair. 1984. *After Virtue.* Notre Dame: University of Notre Dame Press.

Maker, William. 1987. *Hegel on Economics and Freedom.* Macon: Mercer University Press.

Mansfield, Harvey. 1993. *Taming the Prince: The Ambivalence of Modern Executive Power.* New York: Free Press.

Markell, Patchen. 2003. *Bound by Recognition.* Princeton: Princeton University Press.

Marks, Jonathan. 2005. *Perfection and Disharmony in the Thought of Jean-Jacques Rousseau.* Cambridge: Cambridge University Press.

McDowell, John. 1994. *Mind and World.* Cambridge: Harvard University Press.

McGinn, Robert. 1975. "Culture as Prophylactic: Nietzsche's Birth of Tragedy as Culture Criticism." *Nietzsche Studien* 4:75–138.

Mead, George Herbert. 1934. *Mind, Self, and Society: From the Standpoint of a Social Behaviorist.* Edited by Charles W. Morris. Chicago: University of Chicago Press.

Mouffe, Chantal. 1996. "Democracy, Power, and the 'Political.'" In *Democracy and Difference,* edited by Seyla Benhabib. Princeton: Princeton University Press, 245–56.

Moyar, Dean, and Michael Quante, eds. 2008. *Hegel's Phenomenology of Spirit: A Critical Guide.* Cambridge: Cambridge University Press.

Mulhall, Stephen. 2005. *Philosophical Myths of the Fall.* Princeton: Princeton University Press.

Nabais, Nuno. 2006. "The Individual and Individuality in Nietzsche." In Ansell-Pearson 2006, 76–94.

Nehamas, Alexander. 1985. *Nietzsche: Life as Literature.* Cambridge, Mass.: Harvard University Press.

Neuhouser, Frederick. 1990. *Fichte's Theory of Subjectivity.* Cambridge: Cambridge University Press.

———. 2000. *The Foundations of Hegel's Social Theory.* Cambridge, Mass.: Harvard University Press.

———. 2003. "Rousseau on the Relation Between Reason and Self-Love." *International Yearbook of German Idealism* 1:221–40.

———. 2004–5. "On Detaching Hegel's Social Philosophy from His Metaphysics." *Owl of Minerva* 36 (1): 31–42.

———. 2008. *Rousseau's Theodicy of Self-Love: Evil, Rationality, and the Drive for Recognition.* Oxford: Oxford University Press.

———. 2009. "Desire, Recognition, and the Relation Between Bondsman and Lord." In *The Blackwell Guide to Hegel's Phenomenology of Spirit,* edited by Kenneth R. Westphal, 37–54. Malden, Mass.: Wiley-Blackwell.

Norton, Robert. 1995. *The Beautiful Soul: Aesthetic Morality in the Eighteenth Century.* Ithaca: Cornell University Press.

Okin, Susan. 1999. *Is Multiculturalism Bad for Women?* Princeton: Princeton University Press.

Ottmann, Henning. 1999. *Philosophie und Politik bei Nietzsche.* 2nd ed. Berlin: Walter de Gruyter.

Owen, David. 2002. "Equality, Democracy, and Self-Respect: Reflections on Nietzsche's Agonal Perfectionism." *Journal of Nietzsche Studies* 24 (1): 113–31.

———. 2007. *Nietzsche's Genealogy of Morality.* McGill: Queen's University Press.

———. 2009. "Autonomy, Self-Respect, and Self-Love: Nietzsche on Ethical Agency." In Gemes and May 2009, 197–222.

Parekh, Bhiku. 2000. *Rethinking Multiculturalism.* Cambridge, Mass.: Harvard University Press.

Patten, Alan. 1999. *Hegel's Idea of Freedom*. Oxford: Oxford University Press.
———. 2001. "Social Contract Theory and the Politics of Recognition in Hegel's Political Philosophy." In R. Williams 2001, 167–84.
Pelczynski, Z. A. 1984a. "Political Community and Individual Freedom in Hegel's Philosophy of State." In Pelczynski 1984b, 55–76.
———, ed. 1984b. *The State and Civil Society: Studies in Hegel's Political Philosophy*. Cambridge: Cambridge University Press.
Peperzak, Adriaan. 2001. *Modern Freedom: Hegel's Legal, Moral, and Political Philosophy*. Dordrecht: Kluwer Academic.
Pinkard, Terry. 1996. *Hegel's Phenomenology: The Sociality of Reason*. Cambridge: Cambridge University Press.
———. 2000. *Hegel: A Biography*. Cambridge: Cambridge University Press.
———. 2003. "Subjects, Objects, and Normativity: What Is It Like to *Be* an Agent." *International Yearbook of German Idealism* 1:201–20.
———. 2008. "What Is a 'Shape of Spirit'?" In Moyar and Quante 2008, 112–29.
Pippin, Robert B. 1989. *Hegel's Idealism: The Satisfactions of Self-Consciousness*. Cambridge: Cambridge University Press.
———. 2006. "Lightning and Flash, Agent and Deed (*GM* I:6–17)." In Acampora 2006b, 131–46.
———. 2008a. *Hegel's Practical Philosophy*. Cambridge: Cambridge University Press.
———. 2008b. "The 'Logic of Experience' as 'Absolute Knowledge' in Hegel's *Phenomenology of Spirit*." In Moyar and Quante 2008, 210–27.
———. 2010. *Nietzsche, Psychology, and First Philosophy*. Chicago: University of Chicago Press.
Pippin, Robert B., and Otfried Höffe, eds. 2004. *Hegel on Ethics and Politics*. Cambridge: Cambridge University Press.
Pöggeler, Otto. 1999. *Hegels Kritik der Romantik*. Munich: Wilhelm Fink Verlag.
Prosch, Michael. 1997. "The *Korporation* in Hegel's Interpretation of Civil Society." In *Hegel, History, and Interpretation*, edited by Shaun Gallagher, 195–208. Albany: State University of New York Press.
Putnam, Robert D. 2000. *Bowling Alone: The Collapse and Revival of American Community*. New York: Simon and Schuster.
Rawls, John. 2000. *Lectures on the History of Moral Philosophy*. Cambridge, Mass.: Harvard University Press.
Redding, Paul. 1996. *Hegel's Hermeneutics*. Ithaca: Cornell University Press.
———. 2008. "The Independence and Dependence of Self-Consciousness: The Dialectic of Lordship and Bondage in Hegel's *Phenomenology of Spirit*." In Beiser 2008, 94–110.
Reginster, Bernard. 2006. *The Affirmation of Life: Nietzsche on Overcoming Nihilism*. Cambridge, Mass.: Harvard University Press.
Richardson, John. 1996. *Nietzsche's System*. Oxford: Oxford University Press.
———. 2004. *Nietzsche's New Darwinism*. Oxford: Oxford University Press.
Ridley, Aaron. 2007. "Nietzsche on Art and Freedom." *European Journal of Philosophy* 15 (2): 204–24.
Riedel, Manfred. 1984. *Between Tradition and Revolution: The Hegelian Transformation of Political Philosophy*. Cambridge: Cambridge University Press.
Ripstein, Arthur. 1994. "Universal and General Will: Hegel and Rousseau." *Political Theory* 22 (3): 444–67.
Rockmore, Tom. 1986. *Hegel's Circular Epistemology*. Bloomington: Indiana University Press.
Rorty, Richard. 1989. *Contingency, Irony, and Solidarity*. Cambridge: Cambridge University Press.

———. 1998. *Truth and Progress: Philosophical Papers*. Cambridge: Cambridge University Press.

Rosen, Stanley. 1995. *The Mask of Enlightenment: Nietzsche's Zarathustra*. New Haven: Yale University Press.

Ross, Nathan. 2008. *On Mechanism in Hegel's Social and Political Philosophy*. New York: Routledge.

Russon, John. 2004. *Reading Hegel's Phenomenology*. Bloomington: Indiana University Press.

Sandel, Michael J. 1982. *Liberalism and the Limits of Justice*. Cambridge: Cambridge University Press.

———. 1996. *Democracy's Discontent: America in Search of a Public Philosophy*. Cambridge: Harvard University Press.

Schechtman, Marya. 1996. *The Constitution of Selves*. Ithaca: Cornell University Press.

Schiller, Frederick. 2005. *On Grace and Dignity*. Translated by Jane V. Curran and Christophe Fricker. Rochester, N.Y.: Camden House.

Schopenhauer, Arthur. 1969. *The World as Will and Representation*. Translated by E. F. J. Payne. New York: Dover.

Schrift, Alan D. 2000. "Nietzsche *for* Democracy?" *Nietzsche-Studien* 29:220–33.

Sedgwick, Sally S. 2000a. "Metaphysics and Morality in Kant and Hegel." In Sedgwick 2000b, 306–23.

———, ed. 2000b. *The Reception of Kant's Critical Philosophy: Fichte, Schelling, and Hegel*. Cambridge: Cambridge University Press.

Shanahan, Daniel. 1992. *Toward a Genealogy of Individualism*. Amherst: University of Massachusetts Press.

Shaw, Tamsin. 2007. *Nietzsche's Political Skepticism*. Princeton: Princeton University Press.

Shklar, Judith. 1969. *Men and Citizens: A Study of Rousseau's Social Theory*. Cambridge: Cambridge University Press.

Siemens, Herman. 2008. "Yes, No, Maybe So . . . Nietzsche's Equivocations on the Relation Between Democracy and 'Grosse Politik.'" In Siemens and Roodt 2008, 231–68.

Siemens, Herman, and Vasti Roodt, eds. 2008. *Nietzsche, Power, and Politics*. Berlin: Walter De Gruyter.

Siep, Ludwig. 2006. "The Contemporary Relevance of Hegel's Practical Philosophy." In *Hegel: New Directions*, edited by Katerina Deligiorgi, 143–57. Chesham: Acumen.

Skowronek, Stephen. 1993. *The Politics Presidents Make: Leadership from John Adams to Bill Clinton*. Cambridge, Mass.: Harvard University Press.

Smith, Steven B. 1989. *Hegel's Critique of Liberalism: Rights in Context*. Chicago: University of Chicago Press.

Sokoloff, William W. 2006. "Nietzsche's Radicalization of Kant." *Polity* 38:501–18.

Speight, Allen. 2001. *Hegel, Literature, and the Problem of Agency*. Cambridge: Cambridge University Press.

Steinberger, Peter. 1988. *Logic and Politics: Hegel's "Philosophy of Right."* New Haven: Yale University Press.

———. 2004. *The Idea of the State*. Cambridge: Cambridge University Press.

Stern, Paul. 2008. *Knowledge and Politics in Plato's Theaetetus*. Cambridge: Cambridge University Press.

Stern, Robert. 2002. *Routledge Philosophy Guidebook to Hegel and the Phenomenology of Spirit*. New York: Routledge.

Stone, Alison. 2005. *Petrified Intelligence: Nature in Hegel's Philosophy*. Albany: State University of New York Press.

Strauss, Leo. 1950. *Natural Right and History*. Chicago: University of Chicago Press.

Strong, Tracy. 1985. "Texts and Pretexts: Reflections on Perspectivism in Nietzsche." *Political Theory* 13 (2): 164–82.

———. 2000. *Friedrich Nietzsche and the Politics of Transfiguration*. Urbana: University of Illinois Press.

Taylor, Charles. 1975. *Hegel*. Cambridge: Cambridge University Press.

———. 1985. *Philosophy and the Human Sciences*. Cambridge: Cambridge University Press.

———. 1989. *Sources of the Self*. Cambridge: Cambridge University Press.

———. 1994. "The Politics of Recognition." *Multiculturalism, Examing the Politics of Recognition*, edited by Amy Gutmann, 25–73. Princeton: Princeton University Press.

Taylor, Quentin P. 1997. *The Republic of Genius: A Reconstruction of Nietzsche's Early Thought*. Rochester, NY: University of Rochester Press.

Theunissen, Michael. 1991. "The Repressed Intersubjectivity in Hegel's Philosophy of Right." in Cornell, Rosenfeld, and Carlson 1991, 3–63.

Thucydides. 1993. *On Justice, Power, and Human Nature*. Translated by Paul Woodruff. Indianapolis: Hackett.

Tobias, Saul. 2006–7. "Hegel and the Politics of Recognition." *Owl of Minerva* 38 (1–2): 101–26.

Tocqueville, Alexis de. 2000. *Democracy in America*. Translated by Harvey C. Mansfield and Delba Winthrop. Chicago: University of Chicago Press.

Todorov, Tzvetan. 2001. *Frail Happiness: An Essay on Rousseau*. Translated by John T. Scott and Robert D. Zaretsky. University Park: Pennsylvania State University Press.

Tunick, Mark. 1992. *Hegel's Political Philosophy: Interpreting the Practice of Legal Punishment*. Princeton: Princeton University Press.

Velkley, Richard L. 2002. *Being after Rousseau*. Chicago: University of Chicago Press.

Velleman, J. David. 2005. "The Self as Narrator." In *Autonomy and the Challenges to Liberalism*, edited by John Christman and Joel Anderson, 56–76. New York: Cambridge University Press.

Villa, Dana. 2001. *Socratic Citizenship*. Princeton: Princeton University Press.

———. 2005. "Hegel, Tocqueville, and 'Individualism.'" *Review of Politics*, 67 (4): 659–86.

———. 2008. *Public Freedom*. Princeton: Princeton University Press.

Warren, Mark. 1988. *Nietzsche and Political Thought*. Cambridge, Mass.: MIT Press.

Waszek, Norbert. 1988. *The Scottish Enlightenment and Hegel's Account of "Civil Society."* Dordrecht: Kluwer Academic.

White, Richard. 1997. *Nietzsche and the Problem of Sovereignty*. Urbana: University of Illinois Press.

Williams, Bernard. 1993. "Nietzsche's Minimalist Moral Psychology." *European Journal of Philosophy* 1 (1): 4–14.

Williams, Robert R. 1997. *Hegel's Ethics of Recognition*. Berkeley: University of California Press.

———, ed. 2001. *Beyond Liberalism and Communitarianism: Studies in Hegel's "Philosophy of Right."* Albany: State University of New York Press.

———. 2006–7. "Hegel's Critique of Kant." *Owl of Minerva* 38 (1–2): 9–34.

Wolfe, Christopher. 2006. *Natural Law Liberalism*. Cambridge: Cambridge University Press.

Wolff, Michael. 2004. "Hegel's Organicist Theory of the State: On the Concept and Method of Hegel's 'Science of the State.'" In Pippin and Höffe 2004, 291–322.

Wood, Allen W. 1990. *Hegel's Ethical Thought*. Cambridge: Cambridge University Press.

———. 2000. "The 'I' as Principle of Practical Philosophy." In Sedgwick 2000b, 93–108.

Yack, Bernard. 1992. *The Longing for Total Revolution: Philosophic Sources of Social Discontent from Rousseau to Marx and Nietzsche*. Berkeley: University of California Press.

Young, Julian. 2006. *Nietzsche's Philosophy of Religion*. Cambridge: Cambridge University Press.

Zakaras, Alex. 2009. *Individuality and Mass Democracy: Mill, Emerson, and the Burdens of Citizenship*. Oxford: Oxford University Press.

Zuckert, Catherine. 1976. "Nature, History, and the Self: Nietzsche's Untimely Considerations." *Nietzsche Studien* 5:55–82.

———. 1983. "Nietzsche on the Origin and Development of the Distinctively Human," *Polity* 16(1): 48–71.

Zuckert, Michael. 1994. *Natural Rights and the New Republicanism*. Princeton: Princeton University Press.

Zumbrunnen, John. 2002. "'Courage in the Face of Reality': Nietzsche's Admiration for Thucydides." *Polity* 35 (2): 237–63.

INDEX

absolute negativity, 60, 77, 78, 81, 218 n. 42
Acampora, Christa Davis, 114–15, 231 n. 15
actions, ethical, 89
aesthetics
  aesthetic experience, 168
  art as source of pleasure, 150
  art, 238–39 n. 17
  beauty appeals to human freedoms, 161–62
  concept of individual, 236 n. 59
  criteria, 111
  justification of existence, 149–54
  Kant's aesthetic idea, 130, 161
  ladder of the beautiful, 163–66
  See also life, artistically structured
agents, collective, 67
agency
  autonomous, obstacles to, 200–201
  individual, 202
  subjective, 67
Allen, Michael, 215 n. 17
anarchy, 186
Ansell-Pearson, Keith, 213 n. 28
anxiety (Angst), 33
Appel, Fredrick, 181, 245 n. 22
apperception, unity of, 36, 39, 132
Apollonian principle, 113–14
Arato, Andrew, 227–28 n. 44
arête, 56–57
aristocracy, 183, 187
aristocrats, 140, 141
Aristophanes, 242 n. 50
Aristotle, 12, 27, 47, 65, 72, 80, 215 n. 8, 220 n. 4, 223 nn. 37–38
Aristotelianism, 160
Athens, 68, 166
  elites, 33
  Pericles' funeral oration, 83

atomism, 2, 9, 16, 22, 29, 57, 79, 86, 94, 95, 99, 109, 116, 165, 175, 225 n. 19
atomistic cause, 29
atomistic spirit, 15
authority, 8, 9,11, 17,18, 43, 50, 115, 172, 188, 193, 199, 227–28 n. 44
  autonomous, 56
  individual's, 47, 55
  of individuality, 34
  normative, 18, 23
  of reason, 20–21, 244 n. 7
  universal, 66
autonomy, 2, 3, 5, 62, 81, 82, 83, 102, 104, 106, 108, 111, 112, 113, 124, 126, 175, 200–202, 206, 209, 219 nn. 1 and 3, 221 n. 15, 223 n. 39, 232 n. 17, 235 n. 48, 241 n. 43
  agency, autonomous, 115, 119
  atomistic cause, 29
  atomistic spirit, 15
  autonomous judgment, 95
  autonomous self-determination, 103
  bottom-up model, 42, 43, 48
  from conscience, 51
  of individual, 19, 21, 74
  institutional autonomy, 74
  Jesus, example of, 218, n. 49
  top-down model, 42, 47, 48
Avineri, Shlomo, 227 n. 42

Bacon, Francis, 13, 212 n. 7
"bad infinite," 59
beauty, 150–53, 156, 161–62, 166, 241 n. 43, 242 n. 51
  the beautiful, 163–64, 241 nn. 32 and 37
  and eris, 166
  qualities contributing to, 156–58
  See also aesthetics

becoming, stream of, 147–48
Beethoven, Ludwig van, 131, 134
Beiser, Frederick C., 26, 214 n. 5
beliefs, moral, 49
Bergmann, Peter, 178, 245 n. 15
Bernstein, J. M., 220, n. 7
Brandom, Robert, 26, 43, 214 n. 7, 216
    n. 29, 223 n. 35
Burke, Edmund, 74, 109

Came, Daniel, 241 n. 34
capitalism, 101, 203
Cartesianism, 211
categorical imperative, 19
Cavell, Stanley, 211 n.6, 241 n. 36
causes, final 12, 13, 14
character, 56, 114,129, 133, 134, 136,
    137,159, 165, 200, 201, 219 n. 52
    ethical, 89
    formation 48
    "infinite worth" of, 44–55
    requirements of, 111–12
    shaped by laboring, 46
Christian-Cartesian conception, 116
Christianity, 4, 49, 125, 141, 144, 193, 218
    nn. 47 and 49, 234 nn. 33 and 42,
    246–47 n. 32
Cicero, 156
citizen, 213 n. 26
citizenship, active, 26
Clark, Maudemarie, 119, 121, 141,
    229–30 n. 6, 230 n. 12, 231 n. 15,
    233 n. 25
coherence, 36, 49, 51, 55, 135
    narrative coherence 51–53
communitarian movement, 2
community, 4, 5,8, 10, 23, 24, 27–28, 39,
    51, 56, 57, 72, 75, 86, 115, 120, 122,
    123, 124–25, 132, 138, 139, 140–42,
    149–50, 153–56, 158–65, 167–68
    170–172, 174–78, 182, 184–85, 188,
    196, 199, 200, 202, 206, 207, 209, 210,
    234 n. 38, 242 n. 47, 240 n. 28
    ancient political community, 79
    aristocracy of spirit, 141
    eases tension of the bow, 191
    eros and eris in, 162–69
    ethical community, 203; political com-
    munity highest form, 78–83
    ethical views of, 140–41
    and individuals, 77–78; mutual shaping
    of, 141

mistrust in, 162–63, 166, 167
modern ethical, no tension with indi-
    vidual, 84–85
nature of, 63–78; division of labor,
    71–77; good life, 68, 69; mutual
    recognition, 64–66; self-legislation,
    65
ontology of, Hegel and Nietzsche
    differ, 160
origin of, 57–63
overcoming Silenus' truth, 149
political, 156
pre-modern, 8–9
preserved by tradition, 33–34
redemption of, 194
source of authority, 8
universal community of humanity,
    195
Conant, James, 241 n. 36
conformism, social, 57
Connolly, William, 243 n. 1
conscience, 51, 81, 84, 129, 185
consciousness, 59, 80, 96, 232 n. 20, 235
    n. 46
consciousness, self-, 51
    public, 53
conservatives, 199
conservatism, 2
consumption, 59
Constitution, German, 16
constitutionalism, 106
contract, political, 16–17
contradictions, 28, 29, 30, 134, 156
consumption, 37, 39
Cooper, Laurence D., 213 n. 26
corporations, 227 n. 36
court system, 105–6, 228 n. 45
Crittenden, Jack, 211 n.6
Cullen, Bernard, 227 n. 36
culture, 123–24, 132, 150, 152, 182, 183,
    186, 188–89, 190–98, 205, 206, 209,
    240 n. 28
    adversary to state, 183–184, 186
    aesthetic, 209
    artistic, 149, 159, 185
    foundation for ethical life, 151–54
    Hegel and Nietzsche differ on social
    ontology, 205, 171–79
    modern, historical development of,
    171–79
    multitude of, 193
    national, 80

and the state, 244 n. 12, 245 nn. 14, 17, and 20

Dahl, Robert, 204, 228 n. 46
Dallmayr, Fred R., 226 n. 24
Darwinism, 234 n. 31
Dawkins, Richard, 121, 124
death, 29, 33, 47, 109, 146, 157
  fear of, 11, 12, 61, 147
Declaration of Independence, 1
democracy, 187, 247 n. 39
  agonistic, 207, 209, 243 n. 56
  deliberative, 207, 209
  liberal, 170, 171, 191–92, 209
  Nietzsche critical of liberal democracy, 170
democratization, 228 n. 46
democrats, 181, 182, 186
Dennett, Daniel, 215 n. 13
desire, 3, 37, 38, 39, 41, 45,46, 47, 57,
    58–59, 60, 61, 62, 64,65, 66, 80, 91,
    85, 86, 114, 116, 119, 120, 121 124,
    125, 128, 129, 130, 132, 144, 145, 153,
    158, 160, 163,175, 176, 177, 186, 188,
    189, 201, 207
  ethical, 47–48, 90, 94
  expansion of in commercial society,
    90–96
  to be free from nature, 68
  natural, 11, 12–14, 16, 17, 18, 21, 23
  nature of, 88–90
  particular, 47–48, 86, 87,91, 94, 96, 97,
    99, 100, 102, 104
  parts of, 88
  refinement of, 90
  reflective, 144
  spiritual, 88
determinism, 13
deterministic views, 12
Detweiler, Bruce, 181, 245 n. 22
differences, individual, 71–77, 91, 104,
    235 n. 51
Dionysian concept, 113–14
Diotima, 163–164
disintegration, age of, 190
diversity, 132–134,158
doer before the deed, 116, 129, 232 n. 18
doer behind the deed, 201
dogmatism, 141, 145
dogmatists, 142
Dombowsky, Don, 235 n. 51
Dudley, Will, 211 n.8, 214 n.4

Dudrick, David, 141, 230 n. 12
Duso, Giuseppe, 224 n. 7

economic activity
  Hegel's views, 204–05
  Nietzsche's views, 205
economy, British political, 92
ecstasy (Begeisterung), 42
education, 5, 46, 123, 177, 196, 245 nn. 16
    and 22
  German, 112–13
  as liberation, 192–93
  liberal arts, 198
  makes humans ethical, 47
ego, 28, 36, 39, 54, 59, 60, 62, 81, 112, 132,
    201, 216 n. 26, 230 n. 12, 233 n. 29,
    240 n. 29
  reflective, 165
egoism, 96, 175–76, 177, 178, 188
empiricism, 10, 16, 212 n.5 and 10
empiricists, 12, 13, 14, 16, 19, 21, 207
enemies, 182–83
Enlightenment, 144, 198, 211 n. 3
equality, 74
eris, 141, 202, 243 nn. 55–56
  in community, 162–69
  good eris, 165–66
eros, 141, 152, 156, 206, 240 n. 26, 243
    n. 56
  in community, 162–69
error theory, 239 n. 20
essence (Wesen), 32, 53, 59, 79, 147, 154,
    198
estates, 69
  assembly, 106, 107
  as ethical political communities, 96–110
  as mediating institutions, 96–110
  honor in, 102–13
estates, types of
  agrarian, 97
  commercial, 97–98
  universal, 98
esteeming, 122, 124, 141–44, 147, 149,
    151, 165, 191, 237 nn. 4 and 6
ethical good, 68
ethical action, 57, 66, 69,75, 96
ethical life, 56–83, 172, 174, 191
  Hegel's view 57–58
  Sittlichkeit, 57
evil, 30, 118, 122, 143, 146, 147, 149, 172,
    224 n. 9
  problem of, 30, 31

exemplar, 156, 159, 160–61, 164, 165, 167, 168, 174, 185, 192, 205, 206, 207, 241 n. 36, 246 n. 23

fall from grace, 30–31
falsification, 145–46, 153
use by dogmatists, 142–43
family, attachment to damages community, 122
Feuerbach, Ludwig Andreas, 112
Fichte, J. G., 3, 17, 34, 54, 79, 113, 114, 201, 207, 216 n. 26, 221 n. 17
Ferguson, Adam, 92
founders, 156, 158–59, 161
of United States, 195
Franco, Paul, 215, n. 17, 223 n. 38, 224 n. 7, 226 n. 24
freedom, 24, 33, 35, 37, 44, 54, 56, 59, 60, 62, 64, 65, 66, 74, 78, 81, 85, 89, 93, 95, 101, 102, 103, 105, 108, 109, 114, 116, 117, 124, 126, 129, 148, 157, 161, 162, 167, 170, 172, 175, 181, 188, 190, 192, 194, 196, 197, 204, 213 n. 21, 215 n. 17, 221 n. 17, 224 n. 8, 231–32 n.16, 232 n. 17, 234–35 n. 43, 236 n. 59
from desires, 17
from nature, 61, 122
first spiritual characteristic, 31
political, 108
relation to absolute negativity, 32
subjective, 50, 173; definition of, 86
substantial, definition of, 86
through participating in state (Hegel's view), 103
Fries, Jacob Friedrich, 54
French Constitution, 1
Fulda, Hans Friedrich, 224 n. 7

Gadamer, Hans-Georg, 220–21 n. 14
Gardner, Sebastian, 230–31 n. 13, 240 n. 29
genius, 113, 152, 158–60, 162–64, 167, 170, 177, 179, 181, 190, 191, 198, 237 n. 3, 241 n. 36, 242 nn. 46, 52, 246 n. 31
republic of geniuses, 247 n. 38
Gerhardt, Volker, 232 n. 20
German Grundesetz, 1
German Idealism, 221 n. 17
German state, ethical organization (Hegel), 113
German states, 82
Goethe, Johann Wolfgang von, 135, 158, 159, 238 n. 12, 242 n. 52
good, 185, 197

ethical, 98, 103, 107
standard of the, 191
good, common, 85, 86, 88, 89, 94, 96, 99, 102, 107, 109–10, 207, 219 n. 2
good life, 25, 27–28, 56, 64, 66, 68, 69, 71, 80, 81, 82, 84, 85, 89–90, 100, 203, 204, 205, 209, 215 n. 9
Gorgias, 151
Greece, 198
Greek gods, 150, 152, 157
Greek philosophy, 153
Greek polis, 76
Greeks, 68, 83, 123, 124,147, 151, 152, 156, 165, 172, 173, 193, 198, 238 n. 13, 243 n. 50
Greek state, 185
Guay, Robert, 233 n. 24, 240 n. 28
guilds, 97, 98, 99

habituation, 47
happiness, 191, 196, 212 n. 10
Hardimon, Michael O., 214, n. 2, 227 n. 36
harmony, 2, 5, 15, 32, 46, 103, 111, 120, 158, 169, 172, 173, 222–23 n. 33
of individual and community, 84–86
harmonization, 191
Harris, H. S., 226 n. 28, 226 n. 28
Hartmann, Klaus, 227 n. 42
Hatab, Laurence, 231–32 n. 16, 243 nn. 56 and 1
hedonism, 170, 175
Hegel, Georg W. F., 3, 4, 5, 6, 7, 9, 10, 11, 13, 14, 15–17, 20–22, 23, 24, 25–55, 56–83, 84–110, 111–14, 117–20, 122, 124, 128–30, 136, 139, 140, 143, 154, 156, 160, 161, 170, 171, 173, 176–78, 188, 190, 196, 197, 199–209, 211 n. 2, 212 nn. 10, 13, 14, 16, and 19, 213 nn. 27–28, 214 nn. 4–6, 215 nn. 8–9, 11–13, and 15, 216 nn. 18, 20–22, 25, 27–29, 217 nn. 31–32, 34–36, and 38–39, 218 nn. 42–44, and 48–49, 218–19 n. 51, 219 nn. 52 and 57 and 3, 229 n. 4–5, 229–30 n. 6, 230 nn. 8–9, 240 n. 29, 243 n. 3, 247 nn. 36 and 40
on administrative authority, 105
on agency, 67
on art, 219, n. 52
on "beautiful soul," 20
on changes in community rules, 74–75
on the citizen, 227 nn. 39–40
civil liberty, 24
on complete subject, 63

on conscience, 51
on the constitution, 222 nn. 29 and 30
critique of: Kant on ontology of reason
and passion, 217 n. 39; Rousseau,
224 nn. 7–9, 224–25 n. 10; of state,
228 n. 49
on the crowd, 228 n. 48
on defense: of historical individualism,
27–28; of individuality, 84
on definition: of "spirit," 10; of individuality in pre modern society, 10
on desire, 14, 46, 88–90, 92
difference with Nietzsche on individual, 197–98
on duty of institutions, 99–101
duty to serve the state, 183
on economic activity, 204–5
on ego, 28
on elements of human being, 23
on estates, 69, 221 nn. 20–22, 228
nn. 50–51
on ethical community, 79–80
on ethical life, 57–58
on formal individual, 20–21
on freedom by participating in state,
103
on Geek life, 224 nn. 3 and 4
on Greek polis, 85–86
on habituation, 47
on human action, 222 n. 28
on illegal corporations, 226 n. 22
incremental change, 110
on the individual, 15, 55
on individual pluralism, 103–10
on individuality, 25–55, 104, 214 n. 2,
217 n. 35
on individuality, the "concept," 49–50
on intuition, 40
on invisible hand, 225 n. 18
on labor, 37
on legislative delegates, 228 n. 47
on marriage relationship, 223 n. 34
on master-slave relationship, 62–63
on misuse of power by state, 227 n. 43
on money, 225–26 n. 21
on moral norms, 73
on natural individual, 28
on nature, 28, 30–31
Nietzsche connection, 211 n.8
not radical democrat, 109–10
political system result of history, 110
on pragmatism, 214 n. 7
on primitive society, 58–59

on representation, 107
Romanticism, 56
on self-creation, 53–54
on selfish desire, 58–59
similarities to Nietzsche. *See*
Nietzsche, similarities to Hegel
on social institutions, 15
on sphere of politics, 105
on "spirit," 31, 64–65
on the state, 80
on state regulation, 226 n. 26
on the subject, 28, 29, 35–36
on subjectivism, 21
on subjectivity, 216 n. 25
on tension between individual and
community, 84–85
on thought, 221 n. 19
on universal self-consciousness,
64–65
view of Greeks, 83
Heidegger, Martin, 150
Heraclitus, 118, 243 n. 55
Herder, Johann Gottfried von, 17, 80
higher men (höhere Menschen), 117
historical meaning, 75
history, 115, 117, 122, 124, 152, 154–56,
164, 165, 171–79, 182, 195, 206, 207,
247 n. 36
of culture, 247 n. 42
end of, 127, 194
historian, 195
historical basis, 188
historical sense, 173, 174, 192–94,
195–96, 248 n. 45
narrative, 77
personal, 129, 130
shapes humans, 113
Hobbes, Thomas, 9, 10, 11, 13, 16, 186,
212 nn. 5 and 9, 220 n. 9
Homer, 150
Honig, Bonnie, 243 n. 1
Honneth, Axel, 65, 219 n. 1, 220 n. 12,
221 n. 19
honor, 102–3, 107, 222 n. 21
Horstmann, Rolf-Peter, 227–28 n. 44
Houlgate, Stephen, 211 n. 8, 229 n. 4
human beings
development of: distinctiveness of,
121–26; historical conditions, 115,
117; naturalist interpretation, 114–15,
117
modern, 174
natural, 58, 63

humanity, 195
Hume, David, 3, 10, 14, 150, 204
hunger, 29–30, 58–59, 88
"philosophical melancholy," 14
Hurka, Thomas, 185, 246 n. 23
Hussain, Nadeem, 151, 239 n. 20, 245
n. 19
Hyppolite, Jean, 220–21 n. 14

I, 33–34, 35, 44, 49, 59, 64, 116, 132, 159,
164, 207, 217 nn. 31 and 34
and community, 77–78, 66, 71
individual, 41–42, 43, 50, 51, 55
infinite subject, 50, 54
and institutions, 74–75
part of whole, 72, 75
universal subject, 41, 66
identity, 100, 104, 117, 155, 202, 206, 207
ethical, 68
personal, 38, 49, 67–68; compared to nations, 66; use of first person, 38–39,
40–41, 44
universal, 66–71
See also I
Iliad, 165
imperative, categorical, 42
independence, 64
individual, 1, 140–69, 190, 197, 203, 205,
206, 209, 216, n. 21
antipolitical, 170–98
autonomy, 3
definition, 2
ethical, 56–83
ethical view, 3
formal, 3, 9, 17–22, 23, 28, 35, 42, 200
historical, 3–4, 5, 6, 22–24, 114, 200,
201, 208–10; Hegel's defense of,
27–28
independence, 3
modern, 9; contrast with pre-modern, 10
and modern society, 44
narrative, 218–19 n. 51
natural, 3, 9, 10–17, 200; criticism of,
10–11; problems of 11–15
personal uniqueness, 3
political, 83–110
and redemption, 154–62
self-creation, 54
sovereign, 115–17, 231 n. 15
individualism, Hegels' view, 56
individuality, 99, 104, 106, 111–39, 193,
194, 197, 199–201, 203, 206, 214 n. 2,
230–31 n. 13, 234 n. 32

can't precede action, 116
differences between Hegel and
Nietzsche, 197–98
Hegel's defense of, 84
Hegel's definition, 42–43
historical, 3–4, 5, 6; liberal, 1
narrative unity, 129–39
reflective, 172
individuation, problem of, in Nietzsche,
113–17
infinity, 194, 195
instinct, 121, 127, 136, 193, 244 n. 8
institutions
functions of, 226 n. 28
relationship to individuals, 74–75
institutions, mediating, 5, 85, 86, 96, 209,
227–28 n. 44, 229 n. 56
British, 227 n. 37
economic institutions, 204
functions of, 97–99, 100–110
New England, 227 n. 38
See also estates
intuition
Hegel's view, 40
historicization of, 40
Kant's view, 39–40

James, David, 214 n. 2, 215 n. 11, 216
n. 28
Janaway, Christopher, 112
Jesus, 183, 242 n. 52
judgment, 51
common law, 43
Jurist, Elliot L., 211 n. 8, 229 n.4, 240 n. 29
"just," 14
justice, 142–43, 144
justification, 138, 145, 149–54, 179, 180,
184, 185, 207, 237–38 n. 11, 238 n. 13,
239 n. 20, 240 nn. 24 and 27, 241
n. 34, 245 n. 19, 246–47 n. 32

Kain, Philip J., 237 n. 9
kalos, 152, 156
kalos k'agathos, 156
Kant, Immanuel, 3, 9, 17, 18–20, 26, 29,
30, 36, 37, 39, 40, 44, 45, 46, 57, 73,
112, 113, 130, 145, 160, 161, 164, 180,
196, 197, 207, 213 nn. 21 and 27, 215
n. 10, 217 n. 39, 229–30 n. 6, 230–31
n. 13, 231 n. 14, 238 n. 15
on authority, 18–19
categorical imperative, 19, 42
on desire, 46

on history, 19
on intuition, 39–40
on moral norms, 73
on natural individual, 17
on reason, 18
on subjectivity, 216 n. 25
unity of apperception, 36, 38, 39
Kateb, George, 211 n. 6
Kaufman, Walter, 121, 229 nn. 1 and 4
Kleist, Heinrich von, 167
knowers (Erkennenden), 117
knowledge, 144,149, 193, 196
    desire for, 145
    destruction of, 248 n. 47
    tragic, 147, 237 n. 9
Köhnke, Klaus Christian, 229–30 n. 6
Kojève, Alexander, 220–21 n. 14
Kolb, David, 214 n. 6

labor, 60, 74,102, 103, 208
    division of, 89, 203, 225 n. 12
laboring, 37–39, 46
last men, 111, 148, 171, 178, 191
law, 126, 128–29, 240 n. 28
    aesthetic law, 130–32, 136
    constitutional, 15
    ethical, 49, 172
    rule of, 186
    self-legislating, 153
laws, nation of, 81
legislation, Philosopher's, 183
Leibniz, Gottfried, 149
Leiter, Brian, 114–15, 229–30 n. 6, 231
    n. 15, 232 n. 17, 239 n. 20
Lewis, Thomas A., 227 n. 36
liberalism, 1, 2, 87, 96, 106, 140, 188, 192,
    199, 203, 229 n. 55
    liberal democracy, 144
    liberal thought, 226 n. 24
liberals, 141
liberty
    civil, 24
    natural, 24
    notion of, 17
life, artistically structured
    aesthetic unity, 132
    individual compared to artists, 130–32,
        134–36
    goals of self-determination, 132, 135–37
    goal of unity amid diversity, 132–34
    goal of uniqueness, 132, 137–39
life, ethical, 6,86, 94, 95, 124–25, 127
    based on culture, 151–54

Locke, John, 3, 9, 10, 16, 79, 84, 204, 212
    n.5
Losurdo, Dominic, 229 n. 55
love, 142, 160, 242 n. 51
Lukes, Steven, 2

MacIntyre, Alasdair, 229 n. 1
Machiavelli, Niccolò, 10, 24, 167
Mandeville, Bernard, 92, 101, 176, 212
    n. 8, 225–26 n. 21
Mansfield, Harvey, 167
Markell, Patchen, 222 n. 31
Marks, Jonathan, 213 n. 26
Marx, Karl, 11, 85, 112, 226–27 n. 34,
    229–30 n. 6
master-slave relationship, 61–64, 78, 89,
    143–44, 220 n. 7, 221 n. 15, 222 n. 31,
    232 n. 17
    slave morality, 233 n. 26, 237–38 n. 11,
        240 n. 30
    slavery, 234 n. 39
materialism, 229–30 n. 6
McDowell, John, 27
McGinn, Robert, 238 n. 16
Mead, George Herbert, 216 n. 28
meaning, ethical, 200, 203
metaethics, 239 nn. 20 and 21
metaphysics, 113–14
Mill, John Stuart, 5, 56, 84, 92
mixing of class and race, 192–93
Montesquieu, Charles-Louis de Secon-
    dat, Baron de, 80
morality, slave, 128
Mullhall, Stephen, 240 n. 30
multiculturalism, 2, 205

narrative, 140, 153, 155–56, 160, 162, 167
    individual, 202
    narrative history, 196
    self-narrative, 159
    story, individual, 104
narrative whole, 132
natural individual, 212 n. 5
natural law, 27
naturalism, 115
nature, 8, 10–14, 15, 28, 30–31, 37, 45, 58,
    59, 60, 61, 63, 65, 78, 81, 85, 114, 115,
    116, 117–21, 123, 126, 127, 128, 129,
    141–44, 146, 149, 157–59, 161, 174,
    175, 176, 196, 200, 213 n. 21, 215
    n. 15
    biological, 215 n. 13
    state of, 186, 187

nature, second, 48, 100, 115, 123, 124,
    129, 150, 236 n. 58
negation, 215 n. 12
negativity, 109, 208
    of reason, 143, 145
negativity, absolute, 32–35, 108
Nehamas, Alexander, 111, 139, 151, 236
    n. 59
Neuhouser, Frederick, 214 nn. 3–4, 216
    nn. 25–26, 219 nn. 1 and 3, 224 n. 8,
    227 n. 36
Newtonian universe, 28, 29
Nietzsche, Friedrich, 3, 4, 5, 6, 7, 22, 23,
    24, 34, 47, 111–38, 140–68, 170–98,
    199–203, 205–209, 214 n. 28, 218–19
    n. 51, 229 nn. 1–2, 4–5, 229–30 n. 6,
    230 nn. 8–12, 230–31 n. 13, 231
    nn. 14–15, 231–32 n. 16, 232 nn. 17–
    18 and 20, 233 nn. 21–27, 29–30, 234
    nn. 31–42, 234–35 n. 43, 235 nn. 44,
    46–49, 51, 236 nn. 52–56 and 58, 237
    nn. 1, 3, 5–6, 8–9, 237–38 n. 11, 238
    nn. 12–16, 238–39 n. 17, 239 nn. 18,
    20–23, 240 nn. 24–30, 240–41 n. 31,
    241 nn. 32–37, 39, 44, 45, 242 nn. 46,
    48–54, 243 nn. 55–57, and nn. 1–4,
    244 nn. 5–12–13, 245 nn. 14–20 and
    22, 246 nn. 23–26, 28, 30–31, 246–47
    n. 32, 247 nn. 33, 35–40, 42–44, 248
    nn. 45–50
    on ancient world, 124, 134
    on aristocracy of spirit, 141
    on art and culture, 149–52, 159
    on character formation, 129
    on community and ethical life, 124–25,
        140
    on community, 153–54, 154–55, 158–59
    on conscience, 129
    on corruption, 244 n. 5
    critique of knowledge, 153
    on culture, 188–89, 198, 205–6
    on democracy, 247 n. 39
    difference with Hegel on individuality,
        197–98
    on economic activity, 205
    on education, 192, 193
    on ethical life, 127
    on ethics, 117
    on founders, 158–59
    on free will, 116–17
    on freedom, 116
    on genius, 167, 190
    on Greek tragedy, 173

    on Hegel's state as ethical organiza-
        tion, 247 n. 33
    on historical sense, 192–94, 195–96
    on human beings, 112, 115
    on individual life, 132
    individuality can't precede action,
        125–26
    on justification for state, 180
    on knowledge, 244 n. 6
    on liberals, 188
    life like artistic plan, 129–30
    on master-slave relationship, 143–44
    metaphysical views, 230–31 n. 13
    on modern democracy, 170, 187, 191–92
    on modern human being, 174
    on modern world, 170, 190–91, 193–94
    moral system, 232 n. 20
    on natural liberty, 24
    on naturalism, 231 n. 15
    on nature, 117–19, 146–47
    on politics, 125, 179–80, 184, 187
    on power of state, 179
    on promising, 125
    on purpose of state, 171
    on reason, 143
    on role of love in community, 163–64
    on sovereign individual, 231 n. 15
    on state and culture, 179, 180–81, 183,
        184
    on state and individual, 178
    on subjectivity and the will to power,
        128
    on subjectivity, 112, 126
    on suffering, 136–37
    on the beautiful, 164–65, 166
    on the Greek state, 171–73
    on the Greeks, 150–53, 163, 164, 166
    on the table of goods, 160–61
Nietzsche, similarities to Hegel
    on ancient community, 171
    avoids two opposing forms of human
        life, 130
    on freedom, 122
    on the historical individual, 200
    on historical nature of human identity,
        154
    "hostile brother geniuses," 113
    individual life and Hegel's Idea, 241
        n. 44
    on individual and community, 139
    no pregiven substratum in individuality
    reason not separate faculty of mind,
        143

self-determination and Hegel's Idea,
135–36
on slaves and another's reflected will,
143
on subjectivity, 112
sublation and Hegel's term aufheben,
235 n. 47
on superiority of modern to ancient
state, 173
uses Hegel's terms, 136
value of narratives, 202–3
view of will and Hegel's "subject,"
119–20
nihilism, 148–49, 163, 190, 238 n. 14
norms, 32, 39, 43, 45, 47, 48, 49, 50, 51, 50,
66, 91, 85, 86, 89, 91, 100, 115, 123,
124, 126, 129, 136, 137, 142, 153, 172,
173, 201, 207
of conduct, 62
of desire, 93
ethical, 95,178
of good life, 64
normative labor, 39
self legislation of, 245 n. 18
universal, 86, 87, 108, 153

Okin, Susan, 199
oratory, 156
organization, ethical
German state, 113
Ottmann, Henning, 243 n. 3, 245 n. 17
"ought," 12
Overman (Übermensch), 117, 181, 182,
183, 184, 242 n. 53
Owen, David, 112, 246 n. 26

particularity, 84, 86, 90, 94, 95, 96
root of vanity, 91
subjective, 86, 99
passion, 11, 17, 28, 114, 116, 117, 122, 127,
130, 134, 143, 144, 157, 161, 172, 186,
186
patriotism, 85, 103, 104, 226 n. 29
Patten, Alan, 212 n. 14, 218 n. 44
Pelczynski, Z. A., 224 n. 7
Peperzak, Adriaan, 26
perfectibility, 31, 45, 123, 201, 217 n. 38
Pericles, 83, 156, 164
personality, 50, 78, 86, 135, 137, 153, 156,
158, 202
pessimism, 148, 238 n. 16
philosophy, 246–47 n. 32
philosophers, 117, 142, 181, 182, 236 n. 58

Pinkard, Terry, 26, 219 n. 2, 220 n. 7,
222–23 n. 33, 226 n. 27
Pippin, Robert B., 26, 83, 214 nn. 5 and 7,
230 n. 10
Plato, 27, 86, 113, 141, 144, 160, 163, 165,
243 n. 57
Platonism, 141, 152, 160
Republic, 243 n. 3
pluralism, 204
polis, 76, 85, 86, 103, 220 n. 4, 222–23
n. 33, 243 n. 4
politics, 5, 105, 150, 178, 179, 180, 183,
184–85, 196, 197, 203, 205, 206, 243
n. 4
aims of politics, 186, 187
Nietzsche: and Hegel differ, 206–7;
ambivalent toward, 171
role of human beings, 208–09
post-modernists, 2
poverty, causes of, 225 n. 19
power
plastic, 121, 124, 134, 172, 236 n. 55
spiritual, 182–83
practice, historical, 66, 68,
pragmatism, 216 n. 29
promises, 126, 131
promising, 196
property, private, 86, 93, 98, 212 n. 16
right, 38
inequality of, 225 n. 19
property, protection of, 10
prosperity. 204

rabble (Pöbel), 17
no stake in community (Hegel),
104–5
rationalism, Hegelian rational collectivism, 4
rationality, 149, 206, 207
functional, 72–74, 78
instrumental, 58
of state, 85
reason, 12, 13, 39, 45, 142, 143, 145, 146,
151, 153, 161, 162, 180, 207, 230–31
n. 13, 238 n. 15
aims, 22
Nietzsche's definition, 143
passion, ontology of, 217 n. 39
rational being, 18–19
reasoning, Hegel's definition, 41
recognition, 120, 162, 166, 175, 204,
220–21 n. 14, 222 n. 21
as aesthetic justification, 161

recognition of individuals, 102
  by state, 100–101
recognition, mutual, 65–66, 124, 128, 206
reconciliation, 128, 144
  differences between Hegel and
    Nietzsche, 156
Redding, Paul, 54, 220 n. 8, 10 and 13,
  220–21 n. 14
redemption (Erlösung), 154, 162, 195–96,
  240 n. 30
  of community, 194
reflection, 138, 145–46, 147, 202, 207
reflection, rational, lacking in polis, 86
Reginster, Bernard, 121, 233 n. 30, 236
  n. 59,238 n. 14, 239 n. 20
religion, 125, 146–47, 148, 174, 185, 203,
  239 n. 23, 246–47 n. 32
reverence, 162, 165, 167, 198, 242 n. 52
Revolution, French, 22
Richardson, John, 119–20, 121
Ridley, Aaron, 111, 131, 240 n. 28
Ripstein, Arthur, 224 n. 7, 242 n. 52
"right," 16, 19
Romanticism, 56, 86, 213–14 n. 28, 230
  n. 9, 244 n. 10
  and Nietzsche, 114
Rome, 65, 68, 78
Rorty, Richard, 216 n. 29, 223 n. 35
Ross, Nathan, 224 n. 5
Rousseau, Jean Jacques, 5, 9, 11, 17, 24,
  25, 26, 28, 31, 58, 81, 84–85, 86–88,
  90–93, 96, 98, 104, 117, 158, 159, 206,
  208, 212 n.5, 213 nn. 25– 28, 217
  n. 38, 221 n. 19, 224 nn. 7–7, 224–25
  n. 10, 242 n. 52
  critique of modern commercial society,
    87
  on freedom, 17
  historical individual, 23–24
  source of dispute between Hegel and
    Nietzsche, 6
rules, 73–75
  change through history, 73
  mores, 73
  laws, 73
  self-regulated, 73

Savigny, Friedrich Karl von, 27
Schiller, Frederich von, 27, 215 n. 8
Schlegel, Friedrich, 51, 54
Schopenhauer, Arthur, 113, 127, 145, 155,
  158, 159, 179, 187, 230 nn. 8 and 11,
  242 n. 52, 244 n. 10

Schrift, Alan D., 235 n. 51
science, modern, 11–12, 13, 174, 196, 203
self, 5, 116, 150, 160, 230–31 n. 13, 236
  n. 54
  inner, 191
self-consciousness, 47, 51, 62, 102, 125,
  145, 216 n. 20, 220–21 n. 14, 221
  nn. 17–18, 234 n. 35
  universal, 64–65
self-creation, 197
self-determination, 102, 104, 132, 135–37,
  177, 187, 191
  and beauty, 156–57
  political, 85
  rational, 218 n. 44
self-government, 201
self-interestedness, 204
self knowledge, 197, 232 n. 20
self legislation, 183
self-love, 45, 88
self-negation, 61–62
self-reflection, 197
self-satisfaction, 154
self-sovereign, 203
self-understanding, 150, 158, 160
selfish gene theory, 121
selfishness, 57, 65, 73, 84–85, 87, 88, 92,
  94, 99, 107, 124, 220 n. 6, 224–25
  n. 21
Siep, Ludwig, 223 n. 37, 224 n. 8
Silenus' truth, 140, 146–49, 152, 154, 157
Shaw, Tamsin, 179, 239 n. 20, 244 n. 13,
  245 nn. 18–19
Shklar, Judith, 213 n. 26
Siemens, Herman, 247 n. 39
skepticism, 142, 143, 148, 162, 174, 191,
  195
Skowronek, Stephen, 168
slaves, 63, 116
  master-slave relationship, 61–63, 64, 78
  self-negation, 61–62
Smith, Adam, 92, 101, 204
social sciences, modern, 13
  history, Kant's view, 19
social contract, 227 11, 15, 24, 213 n. 27,
  224 n. 8
society, 120, 126, 127, 132, 137, 142, 143,
  150, 174
  ancient, 23–24, 199
  aristocratic, 246 n. 30
  civil, 176–77, 204
  commercial, 176
  modern, 8–9, 2; criticism of, 10

modern commercial, 84–85, 224 n. 5;
  expansion of desire, 87–96
pre-modern, 3, 133
self-legislating, 151
Socrates, 33, 34, 35, 84, 86, 145, 158, 159,
  163–64, 172, 173, 183, 225 n. 11, 238
  n. 12, 242 n. 52
Socratic philosophy, 216 n. 21
Sophocles, 58, 118
Solon, 156
soul, 20, 93, 120, 122, 127, 128, 130, 144,
  146, 160, 171, 182, 185, 189, 192, 201,
  230 n. 10, 234 n. 34
Sparta, 24, 85
Speight, Allen, 54
spirit, 3, 9, 10, 31, 32 41, 53, 54, 64–65,
  78, 80, 193, 215 n. 5, 217 n. 32, 223
  n. 36
  definition of, 27
  Hegel's use, 125
  historical, 230 n. 10
  Nietzsche's use, 124, 126,141
the state, 243 n. 3
  and culture, 244 n. 12, 245 nn. 14, 17
    and 20
  as ethical organization, 247 n. 33
  greed of, 244 n. 13
  preservation of, 247 n. 35
  veneration of, 244 n. 10
state, ancient, 171–72
  hierarchical community, 182
state, modern, 171–90
  advantages and disadvantages,
    173–75
  adversary to culture, 183–84, 186
  Bismarckian, 178–79
  bureaucratic norms, 178
  compared to ancient, 88–90
  corruption in, 176
  function of, 99
  historical development, 171–79
  German state, 98
  power of state, weak understanding,
    179–98
  power of state, strong understanding
    of, 179–80, 181, 184–85
  sustains individual pluralism (Hegel),
    103–10
"state of nature," 11
Steinberger, Peter, 220 n. 4
Stern, Paul, 216 n. 21, 220 n. 11
Strauss, Leo, 112, 211 n. 1
strife, 120

Strong, Tracy, 230 n. 9
subject, 49, 56, 58, 59, 63, 69, 71, 78, 121,
  128, 132, 138, 141, 149, 155,158, 160,
  165, 196, 197 207, 208
  collective, 67–68, 75, 77, 142
  Hegel's definition, 28–29
  Hegel's view, 120
  laboring, 35–44
  reflective, 146
  super-subject, 128
  synthetic, 36–37
  universal, 65, 66,67, 68, 72, 77, 78, 80,
    81
subjectivism, 21
subjectivity, 5, 6, 29, 141–43, 145, 147–50,
  152, 154, 158, 161, 164–66, 201, 210,
  215 n. 11, 220 n. 4, 233 n. 25, 235
  nn. 44 and 46
  Nietzsche on, 110, 112, 117, 121, 124,
    127, 129, 132, 134, 136, 137, 138
  wound in nature of, 207–08
subjectivity, individual, 27, 29–32, 34, 35,
  37–38, 43, 44, 48, 50, 51, 57, 60–64,
  66, 67, 68, 71, 72, 75, 77, 78, 80, 81,
  82, 84, 85, 87, 89, 92, 99, 101, 102,
  103, 105, 108, 172, 185, 190, 195, 196,
  197, 237–38 nn. 11–12
  good life, 27
  Hegel's view, 30
  needs achievement, 29
  subjective agents, 32
sublimation, 229 n. 4, 233 nn. 26–27
subsidiarity, 227 n. 42
substance, 44–45, 46, 86, 90, 109, 121,
  128, 136, 205
  metaphysics of, 114
  relationship with subjects and desire,
    121
suffering, 10, 30, 136–37, 146–47, 155–57,
  159, 174, 185, 195, 236 n. 53, 242
  n. 48
suicide, 33, 148
superego, 51
superstition, 143, 145
synthetic man, 247–48 n. 44

table of goods, 123, 144, 145, 151, 160–61,
  171, 175, 178, 193, 194
Taylor, Charles, 219 n. 3
Taylor, Quentin P., 244 nn. 10–11, 245
  nn. 15, 20–21, 246–47 n. 32
techne, 15
teleology, 28, 77–78, 79, 181

tension, 141–46, 154, 167, 144, 170, 199, 238 n. 13
  between individual and community: Hegel's view, 84–85; solution, bottom-up democratic, 85
  between reverence and mistrust, 163
  of the bow, 191; in shaping community, 141–46; in the bow image, 133
  solution, top-down institutional, 85
theodicy, 137, 149, 152, 247 n. 42
Theunissen, Michael, 227–28 n. 44
thinking, 43, 47, 78, 80, 136. *See also* reasoning
Tobias, Saul, 221 n. 15
Tocqueville, Alexis de, 102, 226 n. 24, 227 n. 38, 229 n. 56
Todorov, Tzvetan, 213 n. 26
totality of whole, 72
truth
  theory of, 233 n. 24
  tragic, 237 n. 10
Tunick, Mark, 215
tyrant, 57

Übermensch, 242 n. 53
understanding, metaphysical, 28
uniqueness, 132, 137–38
  and beauty, 156, 157–58
unity, 132–34, 235 n. 51
  and beauty, 156, 158
unity of apperception, 36, 38, 39
"unjust," 24

values, 191, 194, 196, 197
  origin of, 239 n. 18
Velkley, Richard L., 213 n. 25

Villa, Dana, 226 n. 24, 229 n. 54
virtue, 61, 112, 156, 158, 164, 203
  communal, Achilles example of, 68
  from ethical action, 57
Velleman, J. David, 52
Volksgeist, 80
voting, 103

Warren, Mark, 230 n. 9
wealth, accumulation of, 92–95
whole and parts
  relationship of, 131
  subjective whole, 120
will, 2, 114, 119, 121, 125. 129, 132, 142, 154, 156, 157, 202, 203, 213 n. 27, 216 n. 22, 232 n. 20, 236 n. 56, 240 n. 25
  communal, 172
  freedom of, 135
  free will, 114, 115–16, 201
  structuring, 123
  synthetic, 119–120
  rationality of, 81
will to power, 117–26, 175, 182, 233 n,. 25 and 30, 236 n. 55
will to truth, 141, 142, 145
Williams, Bernard, 90, 229 n. 2
wisdom, 143
Wolff, Michael, 223 n. 2
Wood, Allen, 214 n. 3, 216 n. 26, 219 n. 3

Yack, Bernard, 223 n. 1
Young, Julian, 246. n. 28

Zakaras, Alex, 211 n. 6
Zarathustra, 148, 155–56
Zeitgeist, 112